SOAPY

SOAPY

A Biography of
G. MENNEN WILLIAMS

Thomas J. Noer

THE UNIVERSITY OF MICHIGAN PRESS   ANN ARBOR

Copyright © by the University of Michigan 2005
All rights reserved
Published in the United States of America by
The University of Michigan Press
Manufactured in the United States of America
♾ Printed on acid-free paper

2008   2007   2006   2005   4   3   2   1

A CIP catalog record for this book is available from the British Library.

Library of Congress Cataloging-in-Publication Data

Noer, Thomas J.
     Soapy : a biography of G. Mennen Williams / Thomas J. Noer.
        p.   cm.
     Includes bibliographical references and index.
     ISBN 0-472-11508-1 (acid-free paper)
        1. Williams, G. Mennen, 1911–   2. Governors—Michigan—Biography.
     3. Michigan—Politics and government—1951–   I. Title.

     F570.25.W55N64   2005
     977.4'043'092—dc22   2005004651

PREFACE

I first encountered G. Mennen Williams when I was fifteen years old. Already a political junkie, I overruled my father's desire to watch a rerun of *Maverick* to tune in to the 1960 Democratic convention in Los Angeles. Although I was for Adlai Stevenson (being from Minneapolis, I was still angry that John Kennedy had defeated Hubert Humphrey in the primaries), I thought Kennedy could at least beat Richard Nixon. The only intrigue was who he would pick for vice president. Like other Minnesotans, I hoped it would be our governor, Orville Freeman.

Like many others watching that night, I was stunned when Chet Huntley and David Brinkley announced that Kennedy had chosen Texas senator Lyndon B. Johnson. I didn't know much about LBJ except that he was from the South, and, given the dominance of the civil rights movement in America in 1960, that was enough to alienate me. Announcers predicted a floor fight led by liberals opposed to Johnson's selection, and I eagerly anticipated a rhetorical brawl.

After Johnson was nominated, there was the usual call to make the vote unanimous. The cameras panned to the Michigan delegation and focused in on a tall, gangly guy wearing a polka-dot bow tie (as this was the era before color TV, I didn't know it was green and white) who was pushing toward the microphone. When convention chairman Sam Rayburn of Texas called for a voice vote to nominate Johnson by acclamation, the man from Michigan reared his head back, opened his mouth wide, and bellowed "No!" Rayburn immediately declared the vote unanimous, and the tall guy with the bow tie was left gaping in the middle of the screen of our seventeen-inch Admiral TV. The next morning nearly all the major newspapers carried a front-page photo of "Soapy" Williams screaming his dissent from the nomination of the "master of the Senate" as Kennedy's running mate.

Twenty years later I ran into G. Mennen Williams again while working on a book on American relations with the white regimes of Africa. I spent months in the diplomatic section of the National Archives and in the John F. Kennedy and Lyndon B. Johnson Libraries reading through the papers of Assistant Secretary for African Affairs Soapy Williams. I admired his outspokenness against South Africa's policy of apartheid, his push for a tougher policy toward Portugal for its refusal to allow independence in Angola, and his denunciations of the minority white regime in Rhodesia. I even wrote him a couple of letters, asking about his role in shaping U.S. relations with Africa in the period 1961–65. He responded with brief comments written in green ink on beautiful, personalized white stationery.

Even more interesting than the thousands of memos, position papers, directives, and drafts of speeches in the archives were the photos of Williams in a checkered shirt calling a square dance for African diplomats in the State Department dining room; Williams without a coat (but wearing that same bow tie) wandering into surging crowds during his seemingly endless trips to Africa; Williams on the presidential yacht pointing out the sights along the Potomac to African diplomats; and a blurred image of a white Rhodesian throwing a punch at Williams following his famous "Africa is for the Africans" remarks in 1961, which provoked the wrath of Europeans (and many within his own government). When I finished the book, I felt I knew his policy positions well but did not know much about Soapy Williams before 1960. He was still the tall geek in the bow tie or an ugly plaid shirt.

Over a decade later I was working on a long since abandoned article on the 1948 elections and found a brief summary of Williams's upset victory for the governorship of Michigan. I began to look at some of the secondary literature about Michigan history and politics and found that Soapy was a fascinating character and a very significant figure in American political history. I also discovered that nobody had written his biography.

A year later I made my first journey to Ann Arbor and Lansing, Michigan, to try to get a handle on the vast amount of archival material pertaining to his life. After about three hours plodding through a few of the over fourteen hundred boxes of the G. Mennen Williams papers in the Bentley Historical Library in Ann Arbor, I wandered into the adjacent Mennen Williams Room and looked at the photos of Soapy with Harry Truman, John Kennedy, Lyndon Johnson, Walter Reuther, Martin Luther King, Kwame Nkrumah, and dozens of other national and international figures. I saw pictures of him posed atop the Mackinac Bridge, which he constructed to connect the "two Michigans"; shaking hands in front of the gate of an auto plant during one of his political campaigns; and riding in a convertible with Adlai Stevenson on Labor Day in Cadillac Square in Detroit. Flanking the pictures were cartoons from national magazines and newspapers both lampooning and praising the "boy governor" of Michigan and the New Frontier's most flamboyant diplomat.

When I left Ann Arbor for Lansing, I parked my car next to the G. Mennen Williams Executive Building. A few months later, I found myself in Michigan's Upper Peninsula, driving on the Mennen Williams Highway. Later his widow, Nancy Williams Gram, escorted me on a tour of his study in their Grosse Pointe Farms home lined with political cartoons, correspondence, and photos from 1948 to 1987. It was clear I had a lot to learn about Mennen Williams and his impact on Michigan and the nation. There was far more to him than the bow tie and flannel shirt.

A writer once suggested that while researching a person's life biographers should sing to themselves, "Getting to *know* you / Getting to know all *about* you!" During the past three years I tried this tune while trying to figure out Soapy Williams. (At times I also hummed "Onward Christian Soldiers," the University of Michigan fight song, and the African National Anthem.) I now know a lot about Williams's early life and his career as governor of Michigan (1948–60), head of the State Department's African Bureau (1961–65), and Michigan Supreme Court justice (1970–87). I know his shoe size (15E) and how much spending money his mother sent him at prep school. I can recite the topics of his undergraduate seminar papers at Princeton, as well as the instructor's grades and written comments; I can list the stops for nearly every day of his six campaigns for governor and the speeches he gave at each. If pressed, I can pinpoint where he was and with whom he spoke during almost each day of his career in the State Department and can summarize his handwritten notes (in green ink from a fountain pen) on most of his Supreme Court decisions. I know why he was nicknamed "Soapy," why he wore green and white polka-dot bow ties, what flavor of ice cream he had on his first date with his wife (butterscotch), and that he signed letters to his grandchildren "Bompa."

Despite the detail, I am not sure any biographer "knows" everything about his or her subject. Written letters and documents, oral histories, newspaper articles, interviews, radio and TV tapes, and all the other building blocks of history can answer many but not all questions about a person. As a college freshman I was taught that the "what" always precedes the "why" in history. It is, however, the whys that are the most interesting and most difficult to answer. Mennen Williams lived in an era before e-mail and cell phones, when the written word still dominated and he saved nearly every scrap of paper from his private life and public career (even a sign he used to leave on his desk when he was using the men's room in Lansing and worksheets from the Thursday afternoon French lessons he took when he was in the State Department). Having read and reread most of this mountain of material, I think I have most of the what and can only hope this allows me to at least try to answer the why.

Many biographers suggest that their subjects are persons

filled with contradictions, and with Mennen Williams the disparities are numerous and at times jarring. He was the product
of wealth and privilege, but he embraced an unrepentant social
and political liberalism dedicated to fundamental economic
reform and uncompromising racial equality. A wooden and at
times awkward speaker, he became the most successful campaigner in Michigan history, winning an unprecedented six
straight terms as governor. A Princeton Phi Beta Kappa and
honors graduate of the University of Michigan law school,
Williams was far more comfortable calling a square dance at a
Ukrainian Hall than discussing public policy with academics.
Deeply devout, he ran some of the dirtiest political campaigns
in America, often engaging in vicious personal attacks on his
opponents. Jovial and friendly even with his political enemies,
he managed to provoke the wrath of nearly all of the major
leaders of his party, including Adlai Stevenson, Lyndon Johnson, and John Kennedy. Williams was a master political strategist, whose miscalculations plunged his state into bankruptcy,
destroying his chance for the presidency.

With no experience in international affairs, he managed to
alter significantly American foreign policy toward the third
world and survived the purge of liberals from the State Department during the New Frontier. A bitter opponent of Lyndon
Johnson, he was able to maintain his position after the Texan
became president and continue his influence on U.S. diplomacy. Having never lost an election in his life, he was routed in
his 1966 run for the U.S. Senate from Michigan. He loved
campaigning and the policy battles of government but spent his
final sixteen years above the political fray on the Michigan
Supreme Court, where he became known for compromise and
bipartisanship and an intense effort to modernize and computerize the state's legal system.

Soapy Williams was a militant reformer who advocated dras-
tic changes in America, but he was a strict Victorian in his private life. He created one of the most potent political machines
in American history and was a master of public relations, but he
argued that ideas and issues should not be judged by their political appeal and candidates should never be concerned with

image over substance. He had an insatiable belief in the goodness of people but was convinced that they often made bad choices. He bristled when criticized but was always willing to offer criticism, usually unsolicited, of others. He was always optimistic and confidant and was convinced that God had a plan for him and his life, but he often felt betrayed and frustrated throughout his political career.

Williams's contradictions are part of his appeal. His surface appearance as the idealistic, unrealistic, tireless liberal was deceiving. Behind the bow tie was a man with a clear and unwavering core philosophy that made him one of the most significant and controversial political figures in recent American history. At times the substance was hidden by the flamboyant style, but it was his principles that guided his actions from his sudden emergence on the stage of American politics in 1948 until his death in 1987.

Biographer Catherine Drinker Bowen argued: "Writing a full-length biography is a long and difficult task, during which one is possessed not by dreams of glory, but by anxiety," as authors fear they have not done justice to their subjects. She also suggested that if the writer works hard enough and writes clearly enough, once the book is published "the nightmare dissipates." I only hope that she is right!

ACKNOWLEDGMENTS

I have often found the acknowledgments to be the most entertaining and enlightening part of a book and have discovered
several distinct patterns: One approach is to list and praise every
scholar who has written anything remotely close to the topic in
the hope of deflecting bad reviews. Another is to offer an elaborate discussion of the various theoretical frameworks
employed and the subtle but significant modifications the
writer has employed. A third format is to provide a lengthy
account of the author's heroic intellectual odyssey in overcom-
ing the immense barriers encountered in the long process of
research and writing. Each of these approaches can be fascinating, and I am often in awe of the effort.

Like the book that follows, my acknowledgments are fairly
straightforward. I have no profound intellectual scaffolding to
buttress my effort. My goal was to write a rather traditional
biography that captures both the politics and the personality of
G. Mennen Williams based on archival research, and that aim
has not changed in the past three years. While there were problems during the project, they were largely those common to all
scholars and I suspect not very compelling to readers. As I have
no theoretical insights or unusual burdens to share, my
acknowledgments are almost boringly conventional: an opportunity of offer thanks.

Those of us who spend our lives at small private colleges usually do so because we enjoy undergraduate teaching, small classes, a sense of collegiality, and a general absence of bureaucratic battles. There is, however, a price for such an environment when it comes to research and publication. A heavy teaching load, no graduate seminars or graduate assistants (in fact, no graduate *students*), modest financial resources to support research, and no colleagues working in the same area force us to be more dependent on support from outside our home institutions than are those at larger universities.

The greatest need for all scholarship is time and money. I am grateful to Carthage College for granting a sabbatical leave early in the project and to the Quality of Life Committee for several crucial research grants. Other funding was provided by the John F. Kennedy Library, the Lyndon B. Johnson Library, and the Bentley Historical Library in Ann Arbor.

Despite the belief of most undergraduates, the Internet has not eliminated the need for historians to physically travel to the documents and rely on the expertise of librarians and archivists. Francis X. Blouin, William Wallbach, Karen Jania, and the rest of the superb staff at the Bentley Library were not only incredibly knowledgeable and helpful in guiding me through the vast collection of the G. Mennen Williams papers but also unendingly cheerful and kind. They even found a dentist to fix a broken tooth on a snowy afternoon! I also had the benefit of guidance from the research staff at the John F. Kennedy and Lyndon B. Johnson Presidential Libraries, the Seeley-Mudd Library at Princeton University, the Sterling Library at Yale University, the National Archives in College Park, Maryland, the Minnesota State Historical Society in Minneapolis, the University of Wisconsin Library in Madison, and the Carthage College Library. The increasingly decrepit but amazing rich Wisconsin State Historical Library in Madison was a major source for research throughout the project.

Robert Divine, Professor Emeritus at the University of Texas, Edward Bennett, Professor Emeritus at Washington State University, and the late Kinley Brauer of the University of Minnesota have offered encouragement and assistance throughout my career and on this project. Others who offered suggestions and support include Jerry Simmons of the University of Nebraska-Omaha, John Chalberg of Normandale Community College, and my colleagues at Carthage College, William Gunderson, Bill Kuhn, Stephanie Mitchell, John Neuenschwander, Dean Peterson, and Steve Udry.

I owe special thanks to Nancy Williams Gram for granting me a lengthy interview and showing me Soapy's study in her home in Grosse Pointe Farms. Mary Erwin of the University of Michigan Press was unwavering in her support of the project and provided suggestions and encouragement with grace, tact, and humor.

My greatest debt, as always, is to my wife, Dr. Linda O'Connor Noer, who lived with me and Soapy for three years. She has the rare ability to temper excesses, tolerate obsession, and revive enthusiasm. This book is dedicated to her and to Sophie Elizabeth Bair.

CONTENTS

Illustrations following pages 152 and 296

INTRODUCTION

The Last American Liberal

It was one of the greatest upsets in American political history. Nearly every poll and pundit predicted a sweeping victory for the Republican candidate in 1948. His party was confident and united, and he had massive campaign funds to spend on newspaper and radio ads. In the weeks immediately prior to the election he ran a relaxed campaign, preferring to issue press releases and publicly discuss his new cabinet and legislative agenda. In contrast, the Democratic candidate led a badly divided party. Distrustful of his outspoken advocacy of racial equality and calls for the expansion of social programs, many conservatives had bolted. He was so short of money that he could not afford radio ads, billboards, or even campaign buttons. While the Republican pondered appointments, the Democrat conducted a nonstop personal campaign to bring his message directly to the people. Working eighteen-hour days with up to fifty speeches, he railed against the "do-nothing Republicans" and promised to expand the New Deal programs of Franklin D. Roosevelt.

Despite his energy, the only groups that seemed to respond were African Americans, labor unions, and ethnic organizations. Many of his supporters privately told reporters they had abandoned hope for victory in the contest for the executive and were concentrating their efforts on electing Democrats to Congress. Newspapers, nearly unanimous in their support of his opponent, even prepared headlines announcing a Republican victory.

Despite the polls and predictions, on November 9, 1948, the Democrat pulled off a stunning victory. G. Mennen "Soapy" Williams defeated Republican incumbent Kim Sigler to capture the governorship of Michigan. On the same day, Harry Truman beat Thomas Dewey.

In early 1985, the Episcopal bishop Desmond Tutu of South Africa embarked on a speaking and fund-raising tour of the United States. The most famous critic of South Africa's racist policy of apartheid, Tutu came to America to lobby for support for black rule and racial equality in his nation and to solicit funds to expand the anti-apartheid effort.

After an exhaustive tour in the Northeast, he flew to Detroit for a reception at the Cathedral Church of St. Paul, the home of an affluent congregation that had provided money and support for racial equality in both America and Africa. Tutu was tired and spent only a few moments with each guest. In exchange for their donation, each received a handshake, a smile, and a chance for a photo with the guest of honor. As he worked the room, Tutu was introduced to a tall figure in a green and white polka-dot bow tie. "I am Mennen Williams," he announced, "I was assistant secretary of state for Africa." Tutu smiled and shook his hand without any sign of recognition. "That means Ambassador to Africa," Williams explained. The African nodded and began to move on. Williams's wife, Nancy, followed him and said: "Bishop Tutu, this is Soapy Williams!" Tutu paused, turned around, smiled broadly and shook hands again. "Ah, *Soapy* Williams! You're a great man!"

The new Michigan Supreme Court justice faced a hostile audience. The Economic Club of Detroit was a bastion of conservatism. Its members had been nearly unanimous in their opposition to his policies as governor, and many had campaigned against his election to the court. This elite group of bankers, financiers, and brokers felt he had "betrayed his class" by attacking the wealthy and demanding taxes on income and profits to pay for programs to aid the poor. They viewed him as antibusiness, soft on crime, and an advocate for a more activist and intrusive role for the judiciary. Most expected a speech defending the rights of the accused or a call for stricter regulation of business. Few expected a sermon.

After a brief introduction, the speaker moved to the podium and recited the words of the Old Testament prophet Micah: "He hath showed thee, O man, what is good; and what doth the Lord require of thee, but to do justly, and to love mercy, and to walk humbly with thy God?" The Supreme Court, like all other branches of government, has an obligation to "do justly" and offer "love and mercy," Mennen Williams argued. Removing his glasses, he paused and looked directly at his audience. Man is God's instrument to ensure a just and fair society on earth, he declared. We know what is right and just, and it is our obligation to our God to see that it is done in politics, in business, in the law, and in life.

Critics denounced G. Mennen Williams as a do-gooder, and they were right. Although the term was meant to be derogatory, Williams was convinced that it was his fate and duty to do good in the world. To understand his actions you must know his thoughts, and always at the core of his thoughts was religion.

Religion and politics are often joined in America, and invoking the name of God rarely hurts an elected official. If there are no atheists in foxholes, there are few if any in U.S. politics. While politicians may appeal to a higher power, few were as directly motivated by personal faith as was Mennen Williams. He was convinced that the overriding objective in life is to try to live out the teachings of Jesus and that government is the perfect vehicle to facilitate Christ's admonitions to feed the hungry, clothe the naked, and love your neighbor. To Williams, politics was a noble calling, as it carried with it the power to do good in the world. Such power must be in the hands of "good" people, who will use it to create a better society for all. Civil rights for all races is not only an essential part of the American civic creed as expressed in the Declaration of

Independence, but it is also a moral issue, a divine mandate ordained by scripture. To him, expanded mental health facilities, raising the minimum wage, and building new schools were more than political programs. They were religious activities to move toward the just society that Jesus proclaimed.

Williams never hid his religion. Nearly all of his speeches were laced with biblical references and quotations, and political opponents were often perplexed to hear themselves referred to as "lost sheep" or "forgiven sinners." At political dinners Williams would frequently offer a loud prayer, even after the guests had begun eating. (He would even go into the kitchen to pray for the cooks and waitresses.) His opening words at his first inaugural as governor in 1949 declared: "Not quite two thousand years ago, Jesus of Nazareth said that He came into this world so that men might have life and life abundant. . . . He enjoined men to have a care for one another, not only in matters of the spirit, but in the production and distribution of the necessary goods of this world. . . . It is for this purpose—that men may in fact live together as brothers having a care for one another—that modern democratic states exist." He concluded by saying that in the past Michigan had failed to live up to Jesus's proclamations, but beginning that day it would begin to do so.

Such overt religious imagery and references seemed to some critics to be hypocrisy, as Williams was a tough and at times vicious politician who frequently relied on personal attacks, innuendos, and smears. By portraying his enemies as lost sheep he implied that he alone understood God's intent and he alone could carry out His plan. His opponents were not convinced that God was a New Deal Democrat.

His religious beliefs also led Williams to develop an unshakable belief that he was right and near total confidence that his decisions were correct. Even when his choices led to political disaster he never doubted that they were right. He was certain God was on his side, even if the legislature, the voters, or bureaucrats in the State Department were not. His faith also led him to an unwavering optimism, and he rarely brooded over setbacks, as he was certain he would win the next fight. Politics and policies were a form of divine battle, and he never questioned the ultimate outcome.

If religion was at the core of Williams's political ideology, it was expressed in an unyielding and at times strident liberalism. The Great Depression and Franklin D. Roosevelt's New Deal response shaped his vision of government, and he was faithful to this model until his death. He never moderated his commitment to ever-expansive state and ever-increasing social programs even as the nation moved away from these New Deal assumptions. To Williams, government was the solution to society's problems. It was the instrument with which to achieve racial equality, alleviate disparities in wealth, and empower the masses. America had big problems and needed big government. As the rich had most enjoyed the nation's resources, they should pay the most for programs to help those less fortunate. This may appear to be a rather simplistic political theory, but to Williams it was the essence of good government.

His convictions were consistent, and that was his problem. His belief in governmental power and his refusal to compromise led his state into bankruptcy and destroyed his dreams of occupying the White House. His eagerness to inform others (even within his own party) of their failures pushed him ever farther toward the margins of American political power. "The word *compromise* is not in my vocabulary," he proclaimed, "I am more of a John the Baptist than a disciple." In U.S. politics, however, compromise is often the means to accomplishment and maintaining power, and John the Baptist lost his head.

Mennen Williams's career showed both the strengths and weaknesses of twentieth-century American political liberalism. He was one of the few politicians to adopt and maintain an absolute commitment to racial equality in the era prior to the emergence of a national civil rights movement. He revitalized and reorganized the Democratic Party in Michigan, building a powerful coalition of organized labor, African Americans, academics, and ethnic groups that broke the stranglehold of the Republicans on the state and became one of the most successful political machines in the nation.

His six electoral victories, however, never led to the expan-

sive liberal agenda he advocated for his state. Faced with a hostile Republican legislature, he often chose confrontation over
consensus. If *compromise* was not in his vocabulary, neither was
pragmatism. His accomplishments as governor were impressive
but never all that he hoped for and never enough to make
Michigan into his model for America.

When he shifted from Lansing to the State Department he
proved to be surprisingly adept in adjusting to the different
political environment of Washington and the new arena of
international affairs. He was an unyielding advocate of an
"African first" foreign policy that rejected the prevailing European orientation of American diplomacy. Williams's vocal
opposition to colonialism and continued white minority rule
on a black continent enhanced America's image in Africa and
ultimately led to a significant reorientation of U.S. policies. He
also displayed an ability to understand and survive in the
internecine world of bureaucratic politics while maintaining his
fundamental principles.

His dedication to "Africa for the Africans" and advocacy of a
major U.S. economic commitment to the continent's development, however, had only limited results. As in Michigan, he
refused to accommodate himself to the realities of the situation,
and the continued importance of Europe and the ever-increasing dominance of the war in Vietnam combined to frustrate his
vision of a new American foreign policy and led him to return,
unsuccessfully, to electoral politics.

During the last sixteen years of his life, as a jurist on the
Michigan Supreme Court and later chief justice, he displayed
previously unrevealed skills as an administrator by modernizing
an archaic legal system and showed a new and surprising ability
to work for compromise and consensus. Although his core liberal beliefs remained intact, they were muted in the secretive
and supposed nonpartisan atmosphere of the judiciary. The
uncompromising liberal emerged as the voice of reason, compromise, and camaraderie in the 1970s and 1980s. Age and the
changed mood of the nation transformed the combative
"Soapy" into the conciliatory and revered "Justice Williams."

Williams's career was unique in American politics, as it

involved three distinct areas of government: executive as governor of Michigan, administrative as assistant secretary of state for Africa, and judicial as a member of the Michigan Supreme Court. It also embraced both domestic and international issues. His life provides a vehicle through which we can better understand both the issues and the personalities that dominated America in the decades after World War II. At his best, he was the liberal conscience of the Democratic Party, demanding a clear commitment to racial equality, expansion of the economic reforms of Franklin Roosevelt, and basing political decisions on the needs of the people over the powerful.

The style in which he advocated his liberalism, however, often alienated the very national leaders he wanted to influence. Williams knew well and interacted regularly with nearly every major figure in the Democratic Party from 1948 to 1968. His relationships with Adlai Stevenson, Hubert Humphrey, Estes Kefauver, Averell Harriman, Chester Bowles, John Kennedy, Lyndon Johnson, and others offer an insight into the ideas and actions of these individuals as well as an understanding of Williams. He liked them all (he seems to have liked nearly everyone, even Republicans), but his constant hectoring, refusal to accept compromise, and unsolicited advice managed to anger each of them. At the 1956 Democratic National Convention, he managed to provoke the wrath of Stevenson, Johnson, and Kennedy within seventy-two hours, and they never forgot his actions. (Kennedy and Johnson would become his bosses and Stevenson his colleague when he moved to the State Department in 1961).

Mennen Williams began his career when television was an insignificant aspect of U.S. politics, when black Americans still faced legal segregation, when society dictated that women remain subservient, when Europe ruled nearly all of Africa, and when the global battle against a monolithic communist conspiracy was assumed by nearly all Americans. During his forty years in public office, he witnessed the communications and media revolution, the end of legal segregation, urban riots, black separatism, the feminist revolution, the independence of the third world, the divisiveness of the war in Vietnam, and the beginnings of the collapse of the Soviet Union. The nation and the world had changed and so, too, had American politics. But Soapy Williams did not change. His vision of America, formed during the Depression and New Deal and sharpened during the 1940s and 1950s, was consistent but increasingly old-fashioned during the turbulent 1960s and 1970s.

In an age of political consultants, focus groups, and calculated image, Soapy Williams seems to be of an ancient age. When the word *liberal* is political anathema and both political parties have scurried toward the center, Williams's unending advocacy of *more* programs, *more* spending, and *more* power in government is decidedly out of fashion. His call for an American foreign policy committed to third-world economic development and racial harmony seems equally anachronistic in an era of brutal power politics and military solutions to international issues.

Williams's repeated religious emphasis and flamboyance are perhaps even more distant than his populist policies. He would be a current political consultant's worst nightmare. Who would vote for a skinny, six foot four millionaire in a polka-dot bow tie who loves square dances, quotes the Bible, and is called Soapy? In an era of sophisticated TV ads designed to avoid too clear a position, how could you "package" Mennen Williams? In his era, campaigning began at 4:30 a.m. with handshaking at automobile plant gates and ended eighteen hours and thirty speeches later dancing the schottische at the local Polish American club. Today a candidate's thirty-second TV spot would reach far more people, and the message could be carefully modified and targeted. Bill Clinton may have played his saxophone on MTV in 1992, but MTV has millions of viewers. His folksiness and flamboyance seems calculated compared with Williams's volunteering to sell ice cream cones at a county fair or getting out of his car at railroad crossings to pass out campaign literature. Few U.S. diplomats today would strip to a swimsuit and ride a water buffalo in the Philippines or dismiss the translator so he could practice his French with Emperor Haile Selassie of Ethiopia (who did not speak the language).

G. Mennen Williams was a fascinating mixture of political idealism motivated by religious conviction and a tough, combative politician who used nearly every means to advance his agenda and punish his enemies. He could be a sophisticated intellectual, lecturing his audience on Roman history, Greek philosophy, biblical criticism, Michigan botany, and English common law and then lead his campaign staff in the Mexican hat dance to celebrate his reelection. He was the rich kid from Grosse Pointe, heir to the Mennen cosmetic fortune, who campaigned by attacking the wealthy and the indifference of big business. He got the highest grades in the history of Salisbury preparatory school, graduated Phi Beta Kappa from Princeton, and was awarded the Order of the Coif at the University of Michigan Law School. He did not smoke, drink, or swear, but his greatest support was among the tough blue-collar workers in Detroit's union halls. He went to mass every morning, studied the Bible every night, and spent much of his time battling Jimmy Hoffa and the Teamsters for control of the Democratic Party in Michigan. Williams was occasionally cocky and always ambitious but never pretentious. He built a bridge connecting the two Michigans, he built a new Democratic Party in his state, he tried to build a new American foreign policy, and he built a more efficient Michigan court system. But for every accomplishment in Michigan and Washington, there was a failure. The failures were as often the result of his style and personality as they were his policies. He claimed he could say "hello" in seventeen languages. He had a hard time saying, "I'm wrong" in any.

I

FROM POLO TO POLITICS

The Evolution of a Liberal, 1911–36

> Would to God, I have exceptional powers—was a
> member of a resolute group of similar men striving to
> make the world a better place to live in.
>
> —*G. Mennen Williams, diary entry,*
> *February 3, 1931*

The evolution of Gerhard Mennen Williams from conservative patrician to liberal politician began in Detroit, developed at Princeton, and finally emerged at the University of Michigan Law School. From his birth in 1911 to his completion of a law degree in 1936, Williams achieved brilliant academic success and considered a number of career options (the diplomatic corps, business, and the law among others). His deep religious convictions, the devastating impact of the Great Depression on America, Franklin Roosevelt's New Deal, and the influence of his wife eventually combined to convince him to enter politics, and the same forces led him to the Democratic Party and an uncompromising liberal political philosophy. He was rich, smart, and well connected but became convinced that his role was to be the spokesman for the poor, the uneducated, and those facing discrimination in America. A millionaire and Ivy League graduate, he became the champion of industrial workers, African Americans, the mentally ill, the disabled, and other groups he felt were denied the American dream and the bitter enemy of individuals and groups he viewed as uncaring, selfish, and uncharitable in action and spirit.

Williams was part of a large group of twentieth-century

American patricians who became liberal reformers. Theodore and Franklin Roosevelt, Averell Harriman, Adlai Stevenson, John Kennedy, and Nelson Rockefeller, among others, were heirs to immense fortunes who became progressive politicians. There were two elements, however, that made Mennen Williams unique among his fellow "limousine liberals": his views on race and his refusal to consider political compromise.

Unlike his contemporaries Kennedy and Stevenson and even his political idol Franklin Roosevelt, Williams was an early and unwavering proponent of racial equality. Not only did he consistently attack legalized segregation in the American South long before the Supreme Court declared it unconstitutional, but he spoke out against the more subtle racism prevalent in the North. A half century ago the racial issue was potentially devastating to any American politician, as it risked alienating not only the South but also many whites in the North. Williams was significant for both his early commitment to civil rights and his bluntness and consistent focus on the issue throughout his career.

Williams also refused to adjust his politics and policies to the seeming necessity of compromise. To him, politics was a moral crusade, and one could not abandon principle regardless of the potential political benefits. John Kennedy was willing to select Lyndon Johnson as his running mate as he calculated the need to win the South in the 1960 election. Similarly, Adlai Stevenson agreed to moderate his stance on civil rights to get votes in segregated states and Franklin Roosevelt refrained from endorsing an antilynching bill out of fear of losing the support of southerners in Congress. Mennen Williams viewed such strategic adjustments as a betrayal of ideals. Pragmatism must never include the abandonment of principle. In 1959 his rejection of any compromise with the Republican legislature drove Michigan into bankruptcy, but he remained convinced that he had been correct, as doing what was "right" was better than doing what was "possible." When State Department officials cautioned him against his repeated tirades against white supremacy in Africa and suggested that he restrain his rhetoric to avoid alienating American politicians and European allies, he was stunned by their comments. To him, minority rule was simply wrong and had to be denounced, regardless of the political damage. Silence indicated approval, and how could any person of conviction condone discrimination?

Williams's militant liberalism, his singular commitment to civil rights, and his refusal to temporize his ideas for political gain were a combination of governmental and religious ideology. The spiritual roots were formed in his childhood, but their political expression was in response to America's economic crisis of the 1930s. He found God early and Franklin Roosevelt later.

Detroit, Michigan, in the early twentieth century mirrored the recent transformation of the nation. In the half century following the Civil War, the United States changed from a largely rural, English-speaking, Protestant country to an urban, industrialized, multicultural society. The nation's population tripled in the period 1865–1915 as immigrants fled the poverty and wars of Europe for the dream of a better life in America. At the same time, southern blacks, desperate to escape segregation, and rural whites, lured by the prospects of factory jobs, also flocked to the city.

Detroit was typical of the "great transition" of America. From its beginnings as a fur-trading post, the city quickly developed into a major exchange center between the frontier and the East with the opening of the Erie Canal in 1825. The Great Lakes became the highway for the transport of lumber and grain from the West and manufactured goods from the East. With the coming of the railroad, Detroit rapidly industrialized, and its population jumped from 116,000 in 1880 to 466,000 in 1910. It would more than double to 993,000 by 1920 as European immigrants flocked to its factories. In 1920 nearly a third of its residents were foreign born and it had a significant and growing African American community.

Although Detroit produced a variety of manufactured goods, its identity quickly became linked to the automobile. In 1901 Ransom Olds established an automobile factory in the city, but it was Henry Ford's pioneering assembly line that would transform Detroit into "Motor Town." The automobile companies and their dependent industries quickly came to dominate the city's economy and control the state's politics.

As in Europe, American industrialization produced immense wealth and created vast economic inequities. While African Americans and immigrant workers struggled to survive on the meager wages of the new factories, the nation developed a new moneyed class with previously undreamed of affluence. It was into this economic elite that G. Mennen Williams was born and raised.

Williams's family had money on both sides. His grandfather, Henry Williams, was a Welsh veterinarian who migrated to Canada in 1848 but soon returned to Europe, leaving his wife and two sons in the New World. When he died in an accident, his widow, Letitia, opened a boardinghouse in Windsor, Ontario, just south of Detroit, and the two boys sold box lunches to factory workers. The eldest son, Henry P. Williams Jr., eventually found a job in a Detroit grocery store, and his brother William (G. Mennen's grandfather) and mother soon followed. All three worked in the expanding frontier city and eventually used their wages to buy a six-acre farm on Grand River and Kirby Streets (later known as Williams Square), where they raised fruits and vegetables. Letitia Williams canned jams and processed pickles, and her sons sold them from a push-cart. The business was a success, and they capitalized on the post–Civil War boom by opening a factory in 1865 that later occupied an entire block in Detroit. "Williams' Pickles" flourished, and the family expanded to a national market. (When asked about his nickname, Soapy, an indication of his mothers' connection to the Mennen Cosmetic Company, Williams joked that had he been named after his father's side of the family he would have been called Pickles.)[1]

The Williamses shrewdly used the profits from their pickle factory to finance investments in real estate and by the turn of the century had become one of the wealthiest families in Detroit. In 1910 they sold the factory and lived off the earnings from their properties and investments. In 1880 William Williams married Sarah Phillips (a descendent of an American Revolutionary War hero, Joseph Delezenne, who had served under the Marquis de Lafayette), and they had three sons and a daughter. The eldest son, Henry Phillips Williams, enjoyed the results of his parents' hard work and successful real estate speculations to live a pleasant life of clubs, sports, travel, and philanthropy. He enjoyed riding, sailing, and nearly every other sport appropriate for a gentleman of his class. On Saturdays he played morning golf at the Bloomfield Hills Country Club and evening bridge and poker at the Detroit Club. Henry Williams became a regular at the city's social functions and even had a special ebony and ivory cane commissioned in Paris for opening night of the Detroit opera. Tall, handsome, and wealthy, he was one of the city's most eligible bachelors.[2]

The wealth of the Williams family was substantial, but it was almost insignificant in comparison with that of G. Mennen Williams's maternal side. His mother was the daughter of one of the richest men in America. Elma Mennen's ancestors were landowners in East Prussia who married French women and fled from their estates after being accused of cooperating with the invading French in the Franco-Prussian War of 1870. One group of Mennens settled in Holland, while another faction migrated to the United States.

Gerhard Mennen was fifteen when he and his two sisters arrived in New York City in 1871 and settled in an immigrant German community on First Avenue. Mennen worked as an errand boy, a surveyor's assistant, and finally as a clerk in Emil Lunitz's German Apothecary Shop in Hoboken, New Jersey. He also attended night classes at the College of Pharmacy of New York City. In 1878 he pawned his gold watch and leased a tiny pharmacy in the lobby of the Central Hotel in Newark. Twenty years later he was a millionaire.

Gerhard Mennen's money came from cosmetics he first developed in the back room of his small pharmacy: first, Mennen's Sure Corn Killer; then Mennen's Talcum Infant Powder; and eventually Mennen's Shaving Cream and Aftershave Lotion. He began selling his products in his pharmacy and eventually bought a building to serve as a production center, warehouse, and office and hired salesmen to expand sales into neighboring towns. By 1883, when his daughter Elma

Christina Rebecca, was born, the Mennen Company dominated the cosmetics industry in America.

Gerhard Mennen symbolized the American dream of rags to
riches, and like many successful immigrants he was determined
that his children would receive a proper education and learn the
social skills appropriate for his new class and country. Elma
received private tutoring in languages, art, dance, and music
and an unlimited line of credit in Newark's finest stores. Eventually she entered the National Park Seminary, an exclusive
Episcopal girl's boarding school near Washington, D.C. There
she met Henry Williams's sister Edna, who invited her to visit
Detroit during Easter vacation. Edna Williams introduced her
classmate to her brother, and Henry was smitten. After a year at
Vassar, Elma accepted his proposal, and Henry Phillips
Williams, "the pickle king," and Elma Mennen, daughter of
the "shaving cream king," were married on January 20, 1909, in
Newark. They moved into a house at 19 Merrick Avenue in
Detroit (now a part of the Wayne State University campus).
Two years later, on February 23, 1911, Gerhard Mennen
Williams was born. A second son, Henry, followed in 1912 and
another boy, Richard, in 1921.

Life for the three Williams brothers was typical of the American leisure class of their time. There were live-in servants, a
cook, a butler, and a chauffeur. As a sophisticated easterner living in what she often viewed as the uncultured Midwest, Elma
was determined that her children would attend a prestigious
prep school and an Ivy League college and organized an
exhaustive series of lessons and tutorials to prepare her sons for
their future education. The boys faced a strict schedule of
music, art, speech, and language lessons and weekly classes at
the Annie Ward School of Dancing. Mennen Williams recalled
that his mother "was an absolute perfectionist and demanded
that in others." Elma, who was fluent in French and German,
drilled the boys in the two languages (insisting that they sing
Christmas carols in both) and hired a local actor, Sam Slade, to
give them elocution lessons. The boys memorized famous
speeches and recited them at the dinner table while Elma cor-
rected them. She also lectured her sons about health and once

made Mennen drink an entire pitcher of cream because he seemed too thin. Thursday was "family night," as it was the servant's day off, and Elma cooked and the boys set the table and washed the dishes.[3]

Henry Williams was less concerned with dance and music lessons than with sports and physical fitness. He taught his sons squash, golf, and horseback riding, took them to polo matches, and hired a Detroit boxer named Jack Collins to teach them how to fight. The brothers built a boxing ring and weight room in the basement, and Mennen did far better in the gym than in Elma's endless tutorials. He never mastered the piano, was an awkward dancer (except for the square dances he loved), and was not a polished public speaker. Despite his later political success, even his closest friends noted that he was never a spellbinding orator.

Mennen did, however, become an impressive athlete. He spent several hours a day in the basement lifting weights, working on the punching bag, and reading Charles Atlas's bodybuilding books. He took swimming and rowing lessons at the Detroit Athletic Club and would later become a champion rower (a sport he would continue in prep school and college). He also was a star wrestler, a sprinter in track, and a good boxer. By the age of fourteen he was already over six feet tall and years of weight lifting had given him a muscular frame.

Henry Williams also wanted his sons to learn thrift and hard work. He gave them an allowance of only twenty-five cents a week, and they had to work for any extra spending money. Unlike the immigrant children a few miles away, however, they did not have to go into the factories, as their main job was repairing polo mallets. One of Henry's brothers, Robert, had lived on a ranch in California and had worked as a logger, and "Uncle Bob" took the boys to the family's cottage in northern Michigan every summer for several weeks of camping, hunting, hiking, and fishing.[4]

Both parents shared a deep commitment to the Episcopal Church, and the Cathedral Church of St. Paul on Woodward Avenue was a focus for the Williams family. The parents, children, and servants attended mass every Sunday (even though most of the servants were Catholic). Henry was a vestryman and took the boy's choir on annual picnics in the country. Mennen not only attended Sunday services, where he served as an altar boy and crucifer, but he often went to mass several other times during the week.

His early religious training would shape Mennen Williams's basic ideas for the rest of his life and become the cornerstone of his political philosophy. The sermons and Bible lessons he heard at St. Paul's stressed community and service. The priests argued that Christ demanded his followers not only seek their own salvation but to reach out to their neighbors to meet both their spiritual and material needs. Christians had a duty to be of service to society and to try to help those in their community. As a young boy, Williams became convinced that God has a plan for each person that involves using his or her talents to improve the world. He recalled that "from earliest childhood, I learned that God was a 'bulwark, never failing'" and that "Jesus summed up for us all the law and the prophets in just two commandments—thou shalt love the Lord thy God and thy neighbor as thyself." To Williams, Christianity was not just about individual piety but also involved the creation of a true community on earth through service to others. To Mennen, Christ's command to "love one another" demanded an individual commitment to express this injunction through daily life and social action, and he would later argue that politics was a means of honoring the biblical call for service and Christian love. He would attend mass nearly every day of the rest of his life and remained an active member of the Cathedral Church even while living in Lansing and Washington, D.C.[5]

Williams's early religious training also helped him gain a sense of optimism and self-confidence as he became certain that God had a plan for the world and for each person and would guide him in all decisions. Although he was at times shy and inarticulate, he never doubted that he was destined for greatness and that he would be successful in making the world more closely resemble a true loving community. While his family was politically conservative and did not embrace the reform movements of the Progressive Era, Williams would later translate his spiritual beliefs into a fervent commitment to liberalism.

Although Henry encouraged athletics, it was Elma who dominated the family. Williams later noted: "Mother was a grand dame, no doubt about it. She had a queenly bearing and was to the manor born." To their embarrassment, she kept her sons in sailor suits and "Dutch-cut" haircuts until they were eight. (Mennen hid his hair under a cap as soon as he left home.) She also served as the disciplinarian of the family. Once, however, when Mennen spoke back to her, Henry Williams reached across the dinner table, slapped him on top of his head, and demanded that he show respect to his mother.[6]

Elma Williams dressed elegantly and was one of the leading socialites in Detroit. She became enraged if she was not invited to a function and kept a list of those who had not included her in their parties. Unlike her son, she enjoyed formal dances and afternoon bridge games. To celebrate her wedding anniversary, she threw an elaborate black and white formal ball that her eldest son concluded "was worthy of Marie Antoinette." She loved to attend University of Michigan football matches to socialize rather than to watch the game. She arrived early and sat in a wooden chair outside the stadium, greeting people as they entered the gates until the kickoff, when she left for home. Fearing the servants would cheat her, she would put on her mink coat and have her chauffeur drive her to the grocery store to shop for the family. She was one of the first women to drive a car in Detroit and kept her old electric auto even when her husband bought her a combustible-engine vehicle and hired a driver. Her chauffeur would follow her in the family's new Cadillac while Elma tried to negotiate Detroit's streets in her antique vehicle.[7]

Elma also had strong political opinions. Although her husband was a staunch Republican, he did join the Urban League to help African Americans adjust to Detroit. His wife, however, kept an autographed engraving of Marie Antoinette next to her bed, an excellent symbol of her politics. She was a laissez-faire Republican who felt government should leave her and others alone. She thought taxes were a form of robbery and had no sympathy for reform movements designed to help the struggling poor of Detroit. Her eldest son recalled: "Mother had some very strong and precise ideas as to how the world should run, and very often the fact that the United States Government, for instance, had legislated otherwise, made no appreciable difference." When her son became a liberal Democrat, there were rumors that Elma did not vote for him. She finally told the press that she voted for him but not for any other Democrat. She refused to give him money for his political campaigns, though she continued to pay his annual dues at the Grosse Pointe Country Club in the hope that he would someday return to his upper-class roots.[8]

Amateur psychologists (and psycho-historians) have abundant material to work with in analyzing the relationship between Elma Williams's rigid conservatism and her son's expansive political liberalism. Nancy Williams Gram, Mennen's widow, has argued that her husband's politics were a form of rebellion against his mother. This may be partly true, but Elma's views were typical of her class at the time and there is no evidence that the young Mennen Williams dissented from his parents' politics. He remained a conservative Republican until 1933 and even campaigned for Herbert Hoover in 1932. His evolution to political liberalism came well after he had left home and was a response to the Great Depression and the New Deal more than a revolt against his mother.[9]

One thing Mennen Williams did inherit from his parents was a love of foreign travel. Each year Henry and Elma departed Detroit in late winter for a four or five month trip, leaving the boys under the supervision of their aunt and uncle, Mr. and Mrs. Vincent Stock. The annual vacations included travel to Japan, Russia, China, Germany, France, Italy, Africa, and the Holy Land. When Elma broke her leg on a trip to Africa, she ordered the ship's crew to lower her ashore with a crane. Occasionally they took the boys along on their yearly excursions. As a young child, Mennen and his brothers joined their parents on visits to Cuba, Panama, and Alaska.

Each summer Henry and Elma sent the boys to a ranch in Jackson Hole, Wyoming, and it was there that Mennen got his lifelong nickname Soapy. Ranch hands teased the boys about their wealth from the Mennen Cosmetic Company and in 1925 began to refer to Mennen as Soapy, Henry as Lather, and

Richard as Suds. His two brothers hated the labels and abandoned them as soon as they returned to Detroit. Mennen, however, liked being called Soapy and used the name for the remainder of his life, at times even signing official documents Soapy rather than Mennen Williams. His folksy nickname proved to be the perfect match for his later populist politics.[10]

The Williams brothers enjoyed a life of privilege and comfort but also endured long absences from their parents. Henry and Elma were abroad from January to May each year, and the boys spent a month every summer in Wyoming and several weeks in August in northern Michigan with their uncle. There were few boys to play with in their neighborhood, and Mennen and his younger brothers often had to entertain themselves. Henry developed an interest in carpentry and cars, while Mennen continued to focus on athletics. Richard was ten years younger than Soapy and was only four when his oldest brother went east to school.

To prepare their eldest son for prep school and college, his parents sent him to the best schools in Detroit. He attended the exclusive Liggett School for his first three grades and Detroit University School for the next four years. At the age of fourteen it was time for Williams to go to New England and attend the proper preparatory school. "Both my father and mother were anxious for me to go to Princeton," Williams remembered, but they feared he was unprepared in Latin and English for the demanding standards of the prep schools that channeled students to Princeton. They hired private tutors in both subjects in the hope that the exclusive Hotchkiss School in Lakeland, Connecticut, would accept him. To their disappointment, Hotchkiss found Williams's Latin skills inadequate and suggested he apply again a year later. Elma and Henry did not want to delay their son's admission to Princeton, so Henry boarded the train to visit their second choice, the Salisbury School, also in Connecticut. After meeting with the headmaster, he returned with an agreement from Salisbury that Mennen could enroll in the fall but only if he completed an intensive summer tutorial in Latin. In September 1925, the now Soapy Williams headed east to Salisbury.[11]

Despite his parents' disappointment that he did not get into Hotchkiss, Salisbury was a perfect choice for their son. It was small (one hundred boys), prestigious, and, along with the typical prep school curriculum, emphasized its Episcopal roots and culture. Williams flourished at Salisbury. He excelled in academics, earning the highest grade point average in the history of the school; athletics, where he was the center of the football team, captain of the rowing team, and a member of the skiing, basketball, and track teams; and socially, serving as editor of the school newspaper and chairman of the entertainment committee. At graduation the faculty voted him the school's most prestigious honor, the Headmaster's Medal for "scholarship, character, and leadership," and his classmates selected him for the Crosby Medal for leadership, the highest award for a graduating senior.[12]

Williams's achievements at Salisbury were less the result of innate brilliance than organization and hard work. The curriculum focused on Latin, Greek, French, history, math, and speech. Balancing courses with athletics and extracurricular activities required careful scheduling and hard work, and Mennen Williams had a gift for both. He filled notebooks with careful schedules of study sessions, tutorials, athletics, and club meetings. One of his classmates recalled that "when it came time for his books, you never saw anyone go after the job harder than Mennen did. He didn't work, he slaved. He was not the most brilliant student by a long ways, but he certainly was the most thorough." His instructors noted that his papers were not extraordinarily insightful but were extensively researched and without any construction or spelling errors. Williams's verbal recitations in Greek, Latin, and French occasionally included mispronunciations but were always grammatically perfect. He wrote romantic poetry for the student paper under the name Hymen and often would go through twenty or more drafts before submitting his work.[13]

His academic accomplishments at Salisbury would be repeated at Princeton and the University of Michigan Law School. It was always work, effort, and organizing his time rather than brilliance that led to success, traits that would be duplicated in his political career. When the Salisbury rowing

coach ordered ten extra lengths as punishment after a bad practice, Williams rowed twenty. After he received a low grade in
French (always his weakest subject) he devoted an entire weekend to reviewing irregular verbs, even skipping a football game.
At Salisbury, as at Princeton, at law school, and in his political
campaigns, he simply outworked his peers.[14]

Williams loved the camaraderie of Salisbury and called his
years in prep school "the happiest of my life." In Detroit, aside
from his brothers, "there were few other boys in my neighborhood to play with," but at Salisbury he had "99 friends." Each
Sunday night the school had a formal dinner, with both students and faculty in tuxedos, where they discussed religion,
character, and the need to contribute to society. With his
strong religious background and knowledge, Williams became
a leader at these sessions. Being an accomplished athlete also
contributed to his popularity. Aside from the multitude of team
and individual sports, he continued to lift weights daily, and by
graduation he was six foot three and weighed 210 pounds.[15]

A final element in the Salisbury experience was religion. The
school was staunchly Episcopalian, perfect for Williams. Daily
mass was required of all students and faculty, and Williams
became a crucifer. In his junior year he was selected by the
headmaster to serve as chapel prefect, an honor previously
reserved for seniors. He repeated the role during his final year.
The theology of Salisbury confirmed his earlier religious beliefs
in the importance of service and in the church's role in better-
ing society.

Amid all the success at Salisbury, Williams faced two problems: girls and a career. He had never dated in Detroit,
although Elma scheduled endless dances, tea parties, and other
social events so he could meet girls of his own class. At a birthday dance at the Detroit Yacht Club, he presented the guest of
honor with a large package. When she opened it a live goose
emerged. Williams was sent home, but he thought the punishment was worth it, as he did not have to dance. At Salisbury, he
attended a few dances, but he was tall, gangly, and not very
good on the floor and noted that when it came to girls "I was
not much of a success."[16]

More crucial to Williams than girls was a career choice. Elma had determined that he should enter the diplomatic corps, a profession still dominated by "gentlemen" in the 1920s and one of the few occupations she felt was suitable for a boy of his class. His wealth, language skills (despite his problems with French), and travels made him a prime candidate for the Foreign Service. Elma's plan was for him to take a degree at Princeton's Woodrow Wilson School of Public Affairs and then enter the State Department.

At Salisbury, however, he began to have doubts about his mother's choice of his future career. The theology he heard daily from the pulpit at prep school, like that at the Cathedral Church of St. Paul in Detroit, stressed the need for service and improving society, and Soapy was unsure that a life stamping passports, attending embassy parties, and writing dispatches to Washington was the best means of serving God. His letters to his parents never mentioned options other than the State Department, but he began to think about law and perhaps politics.

A political career was not likely to endear him to his mother, but his father seemed less of a barrier. During one of his summer vacations from Salisbury, Henry Williams took his son to the Cadillac Hotel in downtown Detroit to meet the family attorney, Francis "Frank" Murphy. Williams later called it "probably the most momentous moment in my political life, outside of meeting my wife." Murphy was a superb attorney (he would later be named to the U.S. Supreme Court), but he also was a political activist—a liberal, Democratic, political activist—who would be elected governor of Michigan in 1936. Although Williams had not yet abandoned his mother's dream of the diplomatic corps, when he arrived at Princeton in the fall of 1929, politics was an ever more attractive option.[17]

Williams's superb record at Salisbury made his admission to Princeton a certainty, but he had some doubts about how he would fit in at the sophisticated and class-conscious university. He was academically well prepared, but Princeton also stressed the social life of young gentlemen. Although he had been in Connecticut for four years, Williams was still a midwesterner, and he was apprehensive about how he would adjust to the more cosmopolitan world of college. Like a character in a Scott Fitzgerald novel, he was the naive boy from Michigan entering the heady atmosphere of the Ivy League. In his application, he wrote:

> From a course at Princeton, I, as a "Middle Westerner" expect to get not only a "mens sana in corpore sano" [healthy mind in a healthy body] but also a social background and an insight into the atmosphere of the eastern seaboard states. Besides this, if I have sufficient qualifications, I hope to be trained to be a leader.[18]

As Williams prepared to enter Princeton in 1929, his parents left the family home in Detroit and purchased a house at 180 Provencal Road near Lake St. Clair in the affluent and exclusive suburb of Grosse Pointe Farms. As the eighteen-year-old Soapy Williams boarded the train from Detroit to New Jersey in September 1929, the United States was barely a month away from the end of ten years of unprecedented economic growth. Most Americans assumed that the good times of the Roaring Twenties would continue under the leadership of the new president, Herbert Hoover. As secretary of commerce under Warren G. Harding and Calvin Coolidge, Hoover had presided over a decade of prosperity. In October 1929 it all would end with the stock market crash and the Great Depression, and the nation would enter its greatest crisis since the Civil War.

Soapy Williams was less concerned about economics than social life when he arrived at Princeton. He arranged to share rooms with Stan Backus, one of his classmates from Salisbury, and plunged into a frantic schedule of classes, clubs, and sports. He made the rowing team and set a goal of becoming a member of the 1932 U.S. Olympic team. (He would not be selected.) Academically he found the adjustment from prep school minimal and again displayed an ability to outwork everyone. He avoided the "gut" courses popular among Princeton men, who were assured of a "gentleman's C," and selected offerings in English, Latin, the classics, and history. Later he would include classes on political theory and economics.

As at Salisbury, his hard work led to high grades. One of his professors wrote on the bottom of a paper on "Victor Hugo, Louis Napoleon, and the Coup of 1851" that it "was not very excellent" in interpretation or historical analysis but the exhaustive research made it worthy of an A. Another faculty member summarized Williams's years at Princeton: "He knew how to study and he studied hard. . . . His answers were never long—but everything essential was in them—no padding." Williams would graduate Phi Beta Kappa.[19]

Despite his doubts, he also negotiated the complicated social life at Princeton. Although shy and rather unsophisticated among the eastern elite, Williams's sincerity and openness drew him into a group of friends that often "talked books" all night. He never mentioned his wealth and made sure everyone called him Soapy rather than Mennen. He played squash, tennis, and intramural football and joined his classmates on weekend trips to New York for dinners at Longchamps and Sardis and Broadway shows. (He judged Sardis as having "very nice food, but indifferent music.") Unlike most of the men of Princeton, he rarely drank. He said he had a glass of Scotch once, but "it tasted like soap." Once he and Backus decided to see how long it took to get drunk. They bought a bottle of gin, a bottle of whisky, and a bottle of champagne and checked into a hotel room. After four hours both were drunk and sick, and Williams vowed never to be either again. He also had little contact with women. After attending a morning Episcopal service (he went to mass every day) in which the sermon was on the necessity of sexual abstinence, he returned to campus, where one of his classmates gave him a copy of *Fanny Hill.* Williams was shocked to read the memoirs of a prostitute and felt that the "illustrations were most lascivious." He noted in his diary: "From conversations with Bill, the janitor, I gather that in certain social quarters intercourse in all channels is a regular thing." The janitor argued that, as God gave the sexes different organs, they were to be used and "it makes no difference with whom you copulate." Soapy pondered this casual sexual philosophy and concluded: "I'm not sure that ignorance is bliss, but I don't believe that knowledge exudes happiness."[20]

Despite a heavy class load and two hours a day of rowing,

Williams spent Sundays writing romantic poetry about heroes, honor, courage, and religion. He never published the work but filled pages of his diary with heroic couplets. He also kept a detailed ledger of his expenses. His parents provided $135.00 a month for necessities, and he itemized each purchase: $.49 for a hairbrush; $2.50 for squash shoes, and even $.10 for "an apple and a newspaper." Elma often stopped on her way to visit family and friends in Newark and took her son to dinner in New York to check on his academic progress and to remind him of the family goal of a diplomatic career.[21]

When he returned to Detroit after his freshman year, Williams seemed to have fallen into the same pattern at Princeton as he had at Salisbury: hard work, good grades, and athletic and social success. In the summer of 1930, however, his life changed. Soapy Williams found himself hopelessly in love.

In Detroit, at Salisbury, and during his first year at Princeton he had little interaction with women. He attended the required dances and coed visitations but never dated. During his summer vacation he met Margaret Johnson. "Peg" Johnson was the granddaughter of Abbott Johnson, founder of the Warner Gear Company, a manufacturer of automobile transmissions in Muncie, Indiana. Her father, Ray Prescott Johnson, ran the Borg Warner Corporation, an international automobile supply company. Peg had attended the Mt. Vernon Episcopal Seminary in Washington, D.C., with Williams's cousin and then enrolled in the Grand Central Art School in New York to study fashion design.[22]

The Johnsons had a summer home in Charlevoix, Michigan, and Williams and Peg met at a party at nearby Northport. When he was introduced to Margaret Johnson, Williams was immediately enthralled. The day they met "I stayed up until dawn talking to Peg. The conversation was most serious," he wrote in his diary. The next evening they talked again, and eventually "the conversation became monosyllabic." Uncharacteristically, the shy and inexperienced Williams tried to kiss her, but she rejected him. Embarrassed, he wrote: "I hope that my momentary surrender will not have an unfortunate effect."[23]

He returned to Princeton for his sophomore year obsessed with Peg Johnson, and his diary would trace a long and agonizing account of the changing nature of the relationship and its impact on his future. Peg was two years older than Williams and near the completion of her degree at the Grand Central School. She lived at the Barbizon Hotel in New York, and for the next year she and Williams would become regulars on the train between Grand Central Station and Princeton. She came down for football weekends, rowing regattas, picnics, and auto trips in the New Jersey countryside. He went up to New York for dinners, shows, and long walks in Central Park.

Peg Johnson dominated Williams's diary throughout 1930 and 1931. He devoted pages to describing his feelings, composed poetry and letters to her, and noted every subtle shift in the relationship. On November 6, 1930, he wrote six pages about Peg, love, and a possible marriage:

> The old question, pretty new to me. Am I in love—but first, what is love? If being in love is to have pangs because one can't hear from the other one regularly, I am. If being extremely interested in someone is, I am. If being inspired to better things is, I am. If being worried about it is, I am. If occasionally having the desire to kiss is, I am.[24]

Soapy may have been in love, but he was not sure it was reciprocated. He often mused about her refusal to kiss him at their first meeting and wondered whether this showed she was not as enamored with him.

> Do I think Peg thinks she loves me? Yes. Do I think she contemplates marriage any more than I? No. Do I think I am a damn fool? Yes. Do I think she is mighty fine? Exceedingly. What do I think is going to happen? I believe I shall state to Peg the situation. On her reacting much depends. But I trust that we shall have the same mutual trust, and that I shall continue to believe in her. I don't imagine I shall care for anyone as much as Peg—Certainly I can not admire anyone more. She, surely, is giving me a square deal and more; I hope I can "reciprocate." Pray God almighty give me judgment to reach some good conclusion and strength to act thereon.[25]

During Christmas break of his sophomore year, he spent three days with Peg in Muncie visiting her parents and friends. He was not impressed with Muncie ("I think it is the kind of place that improves with deeper understanding"), but he became even more obsessed with Peg. Being with her in Muncie led to a "gamut of emotions" as he considered "the tragic failure in losing Peg" or "the supreme hope and faith that maybe it might be effected!"[26]

He returned to Princeton pondering the possibility of marriage. Reflections on marriage were new territory for the nineteen-year-old Williams. Marriage would require a steady income and a clear career choice.

> I have always before me the idea of a career to somehow achieve greatness or rather perform a great service. Contradictory ideas arise—a son, a wife etc. . . . . God, if only I could become supremely interested in life so that I should accomplish some worthy service—But I seem to do nothing but muddle around—I could do great things if I could but grow to be worthy of her. Damn it there's the sore spot. I'm so damn pride-bound, I'm afraid I'd rather be a grand success in being a total failure in doing something fine, than a small success in plodding along. Good God make me have a standard of values![27]

He also debated whether he was worthy of marriage. "Help me to help myself to be more cordial, more genial, more social, more friendly, and more of service to my fellows," he wrote. He also noted:

> One other thing, is my fear of consistency and whether I really love Peg as she deserves to be. As for Peg's caring for me, I have every reason to believe she is interested in me, but probably not as a mate. I cannot blame her for this, if it is true, I am certainly no rock for any one to lean on, and no everlasting source of cheerfulness and comfort. I believe she regards me as a brother, but something urges me to know definitely. It is cowardly. Half of my problem would be solved could I know in what light she held me.[28]

Throughout the winter and spring, Williams pondered the joys and pain of his first love and the dilemmas it posed. He remembered the "night I embraced Peg" and the spurned kiss as the most exciting of his life: "There was no God. There was no duty; there was only Peg—That was time, space, every dimension, every ambition, every possibility. There is still Peg, there is still I. There is still my love. I had no more desire than now." He worried, however, that "if we were to embrace, I might not experience what I did. Today has taken away yesterday and substituted nothing—But the hope for tomorrow and the melancholy memory of yesterday. The world is so complex. I can not always think of what is most immediately seeming of importance. I can not do what I desire most to do, I can not even express what that is."[29]

Williams's overwrought prose was partly typical undergraduate angst. His relationship with Peg, however, was a true crisis. A career in the diplomatic corps, law, or politics would require "3 or 4 post graduate years and then a few before I marry," and Peg was twenty-one and might not wish to wait. If, however, this was true love and if God had willed him to be with Peg, he might never achieve the success he was certain was ordained for him without her. And, if Peg spurned a marriage proposal, what flaws in his character were so obvious that she had to reject him? The only solution was to ask: "I believe she regards me as a brother, but something urges me to know definitely." If she said no, he could pursue his diplomatic career or law school. If she accepted, he would have to make other plans. He feared that a formal proposal "might make Peg embarrassed or unhappy" but the longer he hesitated the more he would agonize. He had little experience with women or love and was not sure how to proceed. "The question in my mind," he wrote, "is do I understand people? I guess I don't."[30]

On April 11, after a visit to New York, he considered "the old questions. Do I love Peg, does she love me, and is such a love propitious?" A month later, after she visited Princeton, he offered a tortured rationale for inaction: "I love Peg too much to propose to her because I might not love her enough!" But during a rowing match two days later he found "with each stroke I exhaled Peg, Peg, Peg!" He began to suffer headaches and nosebleeds.[31]

Finally the agony ended. On May 17, Williams took the train to visit Peg in New York. He picked her up at the Barbizon and they went for a walk in Central Park, where he noticed happy young married couples with their children. When they returned to her hotel he went to her room, where they "discussed Omar Kyayam [*sic*]."

> Then we sat silently. I kissed her head and gradually the idea possessed me to kiss her on the lips. I did this, many times, and evidently zestfully, because Peg said I was serious. Soon I noticed that Peg was not responding and looked rather perplexed and not altogether pleased. I asked her what the matter was. She replied I shouldn't be serious. I couldn't quite understand. . . . She said she would tell me someday later.

Williams left and caught the next train back to Princeton, where he "spent much of the night trying to figure this all out." He concluded: "I'm sure she loves me, but probably in another way." He became deeply depressed: "For a time I saw easily how one could kill oneself. At such a moment the immediate emotion is more powerful than all responsibilities of every sort. But doing away with oneself makes nobody better off."[32]

They continued to date throughout the school year, and Williams gave her the oar charm he had won for rowing. When she prepared to return to Muncie for the summer, he presented her with a poem.

> Though time and space may intervene
> And though we seem to part
> Nothing can come between
> Man and what is in his heart.[33]

The next day Williams and his friend Charlie Warner went to the Barbizon to help Peg pack her furniture. After she left, Williams told Warner that he "had more or less come down to facts with her." His friend noted that Williams still seemed "pretty much 'wrapped up' with her" and broke the news that she had another boyfriend at Harvard. "Charlie said she didn't know exactly what she wanted. We saw her as a bit spoiled, used to having her own way, etc. etc. But, in the end, we mutually assured ourselves that she was one of the best women in the world."[34]

Williams and Johnson continued to correspond throughout the summer, but the passion was gone. On September 18, she wrote him "a beautiful letter" in which she explained her actions.

> Do you remember some time ago I asked you not to fall in love with me, or rather, not to tell me that you were in love with me? I didn't give you a reason did I? I will now. I wasn't in love with you. If you had asked me my feelings I would have been afraid to tell you. I was afraid that somehow it might make a difference and that suddenly everything would end. I didn't want that to happen. I care for you tremendously. I still do.

Williams commented: "I should have seen but wouldn't see. I shall not longer have to worry over that. We are now on solid ground and the very best of friends." He later sent her flowers and a series of poems in an attempt to rekindle the flame, but she responded that she wouldn't "play 'Indian giver' and take my words back." Within a year she was engaged.[35]

Peg Johnson did not become engaged to her Harvard beau. While vacationing in Arizona in the winter of 1930, she met a Phoenix department store owner who also had political ambitions. Three years later he proposed, and on September 22, 1934, she married Barry Goldwater. The irony of his college love wed to the country's leading Republican conservative and one of the most vocal critics of Williams was not lost on reporters. During the 1964 presidential campaign they asked the wife of the Republican nominee about her past relationship with the liberal former governor of Michigan and current head of the African Bureau of the Department of State. Margaret Goldwater replied that she had dated Williams a few times and that he and her husband "were not unfriendly."[36]

Neither statement was completely candid. Williams and Peg Johnson Goldwater had dated more than "a few times," and Barry Goldwater would later offer harsh criticism of Williams's liberalism at home and the African-first policy abroad. Goldwater would repeatedly accuse Williams of being a "tool" of corrupt labor bosses, and, when John Kennedy appointed Williams as assistant secretary of state for Africa in 1961 Goldwater joked: "I hear Kennedy has sent Soapy Williams to Africa. That's where I would send him too!"[37]

Infatuation with Peg Johnson did not distract him from academic success. He found, however, that the impact of the Great Depression led him to shift the focus of his studies. The collapse of the stock market and the subsequent descent of America into economic chaos affected even the wealthy young men within the ivy-covered gates of Princeton. In 1931, Williams noted: "My mind is continually confronted with the picture of men out of work, and the ignorance and squalidness of the life of a great many people. Thus I am interested in economics and politics." He concluded: "There must be a social readjustment, a leveling of incomes (I hope this will not mean a standard lower than the one I'm used to)" through passage of "good laws which will enable the average man to have more money." Increasingly he became convinced that he needed to be a part of this response: "What am I going to do about it [the Depression]? Shall I become a lawyer or a doctor? Shall I go into politics?"[38]

Despite the crash and the Depression, Williams was still wealthy. On his twenty-first birthday, his mother gave him 2,800 shares of Mennen Company stock, and he would later receive substantially more. Even his wealthy family, however, was not immune from the economic crisis. His father wrote to his son of the devastating impact of the crash on Detroit. With the collapse of the auto industry, Henry found he could not collect from the tenants living in his real estate holdings and could not rent them even when he lowered prices. One of Williams's friends wrote: "The less said about Detroit's condition the better." The banks were "closed tighter than a Yalesman at a Harvard boat race. Business is in depression."[39]

His studies also led Williams to a more sympathetic understanding of the plight of the poor. He decided to major in history and was struck with Professor Raymond Sontag's lectures on the devastating impact of industrialization on the urban poor in Europe. More and more it seemed to him that a career in government was his destiny, but he was still aware that his mother expected him to go into the diplomatic service. When a friend was appointed to a position in the State Department he noted that it "has raised the old question—shall it be the law at home or Foreign Service?"[40]

In the summer of 1931, Williams, his brother Harry, and classmate Stan Backus took a bicycle trip through France. They later rented a car in Paris to tour Switzerland and eventually took a boat to England. Elma Williams had arranged visits with U.S. diplomats to show her son what his career would be like in the State Department. When they met with an aide to the American ambassador to France, Soapy asked about life in the diplomatic corps. "My boy," the official responded, "you cannot live on what you will make in the diplomatic service. There are parties to give, clothes to buy, expensive gifts to purchase. . . . You must go to your Mama and tell her that if she wants to see her son in the diplomatic service, she will have to foot the bill." Williams already had doubts about a life in the State Department, and the trip confirmed his conviction that his future was in another area. The social emphasis of embassy life and the expectation that he would have to rely on his mother to fund his diplomatic career helped convince him that his calling to "better society" lay elsewhere. That fall he wrote in his diary: "I guess I am no longer going to enter the Foreign Service. There is still the law and politics and even in the background medicine." He later claimed that by his sophomore year at Princeton he had decided to become the governor of Michigan.[41]

The Depression was a significant force in Williams's later decision to earn a law degree and enter politics, but while at Princeton he remained a staunch Republican. As a junior he was elected president of the Young Republican Club and reelected the next year. In 1932 he campaigned for Herbert Hoover's reelection. (He later claimed that he saw himself as a "liberal Republican" while at Princeton but later "I got to thinking that there is no such animal.")[42]

Having decided against the diplomatic corps, Williams applied to the University of Michigan Law School in the spring of 1933. He also began his senior thesis, "The Social Significance of Henry Ford." It was a natural topic for a boy from Detroit, and Williams used his family connections to get copies of the Ford Motor Company's records and statistics. His thesis was a curious mixture of conservatism and his emerging awareness of the Great Depression. Williams was generally sympathetic to Ford, largely ignoring his glaring anti-Semitism. He declared that he was interested in how Ford had succeeded in "building the social structure of a new generation." Ford had made a permanent impact on America by paying high wages, which helped "the further distribution of wealth," and by contributing to the "decentralization of industry and consequently society." By creating auto plants outside of downtown Detroit, Ford had helped reverse migration to the city and begun the flow of industry into suburban and even rural areas, a trend Williams predicted would continue throughout the nation. He praised Ford for his charity work and generous wages but offered some criticism of his undemocratic management style. Williams's generally favorable analysis of Ford was ironic, as less than two decades later auto industry executives would become some of his most bitter political opponents and their employees, unionized during the Depression, among his most fervent supporters.[43]

Williams graduated with honors in history in 1933. He was ranked thirty-seventh in his class of 476 and was selected for Phi Beta Kappa. He also served as president of the Quadrangle Club and regional president of the National Student Federation of America and lettered three years in crew.[44]

The summer before enrolling at the University of Michigan Law School in Ann Arbor, Williams left for a long grand tour of Europe financed by his parents. He wrote lengthy descriptions of the cities, art, and politics of Germany, Hungary, Poland, and the Soviet Union, and his father duplicated them for distribution to friends and family in Detroit. Williams had been moved by the impact of the Depression in America, but he was even more shocked at what he found in Europe. He noted the "frenzy" of Nazi rallies in Germany and the massive unemployment and brutal conditions throughout the continent. Like many young Americans in the 1930s, he was eager to see the Soviet experiment, but, in contrast to a number of other visitors, he found little to admire in Stalin's Russia. He acknowl-edged the rapid industrialization of the country and was impressed with the power of "the people's courts" in adminis-tering justice, but he detested the persecution of religion, the lack of freedom of the press, and the repression of political dis-sent. The Soviet Union had no romantic appeal to the young Princetonian, and, although he would denounce the anticom-munist hysteria of the 1950s, he had no doubts about the threat of communism to global freedom. Like most Americans during the cold war, he was convinced that Russia was determined to spread its system throughout the world and that communists within the United States were part of the conspiracy.[45]

During his four years at Princeton, Williams had fallen in love, abandoned his mother's goal of life in the diplomatic corps, and made a decision to pursue a career in politics. His political ideology was still hazy, but he was convinced that gov-ernment was the instrument that could reform and redeem his nation and the means of dealing with the horrors of the Great Depression. He was also certain that it was the vehicle through which he could "accomplish some worthy service." From his earliest days at the Cathedral Church of St. Paul in Detroit, through his years in chapel at Salisbury, and during his four years at Princeton, he had been convinced that God had ordained man to serve others and that he was destined to fulfill God's intent. In his first year at Princeton he wrote: "Would to God, I have exceptional powers—was a member of a resolute group of similar men striving to make the world a better place to live in. Pray God, however humble my service is, I shall not have lived in vain." He would find his "resolute group" first in Washington, D.C., and later in the rough and occasionally vio-lent world of Michigan politics.[46]

Williams's decision to pursue a law degree indicated his choice of a career in electoral politics. He showed no interest in practicing conventional law but saw the degree as a necessary ticket to electoral office. His choice of the University of Michi-gan rather than Princeton or another Ivy League school sug-gested even more clearly his intent to eventually run for office. Ann Arbor was only an hour away from family and friends in

Detroit. More importantly, if he were to seek election in Michigan, a degree from its state university would be a helpful part of his resume and would allow him to make contacts among those most influential in his home state. His professors and fellow law students would form the first network for his entrance into politics fifteen years later.

Like the rest of the nation, the University of Michigan was caught up in the frenzy of Franklin D. Roosevelt's New Deal reform program. The flurry of legislation in March 1933 raised new questions about government and the law. The National Recovery Act, the Agricultural Adjustment Act, the Civilian Conservation Corps, the Banking Act, the Tennessee Valley Authority, and the other measures of Roosevelt's first hundred days marked a major shift in political power. It was Washington more than Wall Street that now directed the nation's economy, and within Washington it was the White House more than Congress that exercised authority. The so-called second New Deal of 1935 escalated the process as the Social Security Act, the Works Progress Administration, and the Wagner Act marked permanent changes in American assumptions about national government and helped create the "New Deal coalition" that would reelect Roosevelt in 1936.

The activism in Washington led to a major debate among legal scholars over the power of the government to regulate business and be a force in the lives of Americans. When the U.S. Supreme Court declared the National Recovery Act and the Agricultural Adjustment Act unconstitutional in 1935, the relationship between the courts and the other two branches of government became a topic of passionate debate. The controversy over the expanded role of government and the court's response was at the center of heated discussions during Williams's three years in Ann Arbor, and the debate helped move him toward liberalism and the Democratic Party.

In Ann Arbor, Williams continued to gain academic success based on his intense effort and organization. He was always prepared and used massive amounts of research to support his arguments. He was still an awkward speaker, but in his mock trials he cited dozens of precedents to defend his positions. One of his professors at Michigan argued that "his mind was what you might call slow moving" but "as a legal craftsman, he was first class." As at Salisbury and Princeton, his hard work paid off. He graduated in the top 10 percent of his class, received the Order of the Coif, and was an editorial assistant for the *Michigan Law Review*.[47]

It was politics more than abstract legal scholarship, however, that occupied his attention in Ann Arbor. He revived the school's Toastmaster's Club, where students gave short prepared talks or impromptu speeches on national and international issues. Many of the groups' meetings focused on the problems of the Depression and the New Deal response, and Williams found himself supporting Roosevelt and his reform programs.[48]

An even greater influence on Williams was the university's Liberal Club. Neil Staebler of Ann Arbor, heir to a coal and timber fortune, had founded and financed the organization to balance the political conservatism he thought was dominant on campus. Despite his wealth, Staebler was a socialist who had campaigned for Norman Thomas in 1928. The constitution of the Liberal Club stated that its purpose was the "fearless, and broad, and open-minded pursuit of the truth." With Staebler's donations, the group brought speakers of all political persuasions to campus, including Norman Thomas, labor organizers, and pacifists. Williams was fascinated with the range of new ideas and became a regular at the organization's meetings. A decade later, Neil Staebler would be the catalyst for Williams's decision to run for governor of Michigan and would become the state's Democratic Party chairman and Williams's leading political strategist.[49]

After two years of law school, Williams had abandoned his conservative Republican heritage for the liberalism of Roosevelt and the New Deal. He joined a student protest in Lansing opposing a bill that would require students and faculty to sign a loyalty oath. He also began to read political theory and radical critiques of capitalism. While on a cruise to Scandinavia with his mother in early 1935, he read Harold Laski's *State in Theory and Practice*, an attack on the power of unregulated business. Laski argued that economic interests would never share their wealth or power without coercion and either violence or a powerful central government was necessary to alter economic inequities. Williams rejected the need for violence but agreed with the call for more state control. He wrote his father: "Dad, I think you ought to read this book. Indeed, I believe every thinking man should read it."[50]

Williams was also enamored with the flood of intellectuals who migrated to Washington to shape the New Deal. He read a magazine article by a Harvard Law School professor and informal adviser to Franklin Roosevelt, Felix Frankfurter, urging bright young men to abandon the pursuit of their own careers to come to Washington and help reform America. Frankfurter would create a "vast, cohesive, personal empire that spread throughout the executive branch, the White House, and the independent regulatory commissions, where hundreds of Harvard Law School graduates . . . jumped instantly to the command of their former professor." Frankfurter's call for talented men to come to Washington and help remake the nation was a perfect match for Williams. Five years earlier he had written of his desire to be "a member of a resolute group of similar men striving to make the world a better place to live in." Roosevelt and his New Deal seemed to offer this opportunity.[51]

By 1936, Williams had embraced political liberalism but his parents had not. Although Soapy was infatuated with Roosevelt and the New Deal, Henry and Elma Williams were appalled by the multitude of social programs and the high taxes imposed to fund them. When Mennen went to Grosse Pointe for a party, his parents' dentist began to challenge him and his politics and asked how he could justify his switch to the Democrats. Williams launched into a long description of the soup lines in Detroit, the selfishness of big business, the need for reform, and the accomplishments of Roosevelt. "That is why I have become a Democrat," he concluded, and walked out the door. "Well, I'll be damned," the dentist exclaimed, "Did you hear that?" Elma responded: "You asked him, he told you." The next morning Henry Williams told his son that he had a

right to his opinions, as did his parents, but he must "never discuss politics in this house again."[52]

As important as the Depression and New Deal were in
Williams's political conversion to liberalism, there was another,
more personal influence: Nancy Lace Quirk. After his infatuation with Peg Johnson ended, Williams had a few dates at
Princeton and had asked girls to join him at football games or
movies in Ann Arbor but had no long-term relationship with a
woman. In 1935, Nancy Quirk was a sophomore social work
student at Michigan. She was engaged to a man from St. Louis
and had invited him to her spring sorority dance. When he canceled, her friends arranged for Mennen Williams to take his
place. After the dance they walked to Miller's Dairy Bar for ice
cream. Unlike Peg Johnson, Nancy Quirk was informed and
interested in the political issues of the day and knew more
about current social problems than did her law student date.
Her outspoken political liberalism and commitment to reform
appealed to Williams and would shape his political philosophy
directly.[53]

Nancy Quirk's background and good looks were as attractive
to Mennen Williams as her politics. She was the daughter of a
wealthy Ypsilanti, Michigan, banker and had been raised in a
strong Episcopal family. Like Williams, her parents had sent her
east for prep school at the Master's School in Dobbs Ferry,
New York. In 1933, she enrolled in the first class at the School
of Social Work at the University of Michigan. He father was
not very political until Franklin Roosevelt closed American
banks in 1933, at which time he became a critic of the New
Deal. Her mother, by contrast, was a Democrat. In 1928, she
was so angered by the anti-Catholic hysteria provoked by the
nomination of Al Smith that she decorated the family car with
large banners endorsing the New Yorker.[54]

Her daughter inherited her mother's dedication to tolerance
and hatred of religious or racial discrimination. Her social work
courses at Michigan also led her into a concern for economic
reform. In a class called Poverty and Dependence she wrote a
lengthy paper, arguing that "the reformist point of view and the
revolutionary point of view are two methods by which to study

the possible solutions to the problem of poverty." She concluded: "The elimination of poverty requires the reorganization of the very fundamentals of modern industrial society."[55]

She also shared Williams's conviction that God intended humans to create a more just and equal society. "All too often, we accept as morality public prayer and reference to divine guidance," she noted. "This we certainly need. But to make it work, it must be accompanied by translating this prayer into the actions which the Providence expects of a democratic people." She argued that "as long as people are dying of hunger, ridden with disease, living in misery, our mission as Christians is not fulfilled." She was even more blunt in her attack on racial discrimination: "Christ said 'Suffer the little children to come unto me.' He did not say 'Suffer the little white protestant Episcopal children to come onto me.'"[56]

Aside from her liberal politics, her Episcopalian faith, and her Michigan connections, Nancy Quirk was attractive, lively, and athletic. She played golf and tennis, skied, and was an accomplished figure skater. She loved to talk and argue and would prove to be an energetic and skilled campaigner and an important political adviser to her husband. Nancy Quirk was likely more liberal on economic and social issues than Mennen Williams when they met and would be a major influence in his final development of an activist, progressive, political philosophy based on economic reform and racial equality.

In 1936, Williams proposed marriage. He commissioned a local jeweler to design a bronze loving cup with the Quirk family symbol (an oak tree) and the Williams family crest (a lion). He filled it with beer and took it to Nancy at her sorority house. At the bottom of the cup was an engagement ring. (Williams would use the cup throughout his career to toast political victories.) Daniel Quirk, Nancy's father, agreed to the marriage but only if they waited until his daughter graduated. On June 26, 1937, a week after she received her degree from Michigan, they were married at St. Luke's Episcopal Church in Ypsilanti.[57]

Mennen Williams had a law degree and a wife, and his dream of joining the diplomatic corps had long been abandoned. He had decided on a career in politics and government service and had embraced the heady liberalism of the early New Deal. He had determined that he would eventually run for governor of Michigan, but at the age of twenty-five, with no political experience, that campaign would have to wait. To prepare for that effort, he would heed Frankfurter's call and head to Washington to join "a resolute group of similar men striving to make the world a better place to live in."

II

WASHINGTON, WAR, JIMMY
HOFFA, AND THE MICHIGAN
MIRACLE, 1936–48

I'm young. I can take a licking.

—G. *Mennen Williams's response when*
told he had no chance to win the race
for Michigan governor in 1948

Unlike most young Americans looking for work in the middle
of the Great Depression, G. Mennen Williams had a number of
options. He had personal wealth and family connections, possessed a prestigious Princeton degree, and had graduated from
one of the nation's finest law schools. He could have stayed in
Michigan to practice law and prepare for a political career,
worked with his father in Detroit, or, like his younger brother,
moved to New Jersey and joined the Mennen Company. None
of these possibilities appealed to him. Williams had no interest
in the family's real estate and investment business in Detroit or
in working for his mother's cosmetics company: He wanted to
reform business, not be a part of it. He had never wanted to be
a courtroom lawyer, and the prospect of practicing corporate
law seemed both uninteresting and unlikely to further his goal
of being elected governor of Michigan. Washington, D.C.,
rather than Ann Arbor or Detroit, was where the excitement
was. Franklin Roosevelt's 1936 landslide reelection and the
Democratic Party's control of Congress had made the New
Deal a permanent part of American life and led to expectations
for even more substantial reforms. To Williams, a position in
Roosevelt's "brain trust" overseeing the continued evolution

43

of the New Deal would not only be stimulating but would serve as an excellent preparation for his anticipated career in electoral politics.

Williams was determined to secure an appointment in the nation's capital but found it surprisingly difficult to obtain. After completing his Juris Doctorate in the spring of 1936, he began his search for a job in Washington. He had no particular preference except that it be with some government agency in the nation's capital. He first lobbied the dean of the Michigan Law School, Henry Moore Bates, to use his contacts in Washington to find a suitable position. Bates wrote to several New Deal agencies and his friends Frank Parish, an assistant to Attorney General Homer S. Cummings, and former undersecretary of the treasury Dean Acheson, but there were no immediate responses. Williams's father also contacted Michigan senator James Couzens to inquire about an appointment for his son but with no success. There were many other bright young men eager to work in Washington, and, despite his brilliant academic record and the rapid expansion of government under Roosevelt, there was not an abundance of positions available.[1]

Even Elma Williams tried to find her eldest son work among the New Deal Democrats she so despised. Despite her abhorrence of Soapy's new liberal philosophy, she was determined to help him secure a suitable job in government. If Roosevelt and his "band of radicals" in Washington could tax her money, they could at least use some of it to hire her boy. When Bates and her husband did not get results, she took her son to downtown Detroit to talk with Frank Murphy. Murphy would become Williams's political model and for the next decade his mentor and patron.[2]

Murphy had earned both his undergraduate and law degrees at the University of Michigan and had been a member of the firm that handled the Williams family's legal affairs. He had also been an influential figure in Michigan politics. In 1919–20, he served as assistant attorney general for the eastern district of Michigan, from 1923 to 1930 he was a judge on the Detroit Records Court, and in 1930 he was elected mayor of Detroit. A strong supporter of Roosevelt, Murphy served the new president as governor general of the Philippines from 1933 to 1935 and U.S. high commissioner to the Philippines from 1935 to 1936 (three decades later Mennen Williams would serve as U.S. ambassador to the Philippines). In 1936, Roosevelt convinced Murphy to return to America to run for governor of Michigan. He was successful, but lost a reelection bid in 1938. Roosevelt selected him as his attorney general in 1939 and a year later appointed him to the U.S. Supreme Court.[3]

Murphy was a New Dealer but also something of a political maverick. He was adamantly opposed to corruption (a rarity in Michigan politics) and alienated regular Democrats by refusing to tolerate the petty graft common to the state and by championing civil service over political patronage. He also appointed a number of Republicans to prominent positions in Michigan and outraged many in the state when he rejected pressure to use the National Guard to crush the sit-down strikes in Detroit's automobile plants in 1937.

Like the young Mennen Williams, Murphy saw politics as a noble calling and was convinced that officeholders held an almost sacred trust in representing the people. When he met with Williams, Murphy was struck by the young man's sincerity, intelligence, and similar philosophy of government. He was unable to promise an immediate appointment in Washington but assured Williams that he would use his influence to help in the future.[4]

Williams was inspired by his conversation with Murphy, but he still did not have a job. Tired of waiting for others to act, he caught a train to Washington to search for employment himself. He brought with him a letter from J. Douglas Brown, a Princeton dean and a member of the Social Security Advisory Council. The letter led to interviews with the Social Security Board and the Securities and Exchange Commission and job offers from both. Williams selected Social Security. Roosevelt's program of old age pensions was one of the centerpieces of the New Deal and was far more appealing than working on the regulation of the stock market. Preparation for the implementation of Social Security was a massive job involving the central administration in Washington and each of the forty-eight states. Williams explained: "I chose the more active job."[5]

Williams's immediate supervisor was Thomas H. Eliot,

counsel for the Society Security Board and only a few years older than the new Michigan law school graduate. Like Williams, Eliot had political ambitions (he would later become a congressman), and the two spent much of their time discussing politics and campaigns. Political conversations with Eliot proved to be one of the few highlights of Williams's first job.

Williams had been an academic and athletic star at Salisbury and Princeton and near the top of his class at the Michigan law school. In Washington, however, he was only one of thousands of bright young lawyers involved in government. He was no longer the center of attention but a part of a vast bureaucracy with little direct personal power or influence. The Social Security Administration employed over twelve thousand people in Washington and its regional offices, and the agency's central records office covered more than an acre of floor space. Williams's position as an associate attorney at the Social Security Board was routine and often mundane. He was assigned to a section of seven men and one woman to research state constitutions and cases in order to adapt the national social security statutes to each locality. The group also helped draft briefs for the forthcoming Supreme Court test of the Social Security Act. Williams's gifts for research and hard work made for success, but he found he had little power over policies or decisions. Like most low-level administrative positions, it was time-consuming but largely uncreative work.

He did enjoy a close relationship with Eliot. In the fall of 1937, his boss and his wife gave up their apartment and moved in with Williams and Nancy until Eliot left to teach law at Harvard and to prepare to run for Congress. Without Eliot, Williams's job became even more routine and less fulfilling. After a year in Washington, he was restless and eager to be more active and directly involved in politics and was overjoyed in 1938 when his mentor, Frank Murphy, arranged for him to return to Michigan.[6]

Murphy had tried, with limited success, to implement a "New Deal" in Michigan during his term as governor. Although the Republican state legislature frustrated many of his

plans for reform, his activism led to a surge of court cases challenging his programs. Michigan's attorney general, Raymond
W. Starr, and his forty-person legal staff were overwhelmed,
and Starr asked Murphy for permission to hire two new lawyers
to handle appeals. Murphy immediately recommended
Williams, and Starr hired him in 1938.[7]

The position was near perfect for a young and ambitious
politician such as Soapy Williams. He was back in his home
state and working for Frank Murphy, a combination that
seemed ideal for an eventual run for political office. Attorney
General Starr recognized that Williams's talents were not in the
courtroom (he observed that Williams lacked "the harshly
competitive spirit that trial lawyers have to have"), but the
young lawyer was excellent at research and organization, and
he assigned Williams to prepare a milk-marketing bill to regulate the state's dairy industry.[8]

There were over sixty thousand dairy farmers in Michigan in
1938 and continued low milk prices threatened their ability to
survive. They lobbied the state to regulate the industry to raise
wholesale prices, and Murphy was supportive. The governor
was certain that there was a "milk trust" at work in Michigan
that deprived dairy farmers of a fair price and invited Truman
Marshall, head of the Antitrust Division of the Department of
Justice, to come to Lansing to determine the possibility of a suit
against milk producers. Murphy asked Williams to meet with
Arnold to work on the case and to draft legislation regulating
the state's dairy industry.[9]

Soapy Williams was just twenty-six and had been in Michigan only a few weeks, but he showed a strong independent
streak in his discussions with Arnold and Murphy. He argued
that initiating an antitrust suit was premature and warned it
might result in even lower prices by provoking retaliation from
producers that would antagonize farmers. Despite his objections, Murphy was determined to move against the milk industry and launched an investigation. It found no evidence of price
fixing, but the governor was convinced of the need for government regulation and price controls. Williams again dissented.
Typically, he had done his homework by studying the attempts

of other states to control diary prices and pointed out that regulation in New York had actually resulted in higher consumer
prices with little additional income for farmers. Murphy listened patiently but overruled him and ordered the young
lawyer to draft a bill.[10]

Williams dutifully began the laborious job of writing a milk
bill. The governor appointed an advisory commission to help,
but it was unwieldy and Williams relied on the assistance of
O. L. Utley, a professor at Michigan State University, and experts
from the U.S. Department of Agriculture. Republicans in the
legislature eventually gutted the measure with amendments and
the Michigan Supreme Court declared it unconstitutional in
1939, but Williams's energy and effort had impressed Murphy,
and he delegated Williams to draft a bill to allow Michigan to
qualify for federal housing funds and appointed him as the state's
liaison with the Department of Justice's Antitrust Division.[11]

Williams's first efforts in state government showed an independent streak, a willingness to challenge his superiors, and a
continued capacity for hard work. His objections to an antitrust
suit and opposition to a price control bill for the dairy industry
required considerable courage for someone hoping for later
support from Murphy and other Democratic leaders. Murphy,
however, did not object to Williams's opinions and continued
to favor his protégé with important assignments. In November
1938, however, Williams's promising start in Michigan politics
came to an abrupt halt when Murphy was defeated in his campaign for reelection.

Murphy's independence and refusal to play the usual patronage game led many regular Democrats to oppose him in 1938.
He had also alienated many voters by his refusal to use force
against the sit-down strikers and had paid little attention to
developing a political organization outside of Detroit. Combined with the "Roosevelt recession" of 1937, Murphy was
politically vulnerable. In 1938, Republicans swept all the major
offices in Michigan, including the governorship, and Williams's
patron was out of a job. So, too, was Mennen Williams.

During his first two years after law school, Williams had
endured a frustrating year in Washington, D.C., and a much

more stimulating one in Lansing. With Murphy's defeat he faced another career choice: He could stay in Michigan, practice law, and try to build a political base or he could return to Washington to work again for the federal government. He rejected both. Instead he and his wife booked passage on an ocean liner for a lengthy tour of Europe and the Holy Land.

The Republican victory in Michigan blocked any opportunity for a political position in his home state, and Williams was unwilling to return to another routine bureaucratic job in Washington. In 1939, he put his career and political ambitions on hold for six months to await developments. Williams considered himself a biblical scholar and amateur archeologist. (He claimed the single most important event of his generation was the discovery of the Dead Sea Scrolls). He and Nancy toured archaeological digs in Egypt, Jordan, and Palestine and continued on to Italy, Greece, Turkey, and France. In Athens the couple found a cable waiting from Frank Murphy, now Roosevelt's attorney general, asking them to "return at once." They ignored it and continued their travels for another three months. When they finally arrived in New York, a special messenger met them on the dock with a note from Murphy informing them that he was holding a job as his administrative assistant at a salary of $4,800 per year (Williams later found that the previous holder of the position had been paid $7,500). Despite the low pay, the offer was attractive, as it involved working directly with Murphy in a position with considerable power and responsibility. Soapy and Nancy Williams went back to Washington, D.C.[12]

Two years earlier, Williams had been frustrated dealing with the bureaucracy of the Social Security Administration. The size and complexity of the Justice Department was even more imposing. Although Murphy assigned him an office near his, Williams was unfamiliar with the nuances and intrigue of governmental agencies in Washington. There were nearly fifteen thousand lawyers and other officials working for Murphy, and, although Williams had easy access to the attorney general, he was uncertain of the functions of the department and its seemingly endless divisions and committees. He proved to be a quick learner. Within six months he had detailed knowledge of procedures and personnel in the department and, along with Edward G. Kemp, a former law partner of Murphy's, oversaw the attorney general's schedule and screened prospective employees.[13]

Williams also developed a close personal relationship with Murphy. He and Nancy often invited the attorney general to dinner at their apartment, and Murphy indirectly contributed to Williams's most famous trademark. One night when Murphy was seated at the kitchen table Soapy prepared to serve the first course, mushroom soup. As the six foot four Williams leaned over the tureen, his tie dipped into the soup. Nancy rushed to the kitchen to get a cloth to clean up the table and the tie, leaving the dinner rolls to burn in the oven. Williams vowed never again to wear a regular tie and for the rest of his life appeared only in hand-knotted bow ties. (It would be ten years before he would adopt the green and white polka dots that would be his symbol.)[14]

The bow-tie-wearing Williams seemed to be in a perfect position for the eventual move into elected office. He enjoyed a close friendship with one of the most important figures in Washington (who had direct political contacts in Michigan) and had mastered the flow of information and administrative organization to help manage the Justice Department. But less than a year after his appointment as Murphy's assistant it all changed, and he was again searching for work.

In 1940, Roosevelt made the surprising appointment of Murphy to replace Pierce Butler on the U.S. Supreme Court and selected Robert H. Jackson to replace him as attorney general. The elevation of his patron led to a loss of influence for Williams. Jackson had been a vocal opponent of Murphy's Supreme Court nomination and did not want his predecessor's protégé as his assistant. Williams, too, had no interest in working with his mentor's critic. He immediately requested a transfer to the Criminal Division.

The highlight of Williams's brief stay in the Criminal Division was the chance to return to Michigan and get involved directly in the state's political system. In 1941, Jackson sent him to Detroit to lead an investigation of corruption in the Michigan State Liquor Commission. The state-owned liquor industry was a constant source of graft and scandal, as kickbacks to government officials, bribes to distributors, and payoffs to truck drivers (recently organized by the Brotherhood of Teamsters under its leader, Jimmy Hoffa) were the accepted means of doing business. In 1941, the corruption became public when the press published letters linking Frank McKay of Grand Rapids, a Republican national committeeman, to an organized system of payoffs from liquor distillers to ensure placement of their products in state stores. The U.S. Postal Service had delivered the letters soliciting the "goodwill" donations, and this made it a federal case when a grand jury indicted McKay for mail fraud.

Williams and two assistants arrived from Washington to prepare the case against the Republican leader and maneuvered to have the trial assigned to a Democratic judge. The senior judge, a Republican, was outraged and threatened to put Williams and his associates in jail. "He really raised hell," Williams recalled, and he and his assistants carried habeas corpus papers with them in case they were incarcerated. McKay was acquitted, but Williams moved for a second trial, where the Republican leader again was found not guilty. Even though he lost the case, Williams found the McKay prosecution "my most exciting legal experience," and he was now well known in the political and legal communities of Michigan. Five years later his appointment to the Michigan Liquor Control Commission would serve as his stepping stone to the Democratic nomination for governor.[15]

After the McKay case, Williams returned briefly to the Justice Department but, as at the Social Security Board, quickly became bored and restless. With Murphy gone, he was again only one of many ambitious young lawyers with little direct power. He told Linton Collins, an assistant in the department, that he felt he was not being challenged and would soon resign to go back to Michigan. Events would delay his return to his home state for five years.

By 1941, Europe and Asia were at war and the United States

was preparing to enter the conflict. Rearmament finally led to the end of the Great Depression, but it also resulted in rapid inflation. Roosevelt asked Congress for a new law giving him power to regulate prices, and while the House and Senate debated the president established the Office of Price Controls (OPC), headed by the economist Leon Henderson, to try to stabilize prices. One of his assistants was Brunson McChesney, a University of Michigan Law School graduate who had been active in the Liberal Club at Michigan, and he invited Mennen Williams to join him in the new agency. Eager to escape the Justice Department, Williams accepted the new position immediately.[16]

The OPC was so hastily organized that it had no office space. The staff worked out of an abandoned apartment complex in Washington. It later moved to an unfurnished building near Constitution Avenue. With the expansion of government on the eve of the U.S. entrance into World War II, housing was so short that McChesney moved in with Soapy and Nancy in a rented home on Rock Creek Drive. The agency had no official power except for "jawboning" the most obvious examples of price gouging, and Henderson sent Williams and others in the agency on the road to investigate and expose excessive price increases. While most of the OPC's "flying squad" immediately leaked examples of price raising to the press, Williams was more moderate in his approach. He preferred to discuss prices and inflation with businessmen and to appeal to their patriotism to convince them to hold the line and help America prepare for war. Some companies responded to his low-key, diplomatic approach while others refused, noting that the agency had no power to force them to limit their prices.[17]

Within a few months of his shift to the Office of Price Controls, the United States was at war. Williams heard of Japan's attack on Pearl Harbor on the radio and immediately rushed to his office, where he helped draft emergency directives freezing prices to be delivered to the president the next day. He remained in the OPC for several months after Pearl Harbor but eventually decided that he should take a more active part in the war. He met with Frank Murphy, now a Supreme Court justice, who encouraged him to join the armed forces. (Murphy had served in World War I and was so eager to be a part of the war effort that he had been reprimanded for taking a temporary leave from the court to participate in military training in Louisiana). Murphy agreed to write to the director of naval operations to obtain a commission, and in the spring of 1942 Williams left his wife and new son, Gerhard Williams (Gery) and reported to the navy's officer school at Quonset Point, Rhode Island.[18]

Williams was thirty-one years old, but years of lifting weights and rowing had kept him in superb condition and he had no difficulty with the grueling physical training of officer candidates. He also excelled in the academic exams and graduated fifteenth in his class of 750 at Quonset. Williams was fluent in French and German and had traveled extensively in Europe. Naturally the navy assigned him to the Pacific theater. He requested duty in Alaska, where a Japanese attack seemed imminent but was posted to Pearl Harbor as an intelligence officer and then assigned to the staff of Vice Admiral Alfred E. Montgomery, the commander of an aircraft carrier task force preparing to attack Japanese positions in the Pacific.

Williams's job was to collect and analyze the photographs and reports of pilots of the damage caused by U.S. air strikes. For the next two years he served on the aircraft carriers *Yorktown, Hornet, Bunker Hill,* and *Essex* during their attacks on Wake Island, the Marshalls, the Gilberts, the Mariannas, and the Philippines. Interpretation of the hazy photos and exaggerated reports of flight crews was laborious and often inaccurate, but Williams eventually developed a uniform system of photo analysis that was adopted throughout the Pacific fleet.

While her husband was in the Pacific, Nancy Williams also did her part in the war effort. While in Washington, she served as a member of the Red Cross Canteen Corps until her pregnancy led her to return home to Ypsilanti to give birth to their second child, Nancy Lace (Lannie) on June 25, 1943. After her delivery, she drove army trucks from Detroit assembly lines to shipping centers and later volunteered as a nurse's aide.[19]

In December 1944, the navy transferred Williams from sea

duty to the North Island Naval Base in Coronado, California, to work on supply planning for the last year of the war, and Nancy, Gery, and Lannie (who her father had never seen) joined him in a small home at 274 F Avenue. In November 1945, the navy sent Williams overseas for two months to assess the damage of U.S. air attacks on Japan, Singapore, and the Philippines. By the time he was discharged on February 9, 1946, Williams had risen to the rank of lieutenant commander and been awarded ten battle stars, the Legion of Merit, a Presidential Unit Citation, the World War II Victory Ribbon, the Philippine Liberation Ribbon, and the Asiatic Pacific Area Campaign Star.[20]

In the decades after the war, Williams rarely spoke of his military experience. He was always a strong advocate for those who had been in the conflict, holding office in numerous local, state, and national veterans' organizations, and he lobbied aggressively for improved care in veterans hospitals, expanded educational opportunities, and subsidized housing for vets. Like John F. Kennedy, Richard Nixon, and other young politicians who had served in the war, he always mentioned his military record in his campaign literature and speeches but offered few details of his wartime experiences. Few of his close friends were navy colleagues, and he generally avoided reunions of his old units. His letters to Nancy, Frank Murphy, and others during his years of service were generally vague. He said that his job was "interesting" and he hoped to "make a real contribution to the war effort" but offered little more. Only later in private correspondence did he recall the stifling heat, boredom, danger, and exhaustion of his two years in the Pacific and note that several times he had collapsed from fatigue and overwork.[21]

A month before his discharge from the navy, Williams wrote a long diary entry pondering his future. He noted that like "a million or so other returning men" he needed a home, a job, and a direction for his life: "19 years of education, 5½ years attempting to establish a career in public service, 3½ years of war—and now what?" He acknowledged that "a living income is a serious part if not the most vital part" of the problem but was convinced that he needed a job that offered more than just decent pay: "The guts of the matter is getting or making a job that will be part and parcel of my life's work." Before the war he had decided that his life's work would be in Michigan politics, and now he had a chance to begin that effort. "It is my desire to help men achieve an abundant life and human dignity. The achievement of these objectives points in my mind to a life of public service in the liberal and progressive tradition," he wrote. It was time to "get my roots in the soil of Michigan so that I can run for elective office when the time is ripe." Two years later he would judge the time had arrived.[22]

To return to Michigan he needed a job, and again he turned to Frank Murphy. Although Murphy was now on the Supreme Court, he maintained a strong interest in politics, particularly in his home state. He still smarted from his reelection defeat in 1938 and hoped for a liberal New Deal program in Michigan. Williams had already told him of his intent to run for governor someday, and the judge was eager to help him prepare. In April 1946, Murphy arranged for Williams to become deputy director of the Office of Price Administration (OPA) in Detroit. Williams would occupy the position for barely a year, but, as Murphy had hoped, it proved to be an excellent training ground for a campaign for the governorship.[23]

Like many veterans, Williams organized his OPA office like a military operation. He developed "battle plans" for staff meetings and used military time for schedules (e.g., a 3:00 p.m. meeting was to start at 1500 hours). His work was routine, and he spent much of his time discussing Michigan politics and establishing a network of friends and advisers that would help him become governor.[24]

In his year at the OPA, Williams met four people who not only would help him get the Democratic nomination in 1948 but would remain key advisers and operatives during his twelve years as governor. His superior at the OPA was Lawrence T. Farrell, a former administrator of Franklin Roosevelt's Works Progress Administration in Michigan's Upper Peninsula. Farrell was a veteran of Michigan Democratic politics and knew most of the party's officials and activists. Williams told him of his plans to someday run for governor, and Farrell arranged for his young employee to travel throughout the state on OPA business. Officially he was to coordinate the work of local offices with the state office in Detroit. Unofficially he was to get to know local Democrats throughout Michigan to establish a political network for the future.

It was also through the OPA that Williams met an extraordinary married couple, Hicks and Martha Griffiths, who would become two of his closest political advisers. Hicks Griffiths worked in the legal section of the agency, and his wife, also a lawyer, was on the staff of the Detroit Ordinance Office. Both were liberal Democrats appalled by the inertia and corruption of the regular Democratic Party in Michigan and encouraged Williams to prepare to run for governor. They invited their colleague to join their law firm in Detroit and introduced him to liberals and labor leaders in the community. They also encouraged him to visit local ethnic organizations in Detroit, and Williams began to show up to "talk politics" and call square dances at Hungarian, Lithuanian, Polish, German, and other social clubs. With introductions from the Griffiths, Williams recalled that "eventually I went everywhere" in the city in 1946.[25]

A chance encounter on an airplane brought him into contact with an even more important individual: Neil Staebler. In late 1945, a few months before he was discharged from the navy, Williams was on a flight from Washington, D.C., to Detroit. Next to him on the plane was a young woman with two small children, one of whom was ill. Williams volunteered to hold one of the kids on his lap during the flight so the mother could attend to her sick child. He was unaware that the woman was Neil Staebler's wife. Six months later Williams was in Chicago waiting for a train to attend a conference of the American Veterans Association (he was the president of the Detroit chapter) in Des Moines, Iowa, when he met a man at the lunch counter. It was Staebler, founder and financial patron of the Liberal Club at the University of Michigan and a leader of efforts to reform the Democratic Party in his state. Staebler recognized Williams and thanked him for his kindness to his wife on the plane trip months earlier. Over sandwiches, the two discovered that they were headed to the same veterans' conference and shared a desire to remake the Democratic Party of Michigan into a liberal organization. Williams invited Staebler to join him and the Griffiths in Detroit to continue the discussion of the future of Michigan politics.[26]

The chance encounter in Chicago would be crucial for his political career in Michigan, as Staebler had a genius for political organization and would become a master strategist for all six of Williams's election victories. He would also create and direct one of the most effective political organizations in American history when he became head of the Democratic Party in Michigan in 1950. In 1955, *Life* magazine called him "probably the ablest state chairman in the country, Democratic or Republican."[27]

The dapper, mustachioed, millionaire Staebler, in his custom-made hundred-dollar silk suits, did not have the appearance of a reformer, but like Williams his wealth did not determine his politics. The Staeblers of Ann Arbor had made their money in the coal and oil industry and, like the Williams family, had invested successfully in real estate. His father was a political activist who had been elected mayor of Ann Arbor in 1927 and 1929 (Neil had managed the campaigns.) The younger Staebler studied economics, history, and politics at the University of Michigan and after graduating in 1926 went on a trip to the Soviet Union. Like Williams, he was impressed with the economic gains of communism but was disillusioned by the lack of political freedom. He was convinced that America needed massive economic reform but "by a democratic and not by authoritarian means." When the Depression hit Staebler joined the Socialist Party, where he met a young Michigan labor leader named Walter Reuther. In 1932, he ran unsuccessfully for mayor of Ann Arbor on the Socialist Party ticket and with the coming of the New Deal abandoned the socialists for the Democrats.[28]

Staebler shared with Williams a visceral hatred of political corruption. He had witnessed firsthand the common graft in the Michigan oil and coal business and found dishonesty in government "repellent." To Staebler, "politics . . . ought to be

the greatest form of adult education in the nation" but corruption fostered cynicism and apathy. He felt that the Democrats
in Michigan were "as corrupt as the Republicans," though, as
the party had little power, it "was not able to engage in notable
illegalities." Staebler's goal was to end corruption in state politics and to transform the Michigan Democratic Party into a
reformist organization. Williams's liberal politics, sincerity, and
honesty captured him immediately.[29]

Farrell, the Griffiths, and Staebler would emerge as the
nucleus of a network of Michigan liberals who would help
Williams capture the party's nomination for governor in 1948
and win six straight elections. In early 1947, Williams had
another fortunate experience. The Michigan Liquor Control
Commission was charged with regulating the states's complicated and corrupt system for the distribution and sale of alcohol
in state liquor stores. By law, the commission had to have
members of both political parties, and one of the Democratic
officials had left in late 1946. Republican governor Kim Sigler,
a former Democrat, faced a dilemma. An assertive and well-
known Democrat might use the position to disclose the rampant graft in the agency and attack Sigler and the Republican
administration. A less ambitious Democrat likely would reject
the position, as it did not pay much and had little real power
except to receive reports and dispense contracts. Sigler needed
a Democrat who would not use the appointment to develop a
political base and was willing to take a job with minimal
authority and compensation.

The governor and his aides spent several months weighing
candidates until a Detroit newspaper reporter suggested that he
consider a former navy officer in Detroit who had some governmental experience. Williams seemed a safe choice, as he was
a young veteran from a prominent Detroit family with no history of involvement with the state Democratic Party and had
never held electoral office. In February 1947, Sigler offered him
the position. Williams had left the OPA to work in the
Griffiths's law firm and to continue his travels around the state.
He had considered a job with the Bureau of Internal Revenue
in Washington but turned it down as it would mean leaving
Michigan. When Sigler called, he immediately agreed to serve.[30]

The Michigan Liquor Control Commission would be the means of Williams's ascent to the Democratic Party's nomination for governor in 1948. He used the post to forge an informal political network, to become known throughout the state, and to expose the corruption rampant in Michigan. Less than two years later, he would defeat Sigler in the "Michigan miracle," one of the greatest upsets in the state's history.

Williams plunged into his new position with characteristic preparation and energy. Before commission meetings he reviewed invoices, distribution records, and warehouse capacities and knew how many cases of whisky, scotch, and gin had been sold in each region of the state and how consumption varied with each season. He also established a rapport with other members of the commission. Once, when the group was debating liquor licenses for seasonal resorts, one member asked if "a beer chaser is permissible with a drink of liquor." Williams responded that recently at a resort in the Upper Peninsula he had ordered a "crème de cacao" and the bartender had asked, "What will you have for a chaser?" Williams had replied, "I think you can have whatever your heart desires!"[31]

Meetings of the commission were secondary to Williams's major intent: travel throughout the state to assess support for a run for governor. In the past the Liquor Control Commission had usually met for a few days in Lansing or Detroit to receive reports and assign contracts. Williams insisted that the group needed to travel throughout the state to check on supplies and operations. While other members of the commission were reluctant to venture into rural areas, Williams insisted: "I'll just go out and meet them myself." And he did. In 1946, Farrell had arranged for Williams to travel throughout Michigan for the OPA and the Griffiths had organized visits to union meetings, Democratic clubs, and ethnic organizations near Detroit to get his name known in the area. He now began to travel throughout the state in his new role as a member of the Liquor Control Commission.[32]

While Hicks and Martha Griffiths covered his legal cases, Williams spent nearly every day in the summer and fall of 1947 on the road visiting suppliers, warehouse owners, and bartenders who had never before met a member of the Liquor

Control Commission. He would arrive at a warehouse, announce "I'm Mennen Williams, the new Democratic member of the Liquor Commission," ask about their stock, and listen to their complaints. He also stopped in taverns, at times even putting on an apron and serving drinks to customers while asking the owners about their concerns. In a typical two-week trip in May, he covered over eleven hundred miles and visited over fifty warehouses and bars.[33]

Williams also used the trips to establish political connections by meeting with local Democratic officials and activists throughout the state. He never suggested that he was preparing to run for governor but asked them about issues and possible Democratic candidates. He quickly concluded that the Democrats were demoralized, the party was "in shambles," and there was no clear candidate to challenge Sigler in 1948.[34]

If anything, his pessimistic assessment of the Michigan Democratic Party was an understatement. The state's Democrats had generally followed the Jeffersonian ideal of weak government, and most had been unenthusiastic about the New Deal reforms of Franklin Roosevelt. The party had also been consistently ineffective at the ballot box. From 1852 to 1932 no Democratic presidential nominee carried Michigan, and they had been nearly as unsuccessful in campaigns for the governorship. Even in 1932, at the height of the Depression, the Democratic candidate for governor captured only 42 percent of the vote. Democrats had elected Murphy in 1936, but he failed to gain reelection. In 1942, Democrat Murray Van Wagoner, a master of patronage when he had managed the state's highways, had won a narrow victory, but like Murphy he had been defeated two years later.

In 1946, the party reached its nadir. The 1946 elections were disastrous for Michigan Democrats. Sigler defeated the Democratic challenger, Van Wagoner, in a landslide, and Republican senator Arthur Vandenberg won by over 300,000 votes. Only three of Michigan's seventeen congressmen were Democrats. Republican dominance of the state legislature was even greater, as the party controlled the state Senate by a margin of 28 to 4 and the House by an astonishing 95 to 5. There were no

Democrats in any of the state's offices, and in 1946 the party did not even carry Detroit's Wayne County.

After the disaster at the ballot box in 1946, Democrats, in the words of one analyst, "descended from confusion to chaos" and the party's organization was "demolished beyond repair." In many counties and congressional districts there was no Democratic organization, and the few Democrats who were politically active often had an informal agreement with the Republicans not to field candidates in local or district elections in return for a share of state patronage. When Williams traveled throughout the state in 1947, he had lists of supposed party members, but they often pleaded with him not to tell their neighbors they were Democrats.[35]

In contrast, Michigan Republicans were extremely well organized and financed. State Republican chairman Arthur Summerfield, a wealthy Flint Chevrolet distributor, levied an informal "tax" on all General Motors dealers in the state to finance Republican campaigns and used the funds to maintain an efficient statewide organization. Automobile manufacturers also made major financial contributions. As one observer summarized it, Michigan was "a magnificent company store" run by the car industry and the Republican Party.[36]

The Republican dominance continued despite the rapid emergence of organized labor in the 1930s and 1940s, as most unions in the state were either politically inactive or inept. Prior to 1948, the Michigan Congress of Industrial Organizations (CIO), the group that represented most of the major industrywide unions, including the United Auto Workers (UAW), distrusted both major parties and was officially nonpartisan in the state elections. It refused to endorse candidates or allow members to serve as delegates to political conventions in Michigan. In 1944, many within the CIO had tried without success to form a third party, as they saw both the Republicans and the Democrats as too corrupt and conservative. Union membership had grown substantially (in 1948 over one-third of Michigan families had at least one member in a labor union), but they were largely an ineffective political force in the state.[37]

There was, however, one labor leader with a considerable

interest in Michigan politics: Jimmy Hoffa. The specter of Hoffa and his International Brotherhood of Teamsters was decisive in the move by Williams, Farrell, Staebler, the Griffiths, and other Michigan reformers to seize control of the Democratic Party. Hoffa emerged from the tumultuous and violent labor campaigns and strikes of the late 1930s and 1940s as the president of Detroit's powerful Local 299 of the Teamsters and as the unquestioned leader of union in Michigan and throughout the Midwest. Hoffa also became a fierce opponent of the CIO. He used his financial resources and nearly absolute control of his union's members to gain considerable political power in Michigan. In 1945, Detroit UAW vice president Richard Frankensteen ran for mayor of the city, and for a time the CIO became politically active. Hoffa, however, threw Teamster money and votes against Frankensteen and defeated him. Buoyed by this success, Hoffa moved to take control of the state's weak and unorganized Democratic Party. In 1947, the Teamsters' candidate, John Franco, was elected Democratic Party chairman and Hoffa was planning to install Teamster lawyer and public relations official George Fitzgerald as Michigan's national Democratic committeeman.[38]

Hoffa's political activism was not based on ideology but on immediate self-interest. The federal government had long been investigating the Teamsters, and the labor leader feared that indictments of him and his Detroit associates were imminent. Politicians indebted to Hoffa would be crucial in the legal battles he knew were coming. His rapid emergence as a force in Michigan politics served as a major catalyst in moving organized labor toward political activism and in giving momentum to liberals convinced of the need to reform the state Democratic Party. Staebler considered Hoffa "a sinister force" and contended that Democratic Party chairman Franco's "main activity appeared to consist of 'shaking down' postmasters and other appointees." Williams had already clashed with Hoffa and the Teamsters in his work with the Michigan Liquor Commission and saw the Teamster official as a symbol of organized corruption. No individual was more distant from his idealistic view of government as a noble profession than Hoffa. The Teamster leader mocked Williams as a spoiled rich kid from Grosse Pointe who had never gotten his hands dirty. The feud between Williams and Hoffa began in 1947 and would continue for more than a decade.[39]

Hoffa's threat to the Democratic Party had two immediate and significant responses. First, it provoked one prominent labor leader to abandon the CIO's policy of political nonalignment and to help shift the union movement into the Democratic Party. August "Gus" Scholle, a longtime member of the Glass Workers Union and president of the Michigan CIO, had battled Hoffa for over a decade in organizing disputes and was horrified by the emergence of his rival as a power in state politics. Scholle began to argue that labor needed to become involved in politics to meet Hoffa's challenge and had to align itself with the reformers who were trying to make the party more progressive. After six months of intensive lobbying by Scholle and other labor leaders, the CIO's Political Action Committee (PAC) finally abandoned its long-standing nonpartisanship. On March 13, 1948, it passed a resolution.

> Progressives and liberals within the Democratic Party have often been outnumbered by conservative and reactionary elements. The PAC is unanimous in its opinion that the best way of supporting liberalism within the Democratic Party, to conform to the national CIO policy, and to serve the best interests of Michigan labor, is to join the Democratic Party. It is our objective in adopting this policy to remold the Democratic Party into a real liberal and progressive political party, which can be subscribed to by members of the CIO and other liberals. We therefore advise CIO members to become active precinct, ward, county and Congressional district workers and to attempt to become delegates to Democratic conventions.[40]

Labor's endorsement of the Democrats and its commitment to political involvement would be crucial to Williams in 1948 and his next five campaigns.

A second reaction to the Hoffa threat was the celebrated "meeting in the basement" at the home of Hicks and Martha Griffiths on November 21, 1947. The gathering has become a part of Michigan political legend, as it served as the formal beginning of an activist liberal Democratic organization in Michigan and of the candidacy of G. Mennen Williams for governor in 1948. While these were its eventual results, the immediate impetus was to block the rise of Jimmy Hoffa.[41]

For nearly two years liberals had been working to reform the state Democratic Party. Helen "Buffy" Berthelot (a member of the Communications Workers Union and later Williams's campaign manager), Staebler, the Griffiths, and a few others had tried to organize liberal delegates to local and congressional nominating conventions in and around Detroit and Ann Arbor and had been meeting regularly with Williams to discuss reform of the Michigan Democratic Party. Hoffa's sudden prominence led to a new sense of urgency within the group.[42]

Assistant Secretary of Labor John W. Gibson, a former Michigan union official, was scheduled to fly to Detroit from Washington to organize efforts to defeat Hoffa's attempt to gain control of the state's Democratic Party, and Williams suggested to Staebler and the Griffiths that they arrange a group meeting with Gibson to discuss an anti-Hoffa strategy. They invited lawyers Noel Fox and John Boerschenstein from Muskegon; William Kelley, the former mayor of Flint; Peter White of Three Rivers; businessmen Floyd Stevens and John Gerbert from Grand Rapids; Hickman Price, an automobile company executive; and Mel Laliberte, a public relations expert from Flint. After Martha Griffiths served a smothered chicken dinner, the group adjourned to the basement to sip coffee and to talk strategy with Gibson. They all agreed that Hoffa's reach for political power needed to be challenged through a massive revitalization and reorganization of the Democratic Party. Hoffa's victories were a graphic illustration of the weakness of the Democrats in Michigan and the ineffectiveness of the conservative philosophy that dominated the party. Only an energized, liberal, Democratic organization could blunt Hoffa, and they needed to persuade reformers to run as delegates to nominating conventions and to organize voters to back liberal candidates.[43]

As the discussion continued, Williams shifted the conversation to the 1948 gubernatorial election and asked if "it would help any" if he ran for governor. Staebler and others argued that he had the potential for a bright political career and should not waste it in an impossible contest in 1948, but Williams persisted. "I'm young," he responded. "I can take a licking." He suggested that even if he lost his candidacy could serve to focus the reformers' effort to change the Democratic Party. With some reluctance, the group offered their support. Although they did not think Williams could win, they agreed that his candidacy might help energize the party and pave the way for future reforms and victories. Aside from endorsing Williams, the group determined to organize "Democratic Clubs" throughout the state to challenge the party's conservative leadership, to identify liberal candidates, and to contest every election at every level. Discussion of the Hoffa threat gave way to a plan to reenergize and change the political philosophy of the entire Michigan Democratic Party. It was an ambitious agenda for a dozen people in a Detroit basement drinking coffee and munching chocolate chip cookies. The 1948 elections were less than a year away, and they had no money, organization, or party officials in their group.[44]

Although some would later argue that Williams was a reluctant candidate who volunteered to run for governor only to help his reformist friends, it is clear he had called the meeting more with the intent of launching his campaign for the governorship than to talk about Jimmy Hoffa. As early as his sophomore year at Princeton, he had decided he wanted to be governor of Michigan, and he was growing impatient. He had been preparing to run in 1948 since he left the navy, and his extensive travels for the OPA and the Liquor Control Commission had convinced him that there were no other major liberal candidates. In the past two years he had become well known among Michigan's Democrats, and if his liberal colleagues could help him capture control of the Democratic Party he could be nominated. Unlike everyone else in the room, he was convinced he could win.

Despite the Republican sweep in 1946 and the weakness of the Democratic Party, Williams knew that incumbent governor

Kim Sigler was vulnerable. First, Sigler was a former Democrat and had clashed repeatedly with conservatives in the Republican legislature. He also had moved against the corruption dominant in Michigan government and had gained indictments against forty-one Republican officials during his two years in office. As Republicans were certain to maintain a huge majority in the legislature, some party members felt it would be a sound strategy to elect a Democrat in 1948, use their control of the legislature to prevent significant change, and find a "real Republican" to run for governor in 1950. Williams contended that the Republicans thought: "Well, we can take two years of a Democrat, and then we will go back in power." Staebler later agreed and argued that the Republicans wanted Sigler out so they could elect "our kind of guy" two years later.[45]

In his travels around the state in 1946 and 1947, Williams also found that many in Michigan disliked Sigler's flamboyance and perceived arrogance. Kim Sigler was something of a dandy. When he moved from a hotel in Lansing to his new home after being elected governor in 1946, he invited the press to cover the event. The next day the newspapers were filled with photos of Sigler's massive wardrobe, which included more than forty suits and waistcoats, fifty pairs of shoes, and one hundred handmade silk ties. Later he appeared at a veteran's dinner in a sky blue velvet tuxedo, even though the event was to be informal. He also liked to wear a large cowboy hat at public appearances and usually arrived at functions in a limousine with an escort of state police on motorcycles. Sigler was a fervent pilot and would often fly to events in his private plane. Many in the state saw his wardrobe and plane as extravagance and his style as aloof. At Republican functions, he generally spoke only with major leaders, ignoring the rank and file. He also had angered Michigan's hunters and fishermen, a significant voting bloc in the state, with his opposition to conservation and the control of industrial pollution. Williams concluded that conservation was Sigler's "blind spot" and felt he could win the votes of "the duck hunters."[46]

Although he was convinced that the Republican incumbent had some weaknesses, Williams faced the immediate problem of winning the Democratic nomination. "Regular" Democrats hostile to reform vastly outnumbered his small band of liberals, and to secure the nomination he needed delegates to the state convention. In January 1948, Staebler began to organize Democrat Clubs to "talk up" Williams's candidacy and elect delegates to the nominating convention. The new organizations were most successful in Wayne County (Detroit) and Washtenaw County (Ann Arbor). Academics from the University of Michigan, reformist labor leaders such as Helen Berthelot, African Americans (who were generally denied any role in the regular Democratic Party), and liberal lawyers formed the nucleus of the new group.[47]

Williams also drew on his network of friends and colleagues. He contacted classmates from the University of Michigan Law School, family friends from Detroit, and those he had met in his travels for the OPA and the Michigan Liquor Commission to persuade them to join the new reformist organization. In March, Williams, Staebler, and others selected a board of directors to coordinate the Democratic Clubs and prepare for the battle with traditional members of the party for delegates to the nominating convention. Williams also convinced members of the political science department at the University of Michigan to develop a questionnaire to determine the most significant issues for the people of Michigan, and Martha Griffiths distributed it throughout the state.[48]

As important as the efforts of the "new" Democrats were, more crucial was the need to mobilize the support of organized labor. In 1946, the state CIO had raised less than five thousand dollars for Democrats, but its decision to endorse the Democratic Party in March 1948 offered both financial support and a potential army of volunteers and delegates. Williams, however, had had little contact with unions or their leaders. This changed with yet another beneficial coincidence. In early 1948, the Brewery Workers invited him to address their convention in Bay City. He learned that another speaker was to be Gus Scholle, the president of the Michigan CIO and the major force in the group's decision to abandon nonpartisanship. Williams invited Scholle to share a ride to the convention, and during the long trip he told the labor leader of his decision to run for governor and asked for his support. Scholle was impressed with Williams's sincerity and liberal agenda but felt "he didn't have a prayer of being elected." He agreed, however, to arrange for Williams to speak to labor groups in Detroit and to meet with Walter Reuther of the United Auto Workers. Scholle would become crucial in Williams's nomination and victory, and Williams would later call him "one of the less appreciated heroes of our time."[49]

With Scholle's introduction, Williams met with Frank Martel, head of the Detroit–Wayne County Federation of Labor, Harry Southwell of Local 174 of the Auto Workers, and Reuther. The union leaders asked him if he had enough money for his campaign, and Williams replied that his family would not fund his efforts. They then asked if he would run an energetic campaign, and he assured them he would campaign hard throughout the state. Finally, they asked if he thought he could win, and he declared emphatically that he could. His audience was not so sure. Southwell found Williams "a very immature politician. He was big, awkward, shy, something of a shaggy pup, but utterly sincere. He fumbled his words and his gestures looked like he was trying to untie his fingers. I personally did not think he'd win." Winning the election, however, was secondary to stopping the reach for power of Jimmy Hoffa. The labor leaders knew Hoffa would try to nominate his own candidate, and Williams might be able to prevent the Teamsters from controlling the party. Local 174 of the UAW endorsed Williams, and Scholle convinced the CIO's Political Action Committee to donate ten thousand dollars to his campaign, by far the largest contribution he would receive.[50]

The labor leaders' fear of Hoffa was justified. At the national Democratic convention in Philadelphia that summer he used blatant bribery, offering cash and new cars to delegates to elect Teamster attorney George Fitzgerald as Michigan's Democratic national committeeman over anti-Teamster candidate Cyril Bevan. Union leaders and liberals were stunned, and the Michigan CIO launched a massive campaign to elect delegates to the Democratic state convention to block the nomination of a Teamster candidate for governor.[51]

On May 15, Williams formally resigned from the Liquor Control Commission and announced his candidacy for the Democratic nomination for governor. He opened a campaign office in the National Bank Building in Detroit and sent a letter to all precinct delegates in Wayne County asking for their support.

> The situation in Michigan is ripe for change. Our people are
> tired of "bossism." We are sick and tired of a Republican
> governor wrangling with his own Republican officials and
> his Republican Legislature. We are fed up with Republican
> fiddling while the state goes to pot.[52]

Williams had hoped to lock up the Democratic nomination in the summer of 1948 so he could focus his energy and meager funds on the campaign against Sigler in November. Hoffa, however, quickly blocked any easy road to the nomination when he convinced a Kalamazoo lawyer, Victor Bucknell, to challenge Williams in the primary and promised Teamster financial support. To confuse the situation further, regular Democrats, angered by the liberal attempt to take over their party, persuaded Burnett Abbott of Albion to enter the race. Williams had only thirty-two thousand dollars to fund his campaign, and now he would have to spend a sizable portion in a three-way primary fight.

In early August 1948, Mennen and Nancy Williams filled the gas tank of their used DeSoto convertible, left their three young children in Detroit (Wendy Williams [Woo] had been born in 1946), and motored north to convince the people of Michigan to vote for Soapy Williams for governor. They would be on the road without pause for the next three months.

Before he and his wife began their campaign, Williams and Staebler sat down and devised a strategy to win the Democratic nomination. Williams outlined his plan in green ink on a yellow legal pad: He would focus on ethnic groups, veterans, blacks, and union members and capitalize on the anti-Hoffa sentiment in the state. He would try to run up a massive majority in Wayne County and win the usually Democratic Upper Peninsula while breaking even with his two rivals in the rest of the state. His main issues would be lack of adequate schools, housing, and roads, pro-labor issues such as expanding work-man's compensation, and reapportionment (the Michigan leg-islature had not adjusted its districts in thirty years, and rural, Republican areas were vastly overrepresented.) At the bottom of the election plan, he wrote: "I will be in to win and I am going to win!"[53]

The strategy was sound, but he faced the problem of getting his message to the public. His paid campaign staff consisted of Larry Farrell, his former boss at the OPA, and three secretaries. For all the other work of the campaign he would have to rely on volunteers. He budgeted sixteen thousand dollars, half of his total funds, for the primary. Such a meager treasury meant he could not afford radio ads or billboards. His success depended on personally barnstorming the state and bringing his message directly to the people.[54]

Williams had never campaigned for political office before and admitted his shortcomings: "I was anything but a dynamic speaker." One reporter said his voice sounded "like a man chewing slate pencils." He felt his best speeches were "off the cuff," and he asked his speechwriters to sketch out two or three main ideas. He would "ad lib the rest." His problem in the pri-mary was not his speech making or his voice but finding an audience to hear him. The regular Democratic organization supported Abbott and was unwilling to arrange opportunities for Williams to speak. His campaign strategy was to go directly to the people, but he found it hard to find anyone to listen.[55]

In their first tentative efforts to campaign for the nomination Soapy and Nancy Williams were virtually alone. They had no "advance team" to arrange meetings or groups of volunteers to recruit an audience. They would arrive in a town and park on the main street. Nancy would walk around the community handing out green and white flyers (the campaign colors) listing her husband's credentials and ask passersby: "Won't you wait to hear my husband speak?" After a few minutes when there were a dozen or so people lingering on the sidewalk, Soapy would get out of the car and talk for a few minutes. Then they would get back into the DeSoto and Nancy would drive to the next town while her husband prepared for another stop.[56]

'A ten-day trip through the Upper Peninsula from August 7 to August 15 set the pattern for the Williams campaign in both the primary and general elections. They barnstormed through every community of more than five hundred people, relying on local Democrats, union leaders, friends from law school, and associates from the OPA and the Liquor Control Commission to help the candidate find an audience. The first day they made ten stops. By the end of the tour they were speaking to more than thirty groups a day. As he could not afford to buy radio ads, Williams relied on local stations eager to fill airtime by interviewing the candidate for the Democratic nomination, doing as many as five brief broadcasts a day.[57]

Williams did not focus on issues as much as personality. He attacked Sigler for his inattention to the problems of Michigan and promised action to solve them, but his main objective was to let the people of the state get to know him. At a meeting of a Polish-American organization in Detroit early in the primary campaign, one of the officers, Stella Lecznar, told him that he should "not rush in and out" of a meeting, as people wanted to think they were worthy of attention. She advised him to "step into the middle of the hall where everyone can see you. Then introduce yourself: 'I am Mennen Williams. I am running for Governor.' Halfway though your talk, repeat: 'I am Mennen Williams. I am running for Governor.' Then you finish what you have to say and once more you repeat: 'I am Mennen Williams and I am running for Governor.'" Williams found this "priceless advice" and adopted the technique throughout his campaign.[58]

His success at Salisbury, Princeton, and the University of Michigan Law School had largely been the result of hard work, and in the summer of 1948 he again demonstrated his ability to outwork his opponents. With only six weeks until the September 14 primary, his energy was astounding. He quickly developed the technique he would use for the next decade: nonstop campaigning from dawn to midnight. He spoke wherever he could find an audience: veterans' organizations, ethnic clubs, county fairs, Democratic rallies, church socials, dances, auctions, and anywhere else he could find a group of people. At a labor picnic in Detroit, he was mistaken by an official for a volunteer and was given an armband and a stack of raffle tickets to sell. He sold fifty-eight in less than an hour, more than any other volunteer. After breakfast, lunch, or dinner speeches he would head to the kitchen, where, he argued, "the real Democrats were," and greet the cooks, dishwashers, and waitresses. When he returned from the northern part of the state to focus on Wayne County he began his legendary handshaking campaigns at factory gates. He arrived at 5:30 in the morning and returned in the afternoon when the shift changed. He developed a technique of using both hands to greet the arriving and departing workers and would chase down someone who walked by, shouting, "I'm Soapy Williams running for the Democratic nomination for Governor and I just want to shake your hand." He set a goal of a minimum of two thousand handshakes a day.[59]

While Mennen and Nancy set an exhaustive pace on the campaign trail, organized labor mobilized in Wayne County. The CIO leader Gus Scholle, his assistant Tom Downs, and other organizers began a massive voter registration drive and recruited union members to run for election as precinct delegates. Each labor candidate had a brochure with Williams's picture on one side and his or her name on the other. More than 80 percent of the Democratic precinct delegates in Wayne County would be union members, and nearly all had linked their campaigns to Soapy Williams.[60]

Williams's energetic primary campaign and the efforts of Detroit unions were important in his selection as the Democratic candidate, but equally crucial was a split in the antireform movement. Bucknell, the Teamsters' candidate, and Abbott, the choice of the regular party organization, both campaigned against Williams, and some Teamsters were confused and voted for Abbott. The division of the antireform vote and Williams's energetic personal campaign led to a narrow victory. He received only 39 percent of the vote, but, due to a 12,000-vote margin in Wayne County, he won a slim plurality of 8,000 votes out of 285,000 cast. Kim Sigler was unopposed and did not campaign, but he received 430,000 votes in the Republican primary. Williams was the Democratic nominee, but most in Michigan still were convinced he could not win the general election.

Before focusing on his battle with Sigler, Williams faced an unruly Democratic convention and yet another battle with Hoffa. The Teamster leader was outraged that Williams had defeated his candidate in the primary and planned to disrupt the state convention in Flint. Having lost his choice for governor, he hoped to intimidate delegates into selecting his candidates for other state offices. As soon as the meeting opened, several dozen Teamsters stormed into the room swearing and pushing people to the floor. When Hicks Griffiths tried to get the sergeant at arms to evict the intruders, the Teamsters threatened his life. Labor delegates from other unions fought back and evicted Hoffa's men after a brief battle. A few weeks later, when Williams and his wife were back in Flint on the campaign trail, Hoffa came to their hotel and pushed his way into the adjoining room of campaign manager Larry Farrell. The couple heard Hoffa shout: "If you don't do it, I'll have you wiped out!" They rushed into the hall and found Hoffa had left and Farrell was "white as a sheet." The battle between Soapy Williams and Jimmy Hoffa was far from over.[61]

The Teamster invasion was only one problem Williams faced at his party's convention. The Democrats were badly split between the Williams-Staebler reformers and more conservative members of the party. Labor leaders felt they had been crucial in Williams's primary victory and expected him to reward them for their efforts by nominating their candidates. When Williams proposed his Democratic slate, he discovered the depth of the split within his party.

Williams wanted Noel Fox, a Muskegon lawyer and labor mediator and one of the attendees of the November meeting at the Griffiths's home, to be the Democratic candidate for attorney general, but the CIO objected. They felt Fox had not been supportive of unions and united behind Steve Roth, a former assistant prosecutor for Genesee County. Williams reluctantly agreed. To appease regular Democrats and try to unite the party, he offered his primary opponent Burnett Abbott the

nomination for secretary of state, but Abbott refused and
Williams persuaded Fox to accept the nomination. The fight
among labor delegates, reform Democrats, and party regulars
over the nominations became so unruly that Williams repeatedly had to go to podium to ask for order. He left the convention as the leader of a Democratic Party deeply divided by ideology and competing interests.[62]

Williams envisioned a campaign against Sigler that would be
based on clear political issues and different philosophies of government, and that is how it began. Near the end, however, it
became a battle of personal attacks, and Michigan found that
the idealistic Soapy Williams could be an aggressive and tough
political infighter.

Despite the continued efforts of Staebler and others to create
a new Democratic Party in Michigan, Williams knew he had
no effective political organization outside of Wayne County
and very little money. State Democratic chairman John Franco
owed his position to Hoffa and refused to give Williams a single worker or any funding for the campaign. There were only
sixteen thousand dollars left for the general election, which
meant virtually no funds for radio or newspaper ads or billboards. Williams relied on postcards with his picture and record
on one side addressed to anyone identified as a likely Democrat. He also frantically recruited volunteers from the fledgling
Democratic Clubs, organized labor, law school friends, and
those he had met in his travels in the state. Before the campaign, he wrote a memo on a 3 × 5 note card, outlining a strategy to appeal for volunteers. He noted the general apathy
among Democrats but argued that there now was "a compelling ALTERNATIVE" to the regular party organization "MOTI-
VATED BY A FIGHTING FAITH!" To win he needed "door
ringers" to distribute campaign material and get out the vote.
Just as "an engine needs fuel" and "salesmen need a good product," he would run as an unabashed liberal reformer to attract
new volunteers inspired by his message. He hoped that an energetic group of volunteers could overcome his lack of money
and the hostility of the regular party organization.[63]

With faith that his reformist agenda would attract new volunteers and voters to the Democratic Party, Williams and his wife again set out on an exhaustive personal campaign modeled on his successful whirlwind primary effort. He had only six weeks before the November 2 election to get his message to the people, and his efforts were even more intensive and exhausting than in the primary. He began with fourteen-hour days, and by late October he was regularly campaigning for eighteen hours at a stretch, living on vitamin pills and ice cream. He usually began by getting up at 4:30 a.m. so he could be at a factory gate by 5:30, followed by an hour of handshaking with two or three breakfast meetings. By nine he was giving a radio interview or in the downtown shopping area of a community. He would try to attend four or five luncheon meetings of veterans, ethnic, or business groups and then move on to community festivals, fairs, or churches. After another hour spent shaking hands at factories he would move on to dinners, usually sponsored by a local Democratic group, for a more formal speech (always fifteen minutes or less) and spend the rest of the night shaking hands on the street or giving more radio interviews. He never scheduled fewer than sixteen meetings a day and near the end of the campaign was attending as many as twenty-five functions. When his car broke down in Escanaba, he called a friend who had worked with him on the milk-marketing bill and borrowed his Chevy to keep going.[64]

October 13, 1948, was a typical day in the Williams campaign. He got up before dawn to work the factory gates in Grand Rapids and then rushed to breakfast meetings with Democrats in Grand Haven and Holland. He drove north for three stops in Muskegon and lunches in Ludington and Manistee and then east to talk with veteran's groups in Cadillac. He stopped at two county fairs before attending a spaghetti dinner in Big Rapids, rushed back to Grand Rapids to greet late shift workers, and then returned to Muskegon for three dinner meetings and two radio interviews. Between stops he napped while Nancy drove. No crowd was too small. When his car was stopped at a railroad crossing, he would jump out and pass out literature to other drivers waiting for the train to pass. He wrote to his staff in Detroit that "it is doubtful whether there ever was a campaign swing like this one. It is certain there never should be another." He told them he had learned two things: "trust in the Lord" and "keep your car filled with oil!"[65]

Williams offered himself as a youthful, energetic alternative to Sigler and began all his speeches by reminding his audience that he was thirty-seven years old and a World War II veteran with three young children. He made a special appeal to other veterans by emphasizing the lack of housing in the state, the overcrowding of schools and universities, and the absence of an efficient highway system. (Republicans in the legislature appropriated funds for highways in their own districts but not to connect them.) He argued that veterans had won the war but were losing the peace due to the Republican refusal to spend money in the state. Because of continued GOP inaction "family life was in danger." Nancy Williams also stressed the problems facing young families. In a speech in Sault Sainte Marie she reminded the audience that she was a wife with three young children and understood the need for good schools, affordable housing, better health care, and lower food costs. Housing, schools, and highways were effective issues for the thousands of vets who were raising families and using the GI Bill to go to college. His staff also circulated an issue of the military newspaper *Stars and Stripes* with an article on World War II veterans running for office that had a front-page picture of Williams.[66]

He appealed to "the duck hunters" by repeatedly attacking Sigler's record on conservation. In a speech in Bay City on October 14, he mocked the governor's love of aviation and his inattention to the pollution of Michigan's lakes.

> Last night a plane descended from the clouds and brought my
> Republican opponent to the Saginaw region. He went out
> on the ice of Saginaw Bay in the midst of thousands of dead
> fish, victims of steam pollution. I am told he picked up one
> of the many dead fish, posed for his picture and said there
> would be no more steam pollution in Michigan.

A week later in Battle Creek he claimed, "you could tell which way the wind was blowing by the strength of the stench from the polluted Kalamazoo River."[67]

Williams also echoed Democratic presidential candidate Harry Truman's attacks on the "do-nothing" Republican Congress by blasting the inaction of Republicans in Lansing in addressing the problems of housing, schools, roads, and jobs. He suggested that Republicans found schools "irritating," as they had to spend money on them, and reminded voters that they had increased taxes on public utilities rather than big business. "Would you deliberately vote to increase the rate you pay for a telephone . . . for electricity . . . for the gas used in your home?"[68]

Despite warnings from his campaign staff that any mention of race "could get your head knocked off," he made repeated appeals to black voters by denouncing both legal segregation in the South and de facto segregation in Michigan. The civil rights issue had split the Democratic Party at its national convention in 1948, leading southerners to desert Truman and join the "Dixiecrats," and Williams's strategists suggested he avoid the issue. To Williams, however, racism was a sin, a violation of Christ's statement that all are equal in the eyes of God, and he refused to ignore the rampant discrimination in his state.

> The cornerstone of my philosophy of government is my belief in the essential dignity of man. . . . I believe that each individual human being is a child of God—and entitled to be treated as such.

He attacked Sigler's "do nothing for Negroes record" and accused him of cutting the number of black workers in state government and not addressing "the rising tide of discrimination by employers." He called for Michigan to adopt a fair employment bill and ordered his staff to schedule him to speak to black church groups.[69]

At the suggestion of a newspaper reporter, Williams developed another issue: the need for a bridge across the Straits of Mackinac to connect the Upper Peninsula (UP) with the rest of the state. Many in the UP felt they had little connection to their state and identified more with Wisconsin than Michigan. There had been a campaign to build the bridge for more than sixty years, but the Republican legislature was unwilling to fund it, particularly as the Upper Peninsula was one of the few Democratic parts of the state. Williams vowed to complete the bridge, calling it "Michigan's dream." The Republicans dubbed it "Soapy's folly."[70]

In his whirlwind campaign Williams raised a number of significant issues and offered himself as an energetic alternative to Sigler's inattention to the state's problems. He pointed out that "Alabama has its 'Kissin' Jim Folsom as Governor. Michigan has had enough of 'promisin' Kim Sigler" and pledged to increase spending for schools, roads, housing, and hospitals; to clean up rivers and lakes; and to guarantee African Americans and union members fair treatment. As promised, he had campaigned on issues and as a liberal reformer. He soon found another potent issue—scandal and corruption—and the focus of the campaign turned from issues to personal attacks.[71]

In the middle of his campaign, Williams received a letter from a supporter criticizing him for being "too easygoing" in his attacks on Sigler and urging him to "hit 'em in the slats!" He soon began to do so. During the 1948 campaign, Eugene Black, the Republican attorney general, charged that his party had violated campaign laws in the 1946 elections by permitting auto dealers to delay and even avoid payment of the state sales tax on car purchases in exchange for contributions to the Republican Party. According to Black, when a customer traded in a used car, dealers would double or even triple the amount given for the trade-in when they reported the transaction to the state. The customer paid the sales tax on the "real" price of the car, but the dealer paid only on the lower price reported to Lansing. If, for example, a man bought a new Buick for $1,000 and the dealer gave him $200 for his used car, the customer would pay sales tax on the remaining $800. In the paperwork, however, the dealer would inflate the amount of the trade-in to $400 and pay the state the sales tax on only $600. The revenue office in Lansing would overlook the fraud if the dealer kicked back part of the profits to the Republican Party.[72]

At the center of the scheme was the Republican national chairman, Arthur Summerfield, of Flint. On September 18, Attorney General Black served subpoenas on Summerfield and several other car dealers while they were at a Republican fund-

raising dinner in Flint listening to a speech by Wisconsin senator Joseph McCarthy. A month later Black secured grand jury
indictments of four owners of major automobile agencies, and
the alleged scheme became public. Williams had a wonderfully
juicy scandal to utilize in the last weeks of his campaign.[73]

The Democrat wasted no time in exploiting the issue. He
rushed to Summerfield's hometown of Flint and charged that

> emulating from the City of Flint has been one of the most
> corrupt campaigns in the history of the state. Under the
> direction of Mr. Arthur Summerfield, the Republican
> National Committeeman, more money has been raised to
> "buy"—and I mean "buy" this election than was ever raised
> in Michigan before. He is in an unholy alliance with the
> Michigan Auto Dealers [and has raised] . . . an enormous
> slush fund of over $600,000.

These funds were to be used to ensure Sigler's reelection. Gus
Scholle contended that the car dealers had avoided more than
$50 million in sales tax payments and "we have a government
by the General Motors Corporation."[74]

In a radio address the next day Williams linked the scandal to
Sigler. A marriage between a "high-flying governor" and "low-
down racketeers" ruled Michigan, and he vowed "to chase the
automobile dealers out of Lansing and give the state back to the
people." He warned voters not to "let the forty suits of clothes
fool you. Don't let the airplane fool you. . . . Kim Sigler is not
a free man . . . He belongs to someone else. . . . Sigler is a prisoner of the tax fraud racketeers." He began to refer to his opponent as "Cowboy Kim, the airplane pilot" and hammered at the
scandal, claiming: "It is now common knowledge—thanks to
the honest efforts of Attorney General Eugene Black—that
those who contributed to the Republican 'slush fund' were
given special consideration when it came to paying the sales
tax." He promised to make Michigan "free from favoritism, free
from scandal" and to take government "out of the special interests' cloakrooms." His campaign staff quickly circulated flyers
claiming that money for schools had been "siphoned into
Republican campaign funds" and noting that Black, the
Republican attorney general, had now endorsed Williams.[75]

Williams's attacks finally provoked Sigler to action. In contrast to the frantic pace of his Democratic opponent, he had run a leisurely campaign, flying to one event a day and usually returning to Lansing that night. He was convinced he would win easily and spent much of his time considering the appointments he would make following the election. Sixty of Michigan's sixty-one daily newspapers had endorsed his reelection, and a *Detroit News* poll taken on October 28 showed him so far ahead that his victory seemed "assured." Sigler publicly predicted that he would win by three hundred thousand votes.[76]

The slush fund scandal changed Sigler's campaign. He had largely ignored Williams but now began to fight back. He charged that the Democratic Party had been taken over by union bosses and his opponent had become "the Charlie McCarthy puppet on the knee of the CIO-PAC." He described Williams as a millionaire "Grosse Pointe socialite" who knew nothing of the problems of the average Michigan citizen. Unfortunately for Sigler, the press reported that he had labeled the Democrat "a Grosse Pointe *socialist*," and Williams demanded and received a retraction.[77]

The scandal tarnished Sigler and the Republicans, but political experts in Michigan still thought the incumbent would win. Even some Democrats privately told reporters that they had abandoned both Williams and the presidential candidate, Harry Truman, to focus on winning congressional races. Despite such predictions, Williams increased his already frantic pace during the last two weeks of the campaign. He had run out of money and arranged a second mortgage on his home for eight thousand dollars to buy buttons, signs, and a few radio ads. The campaign was so short of lawn signs that staffers asked each county chairman to drive any extras to neighboring towns. He appeared with Truman for one minute on a statewide radio network broadcast and managed to buy some time at a local station in the Upper Peninsula. After a few minutes on the air, he was so exhausted that he announced that the audience "would now hear from my wife." Nancy spontaneously completed the talk.[78]

Despite fatigue and lack of money, some of his supporters began to believe in an upset. Williams's energy, Sigler's overconfidence, and the impact of the slush fund scandal all seemed to be shifting the momentum toward the Democrats, and unions were involved in an unprecedented get out the vote campaign. Jim Lincoln, a partner of Williams and the Griffiths in their Detroit law firm, wrote the candidate that, although it seemed Truman would lose Michigan, "it appears that many people are going to split their votes this fall." He urged Williams to fight hard during the last week.[79]

Lincoln need not have worried as Williams drove himself even harder as November 2 approached. He decided he would devote each of the last seven days to one of the seven congressional districts in Wayne County. He campaigned 20 hours a day in each focusing on union halls, black churches, and ethnic organizations. He determined ethnic groups appreciated being greeted in their own language and claimed he could say "hello" in seventeen languages. He used them all during the final week of campaigning.

November 2, 1948, was clear and cool in Michigan, perfect for the large turnout Williams needed. Unlike the *Chicago Tribune*'s famous headline "Dewey Defeats Truman," the Detroit papers never ran an official announcement of Sigler's victory, although both of the city's major dailies had prepared articles hailing the Republican's reelection. While his staff and volunteers drank beer, ate pretzels, and danced to a polka band, Williams sipped ice water while the votes were counted. When all the returns were in, he received 64 percent of the vote in Wayne County and 51 percent in the states' seventeen other largest counties. He received only 40 percent in the remaining sixty-five rural counties. Although Thomas Dewey defeated Harry Truman by 35,000 votes in Michigan, Williams beat Sigler by 163,000. The press called it "the Michigan miracle."[80]

Soapy Williams would win reelection in 1950, 1952, 1954, 1956, and 1958. He would become a major force in national Democratic politics and a candidate for his party's presidential nomination. He would serve as assistant secretary of state for African affairs and U.S. ambassador to the Philippines. For sixteen years he would sit on the Michigan Supreme Court. Despite his later accomplishments, the stunning upset in 1948 remained the highlight of his long political career.

Nearly forty years later he began preparations for an autobiography he never would write and declared that his first goal would be to discuss the 1948 election. He "wanted to set the record straight on the '48 campaign," as "the few scholarly works I've seen so far come up with a rather simplistic answer that the unions won the election for us." Williams never disputed the importance of labor in his victory, but he argued that his success was the result of more than just labor unions: "We wouldn't have won the campaign without the UAW and the AFL and the CIO. . . . But if that had been all we had we wouldn't have won either."[81]

To Williams, the 1948 victory was a glorious crusade that united workers, blacks, intellectuals, and others who had been ignored by traditional politicians. The campaign served as a reminder to others that "you yourself can be the catalyst that can bring together a movement to achieve the objectives you hold dear and to move America nearer the heart's desire."[82]

He saw the 1948 was a victory for liberalism and reform and an example of how the right ideas and a united effort could overcome the greatest odds. He may have been right, but more than anything else the 1948 victory was a personal triumph for G. Mennen Williams. The decision of labor to throw its support to the Democrats, Sigler's problems with his own party, and the emergence of the slush fund scandal all helped, but without the courage of Soapy Williams to run a frantic and exhausting campaign, it is doubtful Sigler could have been defeated. No other Democrat could have pulled it off. Paul Weber, Williams's sardonic press secretary, in a rare moment of quasi idealism, argued that the one indispensable element in the Michigan miracle was Soapy Williams. "He could have gone out and got a yacht, played around in the Caribbean and had hell of a time," Weber noted, but he "was a rare bird who got into politics for reasons that were almost entirely altruistic." He "was the principal factor in that '48 election. . . . It was a personality election and the key factor was the personality of Mennen Williams." It was his energy and idealism, more than unions and scandal, that led to victory.[83]

III

A NEW DEAL FOR
MICHIGAN, 1948–52

The word compromise was not a part
of my vocabulary.

—G. Mennen Williams on his career as
governor of Michigan

Mennen Williams saw his stunning victory in 1948 as a triumph for liberalism and a mandate to bring reform to Michigan. To Williams and other Progressives the 1948 returns
showed that Americans had not only embraced the New Deal
but had voted to expand the efforts of government to use its
power to create a more just, compassionate, and equitable society. Not only had he won an incredible upset in Michigan, but
other Democratic liberals had succeeded as well. Truman had
defeated Dewey and brought with him a Democratic majority
in Congress. Paul Douglass of Illinois, Herbert Lehman of New
York, and Hubert Humphrey of Minnesota (whose passionate
speech in favor of civil rights at the 1948 Democratic National
Convention had electrified the audience and led to a southern
walkout) had all been elected to the Senate. In addition, Progressives such as Adlai Stevenson in Illinois and Chester Bowles
in Connecticut had won governorships. Williams saw liberalism in the ascent and was certain his role was to ensure its triumph in Michigan.

His postelection euphoria was short-lived, as he was immediately reminded of the reality of Michigan politics. After the
returns were in, George Fitzgerald, Jimmy Hoffa's handpicked

Democratic national committeeman, called Williams to arrange a meeting. Williams and Hicks Griffiths, the new Democratic state chairman, knew what the Teamsters' public relations man wanted to talk about: patronage. In the past, one of the few functions of the Democratic Party in the state had been to dispense political jobs and contracts, and the party's national committeeman expected the tradition to continue. At the meeting Fitzgerald suggested that they divide state and national patronage jobs fifty-fifty. Williams's campaign had been based on a rejection of Hoffa and corruption, and Griffiths replied that the new administration would make no deals with Fitzgerald. Hoffa's man continued to argue, but it soon became clear that he would have no influence in Lansing. Fitzgerald recalled that while Williams was civil Griffiths was the "original Mr. Prick!"[1]

Williams could ignore Fitzgerald but not the Republican-dominated state legislature. Despite his victory, Republicans still controlled the Michigan House by a margin of sixty-one to thirty-nine and the Senate by twenty-three to nine, and GOP leaders assumed that Williams would be a one-term governor. In Staebler's words, the Republicans "were comfortable," as they knew they had Williams "boxed in" and they could prevent any major changes in the state. The Republicans immediately served notice that they were not going to cooperate with the new governor. Michigan was one of only three states that did not have an executive mansion and offered no housing allowance to its governor. The chief executive had to pay for his home out of his own salary. Before Williams was inaugurated, the legislature cut his salary by three thousand dollars while keeping pay for Republican state officials at the previous level.[2]

The salary slash was symbolic of the Republicans' determination to assert their power and let Williams know that they still controlled the state. The Williamses were forced to find a home for themselves and their three small children in Lansing to fit their suddenly lowered income. They eventually moved into a modest three-bedroom house at 615 S. Grand Avenue. It was suitable for their daily needs but inadequate for the entertaining that accompanied the office. The living and dining rooms were so small that when they invited large groups to a reception Nancy would immediately usher them out the back door once they had met the guest of honor, saying: "You've been here, now goodbye!"[3]

Despite their family wealth, the Williamses were determined to live on the governor's salary and adopted a lifestyle that suited their modest home. They had no servants, and their children walked to neighborhood schools. For the first year they even had their number listed in the Lansing phone book. The governor and his wife were often at political functions at night, but the entire family always met for breakfast. Athletics were the major form of family recreation, as they went bowling, boating, and ice skating. (Nancy was an accomplished figure skater, though her husband "had weak ankles.")[4]

The Williamses did enjoy one significant benefit of the office: a summer home on Mackinac Island. During the Depression the state had purchased an abandoned house on the island that was in default for taxes and dubbed it the "governor's summer mansion." It was hardly a mansion, as it was badly in need of repair, was furnished with army cots and bunk beds, and had no dishes or silverware. Despite its shortcomings, the residence became a focus of the Williams family's life and led to a deep love of Mackinac Island. Each summer Nancy would load her car with dishes, bedding, silverware, and children and head north. She soon found that the "mansion" was more than a private home. Vacationers knew it was owned by the state, and she was expected "to entertain every convention at the Grand Hotel." Despite the burdens of hosting hungry and thirsty Michigan citizens, the Mackinac Island home became a much-loved retreat for the family, and they would eventually invite national figures such as Adlai Stevenson, John Kennedy, and Lady Bird Johnson to visit them on the island. Later they enjoyed watching firsthand the construction of "Soapy's Folly," the Mackinac Bridge. After he left the governorship Williams bought a home on the island, and he is buried in a small cemetery there.[5]

For a brief time Williams basked in the glory of his electoral victory. Frank Murphy sent a note that his "Washington Family" was "proud and happy for you," and Truman invited the young governor to the White House. (Soapy gave the president a maroon and gray bow tie.) The governor's enjoyment was short-lived, as knew he was facing a legislature deeply hostile to his liberal agenda. After the election the Associated Press carried a story that, given Republican control of both the House and the Senate, the Democratic governor had no intention of trying to bring "a New Deal to Michigan." Williams responded: "Whoever said that didn't talk to me!"[6]

Williams's intent was precisely to bring the New Deal to his state. His campaign had concentrated on issues such as schools, housing, health, conservation, and civil rights, which he saw as essential if he was to "bring Michigan into the 20th century." His first act after his victory was to create a statewide Committee on Housing, made up of city planners, contractors, architects, and tenants, to prepare legislation to encourage the construction of new homes. In a radio speech delivered at a servicemen's banquet on December 20, 1948, he announced: "I hold no illusions about how this fight was won. It wasn't a popularity contest, won by handholding and pretty speeches." He argued that he had won the election because he was "sincerely interested" in the "close-to-home personal problems" of the people such as housing, education, taxes, pollution, and corruption. Michigan's population had increased dramatically in the last decade, and the state had not spent sufficient money to adjust to its growth. Schools were badly overcrowded, nearly half were more than fifty years old, and teachers were paid less than in any other northern industrial state. State mental hospitals and prisons were also dilapidated and overcrowded, and the Michigan highway system was outmoded. There was an acute housing shortage in Detroit and much of the rest of the state. To Williams, the image of thousands of veterans living in temporary housing (prefabricated corrugated structures he called "steel foxholes") symbolized years of Republican neglect of basic services in the state.[7]

Although Williams was dedicated to bringing Michigan "into the 20th century" by creating a "New Deal" in the state, the Republican legislature disagreed. The conflict between Williams and the Michigan legislature began in 1949 and would continue and intensify over the next decade, eventually driving the state into bankruptcy in 1959. The battle grew out of two radically different views of government. Mennen Williams assumed that government had an obligation to improve society and meet the needs of the people. Both his religious convictions and his political philosophy convinced him the state must provide "necessary" services such as expanded educational opportunities, health care, housing, roads, and conservation. In addition, government must use its power to move society toward racial and economic equality. Williams argued that government must *first* look at the needs of the people and *then* find the revenue to pay for programs to help meet them. The problems and their solutions were obvious, and Michigan must find the money to pay for them. Those who were financially successful, both individuals and corporations, should pay the costs of expanded state services.

Michigan Republicans rejected all of Williams's assumptions. They were dedicated to minimal government and taxation. They were not convinced it was the duty of government to alleviate all the problems of its citizens and argued that its primary obligation was to maintain order and ensure a climate that stimulates private enterprise. The Republicans also reversed Williams's dictum that you first determine the people's needs, develop programs to meet them, and only then find the money to pay for them. They argued that you *first* judge the amount of revenue the state can expect and *then* initiate only those programs this income can fund. They strongly opposed increases in taxes and as a result resisted any expansion of state government.

The philosophical differences between the two parties were only intensified by Michigan's tax structure. Unlike most industrial states, Michigan had no personal or corporate income tax. The major source of state funding was the sales tax, and by law 78 percent of sales tax revenues went to local school districts, leaving only the remaining 22 percent to finance the state's entire budget. Michigan had a very modest corporate franchise tax but with a ceiling of fifty thousand dollars. Even the largest companies, such as General Motors, could not be assessed at a higher net worth. The only other income came from "nuisance" taxes on alcohol, tobacco, and licenses and "consumer taxes" on utilities. Due to the dominance of the automobile industry, Michigan also had only a token gasoline tax, a major source of funding for highway programs in other states.

The duel between Williams and the legislature began in 1949 and continued biannually for a decade. The opening conflict set a pattern that would be repeated throughout his six terms. The governor proposed greatly expanded state services to deal with what he saw as crucial needs (housing, hospitals, roads, schools, civil rights, and other issues) and asked for increased taxation on individuals and corporations to pay for them. The legislature rejected most of his proposals and refused to raise taxes to cover the increased costs of government. Williams responded by creating citizen "commissions" to support his recommendations and appealed his case to the people through speeches and the press, accusing his opponents of being the tools of the rich and insensitive to the human needs of the state. Republicans, convinced they could defeat Williams in the next election, generally ignored his programs and public relations campaigns. They contended that the governor was controlled by organized labor, was promoting class warfare by attacking the rich, and was leading the state toward bankruptcy. Williams would win reelection, and the process would begin again.[8]

The semiannual battle between the governor and the legislature came to resemble a formalized minuet, with each side going through its prescribed motions and the other responding. The dance went on for a decade, until financial collapse ended it in 1959, but the issues and tactics first emerged in January 1949.

As he prepared for his inauguration, Williams knew he faced a hostile legislature, but he was certain that he had been elected to address the problems of the state and could not fail to propose solutions. He had attacked Sigler as a do-nothing executive and was determined that he would be an aggressive leader in reforming Michigan. On January 1, 1949, Williams delivered his inaugural address. Rather than outlining his reform agenda,

he opened with a summary of his ideas about government presented in dramatic religious imagery:

> Not quite 2000 years ago, Jesus of Nazareth said that He
> came into this world so that men might have life and life
> abundant. He spoke, it is true, of the life of the spirit. But he
> enjoined men to have a care for one another, not only in
> matters of the spirit but in the production and distribution of
> the necessary goods of this world. We of the Western
> democracies live in a civilization built upon the teachings of
> the Man of Nazareth. It is for this purpose—that men may in
> fact live together as brothers having a care for one another—
> that modern democratic states exist.[9]

The new governor went on to point out that Michigan had
failed to meet Jesus' injunction to care for each other. He
argued that to do His work the state needed expanded housing,
better schools, higher pay for teachers, pollution controls, a
modern highway system, increased funding for the aged and
mentally ill, expanded workman's compensation payments, aid
to farmers, and guarantees of "first class citizenship for all of our
peoples, regardless of race or color." Those elected by the people had to "forget partisanship" and show "moral strength" to
"co-operate in the public interest."

The religious language and implied expansive social agenda
stunned Republicans. Many felt it was more of a sermon than a
speech and asked what specific programs the governor wanted
and how he planned to pay for them. Five days later Williams
formally submitted his legislative program. To prepare an
agenda to reform and modernize the state, he had called on
John P. Dawson of the University of Michigan Law School and
Samuel Eldersveld, a political science professor at the University of Michigan, to recommend a comprehensive legislative
program. Based on their suggestions, he urged an ambitious
reform package with ten main points, including a state housing
commission to oversee the construction of twenty thousand
dollars' worth of new housing units; expanded rights for workers in collective bargaining; large increases in workman's compensation and unemployment insurance; a major expansion of

funding for junior colleges, universities, and primary schools; a massive highway construction program; an increase in old age assistance grants and aid to the blind; an additional three dollars per month in Aid to Dependent Children payments; modernization of the state prison system; improved veterans benefits; and a fair employment opportunities act to eliminate racial discrimination in hiring. He offered no suggestions as to how the state would pay for his program.[10]

A week later, Williams again addressed the legislature to discuss funding. He estimated that the state would face a deficit of $82 million without new sources of revenue and argued that there were only two choices: cut spending, which would punish "the poor, the sick, and the children" and balance the budget on the backs of "disabled veterans and crippled children"; or increase revenues. He concluded that the "only solution is additional taxation."[11]

He followed by presenting a plan to fund his social program and distributed a ten-page handout with footnotes and five pages of charts documenting existing taxes and showing the impact of new ones. He contended that Michigan's sales tax was regressive, hitting "the poor and middle class" the hardest, and that, as the bulk of it was already designated for local schools, any increase would have little impact. He also argued that the state already derived twice the percentage of revenue from consumer taxes than did other industrial states and that Michigan "can be truly described as a 'soak the consumer' state." He concluded that the only answer to the fiscal dilemma was either a state income tax or a tax on corporations. As the people were already overtaxed, the choice was to tax business. "The state burden upon corporate business is exceptionally light," he contended, noting that "of the ten leading industrial states, Michigan places the smallest burden upon corporations." Due to the fifty-thousand-dollar ceiling on the corporate franchise tax, large corporations were not paying their fair share.

> I therefore recommend legislation to base the corporate franchise tax not on net worth, but on net corporate income at the rate of 4 percent. In plain words, I urge a tax on some-

thing which is taxed in two-thirds of other states but which is virtually untaxed in Michigan—namely corporate profits.[12]

Williams's inaugural reform agenda and call for corporate taxes were clear expressions of his political philosophy: the religious language, the appeals to help injured veterans and sick children, and the idea that wealthy corporations should pay an increased share of the costs of government. Michigan Republicans, however, were appalled by his invocation of Jesus, his emotional appeals to save sick children, and his intent to tax corporations. They characterized Williams as "self-righteous," "a phony idealist," and a "Machiavellian" already maneuvering for reelection. Even his mother, head of the Grosse Pointe Republican Women's Club, denounced his legislative program as "having nothing to help business."[13]

For nearly fifty years the Michigan legislature had been controlled by conservative Republicans financed by large corporations (in particular the automobile industry), and they were not going to allow a thirty-seven-year-old "boy wonder" to change the situation. The legislature would have to approve each of his initiatives and the taxes to pay for them and made it clear it had no intent to do either. In Michigan, no bill could come before the full House or Senate unless it was recommended by a committee. As Republicans chaired every committee, they simply refused to pass on any of the governor's proposals for a full vote.

Although the inaugural address did not convince the legislature of the need to implement his program, it did have one effect. Richard Williams presented his brother with a green and white polka-dot bow tie to wear to the inaugural as a good luck symbol. Green and white were the colors of the 1948 campaign, and Williams used green ink for all of his handwritten notes and messages. The cravat became his trademark for the rest of his life, and he wore it daily, even with formal clothing at John F. Kennedy's funeral. The green and white bow tie became so identified with Williams that in later campaigns his billboards did not even include his name but featured only the famous polka-dot tie.[14]

Williams knew he did not have the votes to pass his program but developed a technique to try to pressure the legislature to act by appointing a variety of "commissions" to study particular problems and suggest appropriate legislation. Even before his inauguration, he created a Commission on Housing and, faced with the intractability of the legislature, began to form other nonpartisan groups.

The use of such informal citizens' groups was both good politics and a reflection of Williams's belief in the importance of direct citizen involvement in the legislative process. He contended that study commissions would "bring government to the people" by allowing groups never consulted by the legislature to be heard and would make them a part of the solution to the state's problems. He claimed: "People by and large are both innately decent and patriotic. They do have an interest in serving, and they welcome an opportunity to help their fellow men." When selecting members for his commissions, he appealed to their sense of citizenship, reminding them of the need to be actively involved in government rather than passive observers of politicians. He also admitted that the commissions were a way to tie members to Mennen Williams, as it was "an opportunity to recognized the various ethnic groups in the state" that had helped in his campaign. In the next decade the governor would establish over fifty study commissions comprised of educators, consumers, members of ethnic groups, union leaders, journalists, and businessmen, including groups devoted to civil rights, veterans' affairs, Native Americans, migrant workers, universities, highways, taxation, hospitals, mental health, agriculture, vocational schools, teacher's salaries, urban issues, reapportionment, conservation, state employees, and the Mackinac Bridge. The commissions held hearings and heard testimony from groups throughout the state, and, although they were bipartisan and occasionally included Republicans, nearly all eventually recommended the legislation the governor wanted.[15]

Study commissions were a vehicle to try to persuade the legislature that the people were in favor of Williams's programs, but they had little impact in 1949. The legislature simply ignored them, as it ignored most of the governor's proposed reforms. Unable to get the legislature to act on his economic agenda, Williams decided to focus on civil rights by persuading Michigan to adopt a fair employment practices act to eliminate racial discrimination in hiring.

Williams's decision to make civil rights his first priority was understandable given his belief that racism was a moral evil and the major blemish on American democracy. In his 1948 campaign he had ignored the advice of his advisers and raised the issue of civil rights, and he would emerge as the leading white advocate of racial equality in the Democratic Party in the 1950s. He would not only denounce segregation in the South as both illegal and immoral (even turning down speaking invitations unless the audience was integrated) but would attack fellow Democrats Adlai Stevenson, Lyndon Johnson, and John F. Kennedy for being too moderate on the civil rights issue. Given his absolute commitment to equality of the races, it was natural that he would demand that his own state move to end discrimination.

Civil rights had emerged as a national issue long before the 1948 elections. The massive black migration from the rural South to the urban North began during World War I and increased dramatically during and after World War II. African Americans in the North had the vote and used it to force politicians to acknowledge the evils of segregation in the South and the prevalence of less formalized discrimination in the North. In 1946, Harry Truman formed a committee to advise him on civil rights, and its 1947 report, *To Secure These Rights,* called for an end of discrimination in housing, employment, health facilities, the armed forces, interstate transportation, and public accommodations. It also recommended making lynching a federal offense, abolition of the poll tax, and creation of a permanent Fair Employment Practices Commission. Truman did ban segregation in the armed forces and introduced legislation against the poll tax and lynching, but he was slow to address the committee's other recommendations. At the 1948 Democratic National Convention, liberals, led by Minneapolis mayor Hubert Humphrey, forced adoption of a platform dedicated to moving America toward racial equality.[16]

Although Michigan had no formal system of racial segregation, the state had a long tradition of discrimination against African Americans and Jews. With its automobile and defense plants, Detroit was a major destination for black migrants during and after World War II. In 1950, African Americans represented 16 percent of the city's residents. By 1960, their numbers had increased to 30 percent and by 1970 to 43 percent. Racial tensions among blacks, older immigrant groups, and southern whites who had relocated from Kentucky, Tennessee, and West Virginia led to a racial riot in Detroit in 1943 and bitter conflicts over housing and jobs. Black church and civic leaders had organized to protest discrimination in the city in 1946 and 1947 and urged Williams to move quickly to deal with racial issues after his election.[17]

In 1947–48, the Michigan Committee on Civil Rights conducted a massive survey of racial discrimination in the state and concluded that it was "an ugly picture." It found that blacks were routinely excluded from skilled jobs throughout the state and were rarely hired for governmental positions. Many communities had no African Americans working in hospitals or other health facilities, and the Michigan State Police had no blacks on the payroll. Most black teachers held jobs only in Detroit and even there rarely became principals or other administrators. Many craft unions barred minority members. The group also found that most resorts in the state denied rooms to blacks and Jews and many Michigan colleges and universities had unwritten but strictly enforced quotas limiting minority enrollment. The Michigan National Guard was segregated by law, and many state hospitals refused to admit black patients. One injured black high school football player was even denied treatment in the emergency room of a Detroit hospital.[18]

Social and housing discrimination was nearly as rampant as it was in hiring. Most restaurants, beauty parlors, and bowling alleys in Detroit, Saginaw, and Lansing denied African Americans admittance. Blacks soldiers stationed at the air force radar station in Sault Sainte Marie were refused service in local taverns, restaurants, and barbershops. A spokesperson for the local Chamber of Commerce explained: "This is a small town. We don't know how to treat them." Michigan real estate agents had a written code that prohibited them from selling property to "members of any race or nationality, or individual whose presence will clearly be detrimental to property values in the neighborhood" and refused to show most homes to blacks or Jews. Public housing projects in Detroit were strictly segregated by building.[19]

Williams knew that the legislature would be hostile to any attempt to use government to end racial discrimination, as in 1945 Republicans had rejected a modest attempt to limit housing restrictions that party leaders had publicly called "the nigger bill." To pressure the legislature, Williams adopted his usual tactic of appointing a commission. The Governor's Advisory Committee on Civil Rights had been formed even before his inauguration. Chaired by Bishop Francis J. Haas of Detroit, the nineteen-member group included labor leaders, academics, church officials, and journalists. Williams was unable to persuade a single Michigan businessman to join. The committee recommended a massive program to combat discrimination in housing, public facilities, government, and employment. Williams decided to focus on jobs as the most crucial issue and the one most likely to secure support.[20]

A week after his inaugural, Williams told the legislature that addressing the prevalence of discrimination in employment was his first priority and urged adoption of a fair employment practices act to create a government agency to respond to complaints of racial prejudice in hiring. He modeled the bill on existing statutes in New York and made it clear that it would not require companies to meet quotas but only to show a lack of racial discrimination. Republicans were not convinced. They contended that the proposal was unnecessary and would constitute an expensive and illegal intrusion of government into private business.[21]

To Soapy Williams it was inconceivable that any elected official would deny another American equal rights, and he was convinced that he could obtain sufficient bipartisan support to pass a moderate fair employment bill. He was naive in his assumptions. After a month of futile negotiations with Republicans, he asked Martha Griffiths, his former law partner and now a state representative from Detroit, and Leo Doyle of Flint to introduce a fair employment bill that would apply to all companies with more than eight employees. Williams then went to the people to muster support. In a speech to the Flint Urban League on February 17 he argued that the right to equal employment was a basic tenet of American democracy, and a few weeks later, in a talk at an AFL-CIO dinner he contended that a fair employment bill was not only a moral duty but would help the economy, as many parts of the state claimed a shortage of labor yet denied jobs to qualified black workers. The Michigan CIO also tried to mobilize support for the Griffiths-Doyle bill by distributing thousands of pamphlets to union members endorsing the proposal.[22]

The governor's public campaign led Republicans to introduce their own version of a fair employment bill, which limited coverage to companies with more than twelve employees, contained no penalties for violations, and would require a state referendum before it could be implemented. The House State Affairs Committee, by a party vote of six to three, refused to recommend either the Griffiths-Doyle or the Republican version of the bill to the full legislature.[23]

Williams was stunned by the Republicans' obstinacy and ignored the suggestion of his advisers that he leave the civil rights issue alone until after the 1950 election. To the governor, the refusal to enact a fair employment act was a rejection of "what a good Christian community should be doing." In 1950, he again asked the legislature to consider the bill and tried to get bipartisan support by inviting Democratic and Republican leaders to meet with him and representatives of the Michigan Civil Rights Commission. The group agreed to form a committee to examine the issue, and, after a long search, Williams found one Republican senator to serve. The tactic had no impact, as the legislature simply referred the entire issue to the Rules Committee, where it died.[24]

The battle over a fair employment act was the beginning of a six-year, emotional struggle between the governor and the legislature over civil rights. The experience embittered

Williams and led him to reconsider his efforts at bipartisanship. After they defeated the proposal in 1950, he denounced the Republican actions as "a record studded with broken promises, political weasel words, the quick brush off and the double cross." His attempt to work with the Republicans had been a failure and convinced him that his opponents did not share the basic idea of equality that had shaped America. To Williams, civil rights was both a moral issue and a question of basic democratic principles, and he vowed that there was "just one thing that I am not going to compromise on; I never have and never will. That is principle."[25]

Frustrated by the legislature's refusal to act on his civil rights program, Williams used what power he had to try to end racial discrimination in Michigan. He ordered the desegregation of the state's National Guard and pressured the State Police to hire black officers. He also lobbied the Detroit Tigers baseball team to sign African American players. In 1950, he appointed Charles Jones to Detroit's Recorder's Court, the first black judge in the state.[26]

The obstinacy of the legislature in dealing with his economic and social reforms convinced Williams that the only way to change Michigan was to win another term as governor. Republicans considered the 1948 election an aberration and saw Williams as an interim governor who would be ousted in 1950. At the time of the Democrat's upset win in 1948, the state was still solidly Republican and the GOP remained much better organized than the Democrats. Williams recognized that he would have to solidify the Democratic Party to prepare for a reelection campaign.

Volunteers, labor leaders, and Staebler's Democratic Clubs had provided the campaign workers for Williams's 1948 victory, but the party was still weak and unorganized in much of the state. In the two years after the election Williams began to form a permanent Democratic organization to work for his reelection and to try to challenge the Republican dominance in the legislature. He appointed Hicks Griffiths Democratic state chairman in 1949 to replace John Franco, and Griffiths began the process of building a permanent party structure. His slogan was "a precinct worker in every precinct, challengers in every poll, and a candidate for every office." Using lists of both regular Democrats and volunteers from the 1948 campaign, Griffiths formed Democratic organizations in every congressional district and recruited candidates to run for the legislature in 1950.[27]

In 1950, Williams nominated Griffiths as probate judge in Wayne County, and the task of political organization shifted to the brilliant Neil Staebler, Michigan's new Democratic chairman. Staebler would serve in the position for eleven years without a salary and would create one of the most powerful political organizations in the nation.

Staebler's stationary had the slogan "People win elections" emblazoned across the top, and he visited every county in the state to meet with local Democrats to encourage them to create a permanent organization and contest every local election. He sent thirty-seven thousand letters to potential Democratic activists, began regular monthly meetings of Democrats in cities throughout the state, and developed a monthly newsletter for the party. He also relied heavily on his vice chairman, Adelaide Hart, a Detroit teacher and Williams volunteer. Staebler noted that Michigan politics had "a distinctly macho tenor." Many meetings were held in bars, and women were an untapped source of volunteers. In 1949, less than half of Michigan's counties had Democratic committees. As a result of Staebler's efforts in 1954, all eighty-three counties were organized.[28]

Staebler found that many in Michigan were eager to contribute to the party but only in exchange for licenses, state contracts, and jobs. Like Williams, he abhorred the usual patronage and corruption in the state and rejected 80 percent of donations offered to the party. Instead he began a system of paid party memberships to finance campaigns and, equally important, promote a permanent commitment to the party. The governor purchased the first membership.[29]

While Griffiths and Staebler concentrated on building a party organization, Williams recruited a group of political operatives and advisers who would remain with him for the next decade. Perhaps his most important appointment was naming Paul

Weber as his press secretary. Weber was a near caricature of the tough, cynical, big city newspaper reporter. He had not been part of the 1948 campaign, but after being named press secretary in 1949 he emerged as the governor's most important political consultant.

The sarcastic, fedora-wearing, Detroit newsman seemed far removed from the idealistic Mennen Williams. Unlike Williams, he hated crowds and campaigns and rarely ventured out of the offices and hallways of Lansing. The governor once persuaded Weber to accompany him on a campaign swing to help write speeches. After sixteen hours in a car with the governor, the press secretary demanded they stop for a meal. Williams handed him a handful of vitamin pills and they continued. Weber never went on the campaign trail again.[30]

Despite their personality differences, Weber became Williams's main speechwriter and political adviser. Weber rarely was involved in policy decisions, but he was crucial in assessing their political impact. His background as a political reporter meant that he knew nearly every legislator and journalist in Michigan, and he used his contacts to ensure press coverage and try to control criticism. The press secretary also was a skilled political infighter and was never reluctant to orchestrate personal attacks on Republican opponents when he thought it necessary. He became so powerful that Republicans would eventually charge that he was the real governor of Michigan.

To be his executive secretary, Williams selected Sidney Woolner, a University of Michigan graduate who coordinated legislation and helped plan the political campaigns. Another staff member, John Murray, had, like Weber, been a reporter with the *Detroit Free Press* and became the governor's "idea man." Murray was paid directly by Williams rather than by the state, and his office was not in the capital. Along with Weber he wrote most of the governor's speeches and organized publicity for the administration.

Weber, Woolner, and Murray were tough political operatives who argued that winning elections was the first step in any program of political reform, as ideas and ideals were useless without victories at the polls. They would provide Williams with a harder edge in his campaigns and were often willing to attack his opponents on personal as well as political issues.

Williams was convinced that his reelection was the only way to prod the legislature to consider the reforms necessary for the state, and he began to take his message to the people long before the election. As one reporter noted: "Soapy has been campaigning 365 days a year since 1948." In his first term he averaged three speeches a week. As in 1948, he spoke to any group that would listen: labor groups, farm organizations, business clubs, county fairs, beauty contests, veterans' clubs, and local Democratic organizations. Weber and Murray wrote most of the speeches, but Williams edited them with handwritten comments in green ink. He recognized his limits as an orator and wrote detailed instructions to himself on the margins of the text: "Slowly," "faster now," "pause here," "raise voice."[31]

In the summer of 1949, he also began weekly three-minute radio broadcasts, which would continue for eleven years. Williams spoke on whatever seemed important to the people of Michigan: the shortage of Christmas trees, the opening of fishing season, the need to reform mental health programs, why eighteen year olds should have the vote, and how to modernize the highway system. One of his most creative efforts was a talk called "Communists and Beans," delivered on April 25, 1950. In it he combined a report on increased bean production with an explanation of why he would not outlaw the Michigan Communist Party.[32]

The linking of bean crops and communists symbolized a serious issue for the governor: anticommunism. Williams had been a severe critic of communism since his trip to the Soviet Union as a student and had repeatedly denounced it as hostile to religion and freedom. Like many Americans, he was also convinced that there was a communist conspiracy to infiltrate and destroy the United States. In 1948, he had worked with Hubert Humphrey to block a takeover of the American Veteran's Committee by communists and had denounced Henry Wallace's third-party campaign in 1948 for its refusal to support U.S. efforts to contain Soviet expansion. He had also joined a new liberal anticommunist organization, Americans for Democratic Action (ADA), a decision that would become a major issue in his reelection campaign.[33]

By 1950, however, denouncing communism and supporting America's cold war diplomacy were not enough. The communist takeover of China and Russia's development of an atomic bomb caused many in the United States to fear that communism was in the ascent. The exposure of Alger Hiss as a Russian spy and the investigations by the House Un-American Activities Committee of communist influence in the entertainment industry led to a rising fear of subversion at home. In February 1950, Wisconsin senator Joseph McCarthy instantly became both famous and powerful with his claim of vast communist infiltration of the U.S. government. Five months later America was at war to prevent a communist takeover of South Korea. Despite his clear anticommunist credentials, Williams had to address the issue of communism within the nation.

As in nearly every other state, there was a strong move in Michigan to outlaw the Communist Party, even though it had less than a thousand members. Williams acknowledged the dangers of communism but argued that Americans had the legal right to belong to any political organization they chose. "Ideas cannot be suppressed by force or killing with a club," he argued. When Republicans demanded that he ban the Communist Party, Williams suggested that the state create a committee of experts to "explore the whole question of legal curbs on Communist activity" and requested fifteen thousand dollars to fund the group. The legislature saw a committee as a way for the governor to avoid the issue and refused to allocate the money, but Williams formed a "blue chip" advisory group by persuading members to serve without pay. The legislature responded by creating a Senate Loyalty Commission, headed by Collin Smith of Grand Rapids, to investigate communist subversion in Michigan. The governor denounced the move as a "secret police system" and a Michigan "Gestapo," but the plan passed by a margin of twenty-seven to nothing in the Senate and seventy-three to four in the House.[34]

Williams also opposed a Republican proposal that a "loyalty oath" be taken by all state employees, contending that it was aimed at college professors and designed to restrict freedom of speech. Again the legislature rejected his argument and passed the loyalty oath program. Though critical of the move, the governor did not veto the measure and tried to demonstrate his own opposition to communism by attacking alleged subversives in his own party. He accused Detroit state senator Stanley Nowak of being involved in communist front activities and vowed to oppose his reelection. Williams also proposed that Michigan's attorney general and the Michigan State Police be given increased power to investigate communist activities in the state. He did, however, refuse to ban the Communist Party and resisted demands from the legislature that he remove anyone found to be a "disloyal or subversive state employee."[35]

In the summer of 1950, while he continued to deal with the anticommunist issue and renewed his attacks on the inaction of the Republican legislature, Williams and his strategists began preparations for his reelection. In a bizarre incident, the governor was nearly killed before the campaign began.

One of Williams's many proposals to the legislature was a plan to modernize the state's archaic prison system. Jails were severely overcrowded, guards were poorly paid, and prisoners had staged several violent riots to protest conditions. In response to the call for increased funding, the legislature *cut* prison allocations and facilities had to curtail spending on food and recreational programs. On July 8, 1950, Williams went to the maximum-security prison in Marquette to personally investigate conditions there. Prisoners in Marquette had repeatedly complained about the food, and there were rumors of a possible riot. The governor decided to make a personal tour of the prison kitchen to sample an inmate meal. Along with Warden Emory Jacques and his bodyguard, state policeman George Kerr, Williams went to the kitchen to taste the day's dinner of ham and lima beans. Suddenly Ralph Stearns, a prisoner serving a life sentence for armed robbery, leaped from behind a door, grabbed the governor, and put a six-inch knife to his throat. "Come on, Soapy, come with us," Stearns yelled. Williams assumed it was a trick meant to draw attention to prisoner complaints, but he soon realized it was an organized and real attack.[36]

Holding the knife to Williams's throat, Stearns forced the governor into an adjoining kitchen as Kerr and an unarmed guard followed. Another inmate, "Crazy Jack" Hyatt, who was serving thirty years for armed robbery, hit Jacques in the face with a four-foot metal potato masher, breaking the warden's arm when he tried to protect himself. Williams grabbed at the knife, but Stearns increased his hold and screamed: "I could kill you, Soapy, but you don't deserve it. I've served 22 years!" As Stearns and the governor struggled, a third prisoner, John Halstead, rushed in and stabbed George Kerr in the back with a butcher knife. Grabbing the knife with his left hand, Kerr pulled his .38 caliber Smith and Wesson pistol with his right and demanded that Halstead drop his weapon. When Halstead refused and yelled "I'm going to kill you!" Kerr shot him in the stomach, killing him, and then turned the weapon on Stearns. He ordered him to take his knife from Williams's throat or he would shoot him. Stearns finally dropped the knife and fell to the floor, crying, "I've served 22 years in these holes. I've served 22 years Soapy!"[37]

Williams was free, but Jack Hyatt leaped across the room and guards had to wrestle him to the floor. Kerr, bleeding from the stab wound in his back, kept his pistol trained on Hyatt, but other prisoners began to stream into the kitchen. Kerr turned to them and announced: "You start something and all of you are going to be dead on this floor!" The prisoners retreated to the dining hall, and order was restored. Guards ushered Williams to his car and Kerr to the prison hospital. The entire Michigan State Police force was put on alert to prevent a riot, but Williams continued with his schedule, attending a square dance that evening sponsored by the Marquette Democratic organization.

Later investigations found that Stearns, Hyatt, and Halstead had tried to escape three years earlier. Hyatt and Halstead were given additional sentences, while Kerr received an accommodation and promotion. Williams and his wife were convinced that God had spared him and immediately proposed raising the pay of state prison guards, though the legislature refused.[38]

The prison attack drew national attention, and the governor generated more press coverage when he refused to extradite one of the famous "Scottsboro boys" to Alabama. In 1931, two white women had accused nine young blacks of rape, and eight were convicted and sentenced to death. Even though one of the alleged victims recanted her story, the Alabama Supreme Court upheld the verdict, and the case became a symbol of southern racism. In 1948, Haywood Patterson, one of those convicted, escaped from a work detail at Kilby prison near Montgomery and fled to his sister's home in Detroit. While hiding in Michigan, Patterson collaborated with writer Earl Conrad on a book about his experiences, receiving an advance of thirteen thousand dollars from Doubleday. After the book was published FBI agents traced him to Detroit and arrested him on June 17, 1950. Alabama officials immediately filed papers for his extradition, and Patterson appealed to Williams to deny the request. The governor emphatically agreed and announced that he would never allow Patterson to be returned to "the injustice system" of Alabama. The U.S. District Court in Detroit eventually overturned Patterson's sentence.[39]

Williams's defiance of Alabama won him the praise of liberals and African Americans across the nation, but Patterson remained free for only a few months. In December 1950, he was arrested for stabbing a man to death in a Detroit bar, and eventually he was convicted of manslaughter and sentenced to a term of six to twelve years. He died in prison a year later.[40]

His narrow escape from death at the hands of a prison inmate and his defense of Patterson enhanced Williams's reputation outside of Michigan, but it did little to help him in his continuing battle with the state legislature. He did manage to win a few modest victories, moving to modernize the archaic Michigan court system, abolishing one-man grand juries, gaining minimal increases in unemployment compensation payments and teacher's salaries, and securing some improvements in the state highway system. He was not, however, able to solve the state's growing financial crisis. On January 5, 1950, he announced that the state was "approaching chaos" in its revenue system and on March 15 called a special session of the legislature to seek a solution.[41]

Republicans had ignored his call for a corporate profits tax and had instead increased consumer taxes by raising rates on gas, electricity, and telephones. Williams denounced the increases as unfair and again called for a profits tax on Michigan corporations. By 1950, the state was seriously in debt. The governor's budget called for expenditures of $340 million, but the legislature appropriated only $270 million. When the legislature again refused to approve a corporate tax, Williams went on the radio and accused Republicans of assuming that they had "a moral right to disregard the needs of the people." He claimed that the new consumer tax "drains money out of the paychecks of the customers who come into the stores and shops of the state. . . . It hits every worker with the effect of a pay cut."[42]

On May 20, he sent another plea to the legislature for new taxes, noting, correctly, that "there is a fundamental disagreement among us." To Williams, the human needs of Michigan were paramount and the only way to address them was through new sources of revenue. He appealed to the legislature to consider the personal costs of the continued lack of funds, reminding them that "behind the columns of figures are living persons. Let us stop thinking in terms of dollars for a few minutes and think in terms of people." He urged Republicans to remember "the children in Caro State Hospital, the tubercular patients at Howell, the disabled veterans who are buying homes" and concluded by declaring that "partisan politics should end when the borders of human decency are reached."[43]

The legislators were unmoved by Williams's emotional appeal. Republicans were still confident that they would regain the governorship in the fall of 1950 and refused to consider a corporate profits tax or any major new sources of revenue. They had learned in 1948 that they needed a strong candidate who would run an aggressive campaign and selected former governor Harry Kelly to challenge Williams. Kelly was a World War I hero, widely known in the state, and had never lost an election. He made it clear that he would attack Williams for his mismanagement of the state's finances and portrayed him as a tool of Walter Reuther and other labor leaders. His fellow Republicans were in no mood to give the governor a legislative victory on the eve of his expected defeat in November 1950.

The Republican charge that the leaders of organized labor controlled Williams was an effective political issue but not completely accurate. By 1950, many Americans were concerned about the power of unions, and Michigan's citizens were particularly upset by the growing dominance of Reuther and the United Auto Workers. One of every four workers in the state relied on the auto industry for his or her job, and the UAW had been extremely successful in negotiating generous contracts for its workers. Reuther was a tough negotiator, and his militancy and threats of strikes had led to a growing antagonism toward unions not only among Republicans but also among many independents and Democrats in the state. In 1945, George Romney, of the Automobile Manufacturer's Association and a future governor of Michigan, called Reuther "the most dangerous man in Detroit." Reuther had been a member of the Socialist Party in the 1930s and was one of the leading spokesmen for the liberal Americans for Democratic Action. Williams recognized his debt to labor for helping him win the 1948 election and often consulted with Reuther and other union officials while in office. When Walter Reuther's brother, Victor, was shot in the face in Detroit in 1949, Williams cabled President Truman, demanding an FBI investigation. When he tried to mediate a strike between the UAW and the Ford Motor Company in May 1949, he was accused by auto executives as being a lackey for Reuther.[44]

The perception that Walter Reuther was the power behind Mennen Williams was, however, an overstatement. The two men rarely met and often clashed on appointments and other political issues. When asked if he "controlled" Williams, Reuther responded that "nothing could be more ludicrous" and noted their frequent disagreements. Williams claimed that attempts to portray him as a puppet of the UAW were only smears by the Republicans intended to drive him out of office.[45]

Despite denials from both, the image of the Democratic governor as under the control of Reuther became a major issue in the 1950 campaign. Even before his nomination, however, Williams had to deal with another labor union and its leader:

Jimmy Hoffa and the Teamsters. Hoffa was still smarting from Williams's defeat of his candidate for governor in 1948 and the removal of Franco as the Democratic state committeeman. In the summer of 1950, the Michigan CIO launched a massive campaign to elect delegates to conventions in six congressional districts in Wayne County so they would have a strong voice in the Democratic state convention to follow. When the local conventions convened, members of the Teamsters showed up with petitions supporting their own candidates. The petitions were clearly fraudulent, as many names and addresses had been copied directly from Detroit and Flint phone books and the same individual had written most of the signatures. When convention officials denied the petitions, violence broke out at five of the six meetings. In the Fourteenth District meeting at the UAW Local 212 Hall, seventy-five teamsters, led by the Democratic national committeeman and Teamster official George Fitzgerald, fought their way into the hall, beating up delegates and security guards. District Chairman Nick Rothe grabbed a wooden club (later described inaccurately by the press as a baseball bat) and waded into the charging Teamsters. Other delegates joined the brawl, and Fitzgerald and his followers eventually retreated to the front steps of the union hall, where he told the press that there had been a "socialist takeover of the Democratic Party by Communistic processes."[46]

The Teamsters' crude attempts to intimidate delegates at the local Democratic conventions failed, but they succeeded in harming Williams. The press focused on the violence at the conventions, and the *Detroit News* condemned "the crude power tactics of Mr. Williams's friends." Many in Michigan identified Williams and his party with violence and undemocratic tactics. The governor, already facing charges that he was a tool of big labor, now had to deal with contentions that his followers had used force to prevent critics from expressing themselves.[47]

As Williams began his campaign for reelection in the fall of 1950, he realized that he faced another uphill battle. The Republicans had already indicated their strategy: to portray him as a radical tool of big labor, dedicated to raising taxes and unable to work with the legislature. They had nominated a well-known and skilled campaigner to run against him. In addition, the labor-liberal coalition responsible for his 1948 victory had shown strains and limitations. In 1949, Reuther and the UAW had mobilized to elect George Edwards of UAW Local 174 as mayor of Detroit, but the racial issue had destroyed his campaign. Efforts to integrate Detroit's housing projects divided union members, and Edwards's opponent, Detroit treasurer Albert Cobo (a future Republican challenger to Williams for governor), warned of "an invasion of Negroes." Many traditionally Democratic voters agreed. Despite the efforts of the UAW, the Detroit Federation of Labor endorsed the Republican Cobo (as did the Teamsters) and Edwards was crushed at the polls. It was clear that the divisive issue of race could triumph over the economic and social concerns of Williams's constituency.[48]

The failure in Detroit illustrated the continued tensions within the Democratic Party. Staebler's efforts to organize the Michigan Democratic Party were progressing but incomplete. Older, "regular" Democrats, labor leaders, and the "new" Democrats of 1948 often battled over candidates and power. Staebler was repeatedly forced to rush to district conventions to mediate among the three groups and to arrange compromises over candidates. The well-funded Republican organization had spent two years preparing to oust the "interloper" Williams, and most observers felt they would be successful.[49]

A final concern for Williams was the mood of the nation. In 1950, the United States was locked into a global cold war with communism, and to many Americans it seemed to be a losing battle. In late 1949, the Soviet Union detonated an atomic bomb, and a few weeks later communism triumphed in China. In June 1950, President Truman sent troops to war in Korea, and, although U.S. forces under General Douglas MacArthur had been successful there, a week before the election China entered the conflict and the war intensified. The frustrations of the "loss" of Eastern Europe and China to communism and the war in Korea led many Americans to believe charges that traitors had been at work and communists had infiltrated the government. The fall of 1950 was not an opportune time to be a liberal, as for a growing number of Americans liberalism was equated with socialism and socialism with communism.

Republicans in Michigan were quick to sense the growing antiliberal sentiment, and Kelly launched an aggressive campaign to portray Williams as a quasi-socialist dominated by radical labor bosses. Unlike the passive Sigler two years earlier, Kelly immediately took the fight to the Democrats. He spent the first several weeks of the campaign on two themes: Williams was controlled by Walter Reuther, Gus Scholle, and other labor leaders, who wanted to "stampede Michigan into socialism"; and the governor's membership in the liberal Americans for Democratic Action confirmed his commitment to socialism. "Socialists dominate the Democratic Party," Kelly charged, and Williams should reveal "the true nature of Americans for Democratic Action." Republicans found that a Democratic candidate for Congress had signed a petition in 1940 to permit the Communist Party to be placed on the Michigan ballot and demanded that Williams repudiate him. "Why doesn't the Governor conduct loyalty tests in his own party?" Kelly asked. He promised that if he ever found a communist in his party he "would have him fired."[50]

Kelly's attack on the power of the unions was expected, but his focus on Williams's membership in Americans for Democratic Action was not. Liberals, stunned by the conservative electoral victories of 1946, had formed the ADA in 1947 as a progressive alternative to socialism and communism. Among its founders were Eleanor Roosevelt, Franklin Roosevelt Jr., theologian Reinhold Niebur, columnist Marquis Childs, economist John Kenneth Galbraith, Ladies Garment Workers Union president David Dubinsky, and Walter Reuther. The group was dedicated to expanding New Deal social programs and promoting racial equality. Although technically it was nonpartisan, the ADA generally endorsed Democrats. Its anticommunist liberalism was attractive to Williams, and, like Chester Bowles, Hubert Humphrey, and other emerging political leaders, he joined immediately.[51]

By 1950, many conservatives were portraying the ADA as a

radical group of leftist politicians and labor leaders committed to promoting a socialist agenda in America. Despite the organization's denunciation of Henry Wallace's Progressive Party campaign in 1948, Republicans contended that it was soft on communism both overseas and at home. Kelly quickly recognized that Williams's membership could be a potent political issue given the rising antiunion and anticommunist sentiment in America in 1950.

The governor was taken back by the vigorous attacks of his opponent and was on the defensive early in the campaign. As in 1948 (and in all subsequent elections), he opened his campaign in Nancy's hometown of Ypsilanti and responded to Kelly's charges. He denied he was a tool of labor, pointing out policy differences with Reuther and others, and defended his membership in the ADA. He noted that the group had a clause barring communist members and stressed that it was dedicated to reforming capitalism rather than promoting socialism. Press Secretary Weber organized an "innocence by association" campaign, distributing lists of famous Americans who were members of the ADA, including a prominent Flint Catholic priest, Father William Flanagan. Ironically, the national ADA released a statement declaring that Williams was three months behind in his dues.[52]

The governor tried to take the offensive against Kelly by duplicating his 1948 marathon campaign, and he began an exhaustive round of eighteen-hour days, beginning with dawn handshaking appearances at factory gates and ending with late-night dinners. Again he concentrated on county fairs, ethnic clubs, and union meetings. "There is no finer response than the smile on the face and the light in the eye of a person with whom you are shaking hands," he noted. Despite the tense racial situation in Detroit, he also focused more directly on black voters, making sure to mention his appointment of Charles Jones as the first African American judge in the state. Staebler predicted that Jones's nomination would be worth "a minimum of 25,000 votes."[53]

As Williams embarked on a seemingly endless schedule of visits to groups across the state, Kelly continued to lash out at the governor. He repeated his charge that the "socialistic" duo of Williams and Reuther were out to destroy capitalism. He also accused Williams of being undemocratic, noting the "baseball bat" incident, and charged that the Democrats had been "buying votes" by holding cash raffles to encourage voter registration. Some old line Democrats who had lost power to the Williams/Staebler faction supported the Republican. Thurman Doyle of Menominee, who had been replaced as the local Democratic chairman, claimed his party had been taken over by "the ADA-CIO socialist coalition" and endorsed Kelly. Hoffa, sensing an opportunity to defeat his nemesis, used Teamster funds to finance "Democrats for Kelly" clubs in Detroit.[54]

As election day neared, Williams began to attack Kelly and the Republicans more directly. He abandoned his earlier stress on the need for new social programs and concentrated on identifying his opponent as a tool of big business and specifically the auto industry. He argued that the Republican refusal to support needed programs was the result of the control of their party by Republican national committeeman Arthur Summerfield and John Lovett, head of the Michigan Manufacturing Association. He repeated his call for a corporate profits tax and denounced the Republican increases in consumer taxes: "Do you want to pay those taxes out of your pocket or do you think big business should begin to share in Michigan through a tax on its record profits?" He sarcastically noted that, while refusing to appropriate funds for housing, education, and mental health, Republicans had allocated eighty thousand dollars for new elevators in the capital so they "would not have to walk up a few flights of stairs."[55]

Williams also stressed the arrogance of his legislative opponents by keeping his proposals in committees and not allowing the full House or Senate to vote on them. How could Republicans call him "undemocratic" when they did not even allow the people's representatives to be counted on an issue? He cited a recent bill that limited finance charges on new car purchases that was to begin ninety days after the legislature adjourned. Republican leaders simply refused to formally adjourn, despite the fact that they had all gone home, to prevent the bill from taking effect.[56]

In the last week of the campaign, both candidates abandoned issues to concentrate on personal attacks. Kelly placed full-page ads in the major state newspapers with his picture surrounded by bold type: "FIGHT SOCIALISM! FIGHT COMMUNISM! VOTE REPUBLICAN!" Michigan physicians and dentists sent a letter to their eight thousand members, accusing Williams of planning to implement "socialized medicine" and urging a vote for Kelly. Business groups took out ads claiming that the proposed profits tax was driving manufacturers out of the state. Kelly also accused the governor of overlooking corruption in the Liquor Control Commission.[57]

Williams fought back, claiming that Kelly had no real issues and so had run "a smear campaign to scare the people." He persuaded leaders of the Veterans of Foreign Wars and the American Legion to join him on the radio to attest to his patriotism and anticommunism. Michigan attorney general Stephen Roth denied Kelly's charge of corruption in the Liquor Control Commission and announced an investigation into kickbacks in the Republican-dominated State Fair Commission. Democrats pointed out that two-thirds of companies that had left Michigan in the past two years had moved to states with *higher* profits taxes than those proposed by Williams.[58]

Throughout the last week both candidates traded insults and accusations. Kelly reiterated his charge that Williams was a socialist tool of big labor, and the governor responded by repeating his accusations that Kelly was a puppet of the auto industry. On the Sunday before the election, the *Detroit News* offered both candidates free space to summarize their issues and positions. Williams attacked the Republican failure to spend money for housing, roads, schools, health, and other critical needs: "Shall the state be run for the benefit of a few. . . . Or shall it be run for the benefit of the majority?" He also denounced the increase in utility taxes and other consumer fees as an example of his opponent's refusal to make business pay its fair share. He renewed his demands for a corporate profits tax and a constitutional amendment to reapportion the state to give equal voice to urban and rural voters. Kelly pledged to fight communism, impose no new taxes, and bring about a return to "harmony" between the governor and legislature.[59]

It was a bruising campaign. Unlike 1948, when Sigler had generally ignored his unknown opponent until the sales tax scandal provoked him in the last week, Kelly had attacked Williams from the beginning. His charges that the governor was a "socialist" were inaccurate, but, given the mood in 1950, they were effective. Even more telling was his repeated linking of Williams with Reuther and other labor leaders. Although unions were politically powerful in Michigan, many in the state felt they were harming business and were concerned only with securing economic gains for their members. Williams's attacks on the conservative legislature and his attempt to label Kelly as a tool of big business did not resonate as well as they had two years earlier, as the generally conservative mood of the country made attacks on business less effective than in 1948. Neither candidate offered a clear program on how to solve the state's growing financial crisis, as both focused on personal attacks.

Williams campaigned even more vigorously than in 1948, driving himself to near exhaustion during the final week with eighteen-hour days. As in the past election, all the major newspapers endorsed Kelly and polls showed the Republican well ahead. In 1948, Williams had been fortunate in having ideal weather for a large turnout, but he was not as lucky in 1950, as heavy rain drenched most of the state on November 7. Williams waited for the returns in his son's bedroom with Weber and Farrell, while Staebler listened to the results on the radio in his home in Ann Arbor. As most of the state did not have voting machines, counting the ballots was a long process. Throughout the night, the lead switched between the two candidates, but by 4:00 a.m. Williams was three thousand votes behind and most of his advisers felt he had lost. A few hours later Staebler called from Ann Arbor and told the governor not to concede, as he had heard of a number of errors in the tabulation and predicted a recount. He urged Williams to contact labor lawyer George Edwards to prepare to contest the results. Edwards worked the phones the next morning and discovered voting errors throughout the state, particularly in Macomb County, a traditionally Democratic area that had gone Republican. On the 1950 ballot was a referendum calling for the legalization of oleomargarine, and a number of votes favoring the butter substitute had been counted as votes for Kelly.[60]

By late Wednesday, November 9, Williams and Staebler were convinced of the need for a recount, but under Michigan law the candidate calling for a recount had to pay its costs, estimated at twenty-two thousand dollars, and the Democrats had no money to hire the legal staff necessary for the process. Williams called his mother for help, but Edna Williams refused to provide financial support. In addition to the economic problem, all returns would have to be certified by the State Canvassing Board, which was controlled by Republicans under the direction of the Republican secretary of state. Most observers thought Mennen Williams's political career was over.[61]

When reporters asked Williams if he would challenge Kelly in 1952, he told them he was going to request a recount of the 1950 results. Kelly, who had left for a Florida vacation, immediately caught a train back to Michigan. Staebler, Edwards, and Woolner began a crash campaign to recruit volunteers in each of Michigan's counties to help in the process, called Democratic activists, and pleaded with them to go to polling places to guard the ballots. They then phoned lawyers around the state and begged them to volunteer to help in the recount, even though the party had no money and they would have to pay their own expenses. They also contacted academics from the University of Michigan and Michigan State University to join the effort. Gus Scholle recruited labor officials and offered union halls to house training sessions for canvassers, and Adelaide Hart convinced schoolteachers to volunteer their evenings. In less than a week several thousand volunteers had signed on to work on the recount effort to save Williams's career.[62]

Even before the official recount began on November 21, preliminary canvassing found a number of errors. The slippery margarine issue was resolved, and the governor picked up nearly seven hundred votes in Macomb County. (Democrats joked, "We are ahead by a slight margarine.") Democrats also found that some local election officials did not check to see if voters had split their ballot: If they had voted for Republicans in other races, they did not look to see if they had broken ranks and voted for the Democrat for governor. An election judge in Oakland County had phoned in the results to Lansing and transposed a 4 for a 9; Williams gained five hundred more votes. As the governor picked up votes, the Republican Canvassing Board, which had opposed a recount, now agreed to a formal canvass, and Kelly also endorsed a recount.[63]

The Republicans hired a team of lawyers to gather in Lansing to oversee the process, while Staebler, Woolner, and Edwards relied on a massive army of volunteers to travel to each of Michigan's eighty-three counties. Every night the Democrats held a phone conference to discuss what procedures had been used, and if a spoiled ballot was thrown out in one county they immediately demanded that the eighty-two others follow the same standard. The governor's supporters also held training programs for all volunteers to teach them how to challenge each type of dispute.[64]

The night before the recount formally began Williams gave his volunteers a pep talk and told them "we have a tough fight with a relentless enemy" and they had to be aggressive. Staebler argued that it was necessary "to keep our eyes glued on every ballot." When the process began, Republicans were shocked to see Democratic lawyers, professors, and union members at every precinct in the state. One Republican official looked across the table at six Democrats and asked: "Doesn't the Democratic party have anybody but PhD professors to send in here?"[65]

After three days of counting, Williams had moved ahead by 1,154 votes and was making gains in nearly each precinct. The Democrats offered to end the recount if the Republicans agreed to a Williams victory, but the Canvassing Board threatened not to certify the election until after the courts had heard a challenge to the recount process. As the counting resumed, Williams continued to gain votes. By the time 68 percent of the vote had been tabulated, his lead was over 4,000 votes and Republicans finally gave in. The Canvassing Board agreed to certify the earlier count and declared Williams the winner by 1,154 votes out of nearly 2 million cast.[66]

The recount victory was the result of an amazing organizational effort by Staebler, Edwards, Woolner, and others. They overcame their lack of money by persuading thousands to volunteer and had organized a brilliantly coordinated effort to contest every error in every county. The victory belonged to Williams, but much of the credit was due to his aides.

Mennen Williams's narrow win provided the only joy for Michigan Democrats in 1950, as he was the sole member of the party to win a statewide office. Attorney General Roth and Lieutenant Governor John Connolly, who had won in 1948, were defeated. In addition, Republicans actually increased their dominant majorities in the House and Senate. It was clear that Williams would have little chance to pass significant reform legislation despite his second victory.

When Williams was sworn in for his second term as governor, the mood in his state and the nation was grim. The Korean War had taken a disastrous turn for U.S. forces with the intervention of Chinese troops, as what had begun as a seemingly minor "police action" had turned into a long and bloody conflict. Williams's second inaugural address reflected the somber cold war reality of 1951.

> The frontiers of freedom are being pushed back hourly by armed hordes of Communist aggression. For the first time since Indian armies ringed log settlements at Detroit . . . we are confronted with the possibility of attack upon our own homes. We must prepare against enemy action not only in far-off battlefields, but in the streets of Detroit, Flint, Grand Rapids, and our other industrial cities. We face an enemy whose philosophy is utterly alien to ours and whose victory would mean the death of our civilization. . . . Communism is attacking the foundations of our civilization, both here in our homeland and abroad.[67]

The governor's bleak portrayal of the foreign and domestic threats to America were not unusual for the time, as many in the nation were frustrated by the stalemate in Korea and alarmed by the assumed communist subversion at home.

Williams, however, attempted to use the anticommunist feeling
to justify economic and social reform. He argued that Michigan
needed new highways for civil defense evacuations and new
schools to teach science and develop "the spiritual strength of
democracy." He also contended that the war with communism
was not just one of armies and weapons but also a battle
between two different ideological systems. To survive, America
needed to be a model of equality and compassion for the world.
The nation had to show its moral superiority and "be faithful to
the moral obligations of a civilized state." The nation could not
"without losing our own souls, abandon our old people, the
patients in our hospitals, our disabled veterans, our homeless
children, and the others who are dependent on our public
care." The United States was "a democracy founded on the
teachings of Moses and Christ" and needed to guarantee equality for all of its citizens if it was to live up to this standard.[68]

Williams's coupling of the cold war and reform seemed to be
a strange marriage, but he was desperate to make the case for
expanding social programs and he recognized that he was oper-
ating from a position of political weakness. He was the only
Democrat on the platform at his inaugural, as Republicans controlled all the other statewide offices and held an overwhelming
majority in the legislature. Many Republicans were convinced
that he had been reelected only as the result of a skilled organization that had orchestrated his successful recount effort. He
had seen how obstinate the legislature could be two years earlier, and linking anticommunism and reform was his only
option to try to persuade the Republicans to consider his program. He acknowledged that his party was a small minority in
the legislature but vowed: "I do not propose to abandon any of
the fundamental principles I believe to be right."[69]

The tactic failed. Three days after his inaugural he sent his
reform agenda to the legislature. It began with a call for more
spending for civil defense programs, a safe topic given the rising
fear of nuclear attack, but then moved to his now familiar list of
necessary improvements in housing, hospitals, schools, roads,
prisons, and health care. He also called again for a corporate
profits tax and a fair employment law, defending it as "integrat-

edly related to the defense effort," as "racial and religious dissemination is ammunition for the enemy."[70]

As in 1949, his first priority was a fair employment bill, but, as was the case two years earlier, the Republicans were adamantly opposed. The governor did find one ally in an extraordinary Republican legislator, Louis C. Cramton of Lapeer. Cramton had long been active in Michigan politics, serving on the Railroad Commission and as a U.S. congressman from 1912 to 1931. He was a Michigan judge from 1933 to 1941 and had been elected to the Michigan House of Representatives in 1948. Economically conservative, Cramton was a liberal on racial issues and while in Congress had been an ardent supporter of Howard University, receiving an honorary degree from the school in 1942.[71]

Cramton had been one of three Republicans to support a fair employment bill in 1949 and was outraged by his party's opposition. On February 8, 1951, at the age of seventy-five, Cramton introduced his own fair employment bill in the House. He admitted that he had little hope for passage but felt it necessary to affirm his own values and called his bill "a law against discrimination." Williams was ecstatic to see a Republican leading the call for equal rights and defended Cramton's measure as both morally right and a practical step to ensure the effective use of all workers in the battle against communism.[72]

Despite the efforts of one of their most experienced and respected leaders, the Republicans refused to vote Cramton's bill out of committee in either the House or the Senate. Business groups strongly objected to the law, claiming it was "socialistic," costly, and would lead to racial conflict in the workplace. Cramton was so outraged that he wrote the Michigan Republican State Central Committee protesting its refusal to support "the fundamental issue of human rights upon which our nation is founded" and vowed to reintroduce the bill at the next opportunity.[73]

Cramton did not have to wait long, as Williams called a special session of the legislature in early 1952 to reconsider the fair employment bill, but it again died in committee. Undeterred, Cramton introduced it for a third time, and on March 6 the

Judiciary Committee voted in favor. For the first time Michigan legislators would have to vote on a plan for fair employment. When Cramton rose to speak in favor of his bill, twenty-
five Republican legislators walked out of the chamber rather
than listen. Cramton broke into tears and told the retreating
legislators: "I never thought I would see the time that Republicans would leave their seats rather than hear a Republican discuss the vital question of human rights." When the vote finally
came, the Republicans returned to the assembly. All thirty-two
Democrats and thirteen Republicans voted for the law, but the
remaining forty-six Republicans voted against it, causing it to
fail by one vote. It would be three more years before Michigan
would adopt a fair employment bill.[74]

The defeat of the bill was a bitter blow to Cramton and
Williams. The governor had hoped that with a prominent
Republican leading the battle the legislature might see the pro-
posal as a moral rather than a political issue. Its defeat left him
with only his executive power to attack discrimination. In
October 1952, he created a seven-member committee to mon-
itor state elections for "racial and religious bigotry" in campaign
ads and materials and continued his efforts to persuade the
Michigan State Police and other government agencies to hire
African Americans.[75]

Williams faired little better in his efforts to secure a corporate
profits tax. He warned the legislature that the state was facing a
deficit of forty million dollars and only a 4 percent profits tax
could resolve Michigan's growing financial crisis. Republicans
proposed a tax on business based on "corporate structure"
rather than profits: all corporations would pay the same amount
regardless of their size. Williams was outraged and threatened a
veto. He denounced the legislature as dominated by "Republican advocates of the 'trickle down' school of thought. They
will tax anybody except big business."[76]

The legislature did agree to the need for some funding for
the construction of a modern highway system and proposed an
increase in the gas tax and a new fee on the purchase of used
cars to fund road construction. Weber wrote a confidential
memo suggesting that Williams allow the gas tax to pass and

then denounce the measure as "taxes on the little guy" followed by "a full scale public relations operation" to show that
"the Governor is the people's champion FOR good roads but
AGAINST consumer taxes." Williams should then demand passage of his corporate profits tax to fund the highway program.
Williams followed the strategy, but the legislature still refused
to approve the profits tax.[77]

He also found it difficult to get support for another of his
major proposals: the Mackinac Bridge. In 1949, he had created
the Inter-Peninsula Communications Commission to study
ways to link the two halves of Michigan and appointed John
McCarthy, head of the State Public Services Commission, to
chair the group. The legislature refused to ratify McCarthy's
appointment, but he agreed to serve without pay. After his
reelection, the governor again raised the bridge issue and
turned for support to W. Steward Woodfill, owner of the
famous Grand Hotel on Mackinac Island. Woodfill cultivated
an aristocratic image, dressing in waistcoats and carrying an
ivory walking stick. More important, he had close ties with the
Republican Party. Williams encouraged him to lobby legislators for creation of an official agency to study the feasibility of
the project. Partly due to Woodfill's efforts, on June 6, 1950,
the governor created the Mackinac Bridge Authority to explore
construction costs and possible financing. In 1951, the group
reported to the legislature that the bridge was feasible, and
Williams asked for two million dollars for additional engineering studies and preparation of a bond issue. The legislature
appropriated a dollar![78]

Both Williams and Woodfill were livid at what they saw as
the arrogance of the Republicans. Members of the Mackinac
Bridge Authority continued to serve without pay, and Williams
gave a blistering speech to the Upper Peninsula Development
Bureau in Iron River, vowing to complete the bridge despite
the Republican insult. He responded to criticism that it would
be impossible to construct such a bridge, as it was "too big," by
arguing that "Michigan is big! The Upper Peninsula is big! We
are not afraid of any task merely because it's big!" There were
only two barriers, he concluded, a shortage of steel due to the

war in Korea and the need to "build a little steel into the back-
bones of some of our more fainthearted citizens!"[79]

The governor and the legislature battled throughout 1951
and 1952 on several other fronts. Williams managed to secure
funding for an expanded junior college system and for increased
money for mental health. He was less successful in his call for
modernization of Michigan's prison system. In 1949, the legislature had cut funding for recreation, education, and food services at state prisons (one of the reasons why Williams had visited the Marquette prison, where he was attacked).
Republicans again refused to increase spending in 1951, and the
one of the results was a violent revolt at the Jackson Peniten-
tiary in April. Prisoners protested the lack of recreation and
education by seizing eleven guards and burning the library and
other facilities, causing more than four million dollars in damage. Ironically, one of the leaders of the revolt was "Crazy
Jack" Hyatt, one of the prisoners who had attacked Williams
two years earlier.[80]

Williams blamed the riot on the Republicans, claiming that
the "unwisdom of the legislature's actions in cutting appropria-
tions" had led to the overcrowding and frustration that had
caused the revolt. He further alienated legislators by agreeing to
the prisoners' demands for more beds, recreational facilities, and
improved medical care in exchange for their release of the
eleven hostages and promised them a meal of steak and ice
cream if they surrendered. Republicans were outraged by
Williams's attempt to blame them for the riot and by his "giving in" to the rioters. The *Detroit News* denounced the settlement as "a deplorable and disgraceful concession by Gov.
Williams to brute force exercised by a group of depraved men.
. . . We should all hang our heads in shame." The newspaper
ran a cartoon showing smiling inmates sitting in the burned
ruins of the prison eating ice cream.[81]

During his second term Williams again faced the problem of
factionalism within his party. There were continuing battles
between the Staebler reform Democrats and labor representatives over nominations and state appointments. The fight
became public when Michigan U.S. senator Arthur Vandenberg

died in 1951. The conservative Vandenberg had been a major supporter of Truman's cold war policies, and Williams had publicly praised his bipartisanship in foreign affairs. When he died the governor faced extreme pressure from different elements within the Democratic Party in naming his replacement.[82]

Union leaders argued that is was time to recognize their importance in twice electing Williams and united behind George Edwards, a leader of the 1937 sit-down strike at the Ford plant in Michigan and one of the major organizers of the 1950 recount victory. Liberals within the party felt that Edwards was too closely tied to labor and his nomination would produce a backlash against the party for being a puppet of the unions. They backed Noel Fox, a leader of the reform movement within the party and twice the Democratic candidate for secretary of state. Leaders of the Michigan CIO had reportedly taken "a blood oath" to fight for Edwards, although Reuther refused any public endorsement. Williams was caught in a political dilemma. If he backed Edwards he would be dubbed a tool of organized labor. If he supported Fox, union leaders would see it as a betrayal. For weeks he refused public comment on the pending appointment, instead polling county chairmen and consulting with Democratic leaders. He finally solved the problem by rejecting both Edwards and Fox. Instead he followed the suggestion of Nancy Williams and nominated Blair Moody, a Detroit newspaper columnist who had never run for office.[83]

Williams later claimed that Edwards was "a very dear friend" who had been crucial in organizing the 1950 recount but that he felt Moody "would do a better job." That may have been true, but Moody's selection was also a way to avoid alienating either of the two major elements in the state party. It showed that Williams was sensitive to charges of being controlled by the unions and also was willing to defy the liberal reform element in his party. He later acknowledged labor's influence by naming Edwards to a seat on the district probate court, provoking strong opposition from Michigan conservatives for his selection of a "known racial labor leader for the bench."[84]

Splits within his party and his upcoming campaign for a third term did not prevent Williams from making his first entrance into national politics in the summer of 1952. Despite his narrow victory in 1950 and his lack of success in passing his legislative agenda, he was still governor of a large state. Candidates seeking the Democratic Party nomination for the presidency in 1952 actively courted his support, as he controlled the Michigan delegation's forty convention votes. It was clear that Williams would be a favorite son nominee at the Chicago convention, but potential candidates were eager to gain his endorsement after he followed custom and withdrew before the balloting. In particular, Governor Adlai Stevenson of Illinois and Senator Estes Kefauver of Tennessee vied for Williams's favor.

Stevenson seemed the obvious choice for a northern liberal like Soapy Williams. He was a fellow Princeton graduate, governed a nearby midwestern state, and had the firm backing of Eleanor Roosevelt and most other prominent liberals. The two governors began corresponding immediately following their victories in 1948, and in 1949 Williams invited Stevenson to join the Eagles Club and attend its convention in Detroit. The Illinois governor responded that he had decided "not to join any organizations" so as to maintain his independence. It was a response puzzling to Williams, who joined nearly every organization in Michigan that asked him. (At one time he was a member of the Elks, Eagles, Moose, Lions, Veterans of Foreign Wars, American Legion, and dozens of ethnic clubs and an honorary chief of the Ottawa Indian tribe.)[85]

Stevenson's refusal to join the Eagles symbolized a major difference between the two governors. Stevenson personified the intellectual in politics, and, although he was an effective campaigner, he often seemed aloof and detached from his audience. While Williams reveled in shaking hands, calling square dances, and addressing ethnic groups in their own languages, Stevenson preferred formal speeches and maintaining a dignified presence. Although they shared a Princeton degree and a liberal agenda, their personalities were clearly in contrast.

The two met in 1950 at a civil defense meeting in Chicago, and throughout the next year Stevenson worked to get

Williams's support for a Democratic nomination. Williams was noncommittal and refused to make an endorsement, telling Stevenson only that he hoped they "could maintain the ideals we believe in."[86]

New York governor Averell Harriman also lobbied for Michigan's support, but Williams did not think he had a realistic chance for the nomination. He was far more enthusiastic toward the coonskin-cap-wearing Kefauver. The Tennessee senator shared with Williams a folksy style and a belief in the New Deal ideology. Kefauver had also been the leader of investigations into organized crime, in particular Williams's bitter enemy Jimmy Hoffa and the Teamsters. Williams also felt that Stevenson was not passionate enough about civil rights and determined that Kefauver, though a southerner, "had the strongest position on civil rights" of any candidate. Like Lyndon Johnson of Texas, Kefauver had distanced himself from the southern caucus in the Senate, which was opposed to civil rights legislation, and had announced that he would not vote for any filibusters to prevent votes on the issue. He had, however, never repudiated segregation and had refused to vote for an antilynching law. Likely it was Kefauver's campaign style and hostility toward the Teamsters more than his civil rights record that appealed to Williams.[87]

Prior to the opening of the convention, Williams was the leading advocate of a strong civil rights platform. Georgia senator and segregationist Richard Russell was the candidate of the South, and Williams and others feared the party would endorse a moderate statement on civil rights to prevent a southern walkout, as had occurred in 1948. Despite Williams's efforts, the platform statement was far weaker than he had hoped for, but he wrote Illinois senator Paul Douglass that "we have lost the battle but I am inclined to believe we are going to win the war."[88]

The 1952 convention dramatically showed Michigan's governor the reality of national politics. His outspokenness on civil rights had already engendered a deep hatred in southern delegates, and he managed to anger them even more when he and Moody demanded a "loyalty oath" from all delegates to endorse the Democratic Party's nominees, a clear reminder of

the Dixiecrat walkout four years earlier. The Michigan governor led a fight to deny the credentials of any delegate who
would not publicly vow to support the party's candidates. The
Credentials Committee originally agreed to the Williams-
Moody plan, but when the convention convened it accepted a
compromise statement that delegates would "exert every honorable means" to see that the Democratic nominees made it
onto the ballot in their states.[89]

Moody nominated Williams as a favorite son, comparing
him to Franklin Roosevelt. The governor then withdrew, and
the Michigan delegation voted for Kefauver. The Tennessee
senator led after the first ballot, with Stevenson second, but
President Truman then began a campaign to shift the convention to Stevenson. He lobbied Harriman to release his delegates, and the New York governor agreed. Williams and
Moody heard of Harriman's decision and feared the convention
would deadlock between Kefauver and Stevenson, paving the
way for the segregationist Russell to win the nomination. They
rushed to Kefauver's suite at the Stockyard Inn and pleaded
with him to withdraw and throw his support to Stevenson.
After a long and tense debate, he finally agreed. Hubert
Humphrey, Moody, and Williams volunteered to escort Kefauver to the podium, where he could deliver his withdrawal statement and endorse Stevenson. When the four arrived at the
stage, Convention chairman Sam Rayburn of Texas refused to
stop the roll call to permit Kefauver to address the convention.
For nearly three hours Humphrey, Moody, Williams, and
Kefauver had to stand at the back of the stage while Rayburn
slowly called on each state for its vote and then asked for individual roll calls. Rayburn, a Russell supporter, was angry about
Kefauver's decision to withdraw, knowing it would lead to
Stevenson's nomination. He was also livid at Williams and
Moody for their "loyalty oath" resolution, viewing it as an
attempt to embarrass the South. Making Kefauver, Williams,
Moody, and Humphrey wait at the back of the platform was
the Texan's punishment.[90]

Although Williams respected Rayburn, he felt he had been
intentionally humiliated in full view of the convention as pun-

ishment for his outspokenness on racial equality. His uncompromising stand on civil rights earned him the wrath of the South, and four years later it would cause a rupture with Stevenson.

Williams's advocacy of a clear commitment to civil rights alienated him from some of the leading figures in his party, but it earned him a national reputation. *Time* put his picture on its September 15 cover and included a four-page article on the leader of "the liberal revolt." Along with Hubert Humphrey and Eleanor Roosevelt, Williams was now a leading spokesperson for an unwavering commitment by the Democrats to racial equality.[91]

It would be two years before the U.S. Supreme Court declared racial segregation unconstitutional, but the Democratic Party was already deeply divided on the issue. Most southern Democrats remained committed to legal separatism of black and white and most northern leaders of the party either downplayed the issue or offered vague sentiments favoring "moderation" out of fear of losing southern votes. Williams was unwilling to remain silent or equivocate on the issue. Although his militant position enhanced his standing among liberals and African Americans, it led conservatives and moderates in the party to dismiss him as unrealistic and unaware of the need for compromise.

The 1952 Democratic convention was Williams's initial encounter with the factions within the national party and the first example of his disdain for temporizing on what he viewed as the great moral issue of his era. He would reprise his role as the "conscience of the Democratic Party" even more strongly in 1956 and 1960.

Williams had tasted the glory of national prominence in Chicago, but to retain his position as the leading advocate for a national pledge to equality he needed to remain governor of Michigan, and his reelection was far from certain. Although he had been on the cover of *Time,* this was no guarantee that he could win another term in Michigan. His 1952 campaign would be a battle both for a third victory in his home state and to remain a force for liberalism within the Democratic Party.

IV

THE "CONSCIENCE OF
THE DEMOCRATIC PARTY"

Toward a National Presence, 1952–56

> Tired, timid, and temporizing is a good policy
> for drunks, but not for politicians.
>
> —*G. Mennen Williams on Adlai Stevenson's*
> *call for "moderation" in the Democratic Party*

Despite his humiliation on the stage at the 1952 Democratic convention, Williams's debut involvement in the internecine struggles of the party was a personal success. He left Chicago as a national figure proclaimed by the press as a leader of the liberal wing of his party. As the architect of the rebirth of the Democratic Party in Michigan, a two term governor of a major industrial state, and the leading white advocate of a clear commitment to civil rights, the young Michigan governor was a potential force in the party and perhaps even a possible national candidate. Even before the convention, the chairman of the Democratic National Committee had mentioned him as a future leader of the party and Williams had declared that he "might prefer seeking a higher office in 1956."[1]

To retain his public position as an advocate for liberalism within his party and to keep alive the possibility of national office, Williams had to continue to win elections. Despite his new national prominence, there were major barriers to gaining a third term in Michigan. In the four years of his governorship, Williams, Staebler, and other "new" Democrats had successfully rebuilt and redefined their party, but serious splits remained. Larry Farrell, Williams's former boss at the OPA and one of his major political advisers, still had strong links to the old Democrats, while Helen "Buffy" Berthelot of the Communications Workers Union had been one of the more prominent leaders in the movement to reform the party. As Williams prepared for his campaign in 1952, conflict intensified between Farrell and Berthelot and the factions they represented.

Farrell was technically in charge of the 1952 campaign, but Williams appointed Berthelot "director of organization" for the contest, and it was unclear who had authority over strategy, volunteers, and finances. After several days of internal conflict, Farrell demanded that Berthelot resign. She refused and stopped talking to Farrell. The two groups could not even agree on which names to list at the top of the campaign stationery. To compound these problems, the Stevenson for President Campaign, led by Margaret Price, argued it should dictate campaign strategy and finances in the state. The three factions fought over access to telephones, mailing lists, and even who used which typewriters. Williams finally intervened personally to clarify the lines of authority, but tensions remained.[2]

Aside from staff feuds, there were other problems in the 1952 effort. Television was becoming increasingly important in U.S. elections, and Williams and his advisers acknowledged that the governor was generally ineffective in using the new media. Williams was uncomfortable on TV and refused to rehearse or use makeup. In his early appearances on television he seldom spoke to the camera but looked at the interviewer or audience and gave lengthy and at times rambling responses that made him appear disorganized. He was most effective in face-to-face meetings with small groups and in radio interviews, where he could ad lib his remarks, and he struggled to master the new force in political campaigns.[3]

There also was a sense of overconfidence among Democrats. Having defeated the Republicans twice, Williams and his advisers felt a third victory would be relatively easy. Despite the frustrations of dealing with the Republican legislature, he was certain he had developed the issues, campaign strategy, and staff to win another term. He was more concerned about working for the election of his Senate appointee, Blair Moody, than his own victory and devoted much of his time and the party's funds to defeating the Republican challenger, Charles Potter.

Despite staff infighting, ineffectiveness on television, and overconfidence, the biggest problem Williams faced in 1952 was Dwight D. Eisenhower. The Republican presidential nominee was extremely popular in Michigan, particularly among World War II veterans, who had been largely support-ive of Williams in 1948 and 1950. It was clear even before the campaign began that Eisenhower would carry Michigan by a large majority, and Williams would have to convince voters to split their ballot between the Republican hero of the liberation of Europe and the Democratic governor.

Having lost to Williams twice, Republicans turned to one of his Grosse Pointe neighbors, former Michigan secretary of state Frederick M. Alger Jr., in 1952. Like Williams, Alger had attended an exclusive eastern prep school and an Ivy League col-lege (Harvard) and had been a decorated naval officer during the war. Alger's family had made a fortune in the lumber industry and had long been active in Michigan politics. His grandfather, Russell Alger, had served as both governor and U.S. senator.

To Williams the issues and tactics in 1952 were identical to those of his previous two campaigns. He would stress again the need for reform in the state and the continued obstinacy of the Republican legislature, and he and Nancy would repeat their blitz of the state with an exhaustive series of personal appear-ances at local festivals, ethnic clubs, county fairs, factory gates, and radio stations. As in the past two elections, he launched his campaign with a "kickoff" dinner in Nancy's hometown of Ypsilanti on September 2 and declared that the main issue was the refusal of the legislature to respond to the rapid growth of Michigan's population with "any comparable progress in state government." The "one-party Republican machine" had been

> blind to the realities of modern life. Their eyes are fixed on yesterday, and their hearts on what they call "the good old days" when the population was small and people didn't expect so much out of life. . . . [T]he noise in Lansing during the last four years has not been the sound of stalemate. It has been the sound of the Republican leadership kicking and

screaming as it was dragged unwillingly along the path of progress![4]

He followed by distributing a campaign flyer called "Building the People's Plant," which listed the major accomplishments of his first two terms: the construction of thirty-seven new community hospitals with fourteen hundred beds, expanded facilities at Detroit's Wayne State University and other colleges, new roads and airports, an increase in old age assistance and workman's compensation, and preliminary plans for construction of the Mackinac Bridge. It concluded: "When we took office in 1949 the state had let its physical plant run down. . . . Governor Williams has reversed that trend with a 'Build Michigan' program."[5]

Williams quickly recognized that the Stevenson campaign was doomed in Michigan. He appeared with the Illinois governor at the traditional Democratic Labor Day parade in Cadillac Square in Detroit (where a photographer captured the famous image of Stevenson with a hole in the sole of his shoe), but when the presidential nominee later returned to Michigan Williams chose not to join him. Instead he invited Estes Kefauver and New York governor Averell Harriman to come to the state to help with his campaign. He also convinced Harry Truman to share a daylong whistle-stop train ride across the state.[6]

As in 1950, the major Republican tactic was to portray Williams as fiscally irresponsible and a tool of Walter Reuther and labor. Alger charged that the governor followed "the Truman policy of spend more, tax more, and go deeper into the red" and claimed that the Democrat's refusal to compromise with the legislature was leading the state toward financial disaster. Alger also criticized Williams's response to the Jackson prison riot, where he "wrecked inmate discipline, shattered the morale of the administrative staff and left the taxpayers of Michigan holding the bag for $2 million . . . while a mob of rebellious convicts feasted on steak and ice cream, compliments of the Governor." [7]

Alger also repeatedly attacked Williams as a puppet of organized labor and a member of the "radical" Americans for

Democratic Action. He began to refer to Williams as "the PACADA Boy," a reference to the CIO's Political Action Coalition and the ADA. Alger contended that Williams had "sold out" the Democratic Party "when he turned it over to the bosses of the CIO." The Political Action Coalition was "socialistic at heart," and Williams was leading Michigan "down the road to disaster just as surely as the Socialistic Labor Party has been leading Great Britain to its collapse."[8]

Two constitutional amendments on the 1952 Michigan ballot dealing with the reapportionment of the legislature helped Republicans label Williams as being under the control of organized labor. The Michigan legislature continued to be heavily weighted in favor of smaller, rural districts (traditional Republican strongholds), and state Senate districts varied in population from 61,000 to 545,000. The CIO led the campaign for more equal representation and managed to get a proposal on the ballot that called for no more than a 15 percent variance among Senate districts. Republicans responded with their own plan, which would freeze existing Senate districts but reapportion the House. The Republican plan strongly favored rural areas and continued to discriminate against Detroit and Wayne County. Most of the state's newspapers joined Williams in endorsing the CIO plan, but Alger and other Republicans charged that it would give political control of the state to Detroit and the CIO. Willis Hall, secretary of the Detroit Board of Commerce, contended that the CIO plan would

> advance the long range socialistic projects of the stooges they
> [the CIO] have put into office. They want to push the
> schemes of Senator Moody, a socialistic puppet of the CIO,
> and Gov. Williams, an agent of the CIO.

Williams continued to endorse the reapportionment plan, but many in the state were convinced that it was a plot by labor to dominate the legislature. Republican charges that he was a radical tool of "socialistic labor bosses" led the president of conservative Albion College to refuse permission for Williams to visit the campus, and many factory owners denied him access to their parking lots for handshaking.[9]

Alger's attacks on the governor's connections with organized labor were effective, particularly when a national coal miner's strike paralyzed the nation. Williams continued to devote his efforts to the election of Moody to the Senate, but when early polls showed Alger with a 54 to 43 percent lead he began to focus on his own reelection and Fred Alger. He returned to the strategy that had been effective in 1948 and 1950 of nearly non-stop campaigning. On a single day he made eight different appearances in southwestern Michigan towns, flew to Detroit for five afternoon functions, attended a dinner at a black church, participated in three labor rallies, gave two radio interviews, and hosted a square dance at a Ukrainian center. The next day he was up at 5:00 a.m. shaking hands at auto plants.[10]

Aside from his typical exhausting campaign style, Williams began to challenge his opponent directly. He charged Alger with using his position as secretary of state to create "a political machine" to recruit campaign workers and with training children to chant "We like Ike" at Democratic rallies. He also claimed that Alger had helped Teamster truckers obtain fraudulent weight slips to avoid road taxes and had been an incompetent and wasteful administrator. Alger was "a phony penny pincher of public pennies" who wanted only to prevent the wealthy from paying their fair share of taxes.[11]

Based on the advice of Weber and other campaign strategists, Williams also stepped up his attacks on the Republican legislature, arguing that Michigan's looming financial crisis was not the fault of its governor but was due to the failure of the legislature to pass a corporate profits tax. Republicans did not understand that the role of government was to provide necessary services for its citizens, not to protect the wealthy. "How can any state be solvent with a legislature like that?" he asked. He warned that if Alger won the election Republicans would impose a bevy of new taxes on beer, soft drinks, auto licenses, hotels, and telephones rather than asking business to pay its fair share.[12]

Alger responded by calling the governor "a liar" who depended on "innuendo, falsehood, smear, and half truths." Williams was running "the dirtiest campaign in the nation" and had turned state government into "a massive public relations machine."[13]

The name calling continued. In a television debate Williams claimed that Alger planned to raid the $50 million Veterans Trust Fund to avoid taxing corporations. (Ironically, six years later, when Michigan was in fiscal ruin, Williams would propose the same tactic.) Alger denied any plans to touch the veterans fund and argued that an Eisenhower victory would lead to massive cuts in the federal budget, which would solve the financial crisis in Michigan. He reminded viewers several times that "a vote for Alger is a vote for Ike!"[14]

Two weeks before the election, new polls showed Williams with a narrow lead, and he intensified his efforts. Democratic candidates for other state and local offices frantically tried to join the governor on the campaign trail. Robert McAllister of Grand Rapids, the Democratic nominee for secretary of state, refused to get out of his car to campaign at a Bay City factory until Williams arrived. "There is no sense going out there without Williams. They want to see him, not us," he told reporters. John Connolly, the Democratic candidate for lieutenant governor, spent three weeks following Williams, often getting less than thirty seconds before the audience, as he felt only the governor could help his victory by drawing a large crowd. The Democratic choice for auditor general, Robert Baker, summed up the view of party candidates when he explained that Williams was "a celebrity and we're all unknowns. We don't shake hands the way Williams does."[15]

As expected, Dwight Eisenhower won a massive victory in Michigan, carrying the state by over 325,000 votes and winning eighty-three of eighty-seven counties. Despite Williams's efforts, Potter defeated Blair Moody by 45,000 votes, and all the other Democratic candidates for state office were crushed. Williams, however, had a slim 7,500 vote lead after the ballots were counted. In a reversal of the results two years earlier, Republicans now demanded a recount. While the State Police guarded ballot boxes, Republicans selected Stanley Battle, a Detroit lawyer who had overseen the 1950 recount, to organize their efforts. Staebler refused to allow Moody to make a concession speech and announced that Democrats would demand a recount of the Senate contest if Republicans challenged the count in the governor's race. George Edwards, the organizer of the 1950 recount effort, was now a judge, so the Democrats picked Albert Fitt, a recent Michigan Law School graduate, to coordinate their recount campaign.[16]

The Democrats immediately set out to duplicate the tactics that had worked in 1950. Staebler sent a self-addressed, stamped letter to every Democratic county chairman asking for the names of volunteers. Detroit unions offered buildings and workers to aid in the recount, and many lawyers and academics who had volunteered two years earlier agreed to serve again. The situation in 1952, however, was far more advantageous for Williams than in 1950. He had the lead, and many Michigan districts had begun using voting machines, making irregularities less common. Equally important, Elma Williams agreed to help finance the recount effort. Despite her continued Republican politics, she argued that it was necessary to have an accurate record of the voter's wishes.[17]

The formal recount began on December 8, and it was immediately clear that Alger would not win. As in 1950, Staebler coordinated a statewide, disciplined network of volunteers and lawyers linked by telephone that challenged every disputed ballot. As the recount progressed the governor gained consistently, and the final results showed him with an 8,122 margin out of over 3 million votes cast. The Michigan legislature refused to approve a recount in the Senate race, and Potter was declared the winner. Moody left the state for Washington, D.C., to host a radio show. During the recount, the press noted that Williams's eleven-year-old son, Gery, had campaigned for his school's student council while wearing a green polka-dot bow tie and had won by a single vote. Republicans complained: "To beat Williams you've got to beat him twice, once in the election and again at the recount!" Hubert Humphrey wrote: "Soapy—Will you please stop doing this to me! You nearly gave me heart failure in 1950, and you just about repeated the performance this year!"[18]

Despite his victory, Williams was bitterly disappointed with the results of the 1952 election. Not only had Moody lost but so had all the other statewide Democratic nominees. Williams would again be the only Democrat in the executive offices in Lansing. In addition, Republicans again dominated the state legislature, and it was clear that most reform programs would again face intractable opposition. As he had done in his first two terms, Williams proposed significant new social programs and lobbied for new taxes to fund them, but he knew there was little chance for their implementation. To finally bring a "New Deal" to Michigan, he would not only have to win another term but also score a decisive victory that would carry other Democrats into office. Even before the recount was completed, Williams and his advisers began to prepare for 1954.

Although he was frustrated with the 1952 results, Williams's victory, albeit narrow, was significant given the Eisenhower landslide and the general Republican gains across the nation. After surveying the general conservative triumph in 1952, Humphrey wrote: "Your reelection was one of the few bright spots in the whole picture. In the next few years that face us, we have a big job cut out for us. We must keep the Democratic party liberal." Williams's successful campaign for a third term made him even more of a national figure in his party, and, aside from pushing for reform legislation in Lansing, he began to venture outside the state to make himself known to Democratic activists and to position himself for a possible place on the national ticket in 1956. Humphrey urged him to "take a more prominent position" in the national party.[19]

In his first inaugural address in 1949, Williams evoked religious imagery to frame his liberal agenda. In 1951, during the grim days of the Korean War, he argued that the global battle with communism demanded racial equality and economic reform to affirm American ideals. At his third inauguration, the governor offered a civics lesson. He reminded his audience that the founders of the United States had wisely created a balance between national and state governments and then addressed Republican complaints about the concentration of power in Washington. To prevent "the unnecessary expansion of federal operations" it was necessary "that the states do their own part."

If the individual states failed to act, the federal government would fill the void and America would be on the road to "centralized government." There were "fundamental" state obligations, such as education, health, civil rights, highways, aid to the mentally ill, and pollution, that demanded action and if ignored would be taken over by the national government. Using rather curious logic, he argued that it would be cheaper for the people of Michigan to have the state deal with these issues than to have the national government do so: "Failure to meet these problems here in Lansing will save our taxpayers nothing in the long run. The same services will be performed out of Washington certainly at no less cost to the Michigan taxpayer."[20]

His assertion that state activism was necessary to prevent a flow of power to Washington was an interesting if tortured argument, but it was unsuccessful, as Republicans were not convinced by Williams's advocacy of state action and appeals to their distrust of the federal government. With a Republican president and Congress in Washington, it seemed dubious to argue that the national government was eager to expand its power and establish new programs.[21]

Legislative leaders dismissed the speech as another attempt by the governor to raise taxes and expand his power. They were even more convinced of their position when Williams followed with a message outlining his agenda for 1953. He announced that there was only "one paramount question" and it was "the problem of our exhausted treasury and the imminent threat of state bankruptcy." He warned that "the situation we face is indeed a desperate one." Michigan anticipated a $65 million deficit, and, due to a rapid rise in school enrollment, it would likely increase. Williams contended that the state could not further reduce public services, as Michigan was already spending less on government than similar states, and concluded: "The only answer to the problem of impending bankruptcy is to raise additional revenues through additional taxes." He renewed his call for a corporate profits tax.[22]

Michigan Republicans disagreed with Williams's analysis of the pending fiscal crisis and his prescription for its cure. They claimed the deficit was due to the governor's insatiable lust for more programs and spending and noted that, despite his dire warnings of impending bankruptcy, he proposed to allocate more money for mental health care, prisons, unemployment and workman's compensation, education, welfare, and aid to the elderly.[23]

Despite the overwhelming Republican majority, Williams was able to enact parts of his reform program. The legislature appropriated $294,000 for a marketing program for farmers, increased unemployment insurance by $5 per week and extended coverage from twenty to twenty-six weeks, raised workman's compensation payments by $4 a week, and boosted old age pensions by $7 a month. It allocated $775,000 for the promotion of tourism and added 76 new prison guards (Williams had requested 163). It agreed to fund the construction of one new prison (the governor had asked for two) and two new mental health clinics for children. It rejected Williams's proposal to allocate funds for two new adult mental health facilities, increased training for psychiatric workers, an expansion of welfare benefits, a raise in the state minimum wage, a guaranteed salary for teachers, and giving the vote to eighteen year olds. It also refused to consider the corporate profits tax and instead raised taxes on licenses, utilities, automobiles, and alcohol.[24]

Given the Republican majorities in both houses, Williams was rather pleased to have enacted at least a part of his program and proclaimed that "during these past five years we have pushed, pulled, hauled, and dragged these reluctant Old Guard Rip Van Winkles into the second half of the 20th century!" He found, however, that he was still unable to prod the legislature into enacting significant civil rights legislation. Although Williams had emerged as one of the leading national spokesmen for racial equality, he again failed to gain approval for a Fair Employment Practices Commission.[25]

On February 1, 1953, the tenacious Louis Cramton again introduced his bill for a Fair Employment Practices Commission. Williams immediately organized church groups, labor unions, and African American organizations to pressure the legislature to enact the plan and proclaimed February 19 "Equal Opportunity Day" in Michigan, but Republicans remained adamantly opposed. Business groups and rural representatives continued to fight against the bill, and one Republican leader argued that passage would encourage thousands of poor uneducated blacks to migrate from Mississippi to Michigan. By a one-vote margin, the Senate refused to vote the bill out of committee. Williams responded by declaring March 3, 1953, "Judge Cramton Day."[26]

The narrow defeat of the legislation led Williams to become more personally involved in the battle for civil rights in Michigan. He had generally deferred to Cramton, hoping that the Republican leader could sway members of his party, but when it was clear that the bill would again come before the legislature in the next session, Williams wrote a personal letter to each member, calling for an end to partisanship and emphasizing the moral necessity of equal rights. He also sent a letter to Eisenhower urging the new president to publicly support the bill. When the *New York Times* ran an article on discrimination against black airmen at the Sault Sainte Marie base and the National Association for the Advancement of Colored People demanded that Michigan take action, Williams blamed the legislature's failure to enact a fair employment law for creating a climate that tolerated discrimination.[27]

When the legislature reconvened in 1954, the House again refused to consider Cramton's bill, but the Senate did approve a version of a fair employment act. Although the House defeated Cramton's motion to dislodge the bill from committee, it seemed that the momentum was finally on the side of the proposal. A year later Michigan would finally pass the legislation.

Republicans in Lansing were far more interested in communism than civil rights. In 1950, the governor had signed the legislature's bill to create a state "red squad" to investigate subversion, but had argued that the attorney general, rather than the chief of the state police, should be in charge of the process to ensure that civil liberties would not be curtailed. In early 1952, Republicans invited the U.S. House Un-American Activities

Committee (HUAC) to hold hearings in Detroit on communist activity in Michigan's labor unions, hoping for revelations
of subversion in a key component of Williams's coalition.
HUAC claimed that more than three hundred communists
were active in Michigan unions and that Ford's Local 600 was
dominated by communists. UAW leaders immediately vowed
to purge the communists from Local 600, and Williams called
for a conference of law enforcement officials to recommend
stronger measures to control subversion. Despite the prompt
response, the state Republican chairman, Owen Cleary,
accused the governor of presiding over an administration of
"commie-coddlers."[28]

The legislature followed with a bill sponsored by Kenneth
O. Trucks of Mason County, based on the national McCarran
Act, which barred communists from public employment,
authorized the state attorney general to publish a list of communist front groups, excluded communists from running for
office, and denied public employees the right to invoke the
Fifth Amendment when called before an investigative committee. Although Williams and many others in Michigan felt the
Trucks Act was unconstitutional, it passed both houses unanimously and he signed it. He also remained silent when University of Michigan president Harlan Hatcher fired two faculty
members and suspended a third for refusing to testify before
HUAC.[29]

Although Williams tried to ensure the rights of freedom of
speech and due process, like most of his generation he believed
that communism posed a serious domestic threat and government needed to respond. He had joined the ADA in an attempt
to maintain a strong liberal platform untainted by communist
influence, and in the early 1950s he accepted the need for a
strong campaign against communism and the Communist
Party. His actions were in part the result of political reality.
Legislation against communism had passed the legislature without debate or dissent, and it would have been political suicide
to oppose such measures, but Williams also believed communism both at home and abroad to be a clear menace to American liberty and felt the state had an obligation to expose sub-

version. While he would later denounce the tactics of Senator Joseph McCarthy, in his first three terms as governor he accepted the need to attack communist influence in his state, although he tried to restrain the extremism rampant in the legislature.

While anticommunism dominated Michigan politics in 1952, Williams remained frustrated by the conservatism of the state legislature and its refusal to enact civil rights and social legislation and began to search for more tangible ways to demonstrate his successful leadership. He became a strong supporter of the Saint Lawrence Seaway plan to link the Great Lakes with the Atlantic, which he felt would stimulate Michigan's economy. When Eisenhower delayed signing the formal treaty that would authorize the project, Williams charged that he was "surrendering to foreign shipping interests" and favoring the East over the Midwest.[30]

More than the seaway, it was the Mackinac Bridge that Williams saw as his most significant accomplishment. He had long been an advocate for the impoverished (and Democratic) Upper Peninsula. After a television speech during which he had stood before a map of Michigan, he showed a rare display of temper and berated his aides after discovering that the UP had been left off. Construction of a bridge connecting the two Michigans had been one of his campaign issues in 1948, and five years later he determined it was time to get on with the project. Although the legislature was reluctant to fund the bridge, Williams continued to push for construction, and despite Republican opposition he ordered engineering studies to determine the feasibility of the structure. Critics claimed that strong winds made a five-mile-long bridge too dangerous, but engineers concluded that modern techniques could create a structure that would withstand more than three times the maximum wind speed ever recorded in the area. In early 1951, the Mackinac Bridge Authority judged the project feasible and recommended that the state issue bonds to finance construction, but a shortage of steel due to the Korean War delayed the project.[31]

In 1953, the legislature agreed to finance the operation and maintenance of the bridge through gasoline and license plate taxes and the state invited New York financiers to send sealed bids on $99 million in bonds to Lansing by December 17. The Republicans, however, made one last attempt to delay the project. The day before the bids were to be opened, Republican state senator Haskell Nichols of Jackson announced that he was petitioning the Michigan Supreme Court to prohibit the sale of bonds for the bridge. Although he claimed he was concerned about the costs, most felt Nichols wanted to delay the project until after the next election so that Williams would not receive the credit. Prentiss Brown, chair of the Mackinac Bridge Authority, was driving to Lansing to supervise the opening of the bids when he heard of Nichols's suit on his car radio and claimed he "nearly drove off the road." Instead he headed directly to Lansing and called Jon Nunneley, the Bridge Authority's legal counsel, and together they went to the Supreme Court Building and persuaded a clerk to phone the justices for an emergency session. That afternoon the court denied Nichols's petition and the bond bids were opened. Construction was scheduled to begin in May 1954 with the Merritt, Chapman and Scott Corporation selected to build the foundations and U.S. Steel the superstructure.[32]

The Mackinac Bridge, completed in 1957, would be Williams's most visible achievement. Years later he would lament that perhaps he should have focused more on "enduring projects like Mackinac" rather than social and economic reforms. Critics in 1948 denounced the plan as "Soapy's Folly," but the unification of the "two Michigans" was both a practical and a symbolic success. Prior to the bridge connecting Saint Ignace and Mackinac City motorists had to wait nearly twelve hours to be ferried across the Straits of Mackinac. During deer-hunting season the wait was often more than twenty hours, and hunters would hire locals to sit in their cars while they spent the day at taverns. The bridge was dear to Williams's heart (he and Nancy could watch its progress from their summer home on Mackinac Island), but he was also aware of the economic impact on the ferry business. As part of the legislation establishing the project, there could be no ferry service within ten miles of the bridge, and ferryboat owners and workers would be ruined. Williams personally arranged jobs for all displaced workers with the state highway department.[33]

The beginning of construction of the bridge contributed to Williams's popularity in Michigan, and he enhanced his appeal in the state through public appearances and effective publicity efforts. Even in nonelection years, he continued an extensive program of travel and speeches throughout the state. In one week in December 1953, for example, he spoke at the Kent County Conservation League dinner, a luncheon of the Michigan Youth Commission, the annual convention of the Michigan Farmer's Union, and the Upper Peninsula Winter Sports Council and gave a major TV address in Grand Rapids. He also continued his weekly radio program.[34]

Williams used other opportunities to keep a visible profile in the state. He began the tradition of attending the annual football game between the University of Michigan and Michigan State University, sitting half the time on each side of the field. Every year he and Nancy sent more than two thousand Christmas cards with a photo of the family. One year the card failed to include the family poodle, Torchy, and hundreds of citizens wrote asking about the dog's health. Williams had to issue a press release assuring the public that Torchy was alive and that the picture had been taken at a local TV station, where "the dog had not been invited."[35]

Aside from keeping his name in front of the voters of Michigan, Williams began to reach out to a national audience. Despite his narrow victories, many groups were eager to invite the young and colorful Soapy Williams to speak. In September 1953, he gave a major address on farm policy to the Democratic National Committee in Chicago, where he charged that Eisenhower was engaging in "creeping Hooverism" by favoring rich farmers and destroying family farms. The next month he was the featured speaker at a Young Democrats of Wisconsin meeting in Madison, where he again attacked Eisenhower. Williams declared that the new president's tax policies favored the rich over the average worker and that he had shown his dedication to "union busting" by endorsing the Taft-Hartley Act restricting political campaigning by labor.[36]

Williams also received national attention when he used the Michigan National Guard to help patrol the state's highways on Labor Day in 1954. During the Fourth of July holiday that year Michigan had led the nation with thirty-three traffic fatalities. Williams ordered seven hundred guardsmen to help local police enforce speeding and drunken-driving laws. The guardsmen could not make arrests, but they could retain suspects until regular police arrived. Critics charged that the plan was expensive (it cost thirty thousand dollars), illegal, and a publicity stunt, but Williams claimed it was a success, as it reduced traffic deaths from thirty-one during the Labor Day weekend of 1953 to twenty-one in 1954. The move led to national coverage, including a favorable editorial in the *New York Times*. Williams used the opportunity to criticize the Republican legislature for failing to modernize Michigan's highway system.[37]

Aside from his continued campaign for stronger support of civil rights, Williams's other major national issue in 1953 was to encourage new approaches to mental health care. His religious faith and his liberal political ideology both convinced him that government needed to be involved directly in new programs for the care of the mentally ill, and he saw mental health as an emerging topic that he could use to expand his reputation beyond Michigan. He had repeatedly lobbied the legislature for expanded psychiatric programs and mental hospitals and argued that money spent for mental health was a wise investment that would avoid higher costs later.

> Each person restored to mental health will repay many times the cost of his treatment in productive contributions to society. . . . There is a social cost in neglecting mental health that is too often overlooked. That is the cost of broken homes, broken bodies, murders, homicides, jail and prison.[38]

In 1953, Williams tried to organize state governors in a unified effort to focus on mental health. He called a national conference of governors to coordinate mental health policy and arranged for staff from the Menninger Clinic in Kansas to attend the program. All forty-eight states sent representatives, and Williams was the keynote speaker. He hailed the meeting as "an historic turning point" in the battle against "sickness of

the human mind." The conference was so successful that attendees agreed to make it an annual event.[39]

His efforts to forge a national program of mental health care
were part of a campaign to position himself as a potential candidate for the vice presidency or even the presidency in 1956 or
1960. Immediately following his election to a third term,
reporters speculated that he would run for the Senate in 1954 to
give him national exposure for future higher office. In July
1954, the *New York Times Magazine* ran an article entitled
"Who'll Head the Tickets in '56?" which listed Williams,
Stevenson, Harriman, and Kefauver as the leading Democratic
contenders for the presidency. Williams was a clear liberal
alternative to Republican conservatism, and as the issue of civil
rights for black Americans became more dominant his outspokenness provided Democrats with a potentially important
issue. Williams was obviously unacceptable to southern
Democrats, but he had a strong appeal to African Americans,
northern liberals, and union members.[40]

Many of his advisers urged him to challenge Republican senator Homer Ferguson in 1954 as an opportunity to position
himself for the vice presidential nomination in 1956. Two years
in the Senate would allow him to deal with national and international issues and would make him a stronger force within the
Democratic Party. Williams seriously considered the possibility.
At a CIO banquet in Lansing in January 1954, he asked: "How
many of you think I should run for the Senate?" After the
crowd roared its response, he asked: "How many think I should
run for Governor?" Again most of the audience stood and
applauded. Williams then declared: "It is clear you want me to
run for *something!*"[41]

Williams eventually decided to seek a fourth term in Lansing
rather than challenging Ferguson. He still wanted to enact his
reform program in Michigan and also felt an obligation to Blair
Moody to let the former reporter have a second chance to win
a term in the Senate. Perhaps even more important, in the
words of his wife, Williams "loved being governor!" Despite
the continuing conflicts with the legislature, he admitted: "I
enjoyed every instant."[42]

To prepare for another campaign, Williams called a meeting of thirty advisers to discuss issues and strategy. In contrast to the narrow victories in 1950 and 1952, he wanted a decisive win to show his electoral power. In the two years since his close contest with Alger, Staebler had continued to develop a powerful and efficient Democratic organization in Michigan. To him, political organization was the key to electoral victories and at the heart of politics was participation. He argued that "humanity has made astounding progress in every other field of human endeavor except politics." To revitalize politics and government it was necessary to mobilize the people into direct involvement in the process: "Politics is a lot of people, good ideas, and coordination of the two. Participation, the widest possible participation, is the answer," he concluded. By 1954, he had mobilized more than ten thousand volunteers for election day, with nearly one-third provided by Michigan's AFL.[43]

Staebler and Williams also made it clear that it was time for the new Democrats to control candidate selection and campaign strategy. To stress the point, the governor asked Helen Berthelot to return from her position as a labor lobbyist in Washington, D.C., to serve as his campaign manager. Berthelot was the first woman to manage a statewide campaign in Michigan. Although there were still conflicts between Berthelot and Farrell, it was clear that "Williams Democrats" would run the campaign.[44]

As Williams prepared for his campaign for a fourth term, he was confronted with an issue that would ensnare him for nearly four years and give critics support for their assertion that he was a puppet of organized labor. In the spring of 1954, the UAW began a campaign to organize workers at the Kohler Plumbing Company in Sheboygan, Wisconsin, and the result was a bitter and violent strike. On July 4, John Guanca from Flint and two other UAW organizers from Michigan arrived to help the Kohler employees and confronted two nonstriking workers, sixty-five-year-old William Bersch and his son. Guanca and the other UAW workers delivered a vicious beating to the two, and the elder Bersch died from his wounds nineteen days later. Guanca was arrested but fled to Michigan before going to trial.

At the time of his arrest he reportedly told police that Emil Mazey, a UAW vice president, "will never let Soapy send me back here." Wisconsin governor Vernon W. Thompson demanded that Michigan extradite Guanca, but UAW leaders argued that the situation in Sheboygan was so inflamed that he would not receive a fair trial and urged the governor to refuse extradition.[45]

Williams faced a difficult dilemma. If he sent Guanca back to Wisconsin, he would infuriate labor leaders on the eve of his reelection campaign. If he rejected extradition, critics would argue that he was so controlled by the unions that he was disregarding justice. Williams stalled by asking Alfred Fitt, the coordinator of his 1952 recount effort and now his legal adviser, to conduct a hearing to determine whether Guanca could receive a fair trial. Wisconsin officials offered to move the trial to an adjoining county, but Guanca's attorneys argued that the case had received so much publicity that there was no part of Wisconsin that would not be biased against the union organizer, and Fitt concurred. Williams decided not to honor Wisconsin's request for extradition.[46]

The Guanca case would drag on for four more years. In 1955, the National Labor Relations Board began action against Kohler and asked that Guanca be brought to Wisconsin to testify, but Williams again refused and proposed that Guanca submit a deposition taken in Michigan. A year later Williams asked James M. Moses, a newspaper publisher from Marshall, Michigan, to assess the possibility of a fair trial. Moses concluded it was unlikely that Guanca could receive justice anywhere in Wisconsin, but Guanca's lawyers later offered to send him back if his trial were moved to Milwaukee. Finally, in 1958 Walter Reuther, testifying before the National Labor Relations Board, suggested that Guanca should be returned to Wisconsin. Williams was incensed with Reuther for not informing him about his statement ahead of time, but when it became clear that Guanca was preparing to flee to Canada he finally agreed to extradition. In June 1959, Guanca was returned to Wisconsin, tried, and sentenced to three years in prison.[47]

The Guanca controversy plagued Williams for five years. His

opponents in Michigan had long charged that he was a tool of Reuther and the unions and claimed the case proved their allegations. Reuther's public shift in favor of returning Guanca, made without consulting Williams, left the governor embarrassed. He claimed he had acted only from a concern about the possibility of a fair trial and contended that both Fitt and Moses had impartially concluded that Guanca would not receive justice. Fitt, however, was a Williams appointee and Moses was a prominent Democrat who had supported the governor in his election efforts. The governor's actions may have bolstered his support among union leaders in Michigan, but his refusal to return Guanca became a continued reference for critics both in Lansing and within the national Democratic Party. His press secretary later claimed that in the Guanca case "we got the worst of both worlds, the heat for not sending him back, the heat when we did send him back."[48]

Although the Guanca case would linger, Williams's immediate concern was his reelection. His initial forays into national politics had convinced him he had a chance for higher office but only if he could deliver an impressive victory in Michigan. Unlike the first three campaigns, in 1954 the Democrats had ample campaign funds and, with the help of Staebler, an impressive political organization. The press reported that Williams was "rolling in campaign funds." Unlike the battered DeSoto he relied on in 1948, he chartered a twelve-seat airplane to whisk him around the state and also had money for a number of statewide television broadcasts. Two of his key constituencies, union members and African Americans, were well organized and committed to a Democratic victory. Labor leaders promised a 325,000-vote majority in Wayne County, and Williams's efforts on behalf of a fair employment act and his appointment of two black judges, Charles Jones and Wade McCree, increased his popularity among African American voters. Polls in 1954 showed that 88 percent of Detroit's blacks intended to vote for him.[49]

Despite a large campaign budget and an impressive political organization, Williams faced two of the same problems that had plagued him in the past: the Teamsters and continued conflicts between old and new Democrats. Hoffa and the Teamsters had been routed by Williams and his reform Democrats in 1948 and 1950, but they reemerged in 1954. With a $56,000 campaign donation from Hoffa, former Teamster official George Fitzgerald challenged Phillip Hart, Williams's nominee for lieutenant governor, in the Democratic primary. Williams had followed a policy of neutrality in past primary battles but abandoned this position in 1954. He accused Hoffa and Fitzgerald of trying to help the Republicans and campaigned hard for Hart. When Hart won the primary by a three to one margin, in the words of Hoffa's biographer, "Hoffa and the Detroit Teamsters abandoned their experiment with the Democratic Party."[50]

Williams faced another challenge to his leadership when conservative Democrat Patrick McNamara entered the primary against Blair Moody. Williams and other "reform" Democrats were incensed, as they saw McNamara's candidacy as weakening a united party and another attempt by "old" party members to prevent reform. Staebler even asked Hubert Humphrey, a liberal colleague of Moody's, to come to Michigan to campaign against McNamara, but the Minnesota senator refused. On July 20, a few weeks before the primary, Moody contracted a fatal viral infection. His sudden death was a personal shock to Williams and particularly to Staebler, a close personal friend. It also provoked controversy within the party, as it was clear that the conservative McNamara would now be the nominee. Liberals such as Staebler, Berthelot, and Hart were convinced McNamara was far too right wing for them to support. Williams finally called a meeting of Democratic leaders, where he lectured McNamara on the need to endorse a liberal agenda, and the senatorial candidate agreed. Staebler was so upset that he turned his chair so he would not have to look at McNamara during the meeting.[51]

Despite Williams's three victories, there was no shortage of Republican challengers hoping to unseat him. Four Republicans entered the primary, and voters selected Donald S. Leonard, former head of the Michigan State Police. Leonard raised the now familiar Republican issues: Williams was a radical tool of organized labor who was leading the state toward financial ruin, and only a Republican governor could work with the legislature to solve the state's financial problems. Unlike previous Republican candidates, however, Leonard tried to appeal to organized labor. He stressed his support of unions, endorsed the right to strike, and called for an expanded workman's compensation program and increased health and safety standards for workers. He also pointed out that he had served as an arbitrator in labor disputes.[52]

Williams's campaign was similar to his previous three efforts, as he again embarked on a marathon of personal appearances throughout the state. One day in Detroit he made twenty-four appearances, including four breakfasts, eight church functions, eight union meetings, two lunches, three dinners, and a barn dance at night. When Leonard told reporters he was "a little fatigued" by the exhaustive campaign, Williams increased his pace. He told reporters he had a new "campaign breakfast" consisting of orange juice, seltzer water, and a raw egg, which gave him more energy. When Press Secretary Weber joined him for a day in central Michigan, the crusty former reporter repeatedly asked when they would stop for a meal and vowed he would not write any more speeches until they ate. He finally announced: "Governor, no eatie, no speechie." Williams gave him a handful of vitamins and a glass of water, and they motored on.[53]

Reporters marveled at Williams's energy and stamina. A *Detroit News* writer sarcastically noted that the governor had spent the day "peering under beds for fugitive hands to clasp." Williams developed calluses on both hands and wore the hair off his arms from shaking hands. Reporters also noted that the governor was now a celebrity and had "bobby sox" followers of teenage girls, who squealed when he arrived and when he asked them to send him their pictures.[54]

Although Williams's now legendary personal efforts were not new, the campaign's use of television was. Although the candidate made a number of TV appearances, it was Nancy Williams who demonstrated the power of the new medium. As in all of her husband's campaigns, she made dozens of daily appearances, particularly at meetings of ethnic and women's groups. At a dinner at a Hungarian church in Detroit, she and Republican senatorial candidate Homer Ferguson were the featured guests. Ferguson insisted on speaking before the meal was served, as he had to be at another function. He quickly listed his accomplishments and left before the audience had eaten. Nancy waited until the meal had been completed and the dishes cleared before addressing the crowd. She offered a personal thanks to the minister for organizing the event and called the cooks, waitresses, and busboys out of the kitchen for acknowledgment. She received a standing ovation.[55]

To capitalize on her speaking ability and popularity, the campaign bought TV time for a program called *Nancy's Scrapbook*. Throughout her husband's three terms as governor she had clipped newspaper stories, headlines, and editorials. The program had her reading from her scrapbooks, noting how legislators and the press had often supported her husband's position on issues but had attacked him personally. She also featured her children and the family dog. (When the poodle ran across the set, she ad-libbed: "Just another member of the family who wants to be on TV!") Unlike her husband, Nancy Williams was excellent on television. She was poised, humorous, and effective. *Nancy's Scrapbook* was so successful that it was repeated in later campaigns.[56]

The governor's main themes in 1954 mirrored those of his earlier campaigns: Michigan needed major reforms, and the legislature was unwilling to spend the money to fund them. He claimed Republicans wanted to return to "the good old days of one party rule," and he blamed the state's fiscal problems on the "bumbling and wrong-headed national economic policies" of Eisenhower and the Republicans. He again proposed an ambitious reform agenda featuring a $500 million bond program for highway construction, greatly increased spending on hospitals and mental health, more new prisons and schools, and no new "consumer taxes." Williams also issued a flyer criticizing Republicans for supporting Joseph McCarthy's anticommunist crusade and his recent attacks on the U.S. Army. "Are you as disturbed as I am about the recent nauseating spectacle between the United States Army and the very junior senator from Wisconsin?" it asked.[57]

As in his previous three campaigns, the 1954 race quickly shifted from issues to personal attacks. In a speech in Grand Rapids, Leonard argued that the Republican legislature had been "taking the wrong tack" and needed to be more aggressive in fighting against Williams's "inept leadership" and insatiable pursuit of personal power. He noted that the public had elected Eisenhower to "clean up the mess in Washington" and vowed he would "clean up the mess in Lansing." Williams responded by noting that Leonard had resigned as head of the Michigan State Police in 1952 largely because the legislature had refused to provide the funds for new officers. "The stalemate in Lansing" was due to the narrowness and miserly spirit of conservatives in the legislature, and Leonard's campaign was, in Williams's words, nothing more than "a fistful of feeble fibs."[58]

Unlike earlier elections, polls showed Williams well ahead. Staebler and his organization organized a massive "get out the vote" drive, and for the first time Democrats had funds for billboards and radio and TV ads. Unlike 1952, Eisenhower was not on the ticket to bolster Republican candidates. Democrats across the nation were eager to be part of Williams's victory, and the governor agreed that Stevenson could join him at several rallies. Williams was so confident of victory that he took two days off late in the campaign to fly to New York for a meeting of the Democratic National Committee.[59]

There was no recount in 1954, as Williams won a smashing victory. He received a stunning 68 percent of the vote in Wayne County and nearly split the rest of the state with Leonard. He won by three hundred thousand votes and carried the entire Democratic slate to victory: Phil Hart as lieutenant governor, James Hare as secretary of state, Tom Kavanaugh as attorney general, Sandy Brown as state treasurer, and Vic Targonski as auditor general. McNamara defeated Ferguson by nearly fifty thousand votes, and Democrats also increased their representation in the state legislature. Republicans still controlled the Senate by a margin of twenty-two to twelve, but the House was equally divided between the two parties.

Williams's landslide victory in 1954 solidified his position as a power in Michigan and the national Democratic Party. During his fourth term he would push again for a major reform of his state and new taxes to solve Michigan's growing financial problems. During the same two years he would be one of the most sought after speakers in the nation and would use these opportunities to advocate his liberal ideology and try to position himself for a place on the national ticket in 1956. His strident approach and uncompromising liberalism would soon alienate Williams from the leaders of his own party, in particular the eventual 1956 presidential nominee, Adlai Stevenson.

As he prepared for his fourth term, Mennen Williams had every reason to believe he was in a position to secure his party's nomination for vice president or even president. He had finally won a landslide victory in Michigan, a large, industrial state crucial to any Democratic victory in a presidential election, and had shown that he had the "coattails" to carry other Democrats into office. With the Supreme Court's decision in 1954 that racial segregation in the schools was unconstitutional, Williams's reputation as an unequivocal advocate of racial equality made him an attractive candidate to deal with the emerging issue of civil rights. He clearly had a strong appeal to union members, a key Democratic constituency, and at the age of forty-three was an energetic and youthful challenger to Republican conservatism.

His strong identification with labor, his refusal to moderate his liberalism, and his lack of mastery of television were drawbacks, but the other potential national candidates also had their weaknesses. Stevenson had lost in 1952; Kefauver and Senator Lyndon Johnson of Texas were southerners and, given the growing importance of civil rights, likely unacceptable to northern Democrats; Senator Stuart Symington of Missouri and Governor Averell Harriman of New York had not shown any national appeal; and Senator John F. Kennedy of Massachusetts was too young and a Catholic. Any Democratic nominee in 1956 would likely be attracted to a young, energetic liberal from a major state as a running mate.

Even before his inauguration there was speculation about Williams's future as a Democratic candidate for national office. Immediately after his election, Democrats invited him to be

G. Mennen Williams as a young boy in Detroit. A member of one of the wealthiest families in Michigan, Williams would become one of the state's leading advocates of liberal reform and racial equality. (G. Mennen Williams Papers, 1883–1988, Box 1-P, courtesy of the Bentley Historical Library, University of Michigan.)

Williams as an undergraduate at Princeton University. At Princeton Williams would excel in both academics and athletics and would decide on a career in politics rather than the diplomatic corps. (G. Mennen Williams Papers, 1883–1988, Box 1-P, courtesy of the Bentley Historical Library, University of Michigan.)

Williams with his mother, Elma, aboard a cruise ship. The heir to the Mennen Cosmetic Company fortune, Elma Williams strongly opposed her son's liberal politics. (G. Mennen Williams Papers, 1883–1988, Box 1-P, courtesy of the Bentley Historical Library, University of Michigan.)

Nancy Quirk Williams as a student at the University of Michigan. Nancy influenced her husband's liberal politics and would become a key campaigner and adviser. (G. Mennen Williams Papers, 1883–1988, Box 1-P, courtesy of the Bentley Historical Library, University of Michigan.)

Williams with fellow naval officers aboard the USS *Yorktown*. During World War II, Lieutenant Commander Williams served as a photo analyst in the Pacific and would earn ten battle stars, the Legion of Merit, and numerous other honors. (G. Mennen Williams Papers, 1883–1988, Box 1-P, courtesy of the Bentley Historical Library, University of Michigan.)

Williams with his political mentor, U.S. Attorney General Frank Murphy. Murphy was crucial in Williams's early political career, securing him a position in the Justice Department and encouraging him to run for governor of Michigan. (G. Mennen Williams Papers, 1883–1988, Box 2-P, courtesy of the Bentley Historical Library, University of Michigan.)

Williams and Harry Truman after their upset victories in 1948. Williams's unexpected defeat of Republican Kim Sigler was called "the Michigan miracle." He would win six consecutive elections as governor. (G. Mennen Williams Papers, 1883–1988, Box 6-P, courtesy of the Bentley Historical Library, University of Michigan.)

Williams in his trademark bow tie in front of the Michigan state capitol. For twelve years Williams battled with the Republican legislature over taxes and reform, eventually leading the state to bankruptcy in 1959. (Photograph by Fred Berk. G. Mennen Williams Papers, 1883–1988, Box 1-P, courtesy of the Bentley Historical Library, University of Michigan.)

Williams in wooden shoes at the Holland, Michigan, Tulip Festival. The governor became known for his flamboyant and energetic campaign style and his appeal to various ethnic groups in Michigan. (G. Mennen Williams Papers, 1883–1988, Box 2-P, courtesy of the Bentley Historical Library, University of Michigan.)

Mennen, Nancy, and their children, Gery, Nancy, and Wendy, on Mackinac Island. The family developed a deep love of Mackinac Island, and Williams is buried in a small cemetery near his summer home there. (G. Mennen Williams Papers, 1883–1988, Box 1-P, Formal Family Portraits folder, courtesy of the Bentley Historical Library, University of Michigan.)

Soapy and Nancy at the opening of the Mackinac Bridge in 1957. Dubbed "Soapy's Folly," the bridge uniting the two Michigans was one of his most successful achievements as governor. (G. Mennen Williams Papers, 1883–1988, Box 4-P, courtesy of the Bentley Historical Library, University of Michigan.)

their featured speaker at the Washington press corps' Gridiron Dinner. The Democratic National Committee also appointed Williams to head the Nationalities Committee of the party, a natural selection given his appeal to ethnic groups but also a position that allowed him to discuss foreign policy and denounce the continued Soviet occupation of Eastern Europe. The party also asked Staebler to chair their National Advisory Committee on Political Organization and share his demonstrated expertise in Michigan with the national party through seminars on grassroots organization, voter registration, and recruitment of volunteers. A *New York Times* feature on possible Democratic nominees in 1956 listed Williams, Stevenson, Kefauver, Symington, and Harriman as the favorites, and Williams was inundated with speaking invitations from state and regional Democratic organizations.[60]

While Williams pondered the possibility of national office, he again faced his annual battle with the Michigan legislature. Although the House was equally divided between the two parties, Republicans were able to organize it, ensuring that they would chair all the committees. Despite this obstacle, Williams's large victory made it more likely that he would get some of his agenda passed. In his inaugural he noted that he had won four straight terms and Michigan was now a "two-party state." He reminded legislators that neither he nor his reform agenda was going to go away. His first three terms had been devoted to "correcting the mistakes of the past," but it was now time to move forward with a bold, new agenda. He renewed his call for a fair employment bill, but he focused more attention on two issues he felt were crucial for the state and likely to receive bipartisan support: roads and schools. He proposed a massive increase in spending on all levels of education, with $150 million over three years for colleges and universities, $750 million over five years for new primary and high school construction, and a minimum salary of $4,000 for certified teachers (those without certification would receive $3,000). He defended the increase by noting that Michigan ranked thirty-third among the forty-eight states in spending on education as a percentage of income and twenty-fourth in expenditures per pupil.[61]

He also claimed it was time for the state to deal with its out-dated road system and recommended a $500 million bond sale to construct new highways and join the unconnected interstate system. Williams also called for an expansion of health, conservation, welfare, and other programs. His budget called for spending $292 million, and he estimated revenues at $248 million. He renewed his demand for a 4 percent corporate profits tax to avoid further debt. Republicans countered with a demand that he cut spending and use the gasoline tax to pay for new highway construction. Despite his victory in 1954, it appeared there would again be a stalemate in Lansing.[62]

While the legislature debated his education and highway proposals, Williams did achieve a major victory with the passage of a fair employment bill. He again wrote to each legislator with a plea to put racial equality "above partisanship" and argued that "the whole community" suffers when one individual is denied equal rights. Republicans tried to claim that the bill would also apply to sexual discrimination in hiring, but experts rejected this argument. Finally, after six years of opposition, both the Senate and the House passed a somewhat weakened version in May 1955. Williams was overjoyed and called the bill "a jewel in the crown of all." At the signing ceremony on June 29, he gave the first pen to Judge Cramton but announced that he would keep the second for himself. "We have written the dignity of man into the law of the state," he concluded.[63]

Williams immediately tried to follow this victory by proposing legislation dealing with other groups in the state. He appointed a Study Commission on Migratory Labor and based on its recommendations introduced a bill calling for health, education, and economic reforms, which the legislature ignored. He also convened a conference on Native Americans and appointed a Study Commission on Michigan's Indian Problems. Finally, after surveys showed widespread discrimination against Jews at Michigan resorts, he barred the Michigan Tourist Council from accepting any advertising that announced a "gentile clientele."[64]

In early 1955, Williams began to accept speaking invitations from around the country to help him gain national exposure and assess the possibility of a vice presidential run in 1956. He focused on two major themes: the need for action on civil rights and the complacency and conservatism of the Eisenhower administration. In a February 19 talk to Kansas Democrats in Topeka, he announced that he was "considering" a run for the presidency in 1956 but refused to answer questions about the vice presidency. A week later Michigan Democrats gathered in Grand Rapids to celebrate Williams's forty-fourth birthday and passed a unanimous resolution, declaring:

> We take note of his rising stature as a national figure and we express our pride that the Democratic Party nationally . . . looks upon Governor Williams as a man capable of higher political office. We support Governor Williams for any office he may seek.[65]

In June, Williams testified before the Senate Judiciary Committee against a call from the American Legion to limit the number of political refugees entering the United States. He asserted that it was "un-American" to deny political freedom to those displaced by communism and that the restrictions would harm the economy by rejecting skilled workers. At the Conference of Democratic Governors, where he was the featured speaker, Williams launched a blistering attack on Eisenhower and the economy. "The administration seems to be satisfied stabilizing our economy at the price that brings prosperity for some but not for all," he argued. Republicans did not care about unemployment as they assumed "everything is hotsy-totsy." He urged America "to get away from the complacency that now exists" and lamented the press's refusal to criticize Eisenhower: "The man who is supposed to be responsible never gets blamed for the things that are going wrong!"[66]

Williams's pursuit of national office in 1955 and 1956 was based on an uncompromising and unabashed liberalism. He had transformed Michigan's Democratic Party from a lethargic, conservative organization into an energetic and reformist group, and he intended to do the same for the national party. Following his fourth inaugural, Michigan Democrats issued a

pamphlet that made clear Williams's philosophy of government.

> The roots of the political philosophy of G. Mennen
> Williams, and of the Democratic Party, lie in a well-inte-
> grated concept of "government for social progress"—in the
> belief that government itself is part and parcel of the com-
> mon urge for betterment, that government reflects the peo-
> ple's desire to make their political system work under chang-
> ing conditions, and work better than before. . . . The
> Democratic Program . . . has been founded on the principle
> that government is built on people and for people—that the
> function of government is to assume those social, economic
> and educational obligations that the people want it to have.[67]

The view of government as an instrument of "social progress"
and part of "the common urge for betterment" was a clear
reflection of Williams's basic beliefs, which stemmed from his
religious convictions and his early enthusiasm for the New
Deal. The stress on a government "built on people and for the
people" was a vision shared by Williams and Staebler of politics
free of corruption and the influence of special interests.

A year later Williams and Michigan Democrats offered a
specific series of programs that flowed from this philosophy
when the party adopted *The Michigan Declaration* in Lansing.
The document was a statement of basic principles for the state
party and a blueprint for Williams's campaign for national
office. It called for "the total elimination of segregation in the
United States" and "the full rights of citizenship without regard
to race, color, creed, or national origins." It attacked the "false
smears and slanders" of McCarthyism and criticzed Republican
support for the Taft-Hartley Act. It condemned the rise of "the
giant corporate farmer" and urged a massive increase in federal
aid to education, with no funding for school districts that
rejected racial integration. It concluded:

> So long as one human being is hungry and we can feed him
> and do not, so long as one person is naked and we can clothe
> him and do not, so long as one person is sick and we can
> minister to him and do not, so long as one worker or farmer

is deprived of a just living and we can remedy it and do not, so long as one person is illiterate and we can educate him and do not, so long as one nation is subjugated by another against its will and we can work for freedom and do not, the American task is not done.[68]

These two documents were a clear articulation of Williams's view of government and the specific programs that stemmed from that vision. It was as a champion of a large, active, reformist government dedicated to racial and economic equality that Williams offered himself to the Democratic Party, and it was these principles that would shape his criticism of other candidates. To Williams, Democrats needed to choose between principle and equivocation, between a view of government as an agent of change and equality or temporizing compromise. His conception of the Democratic Party was clear, and he was unwilling to tolerate those who argued for the need to compromise on its principles. To Williams, compromise and moderation were unacceptable when they denied the basic liberalism he saw as the cornerstone and appeal of his party.

To Williams, the primary goal of government remained "to do good," and he did not understand how others could not agree. In 1955, for example, he submitted a recommendation for expanded facilities for mentally retarded children and was stunned when the legislature rejected it. He claimed the plan was "so just" that he thought it would pass without debate. How could anyone vote against helping retarded children?[69]

As he continued his speaking tour in 1955, he intensified his attacks on the lack of compassion and the refusal to endorse racial equality that he saw as characteristic of Eisenhower and the Republican Party. He repeatedly condemned the president for not enforcing the desegregation ruling of the Supreme Court. When Williams was invited to be the featured speaker at the Alabama State Jefferson-Jackson Day dinner he canceled his address when organizers could not assure him that the audience would be integrated. Alabama state law prohibited interracial functions, but local Democrats had assured Williams they would sell tickets to both races. When they admitted that the police might enforce the segregation law, Williams announced that "in good conscience" he could never speak at a segregated meeting. The *New York Times* dubbed him "the conscience of the Democratic Party."[70]

He also attacked Eisenhower for refusing to expand aid to education and proposed a $16 billion, five-year program of federal aid that included $1 billion a year for school construction and $500 million annually for college scholarships. He claimed that raising the maximum corporate income tax rate from 52 to 58 percent could finance the project. Eisenhower proposed lowering the tax rate. Williams also publicly contended that Ike lacked energy and was "too old" for a second term. It was bad timing, as a few days later the president suffered a heart attack and Williams had to apologize.[71]

Despite criticism of his attack on Eisenhower's age, his speeches succeeded in gaining him national attention. Democratic House majority leader John McCormick of Massachusetts named Williams as one of the leading contenders for the next presidential nomination, and former Minnesota governor Harold Stassen, Eisenhower's special assistant for disarmament, predicted a Harriman-Williams Democratic ticket in 1956.[72]

Throughout 1955, Williams was on the road urging a commitment to civil rights, attacking Eisenhower, and letting it be known that he was available for the national ticket in 1956. This was the first time he had been separated from Nancy since the war, as she remained in Lansing to be with their three children. The relationship between Mennen and Nancy Williams was unique. Unlike most political wives in the 1950s, Nancy was an important and active campaigner, from the lonely initial efforts in 1948 through all of his contests for governor. She also was a key political strategist who often influenced her husband's policies and appointments. For twenty years they had rarely been apart, but in 1955 Williams was in Michigan for only a few days a week. In August 1955, in a reversal of roles, Nancy was out of town and Soapy was left alone in their home in Lansing. He wandered through her study, looking at family photos and her massive scrapbooks of newspaper clippings, and took out a yellow legal pad and in his trademark green ink wrote a love letter to his absent wife.

Sunday, August 22, 1955

Darlingest:

Tonight I am all alone for an hour or two in your study. It's almost as hot—no it's hotter than those years in the South Pacific.

When I look up I can see the Nancy that I married in her bridal veil. All around are pictures of the family first two and small then three and growing all the time. Next year's Xmas picture will show Gery towering over us all. By the other wall under the table a dozen folios of clippings, a gargantuan labor.

Do you remember the day we first met? I remember it so well—and your pert straw sailor's hat, that's why I like the one you have now so much. Remember our walk and ending up at Miller's? And our talk?

Somehow all the things in these pictures and in these clippings were spoken in that little walk, or at least so it seems to me. The Christmas pictures were there. The other things aren't exactly in the clippings but I hope they're in the lives of men and women because of the things we've tried to do that those pictures in their own strange way talk about.

No I can't say I am alone, nor will I really ever be. As I've heard you say, unless there were something more than and over us moving in our lives, we wouldn't be doing what we are. Even before this bridal picture, even before the tennis picture on my bureau, I bid loneliness goodbye. Darlingest, it's been a great adventure together. Whether it was the battered old red convertible; the sands at Quonset, at Alice's, or even halfway round the world at sea, or tonight—or the fourth inaugural, or being battered at Chicago—I've never felt alone.

Well, honey, it won't be long now. Maybe even I'll see you before you get this. But I want to say this silent house speaks of you, everything speaks of you—everyone speaks of you—my dearest, Michigan's first lady, the first lady of my heart—God love you.

All my love, Soapy[73]

Throughout the fall of 1955 and into early 1956, Williams continued his speaking tour and focused increasingly on the volatile issue of civil rights. In the two years following the *Brown v. Board of Education* decision, the issue of segregation split the Democratic Party. In response to the Supreme Court's ruling, the South vowed "massive resistance" to integration, and, as the court had mandated an end to segregation in a vague timetable of "all due speed," the process of ending racial separatism moved slowly. With the Montgomery, Alabama, bus boycott in December 1955, and the emergence of Martin Luther King as its leader, the white South faced a more organized movement to end segregation and politicians in both parties were forced to take a position on the issue of racial discrimination.

To Williams, the response to *Brown v. Board of Education* and black efforts to challenge segregation was clear: America and the Democratic Party needed to unequivocally endorse the immediate and total end of racial discrimination. To Williams, the issue allowed no room for compromise, as racism was both a moral sin and a repudiation of America's basic tenet of equality. He was determined to force his party to accept a strong civil rights platform in 1956 and to select candidates dedicated to the immediate and total end of both segregation in the South and discrimination in the North. His unyielding commitment to civil rights would work to make Williams even more of a national figure but would also eventually alienate him from many in the Democratic Party.

Williams kept a detailed file on examples of racial discrimination throughout the nation and statements by all the Democratic presidential contenders on segregation and racism. In January 1956 in Los Angeles he gave his strongest speech on civil rights to date, denouncing segregation in housing, schools, and public facilities.

> There are neighborhoods in every community . . . in which some of our citizens are not permitted to live. . . . There are schools which children are not permitted to attend, despite the recent Supreme Court Decision. There are restaurants in which they may not eat, hotels in which they are not accepted as guests, trains and buses in which they dare not ride. . . . There are whole communities in which there is one law for one race, a different for another. . . . [D]iscrimination is repugnant to democracy. The denial of equal opportunity

. . . plays directly into the hands of those who would destroy us.

Racism was also a defiance of God, as every individual was endowed "BY THEIR CREATOR" with the unalienable right to equality. Williams warned the Democratic Party that in its zeal to win votes in the South it risked losing more votes in the North.[74]

In an address to the New York Police Association he argued that racism and discrimination were the major drawback in America's global battle with communism and cited the murder of black teenager Emmett Till in Mississippi, a riot in Chicago over integrated housing, and the recent attempt to enroll black students at the University of Georgia.

> Picture a little colored boy murdered without rebuke in Mississippi, a mob throwing a man's furniture through the windows of his apartment outside Chicago because he happens to be a Negro, and stones being thrown at a colored girl because she insists upon the right to the kind of education she wants in a university of her choosing.

Each incident, he argued, showed the world an image of America as a nation of violence and intolerance rather than as an example of freedom.[75]

Williams urged the Democrats to adopt a strong civil rights platform to "lead the way to the complete elimination of segregation," including the end of the poll tax, an antilynching law, a fair employment statute, and even a refusal to seat any member of Congress elected in districts that discriminated in voting. When he was invited to appear on the *Today* show in May to publicize "Michigan Day," he used the television program to lobby for a strong civil rights platform.[76]

His blunt rhetoric on civil rights not only angered southerners but also eventually caused a major split with the leading contender for the Democratic nomination in 1956, Adlai Stevenson. Williams had been a reluctant supporter of the Illinois governor in 1952, and he was even more hesitant to endorse him in 1956. He feared Stevenson was too passive on the issue of race and would equivocate on civil rights to gain support from southerners. Williams clipped a November 1955 *Newsweek* article by Ernest K. Lindley entitled "A 'Moderate' Stevenson" and wrote in the margin in green ink: "He *is* a moderate—both in his political philosophy and usually in his discussion of specific issues!" To the Michigan liberal, the term *moderate* was a pejorative.[77]

When Stevenson sent Williams a letter in December 1955 enclosing a copy of the speech announcing his bid for the presidential nomination and asking for support, the Michigan governor refused to commit to his candidacy, responding only that he would "read and study" the speech. Harriman, Symington, and Kefauver joined Stevenson in courting Williams's support for 1956, and it became clear that he would again back the senator from Tennessee. As in 1952, Williams was convinced that Kefauver would be the strongest advocate of civil rights. In addition, he was the candidate most likely to consider Mennen Williams for the vice presidency. If Stevenson were nominated, it was clear he would not pick another midwestern governor as a running mate. As a southerner, Kefauver might well seek to balance the ticket with the liberal from Michigan.[78]

Tension between Stevenson and Williams increased dramatically when the Illinois governor made a comment in Chicago that "moderation is the spirit of the times" and the Democratic Party needed to pursue compromise on major policy issues. Williams was incensed by the call for moderation and in a speech to the National Young Democrats accused Stevenson of giving in to the Republicans. He denied that there was a "state of war" between himself and Stevenson, explaining that the Democratic Party "is big enough to have differences," but refused to repudiate his comments.[79]

In April 1956, the conflict between the two Democratic governors escalated into an open battle. Bob Considine, a writer for the Hearst newspapers, published a long article quoting Williams's speech to the Colorado Young Democrats attacking Stevenson for his call for moderation. Williams contended that it would be "craven cowardice" if Democrats allowed the 1956 campaign to "degenerate into a spineless and self-defeating formality" by accepting the views of "temporizers." He argued that

the Eisenhower Administration can be beaten—but only by a
militant Democratic party offering the people an opportunity
for a better future. The Republicans can sometimes win by
pretending to be like Democrats, but I don't think the
Democrats can win by pretending to be like Republicans.
That is why I have been so critical of so-called moderation
and compromises on the issues. . . . If the voters are presented with a choice between tweedledum and tweedledee,
they may well choose to bear the ills they have had.

The article also quoted Williams as saying "tired, timid, and temporizing is a good policy for drunks, but not for politicians."[80]

Stevenson and his advisers were outraged by Williams's public attack on the likely Democratic nominee. Stevenson's aide
William McCormack Blair wrote Staebler that he "could
hardly believe that Governor Williams said this" and asked
Staebler to urge Williams to repudiate his comments. Staebler
replied that he was "astonished" at this request, as most of the
speech had focused on criticism of Republicans, and Williams
refused to disavow his remarks. On the eve of the Democratic
convention, the two governors were not speaking.[81]

His frosty relationship with Stevenson did not deter Williams
from pushing for a strong civil rights plank and actively seeking
the vice presidency at the 1956 convention. He successfully
lobbied for inclusion of Detroit congressmen Charles Diggs on
the Platform Drafting Committee to make sure there was an
African American voice in the group. Throughout 1955 and
1956, Williams had received hundreds of letters from across the
nation urging him to run for president in 1956. He responded
by thanking them for "their flattering comments" about "the
possible role I might play in the future" but claimed his major
role was to help with the "development of a strong Democratic platform."[82]

Despite his claim that he was only interested in securing a
liberal platform, Williams still held out hope for the vice presidential nomination. Staebler requested extra floor passes for
"persons who are not members of the delegation" so Williams's
aides could work the floor for his nomination and prepared
hundreds of cardboard green and white polka-dot bow ties to
distribute to the delegates. On July 31, however, Kefauver sent

Williams a telegram announcing that "after prayerful consideration" he was withdrawing from the battle for the nomination
and urging support for Stevenson. A Stevenson nomination
ended any chance of Williams being on the national ticket. Not
only had their public feud strained the relationship but also
Stevenson would need to balance the ticket with someone
other than another liberal midwestern governor. Williams
would have to wait until 1960 to win a spot on the national
ticket[83]

Having alienated the likely Democratic presidential nominee
with his attacks on Stevenson's "moderation" comments,
Williams managed to antagonize two other national leaders of
his party at the convention. When the "Michigan Special" train
pulled into Chicago's decrepit Dearborn Station on August 11,
1956, Williams had total control of his state's forty-four delegates. He would be nominated as a favorite son, and Michigan
would vote for him on the first ballot, but in later roll calls he
could shift his delegates to any of the leading candidates:
Stevenson, Harriman, Lyndon Johnson, or even the now withdrawn Kefauver.

Lyndon Johnson and Mennen Williams were both tall and
both Democrats, but they had little else in common. As the Senate majority leader, Johnson was the master of the political deal
and parliamentary procedure, and his ability to use power to
force compromise was already legendary. His blunt, profane
style and his behind the scenes maneuverings were the direct
opposite of Williams's approach to politics, and the two had
never established a rapport. Williams had made a number of trips
to Washington to lobby for programs to help Michigan and had
publicly praised Sam Rayburn, the Speaker of the House, but he
noted only that he had "met with Lyndon Johnson."[84]

More important than his style, Johnson was a southerner, and
even though, like Kefauver, he had tried to distance himself
from his region's segregationists by refusing to attend the southern caucus, Williams and other northern liberals were convinced
that he was weak on civil rights. At the platform hearings,
Williams and ADA chairman Joseph Rauh of Washington,
D.C., proposed a clause pledging delegates to "carry out" the

Supreme Court's decision banning segregation. Other liberals, particularly Hubert Humphrey, opposed the move, as they saw it as weakening party unity, but Williams persisted. The clause failed, but to Williams, Rauh, and other liberals civil rights was "the great issue of 1956."[85]

Despite their differences in ideology and style, Johnson was counting on Mennen Williams in Chicago. The Texan's strategy was to prevent Stevenson from gaining a first-ballot victory. If Stevenson could be stopped, Johnson, southerners, and his Senate colleagues could perhaps broker the majority leader's nomination on later ballots. The key to Johnson's tactics was to keep favorite sons such as Williams in the first round of balloting. While Stevenson, Harriman, and other candidates scurried from one state caucus to another, Johnson remained in his suite in the Conrad Hilton hotel working the phones with party leaders. He was convinced that Stevenson "had too much lace on his drawers" to ever defeat Eisenhower and that the party would turn to him as its best chance for victory. Stevenson's campaign manager, James A. Finnegan, was aware of Johnson's strategy and used liberal fears of a compromise on civil rights to work against the Texan. He agued that unless Stevenson won on the first ballot the convention would shift to the control of southern conservatives, who would either force the Illinois governor to adopt a softer position on civil rights or nominate Johnson. Favorite son candidates such as Williams needed to release their delegations so they could vote for Stevenson on the first ballot.[86]

On Monday, August 13, the first day of the convention, Stevenson and Eleanor Roosevelt met in a closed-door session with the Michigan delegation. After the meeting Williams told the press that the convention faced the possibility of a deadlock and "a minority power" might select the nominee. He leaked the news that he would release his delegates after his nomination so they could vote for Stevenson on the first ballot.[87]

At 5:00 a.m. the next morning members of the Michigan delegation told Johnson operative Jim Rome of Williams's decision. He woke the majority leader and told him the Michigan governor would release his delegates to vote for Stevenson on the first ballot. Johnson was stunned. "I don't believe it," he told Rome. Six hours later he was forced to believe it, as the Michigan delegation caucused and Williams announced that it would cast a unanimous vote for Stevenson on the first ballot. Other favorite son candidates followed Michigan's lead, and Stevenson's first-ballot victory was assured. Johnson was perplexed and incensed. He could not understand how his political instincts had been so wrong and did not hide his anger with Williams for orchestrating the shift of favorite son delegates to Stevenson.[88]

Having angered Johnson, Williams managed to infuriate another leading Democrat two days later. After Stevenson's nomination it was clear that Williams would not be considered for vice president, but when the nominee announced that he would leave it to the convention to select his running mate there was a frantic day of maneuvering by other contenders. John F. Kennedy and Estes Kefauver were the front-runners, and Kennedy operatives assumed that Michigan would support their candidate over the southerner. Williams, however, felt that Kennedy was "soft" on civil rights and had criticized the Massachusetts senator for suggesting that the Supreme Court decision outlawing segregation needed to be implemented slowly. When Kennedy aides approached Williams he told them the Michigan delegation would vote for Kefauver. As Williams was leaving the convention, "a very exercised Bobby Kennedy" confronted him and demanded: "Why are you against my brother?" John Kennedy later acknowledged that the vice presidential nomination in 1956 would have been a blunder and even thanked Williams for not voting for him, but he and his brother never forgave Williams for summarily rejecting their overtures.[89]

As Williams boarded the train to return to Lansing, he was pleased with his efforts in Chicago. As in 1952, he had made headlines for his advocacy of a strong civil rights platform and for trying to force delegates to accept publicly the Supreme Court's ruling on desegregation. His shift of the Michigan delegation to Stevenson seemed to have blocked a brokered convention, which might have nominated Johnson, and he had been influential in securing the vice presidential nomination for his friend Kefauver. His disappointment with Stevenson's call for moderation did not prevent him from sending the Democratic nominee an unsolicited five-page note outlining a campaign strategy. Stevenson did not respond.[90]

Williams's notoriety had a price. In less than a year he had managed to alienate Stevenson, Johnson, and Kennedy. Although later Kennedy and Johnson would be his superiors and Stevenson his colleague when he served in the State Department, the strains of the 1956 convention endured. Four years later he would be the only prominent Democrat to publicly vote against the nomination of Johnson for the vice presidency, further angering both the majority leader and Kennedy. When Williams left Chicago he heard train whistles, but perhaps he should also have been aware of burning bridges.

In the summer of 1956, however, Williams was confidant that he had not only served as the conscience of his party on civil rights but would be a leading contender for the presidential nomination four years later. If, as expected, Stevenson lost again to Eisenhower, the 1960 Democratic nomination was open to a number of candidates. Given his now national reputation, repeated electoral success in Michigan, liberal ideology, and strong ties to African Americans and unions, no Democrat seemed to be in a more favorable position for national office. He was unaware that three years later both the state of Michigan and his presidential ambitions would be bankrupt.

V

MICHIGAN'S FINANCIAL CRISIS AND THE PURSUIT OF THE PRESIDENCY: 1956–60

I think I'm more a John the Baptist than a disciple.
Maybe I had too much courage and not enough
common sense, maybe too much idealism
and not enough practicality.

—G. *Mennen Williams reflecting on his*
years as governor of Michigan

Mennen Williams's career as governor of Michigan can be divided into three stages: His first three terms were largely devoted to political survival. He was a young political novice who scored an unexpected upset in 1948 and narrow recount victories in 1950 and 1952. The overwhelming Republican dominance in the legislature generally blocked his plans for a "New Deal in Michigan," and he spent much of his time building a new Democratic Party in the state. His decisive triumph in 1954 moved him into a second phase with considerably more power, as he not only won a landslide victory but also carried with him the entire Democratic slate. He was finally able to pass a fair employment bill and other reform legislation, despite a still hostile legislature, and gained national attention through his unabashed liberalism and outspoken advocacy of civil rights. By the 1956 Democratic National Convention, he was dominant in his home state and a major force in the national party. In the fall of 1956, Williams entered a third era, in which his focus was less on Lansing than on Washington, D.C., as he was convinced he could gain the 1960 presidential nomination, win the election, and lead America into a new era of liberal reform and racial harmony.

In retrospect, Williams's 1960 presidential ambitions seem rather naive. His strident liberalism and open criticism of other leaders of his party had alienated many influential Democrats. He had no experience in foreign affairs, and his continued battles with the Michigan legislature showed an unwillingness to engage in the political compromise seemingly necessary for national office. Williams did not have the elegance and television persona of John Kennedy, the rhetorical skills of Hubert Humphrey, the intellectual polish of Adlai Stevenson, or the behind the scenes political skills of Lyndon Johnson.

But such hindsight ignores the situation in the fall of 1956. Williams had proven his ability to run aggressive and successful campaigns in four elections in Michigan and had strong support from African Americans, labor, and liberals within the national party. Kennedy was seen as too young, and a Catholic had never been elected to the presidency. If, as expected, Stevenson lost to Eisenhower in 1956, it was doubtful that Democrats would offer him a third nomination. Many within the party viewed Humphrey as too emotional, soft, and unelectable. As a southerner, Johnson was anathema to blacks and liberals in the party, and Missouri senator Stuart Symington and New York governor Averell Harriman did not have strong national reputations or organizations. Williams had every reason to be optimistic about his chances in 1960. As civil rights continued to develop as the great national issue in America, the Democratic Party might well have turned to its leading spokesman for racial equality in its bid to capture the White House.

Two major concerns jeopardized Williams's presidential ambitions: his militant liberalism and the mounting financial crisis in his state. Southerners and moderate Democrats saw the Michigan governor as far to the left of most in their party and too closely identified with labor and civil rights to be elected. Michigan's continued fiscal problems raised questions about his management skills and leadership ability. If he could not solve the economic problems of his state, how could he govern the nation?

Williams made no attempt to moderate his political liberalism, as he was convinced that only a Democrat clearly committed to racial and economic reform could win in 1960. The situation in Michigan, however, was potentially perilous for his run for the presidency, and it would be state finances more than political ideology that would eventually doom his dream of occupying the White House.

Williams temporarily put his presidential ambitions on hold as he prepared for yet another campaign in 1956. As he did not enjoy the luxury of governors who ran every four years or senators who had six-year terms, he had to devote nearly half of every other year to exhaustive campaigns for reelection. To retain the nation's attention and solidify his position as a presidential candidate in 1960, he not only had to win another term but score a massive victory, as he had in 1954.

In the spring of 1956, he called a conference of his key political advisers at Haven Hill, a lodge in western Oakland County, to plan campaign strategy. The press heard of the gathering and questioned Paul Weber about the meeting. He told them the governor was delivering a lecture on "rare forms of flora and fauna found in the park." Reporters laughed, but Weber was telling the truth, as for the first hour of the meeting Williams displayed a variety of plants from the region and summarized their characteristics. After his botany lecture, the discussion shifted to the upcoming campaign. As Eisenhower was running for a second term and remained extremely popular, they would again have to convince voters to split their ballots between the Republican president and the Democratic governor. Although he again appointed Helen Berthelot to manage the campaign, he sent a note to Weber and Woolner, explaining that while "Buffy" would coordinate scheduling and supervise the staff they would be in charge of election strategy and tactics. Weber and Woolner would orchestrate Williams's most aggressive, vitriolic, and successful campaign.[1]

Williams officially announced his bid for reelection on May 9. He claimed that "on the basis of what has been accomplished, I would feel free to leave office with a quiet conscience and a conviction that I have done my best to carry out my promises to the people." Michigan, however, faced new challenges and changes such as the Saint Lawrence Seaway, the

Mackinac Bridge, and the emergence of atomic power. As the Republican Party was "dedicated to the past" rather than change, he had to run again. Following his announcement, he called the legislature into a special session to deal with highway construction, to fund a polio vaccination program, and to raise unemployment compensation.[2]

To try to dislodge Williams from Lansing, the Republicans turned to Detroit mayor Albert Cobo. During his seven terms as city treasurer and six years as mayor of Michigan's largest city, Cobo had earned a reputation as a "doer" and a "builder." He had organized the reconstruction of Detroit's highway system and undertaken a massive building program that included slum clearance, new parks, and downtown construction. Unlike the state, Detroit was free from debt, and Cobo had strong support from the city's business community. He vowed he would install a "business administration" in Lansing that would cut spending and engage in "harmonious cooperation" with the legislature. Like previous Republican challengers, Cobo accused Williams of being controlled by organized labor and promised "government without favoritism." At the Republican National Convention, he was introduced as "the next Governor of Michigan" and addressed delegates during the evening to ensure network TV exposure.[3]

Cobo was a formidable challenger, but Michigan Democrats were confident that they could repeat their 1954 landslide victory. Berthelot noted: "By this time, we had a reputation for knowing what we were doing. As a matter of fact, we *were* getting pretty good." Earlier campaigns had been heavily dependent on Williams's barnstorming throughout the state, but "the 1956 campaign was nothing like the previous ones. It seemed that we suddenly had grown into a big operation."[4]

Overseeing the big operation was Staebler. By 1956, he had built the Michigan Democratic Party into an incredibly efficient machine. He had a professional organization with a paid staff in each of Michigan's eighty-three counties and, with the help of labor volunteers, had conducted massive voter registration drives throughout the state. In 1956, he assigned each county a "quota" of 115 percent of the vote they had delivered for Williams in 1954 and made it clear that they were expected to meet it. Several hundred "released time" union members worked full time on the campaign and provided 25 percent of the clerical staff.[5]

Democrats also had raised ample funds for the reelection effort. To help finance a repeat of the successful *Nancy's Scrapbook* TV show, Adelaide Hart sent a letter to women leaders in each county setting a minimum financial goal to "pay production costs" of the show. Hart suggested bake sales, potluck dinners, and "throw your hat into the ring" parties, where women would pay a dollar to enter a contest for the most outlandish hat. Women in Grand Rapids raised more than ten thousand dollars for *Nancy's Scrapbook* and penned a song that began:

> On your scrapbook pages, truth is plain to see.
> We'll pitch in and find the dough to put it on TV![6]

With Staebler's organization in place and abundant financial resources, Williams was confident when he began the campaign at the traditional kickoff dinner in Nancy's hometown of Ypsilanti. He promised a "grueling, surging, hectic, campaign" and quoted from Shakespeare's *Henry V,* describing Michigan Democrats as: "We few, we happy few, we band of brothers!"[7]

As in all of his campaigns, he immediately embarked on an exhaustive series of appearances throughout the state, with the usual dawn visits to factory gates and dozens of other daily events. He also openly championed a clear commitment to racial equality. He had been touring the nation demanding an end to discrimination and continued his call for equality in his home state, stressing Republican opposition to the Fair Employment Act.

> If the Republican Party is on the side of the Negro, why is it that Republicans almost uniformly oppose civil rights measures? The Republican party is no more on the side of the Negroes than Lucifer is on the side of Gabriel![8]

Even more than in 1954, the campaign made extensive use of television. Not only did Nancy Williams repeat her highly successful *Nancy's Scrapbook* show, but the governor bought thirty minutes of time each Monday evening in September and October to speak to the people and to counter what he called the "one-party press." Woolner developed a series of ten-second TV spots with the jingle: "Make it emphatic, vote straight Democratic!" and prepared brief ads on "How to Use a Voting Machine." Democrats also bought daily radio time throughout the state, featuring highlights from Williams's past weekly radio shows.[9]

Cobo began his campaign by attacking Williams's inability to solve Michigan's financial problems and his continued battles with the legislature. He claimed he had the ability to "get things done," while the governor's personal conflicts with lawmakers in Lansing had led to governmental stalemate. The Republicans also mocked Williams's grandiose promises of sweeping reform by running a newspaper ad that featured a cartoon character wearing a large bow tie and emitting soap bubbles labeled "previous campaign promises."[10]

The Detroit mayor also charged that the aristocratic Williams was out of touch with the average taxpayer and pointed out that the governor wore expensive, custom-made shoes. On the advice of Weber, Williams used the "shoe issue" in the first TV debate. After Cobo's opening remarks, Williams removed his shoes, held them up to the camera and said: "Now having gotten my opponent's chief issues out of the way, we'll move on." He explained that he had big feet (size 15E) and needed to have his shoes handmade or they would hurt. Weber later noted that "we got the votes of everybody with sore feet!"[11]

The humor of the shoe issue soon gave way to aggressive personal attacks on Cobo. James Lincoln, a former law partner of Williams, was a member of the Detroit Common Council and secretly sent Weber materials to be used against the Detroit mayor. Lincoln forwarded copies of the annual reports of Cobo's real estate agency and dry-cleaning business so Weber could search for customers who had received favorable treatment from the city. A city clerk provided the Democrats with a list of all the mayor's real estate deals. Lincoln also discovered a scandal in 1936, when Cobo was city treasurer, involving a shortage of $349,000 in the city's trust fund and an eventual suicide. Although there was no evidence that Cobo had profited from the incident, Democrats charged he should have noticed the error. Williams's aides also obtained details of Cobo's divorce and the financial settlement with his former wife and leaked them to the press. When Cobo denounced plans by farmers to picket dairies to try to raise the price of milk, the Williams campaign claimed that he had plans to "jail farmers." After a Republican member of the Detroit Common Council appointed Jimmy Hoffa to the Wayne County Board of Supervisors, Democrats published a flyer entitled "Hoffa Backs Cobo," despite the fact that the Republican had repeatedly repudiated the Teamster leader.[12]

The most successful personal attack on Cobo involved his purchase of a home in Tucson, Arizona. Williams's operatives found a photo in the *Tucson Daily Citizen* of Cobo sitting in an armchair outside his Arizona residence with the caption "I love Tucson!" The accompanying interview quoted the mayor as saying he had invested in Arizona real estate because he was unsure whether property in Detroit would increase in value. Democrats immediately leaked the story to the press, claiming that Cobo favored Arizona over Michigan, and Detroit papers ran the photo of Cobo in front of his Arizona home. Staebler wrote to the head of the Democratic State Committee in Arizona, saying how "elated our publicity people were" with the Cobo photo and requesting the "exact wordings of headlines showing preference for Arizona" and dates of any other such material.[13]

Cobo was indignant at the Democratic effort to make an issue of his Tucson home and explained that he had bought the residence because his wife suffered from arthritis and was more comfortable in the dry desert climate. Campaign aide John Murray wrote a memo suggesting that they should approach the topic "with caution" as it might generate sympathy for Cobo's wife, and the Democrats dropped the issue.[14]

The often vicious attacks on Cobo showed the deep desire of Democrats to win a landslide victory in 1956. Polls showed Williams ahead from the beginning of the campaign, but Weber, Staebler, and others wanted a decisive triumph to position the governor for the 1960 presidential nomination and were willing to engage in personal innuendo to help ensure a massive victory. They argued that Cobo's attacks on Williams's custom shoes had begun the mudslinging and the mayor had engaged in other personal attacks when he criticized the governor's mother for moving a Mennen Company plant from Newark to Morristown, New Jersey, following a labor dispute.

Near the end of the campaign a Republican operative infiltrated the Democratic Party headquarters and stole a mailing list of Michigan's African American leaders. He then sent them a fake letter urging Democrats to vote for Stevenson, as he would appoint Democratic segregationist judges to the federal courts. The letter was signed "Friends of James Eastland and Strom Thurmond." Williams, Detroit congressman Charles Diggs, and black union leaders immediately exposed the letter as a fraud, identified the undercover agent, and attacked Republicans for conducting a smear campaign. Williams would win over 85 percent of the black vote in 1956. When pollster Samuel Lubell interviewed prospective Michigan voters he found that "of the ninety-nine Negroes interviewed, all but two were for Governor Mennen Williams."[15]

Early in the campaign, Williams concluded that the Stevenson challenge to Eisenhower was doomed in Michigan. He was correct, as Eisenhower carried the state by 350,000 votes. Williams, however, crushed Cobo by more than 300,000 votes and again carried the entire Democratic slate to victory. As in 1954, his victory was due to capturing 67 percent of the vote in Wayne County and 49 percent in other urban areas. Cobo won 56 percent in the rural areas. Despite the Democratic landslide, Republicans retained control of the state legislature due to the archaic Michigan districting system, which heavily favored rural areas.

His impressive victory seemed to confirm Williams as a leading candidate for the 1960 Democratic presidential nomination. Winning a fifth straight term in a major industrial state that had been traditionally Republican demonstrated both his personal campaign skills and the effectiveness of the Democratic organization he had forged in Michigan. To Williams and his advis-

ers, the landslide win solidified his position as the leading
spokesperson for liberalism within the Democratic Party. To
further convince Democrats that he was a serious presidential
contender, Williams renewed his outspoken criticism of
Republican conservatism and his demands for a clear national
commitment to racial equality.

Although he was eager to focus on national issues, Williams
first faced the mounting fiscal crisis in Michigan. For eight years
he and the Republican legislature had offered fundamentally
different conceptions of government. Williams argued that
Michigan needed new sources of revenue to pay for necessary
state programs while Republicans called for cuts in spending to
avoid new taxes. It had been a bruising battle, and both sides
claimed a partial victory. Republicans had resisted Williams's
repeated demands for a corporate profits tax while the governor
had managed to dramatically increase state spending by borrowing funds to pay for his programs. Both sides, however, recognized that the stalemate was leading Michigan toward a day
of reckoning, as continued budget deficits would eventually
push the state into financial disaster.

The battle was renewed in January 1957 when Williams submitted a proposed budget of over $500 million with significant
increases in spending for education, mental health, and welfare,
all to be funded with a corporate profits tax. The legislature
countered by appropriating only $330 million and again reject-
ing any new taxes. It seemed that Williams's electoral triumphs
meant little to Republicans in Lansing. The governor quickly
refigured his numbers and offered what he called "one of the
tightest budgets in the history of Michigan," totaling $411 mil-
lion, claiming that it represented the "minimal acceptable
amount" necessary to run the state, but Republicans rejected
his plan. Despite high employment and strong economic
growth, Michigan would run a deficit of $81 million in 1957
and would continue to borrow to pay its bills.[16]

Republicans found an ally in their battle with Williams when
Harlow H. Cartice, the president of General Motors, issued a
statement attacking the governor's proposed profits tax, claiming that it would force GM to move auto plants to states with a

more favorable tax structure. Williams, on a speaking trip in Oregon, denounced Cartice's statement as "politically motivated." When he returned to Lansing, the governor accused the GM executive of trying to "dictate government from the offices of corporate management" and noted that thirty-two other states had a corporate profits tax. At a press conference he presented statistics showing that Michigan had been successful in attracting new industry during his years as governor. "There is no grass in our streets and there won't be," he concluded. Williams charged that Cartice was a puppet of the Republicans and was using threats to blackmail the legislature into avoiding necessary new sources of revenue. Cartice finally issued a statement, claiming that he had been "misunderstood" and GM had no plans to move production outside of Michigan. Williams may have won the verbal contest with Cartice, but he was unable to stem the mounting financial deficit in his state. Borrowing to cover the revenue shortfall was successful in the short run, but it only postponed the inevitable economic crisis in the state.[17]

Although he did not solve Michigan's fiscal problems, Williams was increasingly looking to the national stage in 1957 and 1958. To gain more exposure, Williams and New York governor Averell Harriman, another potential presidential candidate in 1960, formed the Democratic Advisory Committee in early 1957. The DAC was intended to act as the voice of liberalism within the party by discussing and addressing the major political issues. Democratic national chairman Paul Butler explained that the group had the power to "formulate and interrupt Democratic policies between conventions." The Advisory Committee included a number of prominent Democratic officials, including former president Harry Truman, but the dominant voices were those of Williams and Harriman. Conservative Democrats, including Speaker of the House Sam Rayburn and Senate majority leader Lyndon Johnson, refused to meet with the group and made it clear that it represented only a small portion of the party. Presidential hopefuls Humphrey, Kennedy, and Symington also declined membership.[18]

For the next three years the DAC would meet regularly and issue statements condemning the Republicans and advocating a liberal political agenda that made the front page of most national newspapers. The group demanded a stronger commitment to civil rights, expanded welfare programs, statehood for Hawaii and Alaska, and increased taxes on corporations and wealthy individuals. It also attacked Eisenhower for the failures in America's space program, the inability to achieve a permanent peace settlement in the Middle East, and the lack of a commitment to the decolonization of European empires in Africa and Asia.[19]

Both Harriman and Williams saw the DAC as a way to nourish their presidential ambitions. The two governors were rivals for the 1960 nomination, but it was an extremely friendly contest. Both were wealthy liberals who greatly admired Franklin Roosevelt and wanted the Democratic Party to reflect the humanitarianism and commitment to reform that they saw as characteristic of the early New Deal. In 1957, they formed a second organization to encourage liberalism and enhance their national status, the Committee of Governors for Civil Rights. The group was limited to governors of states that had passed significant civil rights legislation and was designed to counter the existing Southern Governor's Conference. Twelve states were eligible for inclusion, and six sent delegates to the group's first meeting in New York. They elected Williams as president in honor of his outspokenness, and he announced that he hoped someday the group would become "a committee of forty-eight!"[20]

As he tried to position himself for the presidency in 1960, Williams renewed his extensive speaking campaign across the country. His major issues were civil rights, the Republicans' conservative economic policies, and America's failures in the space race with the Soviet Union.

Williams had been the leading advocate within his party of a clear commitment to racial equality since the 1952 Democratic National Convention, and he repeated his demand for civil rights in 1957. In May three of the leading candidates for the 1960 nomination, Kennedy, Harriman, and Williams, spoke at a meeting of the Democratic National Committee. Williams's talk combined a combative assault on Republicans with a near utopian vision of a global reform program led by the United States to achieve Christ's call for equality and brotherhood. After Kennedy and Harriman offered rather gentle criticism of Republican policies, Williams launched a blistering personal attack on Eisenhower, denouncing the president as an example of "dynamic do-nothingism." He asserted that "the nation cannot exist half modern and half Republican" and promised that

> we will go ahead and fight—even if the President won't—for civil rights, for education, for the little businessman and against monopoly, for the revival of depressed areas, for further improvement of social security, for extension of minimum wage coverage.

Williams then abandoned his assault on the Republicans and offered his dream of a New Deal for the world. He contended that the United States was so wealthy and powerful that

> for the first time in human history it is within the grounds of possibility to make a world in which the ancient scourges of humanity—poverty, pestilence, famine and war—will be things of the past. . . . America cannot escape from her destiny. . . . We must either lead the world forward or go down in a colossal wreck of modern civilization.

The nation had the power to end poverty, war, and disease but lacked the leadership to do so.[21]

Williams's was a grandiose vision of a world free of war, disease, hunger, and poverty and the ultimate expression of his goal of fostering a world community based on Christ's injunctions. If, however, America was to lead the world into an epoch of peace and justice, it first had to solve its most obvious problem: the shame of racial discrimination.

When Arkansas governor Orville Faubus blocked an order integrating Little Rock's Central High School in the fall of 1957, Williams lead the assault on Eisenhower's initial inaction, charging that the president had "failed in his duty" to enforce the Constitution and that his "hesitation and confusion" had done "damage to the prestige and dignity of the United States."

The Nation asked Williams to write a piece on the crisis, and in an article entitled "Little Rock: Challenge to the Democratic Party" he used the conflict to challenge his party to make an unequivocal commitment to racial equality. Civil rights, he argued, was a test of "the spiritual integrity of the Democratic Party," a moral issue that should not be viewed in terms of political calculations. Racial discrimination was the most important issue facing the nation and could not be addressed by "counting votes in the next election." He concluded: "[W]e do not want to drive out the South, but the Democratic Party simply must stand on its own principles, whether the stand results in political gain or political disaster." When Eisenhower finally sent troops to Little Rock, Williams hailed the action as long overdue.[22]

The Soviet Union's successful launch of the space satellite Sputnik in October 1957 gave Williams a second issue on which to attack the ineffective leadership in Washington. He claimed that the Russian success had been the result of the Eisenhower administration's lack of creativity, failure to appropriate the necessary funds, and general apathy. He even penned a poem mocking the lack of U.S. success in space, which was widely printed in the press

Oh little Sputnik
With made-in-Moscow beep,
You tell the world it's a Commie sky.
And Uncle Sam's asleep![23]

He even managed to link Sputnik to the civil rights issue, arguing that racial prejudice excluded many young African Americans from higher education. As a result, the United States was ignoring a vast pool of potential scientists and engineers who could help it catch up with the Russians: "The youth discriminated against in education today might tomorrow be the scientist who saves Western civilization."[24]

Williams also made some tentative attempts to address foreign policy issues, as it was clear that if he were to run for the presidency he would have to develop some expertise in international affairs. He wrote Stevenson asking for help in writing a speech on foreign affairs that would stress "the peace theme" and appointed a group of Michigan academics to help him develop positions on foreign issues.[25]

His efforts to "look presidential" by discussing foreign policy were sporadic. He repeatedly condemned Eisenhower and Vice President Richard Nixon (the likely Republican nominee in 1960) for their failure to solve the continued problems of the Middle East and for an inability to create a stable and peaceful world. In typically rather tortured rhetoric, he asserted: "We have set booby traps on every perch the dove of peace might land on."[26]

When Eisenhower aide Sherman Adams was accused of accepting gifts from business leaders, Williams asserted that the incident "indicates what many people have said, that this administration is hypocritical, it is immoral, and it is corrupt at the same time." His portrayal of the Republicans as immoral and corrupt finally provoked the wrath of the GOP national chairman Meade Alcorn, who charged that the "the effective control of the Democratic Party is in the hands of left-wing extremists" and cited Williams and Oregon senator Wayne Morse as the leading examples.[27]

His relentless criticism of the Republicans, his demand for action on civil rights, and his five electoral victories succeeded in attracting the attention of the national media. In late 1957, the *Saturday Evening Post* ran a long flattering piece titled "Soapy, the Boy Wonder," which praised his energetic campaign style, his commitment to civil rights, and his academic success at Princeton and Michigan and concluded that he was a "major contender" for the 1960 Democratic nomination. *Time* predicted a Democratic ticket of Williams for president and Kennedy as his running mate, and *U.S. News and World Report* concluded that given his "vote-getting record few would rule 'Soapy' Williams out" in 1960. Writing in *The Reporter,* D. D. Lloyd listed Williams along with Kennedy, Humphrey, Stevenson, and Symington as the front-runners for the Democratic nomination.[28]

It seemed that Williams had succeeded in positioning himself as the potential standard-bearer of his party in 1960. In November 1957, he temporarily abandoned his national speaking campaign to return for the fulfillment of one of his major dreams: the opening of the Mackinac Bridge. He had first proposed uniting the two Michigans in his 1948 campaign, and nine years later the structure was finally completed. It was his most obvious achievement as governor, and he was eager to drive the first car across the bridge on November 1. The official dedication was to be in June 1958, as there was fear that the weather in November might disrupt the ceremony. As it turned out, the weather was ideal as a smiling Williams in shirtsleeves and green polka-dot bow tie got into his car to lead the procession across the five-mile structure. He soon discovered that he had not brought his driver's license, so Nancy took the wheel for the symbolic crossing. When they got to the tollgate, he found that he had not only forgotten his license but had failed to bring any money, but the guards agreed to let the couple cross without payment. The governor was scheduled to be the concluding speaker at the ceremony midway across the bridge, where he was to pull a cord revealing a plaque commemorating its completion. An earlier Republican speaker upstaged the governor by uncovering the plaque before Williams's remarks and he had to delete the final paragraph announcing the unveiling of the monument. He was incensed that the Republicans had denied him the honor of commissioning the plaque for "his bridge," and aides reported that they had "never before and never again" seen him so angry.[29]

Despite the embarrassment at Mackinac, the eighteen months after his 1956 reelection were one of the high points of Williams's career. He had followed his landslide victory by forming two groups (the Democratic Advisory Committee and the Committee of Governors for Civil Rights) to foster his liberal ideology and encourage his consideration for the Democratic nomination in 1960. His continued work as chairman of the Minorities Commission of the party also kept his name in front of potential delegates. Perhaps most significant, the crisis at Little Rock had focused the attention of the nation on the issue of civil rights and Williams, long a leading advocate for racial equality, had emerged as a major spokesperson for the end of segregation. Combined with his continued criticism of Eisenhower and the Republican administration, this gained Williams the attention of the national press. But, in stark contrast to the successes of 1957 and early 1958, the next two years would prove disastrous for Williams and his presidential ambitions.

Most of Williams's advisers were convinced that the road to the White House ran through the U.S. Senate. Immediately after his 1956 victory Staebler and others urged him to run against Republican senator Charles Potter in 1958 as a stepping-stone to the presidency. As a senator, Williams would receive even more press attention and develop some experience in foreign affairs, a necessity for a run at the nomination. In addition, Washington would provide an escape from the mounting fiscal problems in Michigan. Nearly everyone in the state recognized that the financial dilemma could not be ignored much longer, and if Williams ran for a sixth term as governor he would be embroiled in the inevitable economic crisis.[30]

Williams pondered the possibility of leaving Lansing for the Senate. He later admitted that "many of my counselors" had urged a run against Potter and it "was a very close question," but ultimately he had decided to seek a sixth term as governor. A number of factors influenced his decision not to challenge Potter. As the junior senator from Michigan he would have little power in Washington, and he determined that it would be better to be one of forty-eight governors than one of ninety-six senators. Williams also was aware that no Michigan governor had been elected to six terms, and he was intrigued with the notion of securing a place in the state's history. Finally, he loved being governor. He enjoyed the attention and power and remained convinced that he could work out a solution to Michigan's budget problems. On May 1, 1958, he ignored Staebler's advice and announced that he would seek a sixth term to prevent the Republicans from destroying the "progress of the last ten years." Phil Hart would challenge Potter for Michigan's Senate seat.[31]

Following his reelection announcement, Williams faced a personal crisis. At their summer home on Mackinac Island,

Nancy Williams developed sharp pains in her legs, and doctors determined that she was suffering from Guillain-Barre syndrome, a severe nervous disorder that could lead to paralysis of the arms, legs, lungs, and heart. They rushed her to Lansing for treatment, where for the next six months she would undergo massage and exercise therapy. Nancy Williams's illness was not made public until 1976, when she revealed to the press her attack eighteen years earlier. Williams did write to his son, a freshman at Princeton, informing him of his mother's disease and noting that she was confined to "a long siege in bed." Nancy Williams would recover, but for the first time she was unable to campaign with her husband.[32]

Personal problems were followed by political dilemmas. In 1958, the nation was in the midst of a severe recession. The economic setback was both a benefit and problem for Williams, as it offered him the chance to attack Eisenhower and the Republicans for their economic mismanagement but also had a disastrous impact on the economy of Michigan. The automobile industry, still the major employer in the state, was hit hard by the recession, and massive unemployment lowered tax revenues and drained unemployment funds, deepening the state's already disastrous financial situation.

Williams responded aggressively to the "Eisenhower recession," calling it "a major economic disaster" and demanding that the president provide federal funds for unemployment compensation and develop "a practical program" to put people back to work. He claimed that the economic problems in Michigan were the direct result of "this national Republican recession."[33]

Despite his attempts to blame the Republicans in Washington for Michigan's economic problems, many in the state put part of the blame on Williams. Adviser John Murray conducted extensive polls in Michigan and found that many thought Williams had created "a bad business climate" in the state. Eisenhower was still immensely popular, and most in Michigan felt that the government should do more to "help business" rather than blaming the president. Murray also noted that a vast number of voters were unaware that the Republicans con-

trolled the legislature and thought Williams had no real opposition in Lansing. Similarly, aide John Abernethy informed the
governor that "surveys show an astonishing number of Michigan's citizens believe Democrats control the Legislature because
we have a Democratic governor and Ad. Board." Democrats
rushed to prepare a pamphlet entitled "Know Your Opponent:
Republican Voting Record," documenting the ten years of
GOP opposition to Williams and his programs.[34]

Despite the disturbing polling data, Michigan Democrats
were supremely confident in 1958. Williams's last two landslide
victories had convinced them that he was unbeatable in the
state. After ten years in office he was so well known that billboards did not even include his name: They simply showed a
giant green and white polka-dot bow tie with the phrase
"Keeping Michigan Strong!" Aides argued that the national
press would flock to Michigan to assess the governor's presidential prospects and they should be certain "to give them a
view of Williams in action." Staebler invited prominent
Democrats Harry Truman, Hubert Humphrey, Wayne Morse,
Senator Al Gore of Tennessee, Governor Edmund Muskie of
Maine, and Governor Orville Freeman of Minnesota to meet
with Williams in 1958 and observe his energetic campaign
efforts in the hope that they would see a candidate who could
win the White House in 1960.[35]

Michigan Democrats moved from confidence to cockiness
when the Republicans nominated an unknown Michigan State
University speech professor, Paul Bagwell, to run against
Williams. Bagwell was a political novice and seemed to be a
sacrificial candidate with little chance to defeat the entrenched
Soapy Williams. A confidential staff memo argued that Bagwell
would "be lost" trying to deal with complex political issues, as
he "does not understand these things." Williams should stress
his knowledge of details and issues and make it a contest
between "the inexperienced professor and the experienced
Governor." Bagwell was "desperate to get his name known"
and may try some "circus stunts," but he was no match for
Williams or the Democratic campaign organization. As there
was no chance that a Republican could win the governorship,

Bagwell "should be ignored as much as possible" and Williams should focus on helping the Democrats win control of the legislature and aiding Hart's election to the Senate. Most political observers shared the optimism of Williams's advisers. The *New York Times* spoke for much of the national press when it predicted "an easy win" for the governor.[36]

At the Democratic state convention in Grand Rapids delegates unanimously nominated Williams, and he responded by calling his party "the most effective political instrument for progress in the history of Michigan." Euphoric delegates sang a tune to the melody of "Seventy-Six Trombones" that concluded:

> Governor Williams will lead the big parade.
> With the Ad Board close at hand.
> Followed by rows and rows of the finest politicos
> Ever joined in a Democratic Band!

Despite the state's grim economy and massive budget deficits, Williams's acceptance speech called for major increases in spending on roads, schools, agriculture, conservation, workman's compensation, hospitals, and highways. He also urged a doubling of funding for the state's junior colleges. He made no mention of how Michigan would fund his proposals.[37]

Before confronting Bagwell, Williams faced another, older enemy. In the summer of 1958, there were rumors that Jimmy Hoffa was again trying to gain influence in Michigan's Democratic Party to help him in his legal battles with the federal government. Williams was quick to repudiate the Teamster leader and warned Democrats not to accept any funds from the disgraced union official.

> Jimmy Hoffa has been over in the Republican corner for the
> last six years. He went over to the Republicans when he
> found that supporting the Democratic Party bought him no
> influence in the government. It is possible that Hoffa is now
> attempting to buy his way back into the Democratic Party.
> We want no part of Jimmy Hoffa.[38]

As soon as the campaign began it became clear that the Democrats had underestimated Bagwell. The speech professor was an articulate and poised campaigner and extremely effective on television. He mocked Williams's campaign style, claiming that the governor was more interested in personal appearances than discussing the issues. Because of Williams the people of Michigan "now expect their candidates to be seen eating spun candy at county fairs and judging quilts at church bazaars" rather than explaining their ideas about government. When Williams, recognizing Bagwell's verbal skills, refused a direct TV debate, the Republican charged that he was afraid of the facts and offered "propaganda" instead of programs.[39]

The main Republican issue in 1958 was the faltering economy and the impending financial crisis in Michigan. Bagwell demanded an independent agency survey the business climate of the state to determine whether Williams's policies were discouraging economic growth. When the governor refused, Bagwell claimed "he is afraid that the truth will tear down Williams" and charged "it is political cowardice for the governor to refuse this challenge." Democrats responded with statistics showing that Michigan had created 315,000 new jobs in the past two years and blaming the economic problems in the state on Eisenhower and the Republican recession. Williams reminded voters that Republicans had controlled the legislature for the past decade and declared that the state's budgetary problems were the direct result of their obstinacy.[40]

Stung by Bagwell's charge that he was antibusiness, Williams accused his opponent of "running down the state" through negative campaigning and charged that the Republicans were "willing to ruin Michigan if that will help them rule it." Bagwell's campaign was designed not to solve the state's economic problems but "to destroy the capacity of Michigan labor unions to bargain effectively." The main cause of the weakness in Michigan's business was the "Republican recession." Like Herbert Hoover in 1929, Eisenhower had blundered into economic collapse and refused to accept responsibility or undertake programs to encourage recovery. Michigan Republicans were "trying to cover-up their party's responsibility for the national recession by running down their own state."[41]

Although Williams refused to debate Bagwell, his campaign

did make intensive use of television in 1958. Nancy's illness prevented a repeat of the successful *Nancy's Scrapbook,* but the Democrats hired W. B. Doner and Company to produce a series of TV ads hailing Williams's accomplishments and attacking Republicans for causing the recession. One spot, which featured the Mackinac Bridge, claimed: "Republicans sneered at the bridge and called it 'Soapy's Folly' but under Mennen Williams the two Michigan's are now one!" Another, which showed a photo of a crowd, claimed that more than a thousand Michigan residents were alive as a result of the construction of new and safer highways. Williams also appeared in many ads, using a teleprompter for the first time. Although he occasionally used his spots to attack Bagwell, most of his TV efforts were devoted to campaigning for Hart against Potter in the race for the Senate and for other statewide Democratic candidates, particularly the nominee for lieutenant governor, John Swainson, who would succeed him as governor in 1960.[42]

Williams's emphasis on helping Hart, Swainson, and other Democrats rather than focusing on his own reelection illustrates the overconfidence that marked the 1958 campaign. Having won five contests against more prominent Republicans, Williams, Staebler, Berthelot, and Weber dismissed Bagwell as only a token candidate, but the continued impact of the recession and the professor's surprisingly aggressive campaign prevented the expected third consecutive landslide. Williams won 54 percent of the vote, but his margin was only 139,000 votes, less than half of his totals in 1954 and 1956. Hart defeated Potter by 172,000 votes, and Secretary of State Jim Hare won by over 300,000 votes. The victory kept Williams's presidential hopes alive but was far from the impressive triumph most had expected. His easy wins in the past two elections had provided momentum for his national efforts, but his 1958 victory did little to sustain his image as an unexcelled campaigner who could lead the Democrats to the White House in 1960.

Williams's unexpectedly narrow victory was even more surprising because the Democrats enjoyed great success across the nation in 1958, picking up thirteen Senate seats, forty-six in the House, and five governorships (although Williams's friend and

liberal ally Harriman lost to Nelson Rockefeller in New York).
In retrospect, Staebler had likely been correct when he urged
Williams to run for the Senate. Williams himself later wondered whether he "did the right thing" when he decided to run
for the governorship again.[43]

Despite his disappointment with the 1958 results, Williams
remained convinced that he would be a major contender for
the presidency in 1960. He was by nature an unwavering opti-
mist, and, though damaged by Bagwell, he was certain that he
had as good a chance as any rival for his party's nomination.
Immediately after his reelection, his operatives approached
Democratic activists who had been involved in the 1956
Stevenson campaign to obtain their support in 1960. Williams
flew to New York for a private meeting with Harriman, former
senator Herbert Lehman, Truman's former secretary of the air
force Thomas Finletter, and the leader of New York's infamous
Tammany Hall, Carmen De Sapio, to discuss his presidential
prospects. It is ironic that Williams, the leading critic of graft,
who never had a trace of scandal in his entire public career,
would court De Sapio, the head of one of the premier symbols
of political corruption. It was an awkward meeting. Harriman,
Lehman, and Finletter were out of office and held little political power, and, although De Sapio agreed to list Williams as
one of the top four contenders for the 1960 nomination (along
with Kennedy, Symington, and Johnson), he did not offer an
endorsement.[44]

Two weeks later the governor again flew to New York for a
major address to the Lexington Democratic Club, a liberal,
reform group dedicated to fighting De Sapio and Tammany
Hall. Eleanor Roosevelt was the honored guest and Williams
the featured speaker. He began by praising Franklin Roosevelt
and, looking directly at Mrs. Roosevelt, argued that the
Democrats needed another FDR in 1960, someone who could
offer the American people a "sense of participation" and "a
vision for America." He then proposed three major points as
the basis for the Democratic Party's campaign to capture the
White House: an end to all forms of racial discrimination, a federal program to eliminate poverty, and a foreign policy dedi-

cated to peace not war. It was a long, rambling, and unsuccessful effort. The applause was tepid, and Mrs. Roosevelt was
unenthusiastic. Most in the audience told reporters they preferred Hubert Humphrey in 1960.[45]

Undeterred, Williams returned to Michigan to meet with
Staebler and other aides to discuss their prospects in 1960. They
agreed that they should designate "3 or 4 people" to work for
Williams's nomination and reassess their prospects at the end of
the year. By the end of 1959, his chances for national office
were bleak, as he faced the financial crisis that had been growing in Michigan for over a decade.[46]

Since his first victory in 1948, Williams had argued the need
to expand Michigan's tax base to fund the programs he saw as
essential to modernizing the state. He had repeatedly called for
a corporation profits tax to balance the state's budget. Republicans had been consistent in their opposition to a profits tax or
any other new taxes and had called on Williams to cut state
spending instead. Both sides recognized that Michigan could
not continue to borrow to meet its debts but disagreed on the
solution to the problem. In early 1959, ten years of conflict
escalated into a political war that would bankrupt the state and
destroy Williams's presidential ambitions.

Michigan's financial crisis began even before Williams was in
office. In his final message to the legislature in 1948, outgoing
Republican governor Kim Sigler warned that the state was
headed toward financial distress and argued that Michigan
needed either new taxes or a reduction in services. The state
did neither. Over the next decade Republicans in Lansing
grudgingly enacted parts of Williams's aggressive agenda of
social programs but rejected his call for new taxes to pay for
them. The governor had managed to patch together annual
budgets by employing a creative system of borrowing and shifting funds among various accounts each year, but the 1958
recession put new strains on the state. Unemployment in
Michigan soared to over four hundred thousand, greatly
increasing the welfare rolls and claims for unemployment insurance. The economic slump also led to sharply lower revenues.
In 1958, the state took in $47 million less than the previous

year, and there was a projected deficit of over $110 million for
1959. Michigan faced the consequences of ten years of deadlock
between the governor and the legislature and a decade of creative accounting and borrowing.

Perhaps bipartisanship and compromise could have solved
Michigan's economic woes, but both were absent in Lansing.
Williams had spent ten years battling the legislature over his liberal agenda and the need for new taxes. As the state's first six-
term governor and a leading candidate for the presidency, he
felt it was time for Republicans to acknowledge his political
power and finally accept the need to increase revenues. His
opponents saw the pending financial crisis as a golden chance to
embarrass Williams and frustrate his presidential ambitions.
Although the Michigan House was evenly divided, Republicans controlled the Senate by a margin of twenty-two to twelve
and could block any new taxation or spending. The budget
conflict in 1959 was more than a battle over political philosophy; it was the final war of wills between G. Mennen Williams
and his Republican opposition. Both sides were eager for a
showdown, and neither considered a compromise.[47]

Williams began the confrontation at his sixth inaugural. He
insisted on a modest ceremony without a ball or formal reception to dramatize the state's financial plight and warned the legislature of the need for immediate and dramatic action to avert
bankruptcy. Two weeks later he sent a message to the legislature outlining the severity of the crisis.

> There is no room for recrimination and no excuse for parti-
> sanship in the situation we face. The future of Michigan is at
> stake. . . . We simply do not have time for bickering over
> past disagreements. Let the dead past bury its dead.

He then produced a chart showing that the current deficit of
$34 million would escalate to over $70 million by May 15.
Unless the legislature agreed to new taxation, he warned, "we
will not be able to meet such essential obligations as payrolls
and welfare costs."[48]

On February 4, the governor sent his plan to solve the state's
economic crisis to the legislature. To meet the long-term fund-

ing problem he called again for a corporate profits tax but also offered a new proposal: a graduated state income tax. He suggested that these new taxes would eventually put the state on a solid financial footing but that Michigan still faced a severe short-term cash flow crisis. To cover this immediate shortfall he proposed borrowing from the $50 million Veterans Trust Fund. The money would be paid back over the next few years out of the new revenues generated by the profits and income taxes.[49]

The plan was a major political risk. In 1952, Williams had strongly criticized his opponent, Frederick Alger, for suggesting that the state tap the lucrative Veterans Trust Fund, accusing Alger of betraying those who had fought for America by draining money set aside for them. In addition, most labor leaders, including his close associate Gus Scholle, were firmly against a state income tax. Republicans were gleeful, as they could charge Williams with hypocrisy on the veteran's fund issue and encourage conflict between the governor and organized labor, one of the groups most responsible for his electoral victories [50]

Senate Republicans claimed that Williams was exaggerating the state's cash flow shortage and suggested that the simplest solution would be to just cut spending. They then proposed a "flat rate" rather than a graduated personal income tax. When Williams denounced such a plan as favoring the wealthy, Republicans countered with a plan for a 1 percent "use tax," a rhetorical phrase for an increase in the state sales tax. Michigan's constitution limited the sales tax to 3 percent, but Republicans argued that a new 1 percent tax on all sales was legal, as it was a "separate tax." They also demanded a state referendum in which voters would have to approve any new taxes and borrowing from the Veterans Trust Fund. Williams was outraged and called his opponent's actions "complete and reckless irresponsibility." Michigan inched ever closer to bankruptcy.[51]

On April 27, it seemed a compromise would be possible when the Republicans agreed to permit temporary borrowing from the Veterans Trust Fund to cover the immediate cost of government while the legislature continued to debate use tax and income tax. The next day, however, the Republicans reversed themselves and announced that any use of money from the veteran's fund had to be combined with their proposed increase in the sales tax. Williams charged that the Republicans had violated their agreement, and even the conservative *Detroit News* agreed. The paper had been a vocal critic of Williams for ten years and had originally blamed him for the state's financial woes, but now it concluded that it was the twenty-two "Senate Bourbons" who had "crushed the rare and delicate flower of compromise." The paper contended that Michigan was becoming the laughingstock of the country and that "the dubious honor for this publicity goes entirely to the Republican majority in the State Senate."[52]

Editorial writers fumed, but Michigan Republicans were delighted. As they had hoped, Michigan's looming bankruptcy was a major embarrassment to Williams and his presidential ambitions. Lobbyists from General Motors, Dow Chemical, and other major corporations mounted aggressive campaigns in support of the Republican opposition to new taxes. A spokesman for the Michigan Manufacturing Association sent a telegram to all twenty-two Republican senators that praised their refusal to give in to the governor: "You have him over the barrel for the first time in ten years. Keep him there 'till he screams 'uncle.' God bless each of you!"[53]

Williams had finally had enough of both the Republicans and business lobbyists, and he decided to call their bluff by letting the state go bankrupt. When the people of Michigan saw that the state could not pay its bills they would understand that the responsibility was that of the Republicans and their corporate allies and would force his opponents to abandon their obstinacy and agree to his plan for borrowing from the veteran's fund and imposing new taxes. The decision proved to be his greatest political blunder.

In 1995, President Bill Clinton, locked in a similar battle with the Republican House of Representatives, allowed the government to close offices, parks, and monuments in a temporary bankruptcy. He then assailed the Republican Congress for permitting the shutdown of government and forced his opponents to accept his budget. Nearly three decades earlier, G. Mennen Williams had adopted the identical tactic but with disastrous results.

Staebler, Lieutenant Governor Swainson, and other advisers agreed that only a shutdown of public services would prod the legislature into action. Staebler argued that many Republicans were "pooh-poohing the idea that there was a crisis" and needed to be jarred into taking responsibility. Swainson contended that unpaid state employees would pressure the legislature into accepting Williams's proposals. The governor wrote to his wife.

> We have been having quite a time here with the Republicans. We have really gone a long ways to co-operate and they have the unmitigated gall to say we have refused to cooperate. All we have refused to do is to go for a sales tax. They have refused to go for anything else.[54]

On April 29, 1959, the state of Michigan withheld checks from selected government employees. Williams announced that the Republicans were "determined to have payless paydays and now they have their wish." More than three hundred government workers, including members of the state legislature and Supreme Court, did not receive paychecks. Williams further infuriated Republicans by announcing his priorities for state payments, with welfare recipients at the top of his agenda. Republicans were quick to point out that the governor was continuing to issue checks to welfare recipients but not to legislators and Supreme Court justices. Williams responded that those on welfare needed the money more than judges and members of the legislature.[55]

The next day Williams debated Republican senator Edward Hutchinson of Fennville on statewide television. The governor called the payless paydays a "contrived crisis" and a "deliberate disaster" provoked by the Republicans. Hutchinson responded that the problem was Williams's insatiable addiction to spending and taxing the people of Michigan and repeated the Republican vow to oppose any new taxes except the use tax. The next day the governor accused the Republicans of trying to "blackjack" Democrats into accepting their unjust sales tax. He announced that payless paydays would continue and he was assigning each of the seven members of his Administrative Board to work with a different government agency to help them deal with the crisis. He also asked the state's largest employers to pay their taxes early, but few companies complied and he was forced to transfer $19 million from the State Liquor Control Commission to the general fund to cover welfare payments.[56]

As the financial crisis continued, the *Detroit News* asked three Detroit psychiatrists to analyze Williams and his legislative opponents. They concluded that the governor was often "aloof" and arrogant in his dealings with the legislature. Rural Republicans subconsciously "envied Williams" as a popular "urban father figure" and were so blinded by their hatred that they were "unable to assess the realities of the situation." None of them offered a solution to the crisis.[57]

Banks and credit unions began to offer interest-free loans, and Detroit grocery stores promised free credit to government employees. The University of Michigan announced that it would have to borrow $4 million to cover payroll checks in May, and Michigan State University declared that it needed $2.6 million. The press ran cartoons of a man labeled "Michigan" in front of a pawnshop, and residents joked about a new state cocktail: "Michigan on the Rocks."[58]

On May 7, after a second payless payday, Williams requested a personal appearance before the legislature. As he often did when he was angry, he spoke very slowly and declared: "This is truly a disgraceful condition to which a great State has been reduced!" He further contended: "There is no further advantage to anyone in continuing this deadlock." He proposed that both the House and Senate work together to write a tax bill and immediately release the Veterans Trust Fund to cover current expenses, but the Republicans refused. Seething from the rebuff by his opponents, Williams and his aides met to ponder the next step. They considered calling for a referendum on the corporate profits tax or an initiative to force the immediate redistricting of Michigan's gerrymandered legislature. Some advisers suggested that they summon corporate leaders to Lansing and demand that they curtail their lobbying. None of these steps were realistic, and the administration had no other ideas to force an end to the stalemate.[59]

Williams's decision to withhold paychecks was intended to show the public irresponsibility of his Republican opponents, but as the crisis continued most of the criticism was directed at the governor. Nearly all major national news magazines, including *Time, Newsweek, U.S. News and World Report,* and *The Reporter,* ran lengthy stories on the fiasco in Michigan and placed much of the blame on Williams. The *New York Times* concluded that "the Governor's prestige appears to have suffered a serious blow as a result of Michigan's continued fiscal crisis," as to those outside the state "the plight is considered his responsibility." When Michigan Democratic Committeeman Tom Quimby and Committeewoman Margaret Price went to the Conference of Western Governors in Denver to lobby for Williams's nomination in 1960, they "were kept busy explaining Michigan's fiscal troubles." They distributed a pamphlet claiming that it was the Republican legislature that had forced the crisis, but the Kennedy and Johnson representatives argued that Michigan's fiscal problems were the result of Williams's mismanagement and his dedication to a "welfare state"[60]

Republicans sensed that the public was increasingly placing responsibility for the disaster on Williams's shoulders and mounted an intensive public relations effort to show it was the governor who had closed down the government. Staebler later admitted: "We underestimated the publicity skills of the Republicans." He recalled that the hope that unpaid state workers would blame the Republicans "didn't work out" and "the desired result did not materialize." The usually buoyant Williams became increasingly depressed. Berthelot wrote him a long letter on May 12 urging him to continue the fight and "hurry up and settle those Michigan Republicans so I can get your D.C. Williams for President Committee in session." Williams responded that "these last few weeks have been rugged ones indeed" and "we have had a lot of bad public relations breaks." He noted that sometimes it is "more important to be a servant in the house of the Lord than to sit in the seats of the mighty." He wrote his wife that "the Republicans have finally forced the state to miss paydays, we are locked in a stalemate. . . . The Republican Senators seem to be willing to force the state to its knees by this kind of blackmail. As you can well imagine, it has been a pretty strenuous time."[61]

Williams was convinced that the national Republican Party was encouraging the obstinacy of the legislature in order to destroy his presidential chances and block liberal reform. In a speech to the Michigan Jefferson-Jackson dinner in May he charged that conservatives, led by Arizona senator Barry Goldwater, had made Michigan their "number one national target" in a campaign against progressive policies. "We're fighting against the desperate moves of the reactionaries . . . to destroy Michigan's reputation for liberalism."[62]

Despite Williams's aggressive rhetoric, when it became clear that the Republicans were adamant in their refusal to compromise and sensing the possible collapse of his presidential campaign, he finally capitulated. In late August he agreed to sign the Republican proposal for an increase in the sales tax if they would agree to an increase of $8.5 million in the business activities tax. He would also withdraw his proposals to create an income tax and borrow from the Veterans Trust Fund. Like many others, Williams was convinced that the boost in the sales tax was unconstitutional, and he was right. In late October the Michigan Supreme Court ruled against the "use tax," and the state again faced financial ruin. Finally, on December 18, after nearly a year of bickering and bankruptcy, the legislature cobbled together a bill raising "nuisance taxes" on cigarettes, beer, liquor, telephones, telegrams, and licenses to try to keep the state solvent.[63]

Michigan's yearlong financial crisis was a severe blow to Williams's presidential prospects, as his critics argued that he could not be trusted to run the nation when he could not even manage his home state. The turmoil also enhanced his image as an extreme antibusiness liberal addicted to spending and expanding welfare. Finally, the conflict kept him in Michigan while many of his rivals crossed the nation making speeches, raising money, and seeking delegates. While he languished in Lansing, Kennedy, Humphrey, and Symington were on the road courting support.

It is clear that Williams underestimated the tenacity of his

Republican opponents and did not anticipate the disastrous impact of payless paydays. It is more difficult to explain how such a successful politician could have so miscalculated the response to his policies. A number of elements entered into his disastrous decision. Williams was supremely confident in 1959 and totally certain that he had the political power to force his will on the legislature. His overconfidence was first evident in his 1958 campaign against Bagwell, and, despite the narrowness of his victory, it carried over into 1959. Second, his advisers encouraged him to take a strong stand against the legislature to show his leadership and finally crush the opponents who had repeatedly frustrated his liberal agenda in Michigan. Staebler and others were certain that the Republicans would capitulate if the governor were persistent. Williams also assumed that the public would see that it was the Republicans, not the governor, that had brought the state to ruin. His faith in "the people" was an essential part of his political philosophy, and he was certain they would rally to his support. He was wrong. Finally, Williams had spent nearly two years positioning himself for a run for the presidency in 1960 and had neglected politics in his home state. He assumed that as a potential president he need not worry about twenty-two rural Republicans and did not have to consider any form of compromise. How could his own state reject a possible occupant of the White House? When the Republicans refused to accept his proposals he was certain that payless paydays would force them to capitulate. When, to his dismay, they continued to oppose him, he had no alternative or fallback position. In the end it was Williams, the potential president, who gave in to the Republican senators.

The disaster in Lansing was a serious setback to his presidential ambitions. Not only was he faced with the charge that he could not govern his state, but his rivals for the nomination had grown stronger. While Williams battled Republicans in Lansing, Kennedy and Humphrey had gained momentum. Kennedy had nearly unlimited financial resources and had put together a skilled campaign organization while Humphrey had moved to take the liberal wing of the party away from Williams. It would be a difficult struggle for the Michigan

Democrat, as he did not have Kennedy's money or staff and had lost many of his most fervent supporters to Humphrey.

Soapy Williams, however, was almost always optimistic and assumed that he still had a good chance to win national office. Despite the financial fiasco, he was still a possible Democratic selection in 1960. He was only forty-eight years old, and if he could not gain the presidency there was always the possibility of a vice presidential nomination. He still felt he could make a strong run for the presidential nomination, but he faced a difficult dilemma. He and Humphrey were both midwestern liberals with strong records in support of civil rights. It was obvious that Humphrey would challenge Kennedy in the state primaries in early 1960, and if he were successful he would be the clear "liberal" candidate. If, however, Kennedy triumphed in the primaries, Williams would be a liberal alternative or a possible running mate. Ironically, the liberal Williams's only hope was for Kennedy to defeat his ideological twin from Minnesota. To further complicate the process, if Kennedy won decisively he could lock up the nomination before the convention. Williams's chances for the nomination depended on an unlikely scenario of Humphrey and Kennedy fighting to a stalemate in the primaries, leaving the Michigan governor as a liberal alternative to the moderate Symington and the southern candidate, Lyndon Johnson. Williams viewed the other possible Democratic nominee, Adlai Stevenson, as vacillating, lazy, and unable to defeat any Republican.[64]

After finally passing a budget in Michigan, Williams tried to resurrect his presidential campaign. At the Midwest Governors' Conference he met with Humphrey to work out a liberal platform and a strategy to defeat Kennedy. During the budget battle he made a rare effort to demonstrate his knowledge of foreign policy when he engaged in a public debate with Soviet deputy premier Frol Kozlov in Detroit. Kozlov was in Michigan to tour automobile plants, and Detroit mayor Louis Miriana refused to see him. Williams had long used his position as head of the Democratic Party's Committee on Minorities to denounce the Soviet occupation of Eastern Europe and quickly agreed to meet with the Russian official. As reporters listened,

Williams lectured Kozlov about the denial of freedom in East-ern Europe, and when the two met privately he demanded that the Soviet Union agree to international arms inspections as a first step toward disarmament. Williams then leaked a summary of the conversation to the press, implying that the deputy pre-mier had agreed to his proposal. Kozlov was outraged and told the press he had assumed the conversation was "off the record" and that "Governor Williams is not well informed on foreign affairs."[65]

Williams also returned to the lecture circuit, accepting an invitation from Oklahoma Democrats to join Kennedy, Symington, and California governor Pat Brown in addressing their Jefferson-Jackson Dinner, where he accused Republicans of "behaving like beatniks" by refusing to take responsibility for their actions. He also was one of seven presidential contenders to address a New York dinner honoring Eleanor Roosevelt. In January 1960, he was a featured speaker at a hundred dollar a plate Democratic fund-raising event in New York City and attacked Eisenhower and Nixon for their "lack of creativity" in foreign policy. Neither the audience nor reporters were impressed, and one writer judged it a "pedestrian effort." Williams's reappearance on the national scene did lead the Southern Governors' Conference to release a statement indi-cating that only two Democratic presidential candidates were "unacceptable"· Humphrey and Williams.[66]

He also commissioned Chicago journalist Frank McNaughton to write a campaign biography, *Mennen Williams of Michigan, Fighter for Progress*. McNaughton began the book before the fiscal crisis in Michigan began, and he had to hastily revise it to include coverage of the budget battle. His opening chapter was a defense of the payless paydays strategy and a strong attack on the legislature. Even McNaughton, however, had to admit that "at times the Administration seemed confused and paralyzed by its own inability to choose some path out of the dilemma" and acknowledge that the governor had "made a number of monu-mental miscalculations of strategy." Such criticism was rare in a commissioned campaign biography and illustrated the defensive nature of the Williams's campaign following the 1959 financial disaster. The rest of the book stressed Williams's academic achievements, energetic campaign style, and advocacy of civil rights. McNaughton devoted a large section to countering arguments that the governor was a tool of labor leaders. Published in January 1960, the book suffered minuscule sales and rare and lukewarm reviews. The *New York Times* concluded that, even for a campaign biography, it was too strongly pro-Williams: "The forces of light are made too light and the forces of darkness are too dark."[67]

As Humphrey and Kennedy began their primary battles, Williams's candidacy was floundering. At the California Democratic Convention in February, Governor Pat Brown read the names of the Democratic contenders to the audience. Stevenson and Kennedy received loud standing ovations. Johnson's name was booed. Williams got only "moderate hand clapping."[68]

Another blow to Williams was the reemergence of the John Guanaca case. Republican members of the Senate Rackets Committee, headed by Barry Goldwater, opened hearings on corruption in the United Auto Workers union by resurrecting the Guanaca incident. Goldwater asked a UAW official: "Are reasonable people to believe that the Governor of Michigan was acting voluntarily in denying such extradition? Or rather, is it not true that Guanaca was protected by the umbrella of immunity given all thugs and hoodlums employed by the UAW?" The hearings generated national coverage (though no comment from "Peg" Johnson Goldwater), and Williams again faced charges that he was a tool of Reuther and other labor leaders.[69]

Aside from the grim political news Williams also faced a family crisis. His son Gery had enrolled at Princeton but found it difficult to duplicate his father's academic and athletic success. In 1960, he was placed on academic probation for low grades and missed classes. The elder Williams wrote his son that probation "was a failure on my part as well as yours," as he had spent so much time dealing with politics in Michigan and running for the presidency that he had ignored his family responsibilities. The governor offered to contact his son's professors, and when Gery did not respond he wrote to the dean asking for suggestions to improve Gery's grades.[70]

In a final attempt to revive his sagging campaign, Williams sent Tom Quimby to Washington to assess his chances for the nomination. Quimby and Berthelot contacted the noted capital hostess India Edwards, a former vice chair of the Democratic National Committee, to organize a party for potential supporters. It proved to be a disaster. After Edwards introduced Quimby, one of the twenty guests asked about Michigan's financial crisis. Liberal economist John Kenneth Galbraith and conservative economist Leon Keyserling then began a lengthy argument about fiscal policy. While the two debated, most of the guests quietly left.[71]

Kennedy's success in the West Virginia primary finally convinced Williams that he had no chance for victory. He phoned potential delegates, and "my survey indicated to me that I wouldn't be able to prevail against Kennedy." He concluded that his run "would be an empty gesture." As he had never officially announced his candidacy, he did not formally announce his withdrawal, but by April 1960 Soapy Williams was no longer a candidate for the presidency.[72]

Williams had been actively running for national office since 1952. After his stunning victories in 1954 and 1956, he seemed to be as strong a prospect as any other candidate, and the collapse of his presidential effort was a bitter blow. Certainly the contentious and drawn-out battle with the Michigan legislature was a major disaster. Berthelot argued that the financial crisis "quickly ruined his chances." There were, however, other factors that contributed to his failure. His decision to seek a sixth term as governor rather than run for the Senate seems in retrospect to have been a blunder, as he could have avoided the budget war of 1959 by escaping to Washington. He also was never able to overcome his image as too strident, too liberal, and too closely identified with organized labor and was unable to demonstrate why he, rather than Humphrey, was the best candidate of the liberal wing of the party. Williams also was incapable of restraining his criticism of fellow Democrats. His 1956 attack on Stevenson was followed by verbal assaults on Kennedy and Johnson for their lack of support of civil rights. Civil rights was the ultimate moral issue for Soapy Williams, and he felt he could not silently watch the leaders of his party equivocate over racial equality. His outspokenness may well have been morally correct, but it was politically destructive.[73]

Williams was disappointed in the collapse of his quest for the presidency, but he never stayed depressed for very long. Having abandoned his own campaign, he was now courted by the remaining contenders for the nomination. He controlled the Michigan delegation, was a proven vote getter, and still was a possible vice presidential selection or a candidate for a major cabinet appointment. Many of his advisers urged him to run again for governor, but he had no desire for another battle with the Michigan legislature and was convinced he would face a rough reelection battle, as the Republicans had "really hammered" him on the payless paydays and would certainly use the issue against him. On March 2, 1960, he announced that "with a heavy heart" he had decided not to seek reelection and the next evening addressed the state on television to declare that he now wanted to work "for the advancement of peace" both at home and abroad. Williams's future was now in Washington, D.C., not in Lansing.[74]

Surprisingly, it was Lyndon Johnson rather than John Kennedy who first explored the possibility of seeking Williams's support for the 1960 nomination. Johnson knew of Williams's deep distrust of his civil rights record. In 1959, Williams had made headlines when he refused to stay in a segregated hotel in Houston while on a speaking tour. When he met with reporters to discuss the incident, they asked about Johnson's presidential chances and Williams declared: "The people of Michigan would not even consider him a serious candidate."[75]

Despite Williams's known hostility to Johnson, the majority leader was convinced that politics was about making deals and ideology was often abandoned when it conflicted with power. His aides felt they might be able to gain some support in Michigan after Williams's candidacy failed and perhaps even convince the governor to steer his state's delegates to Johnson. In March the Texan sent one of his political operatives, Eugene Locke, to survey the situation in Michigan. Locke reported that

Williams's popularity among the state's Democrats was "amazing" and the only chance Johnson had "would be to make a trade with the Governor." Locke concluded that Williams "would like to be Vice-President, or in the absence of that, Secretary of Labor." Although his liberalism would make any trade-off difficult, he "wanted to be with a winner" and "might go for a deal."[76]

Encouraged by Locke's report, Johnson considered making a speaking trip to Michigan in the late spring to meet with Williams. His aides assured him that despite Williams's liberalism most Michigan delegates understood practical politics and were "not like those ADA nitwits in Texas." Johnson never went to Michigan, but he still had hopes of gaining some of the state's delegates. Locke predicted that if Williams turned the delegation loose "LBJ might do something here!"[77]

It is unlikely that Williams ever considered working with Johnson. His vice presidential ambitions were real but not worth abandoning his decade-long advocacy of civil rights. It was John Kennedy, more than Lyndon Johnson, who seemed to offer the best opportunity for the second spot on the ticket or a significant cabinet post.

John Kennedy and Mennen Williams were both from wealthy families, had Ivy League degrees, had been decorated naval officers in World War II, and wanted badly to be president. Their characters and personalities, however, could not have been more different. Kennedy was cool, calculating, aloof, and politically shrewd and ruthless. He had never embraced the militant liberalism of Williams or viewed civil rights in moralistic terms. Williams's religion was at the core of his life and politics and shaped nearly all his personal and political decisions, while Kennedy's Catholicism was at best superficial and had little impact on his ideology. It is nearly impossible to imagine John Kennedy in a polka-dot bow tie calling a square dance in an ethnic club and equally absurd to envision Soapy Williams consorting with Mafia dons and prostitutes in Palm Springs. Kennedy's nearly insatiable sexual appetite and countless affairs were in marked contrast to Williams's belief in the sanctity of marriage and lifelong dedication to blissful monogamy.

Despite their polar personalities and behavior, it was basic political issues that most divided the two in 1960, as Williams had long doubted Kennedy's liberal credentials. When they first met in the early 1950s, Kennedy had told him: "I wish I could be a liberal like you and Hubert Humphrey, but you can't do that in Massachusetts." Williams, however, was convinced Kennedy's conservatism was more than the need for political survival in his home state: It stemmed from a thirst for power that overrode any firm convictions or principles. He felt Kennedy had no personal commitment to civil rights and was far too willing to compromise on the issue for political gain. When the Supreme Court declared that segregation must end "with all due speed," Williams denounced the phrase as "weasel words." Kennedy, by contrast, declared that the court "does not need any assistance from any of us" in enforcing its decisions and refused to call for an immediate end of racial separatism. Williams also was convinced that Kennedy had not supported a strong platform on civil rights at the 1956 convention out of fear of losing support in the South.[78]

For his part, Kennedy was still angry with Williams for refusing to even consider his run for the vice presidential nomination in 1956. He also had difficulty understanding Williams the man. He knew that Williams, Staebler, and Reuther controlled the Michigan delegation and was convinced that Staebler would back a "winner" rather than quibble over issues and Reuther would support Kennedy if he was assured that he would have the "ear of the president." Williams, however, was different. Kennedy and his aides viewed him as "strange" and "quirky" and were unsure how to approach him for support. One of Kennedy's advisers wrote an appraisal of the Michigan governor in early 1960.

> Everyone seems agreed that Williams is a man of strong convictions. He takes himself very seriously and believes that he is an instrument of God's will in furthering liberal, humanitarian causes. He is a devout Episcopalian and will show moving pictures of his trip to the Holy Land at the drop of a hat. Williams apparently sees himself as having been tapped to put the Sermon on the Mount into governmental practice.

This is not a pose but reflects a sincere, if unusual, conviction. I go into this in some detail because I think any
approach to him which overlooks this strong religious
drive—which is completely intermeshed with his personal
ambition—will miss the mark.[79]

Ever since the 1956 election Kennedy had courted support in
Michigan from "anti-Williams" Democrats led by former governor Murray Van Waggoner. In 1959, he sent an aide,
Theodore Sorensen, to meet with local labor leaders to assess
the possibility of their endorsement of Kennedy should
Williams's presidential campaign fail. The senator's operatives
found that the state's Democrats were solidly behind Williams
and would follow his lead in voting for any other candidate.[80]

Recognizing the Michigan governor's control of his state's
delegation, Kennedy decided to approach Williams through a
mutual friend, Donald Thurber, a Harvard classmate of
Kennedy who Williams had appointed to the University of
Michigan Board of Regents. In late 1959, Kennedy asked
Thurber to meet with him in White Plains, New York, to discuss Mennen Williams. The two met for forty-five minutes,
and Kennedy immediately asked if Williams would continue
his pursuit of the presidential nomination. When Thurber suggested he would, Kennedy responded: "He has no chance."
Kennedy admitted that he did not know Williams very well
and asked about the governor's politics and personality.
Thurber offered to set up a meeting between the two.[81]

After Williams's presidential campaign collapsed in the spring
of 1960, Thurber called Kennedy's brother-in-law Stephen
Smith and speechwriter Ted Sorensen and told them that
Williams would like to meet with Kennedy. The senator
immediately rearranged his schedule to include a trip to Michigan. To prepare for the meeting, Kennedy's press secretary,
Pierre Salinger, approached Frank Blackford, a legislative aide
of Williams who had worked with Robert Kennedy on investigations of the Teamsters. Salinger met with Blackford at a
convention in San Francisco and questioned him about
Williams and what Kennedy needed to do to gain his endorse-

ment. Smith then phoned Thurber and asked: "What does Soapy want to talk about? Jack does not need to beg at this point. We'd like to know in advance what Soapy is likely to say so that Jack will not be taken by surprise." What Soapy "wanted to talk about" was civil rights.[82]

On June 2, Williams and Kennedy met at the governor's summer home on Mackinac Island, and their discussions clearly illustrated their major differences in style and politics. The pragmatic Kennedy asked what Williams "wanted" in return for an endorsement and delivering the Michigan delegation. The idealistic Williams responded that he wanted "good government!" Williams and Staebler then questioned Kennedy for nearly an hour about the depth of his dedication to civil rights and whether he would continue the liberal Democratic Advisory Council. Williams recalled that he wanted to be certain Kennedy was not a "Curley politician," a reference to James Curley, a former Massachusetts governor who had been jailed for corruption. "We were ideologues . . . and we probed John Kennedy," he explained. Although he still favored Humphrey and remained unconvinced of Kennedy's commitment to racial equality, Williams determined that Kennedy was the best hope for a Democratic victory in 1960.[83]

After their meeting Williams ushered the Massachusetts senator to a press conference and announced that he would allow his name to be submitted as a favorite son but would immediately withdraw and the Michigan delegation would vote for Kennedy. He hailed Kennedy as "a liberal Democrat, dedicated to the great tradition of Democratic liberalism" and pointedly stressed the senator's commitment to civil rights: "He will pursue the specifics of human dignity," and his administration would be "intellectually dynamic and spiritually dedicated."[84]

Unfortunately, Williams's endorsement had been leaked to the Washington press that morning by Senator Phil Hart, and journalists from the nation's capital who had traveled to Michigan felt they had been "scooped by colleagues back home." Williams dominated the press conference, fielding questions about the leak, while Kennedy stood "in quiet agony beside him."[85]

Soapy Williams's endorsement was important in Kennedy's drive to secure a first-ballot victory, and his support also seemed crucial for a victory over Nixon. Kennedy aide Harris Wofford, who had been working on the civil rights issue, suggested that a letter from Williams to African American leaders would be extremely influential in gaining their support in the fall and urged Kennedy to push the governor to follow his endorsement with a public statement applauding the senator's commitment to civil rights.[86]

Williams's pledge to support Kennedy at the Democratic convention, however, provoked unexpected criticism from African American leaders in Michigan, who were still highly skeptical of the senator's commitment to civil rights. As a result of their concerns, Williams arranged a second meeting with the likely nominee at Kennedy's Georgetown home on June 20. Former Connecticut governor Chester Bowles, who had been working all summer with Williams on a strong civil rights platform, joined the governor and seven others from Michigan. It was a stormy session. Williams; Charles Brown, a black member of his staff; and Damon Keith, head of the Michigan National Association for the Advancement of Colored People (NAACP) demanded that Kennedy promise to use the power of the federal government to immediately integrate southern schools, endorse the sit-in movement as a necessary tactic to end segregation, send federal marshals to the South to oversee voter registration, and agree to enforce open housing in all federally funded residences. They also demanded that he explain his 1959 visit to the home of segregationist Alabama governor John Patterson. Kennedy was "visibly affected" by the aggressiveness of the questions and angry with Williams for repeatedly interrupting his answers. He agreed that civil rights was of "overwhelming moral significance" but refused to commit to any specifics.[87]

Williams and Brown continued to press him to endorse the sit-in movement as a legitimate tactic to demonstrate the injustices of segregation. Kennedy had stated that he supported the participants in sit-ins as long as "they act peacefully." The Michigan delegation argued that this seemed to blame the pro-

testers for the violence in the South. After a break for an outdoor brunch hosted by Jackie Kennedy the group met again.
After a long silence Williams finally stood up and spoke.

> Well, Jack, as I understand what my Negro friends are trying
> to say is that you're insisting on including this 'by peaceful
> means' . . . it's as if you issued an invitation to them for din-
> ner and said, 'Please come to dinner, but wash your hands
> before you sit down.' Obviously you would expect your
> guests to wash their hands . . . and you would be insulting
> them if you said that. And by saying this 'by peaceful means'
> you are doing the same thing.[88]

Kennedy was incensed at the hectoring tone of the meeting
and thought Williams had been patronizing in his approach to
his party's presidential nominee. Williams, however, was
delighted. He judged the visit "a most successful operation"
and found "the discussion honest and hard hitting with no
punches pulled and no quarter asked." He concluded:
"Kennedy was given new insight into a very important situation and is prepared to do what is necessary."[89]

Williams was in high spirits as he prepared to attend the 1960
convention in Los Angeles. Despite his own failed presidential
run, he was certain he had influenced Kennedy to take a
stronger stance on civil rights and was convinced that there
would be a major cabinet position for him in the new administration. He had two main goals in Los Angeles: to push his party
to endorse a strong civil rights plank in the platform and to help
Kennedy win a first-ballot nomination. Throughout June and
July he worked with Bowles and other liberals to draft a civil
rights platform based on a clear commitment to ending segregation throughout the nation. When he testified before the
platform committee he concluded as follows.

> I cannot stress too greatly my feelings that the times demand
> that the Democrats must stand up and be counted on this
> central question of contemporary civilization. It is my deep
> belief that discrimination is immoral. In the deepest sense un-
> American, and where ever the government is involved, it is
> unconstitutional.

A few days later Williams's photo would be on the front page of nearly every American newspaper, not for his support of civil rights but for his defiant opposition to Kennedy's selection of a vice presidential nominee.[90]

Although he had endorsed Kennedy, Williams accepted a favorite son nomination, but he withdrew his name before the voting. Despite challenges from Stevenson and Johnson, Kennedy secured his first-ballot victory with the aid of a unanimous vote by the Michigan delegation. The convention awaited his vice presidential selection. Like most in Los Angeles, Williams expected Kennedy to pick Symington, Humphrey, or Minnesota governor Orville Freeman. He had announced earlier that he would support any nominee "with the possible exception of Lyndon Johnson."[91]

The day after his nomination, Kennedy invited Williams to his Biltmore Hotel suite. As the room was crowded with aides and Democratic leaders, they adjourned to the bathroom. As a courtesy, Kennedy asked Williams if he were interested in becoming his running mate, though both knew this was not an option. When Williams declined, Kennedy asked if Michigan had "any particular candidate." The governor responded that Michigan's only requirement was "that it not be Lyndon Johnson," as the Texan was "the antithesis of the program we had developed." Williams returned to his hotel and told the Michigan delegation that Johnson was not an option.[92]

A few hours later, Robert Kennedy knocked on Williams's hotel room door. Williams noted that the younger Kennedy "seemed somewhat crestfallen and woebegone" and looked "sort of forlorn." He told Williams that his brother had decided on Johnson as his running mate. Williams was stunned and felt Kennedy had betrayed him. "It was a great shock to me," he recalled, as just a few hours earlier he had been "assured that it was not going to be Lyndon Johnson." He felt Johnson was "ideologically wrong on civil rights" and his selection was "out of this world." Nancy Williams "went wild" and threw her Kennedy for President button on the floor.[93]

Williams made an immediate decision to fight the Texan's nomination, though he knew the chances were "99 out of 100" that he would fail. He later recalled that "we had given our life's blood to get Kennedy in and just weren't able to take it lying down." Most of the Michigan delegation had already left for the convention hall, and Williams sent word that there would be an emergency caucus in a small room off the convention floor. He also sent "runners" to contact the California, Minnesota, and District of Columbia delegations to try to organize an open campaign against Johnson.[94]

When members of the Michigan delegation finally straggled into the crowded room, Williams informed them of Kennedy's decision. There was a "universal reaction" against Johnson. Williams was by now "furious" at Kennedy and "just emotionally upset about the whole thing." Staebler and Margaret Price reported that although many liberals were outraged at Johnson's selection only Joe Rauh of Washington, D.C., would join a floor fight against the nomination.[95]

Hearing of the Michigan governor's plan to publicly attack his nominee, Kennedy sent his brother to inform Johnson that "the liberals will raise hell. . . . Mennen Williams will raise hell." Johnson responded: "Piss on Mennen Williams! The only question is—is it good for the country and good for the Democratic Party?" Kennedy then asked Leonard Woodcock of the UAW to try to talk Williams out of publicly opposing Johnson, but there was no reasoning with the Michigan governor. For over a decade he had been the leading voice for a clear stand in favor of civil rights, and he felt he had personally forced Kennedy to take a stronger position for racial equality. Johnson stood for everything he had fought against in the Democratic Party, and, though he felt "terribly let down" that other liberals had not joined him, he decided he would vote against the Texan even if he were the only voice of opposition.[96]

As a furious Williams stormed onto the convention floor, delegates and TV and newspaper reporters had heard that he would oppose Johnson. Dozens of journalists followed him across the floor, asking if he would vote no, but he refused to comment and continued his walk toward the Michigan delegation. Convention chairman Sam Rayburn knew that Williams planned to speak against the majority leader and arranged a motion to nominate Johnson by acclamation, avoiding a role call vote. When Rayburn asked for a voice vote, Williams seized the microphone and at the top of his voice screamed "No!" Rayburn calmly ignored him and declared the vote for Johnson to be unanimous.[97]

All three television networks focused their cameras on Soapy Williams standing at the microphone bellowing "No!" The next day a photo of the tall, gangly, Michigan governor in the polka-dot bow tie yelling his objection to the vice presidential nominee of his party was on the cover of nearly every major newspaper. He was the only delegate to publicly oppose Kennedy's selection of Johnson.

In some ways, Williams's lonely dissent in Los Angeles was his finest hour. While many other Democrats were also outraged by the choice of Johnson, Williams was the only one to act, as no other delegate was willing to incur the wrath of Kennedy, Johnson, and nearly every other leader of his or her party by opposing the nomination. If politics is to be based on sincere conviction and core beliefs are too important to compromise for personal gain, Mennen Williams's action was the epitome of principle in American politics.

But there is also another side to American politics, the need to compromise to obtain results, to maintain good relationships with those in power, to show restraint when your comments and actions may harm you, and to retreat when it is clear you cannot win. Compromise, restraint, and retreat were absent in the makeup of G. Mennen Williams. He may have been long on principle, but he was often short on pragmatism. Venting your rage against the future president and vice president on national television was not the best way to secure a major appointment in the new administration.

His actions at the convention were consistent with Williams's refusal to curtail his criticism of fellow Democrats, despite the political cost, when he was determined that they had put politics above principle. In 1952, he alienated much of the South by pushing for a commitment to civil rights, knowing that it had no chance of success. Four years later he antagonized Stevenson by attacking his call for moderation, angered

Johnson by withdrawing as a favorite son candidate, and incurred the wrath of Kennedy by refusing to support his run for the vice presidency. In 1960, he took the final step in distancing himself from the leaders of his party. It was the logical culmination of a decade marked by his frequent outspokenness, open criticism of those he judged as wrong, and an adamant refusal to accept compromise. Whether dealing with the Republican legislature in Lansing or his own national party, Williams never hesitated or wavered in his convictions or in the belief that he was right. It was his greatest strength but also his most telling political weakness. He later ruefully admitted: "I think I'm more a John the Baptist than a disciple. Maybe I have too much courage and not enough common sense, maybe too much idealism and not enough practicality." His self-assessment was amazingly accurate.[98]

Williams's dissent from the nomination of Johnson made him a hero to many liberals who shared his distrust of the Texas senator, and when he returned to Lansing he found hundreds of telegrams from African Americans, labor leaders, and academics applauding his action and commending him for his courage. His actions in California had quite a different impact on Democratic Party leaders, who felt he had embarrassed Kennedy and jeopardized party unity in the upcoming campaign, and some speculated that he had destroyed any opportunity for a major cabinet position should Kennedy win in November.[99]

In the fall of 1960, for the first time in a dozen years, Soapy Williams was not running for office, but he was preparing for an exhaustive campaign in his home state and across the nation. He was the greatest vote getter in Michigan history and was determined to help elect his political protégé, Lieutenant Governor John Swainson, to ensure continuation of his program of liberal reform. In his final address to the state legislature he noted that "the 'Fabulous Fifties' or the 'Frustrating Fifties'" had given way to either "the 'Sorry Sixties' or the 'Splendid Sixties.'" He argued that the new decade held immense potential for the state but only if Michigan addressed its continuing social problems. He refrained from discussing the financial stalemate and disaster that had plagued his last year in office but made it clear that he was still committed to enacting sweeping economic and social reforms. The election of Swainson was a personal challenge, as it would ensure his legacy and continue his struggle for a New Deal for Michigan.[100]

Williams faced a second campaign in 1960. Despite his actions in Los Angeles, he was convinced that Kennedy was indebted to him for the nomination and would name him to a major cabinet position. Labor leaders promoted him as a potential secretary of labor, and other liberals in the party saw him as a perfect candidate to head the Department of Health, Education, and Welfare (HEW). Congressman Charles Vanik of Ohio wrote him: "You could be the greatest Secretary of H.E.W. in history—and President later!" In a press conference after the convention, Williams announced that he would "welcome" an appointment in the Kennedy administration and would be "happy" to head HEW. Although he was not on the ballot in 1960, Williams was campaigning for a cabinet position.[101]

To gain a major appointment, Williams needed a Kennedy victory, and he made it clear that he was willing to work for the nominee anywhere in the nation. He called Kennedy several times with unsolicited suggestions for campaign strategy and volunteered to work for a Democratic victory. Williams was stunned that Kennedy had arrived in Los Angeles without a prepared acceptance speech. Although he had given a successful talk, Williams cautioned him that "from now on each appearance is an act of state. A single slip can lose more than many high moments of inspired brilliance." He urged Kennedy to focus on ethnic groups (as Williams had done in Michigan) and gave him the dates of the Pulaski Day celebrations in Michigan, the Polish Congress in Chicago, and von Steuben Day in New York.[102]

In August the Democratic nominee summoned Michigan's governor to meet with him in Hyannis Port to discuss campaign strategy. Williams was delighted to have the ear of the candidate and the opportunity to gain his approval for a position in the new administration. On August 5, Williams flew with Kennedy in a small plane from New York City to Cape

Cod. The noise of the engine was so loud that they often had to communicate in writing. Kennedy asked for advice about the proposed TV debates with Republican nominee Richard Nixon, and Williams replied that specific issues are not as important on television as who "the people [are] going to believe is sincere." When they landed Kennedy's aides told Williams that they would use him as a major force in the campaign, with particular stress on California, Illinois, and New York, states with large black populations and a tradition of political liberalism. Williams was also to use his appeal with ethnic groups to attack Nixon for Republican failures to work for the freedom of Eastern Europe.[103]

Despite his actions at the convention, Williams seemed to be back in the good graces of Kennedy and plunged into the campaign with his usual energy and forcefulness. He divided his time between working for Swainson in Michigan and for Kennedy in California and New York. In both states he gave speeches on civil rights and economic growth and attacked those who used Kennedy's Catholicism as an issue. He also sent the nominee lengthy reports on his prospects for victory. He was pessimistic about Kennedy's chances in New York and urged him to utilize Stevenson and Eleanor Roosevelt. He also noted that "the Negro community is generally apathetic—dissatisfaction with Johnson" and called for Kennedy to publicly meet with Martin Luther King. He was more optimistic about California, despite the lack of effort from "the Stevenson people," and predicted that "the state "will probably go for Kennedy."[104]

His assessment of Kennedy's chances in Michigan stressed the fact that Johnson's selection had alienated blacks and union officials. The Texan "was some load to bear," but he might appeal "to the hillbillies from Kentucky and Tennessee" who had migrated to the state in the past two decades. Williams promised to deliver the state for Kennedy if he and his organization were allowed to run the campaign. He told the nominee to make sure to have his brother and campaign manager Robert Kennedy "stay the hell out of here" and leave the Michigan effort to local Democrats.[105]

Williams would eventually spend two weeks campaigning for Kennedy in New York and a week in California. He also gave speeches promoting the ticket in Indiana, Illinois, Wisconsin, Pennsylvania, Kansas, Colorado, and Ohio. As instructed, he attacked Nixon and Eisenhower for not supporting the liberation of Eastern Europe and for not confronting Soviet leader Nikita Khrushchev with a congressional resolution on captured nations. He claimed that Nixon "talked tough" but took no action against the Soviet Union. He also criticized the vice president for his refusal to criticize the anti-communist campaign of Joe McCarthy, for not working for disarmament, and for a lack of commitment to civil rights.[106]

Between campaign stops for Kennedy, Williams shuttled back to Michigan to work for Swainson, Senator Pat McNamara, and the national ticket. On Labor Day, he met Kennedy at the Detroit airport, rode with him during the traditional parade through downtown, and introduced him at a speech delivered at Cadillac Square. On October 13-14, Williams joined Kennedy and Swainson on a two-day campaign swing across the state by train, culminating with a speech on the steps of the Kalamazoo City Hall. He endured an awkward moment when he had to introduce Eisenhower at the opening of the Detroit Auto Show, but refrained from attacking the outgoing president, claiming that cars were "bi-partisan."[107]

The 1960 returns were a triumph for Williams. Kennedy's narrow victory included success in Michigan and New York, the states where Williams had campaigned most actively. Swainson and incumbent Democratic senator McNamara both scored impressive victories. Williams had proven to be an effective national campaigner and was convinced his efforts would lead to a significant position in the new administration. He knew there was still distrust of Kennedy among liberals and African Americans, and he seemed to be the perfect man to reach out to these groups.

Kennedy and his aides were aware of Williams's contributions to securing a first-ballot nomination and in the victory over Nixon, but they were still distrustful of his unwavering liberalism. His narrow margin in the election and the continued control of most congressional committees by southerners made Williams's appointment to the cabinet a risky proposition. When Kennedy met with his transition team on Cape Cod after the election, he told his advisers that there were four men he particularly wanted in his administration: Orville Freeman, former congressman George McGovern of South Dakota, Frank Coffin of Maine, and Williams. But it was unclear just what post best suited the Michigan governor.[108]

The two natural positions were secretary of health, education, and welfare or secretary of labor, but Kennedy was convinced that Williams was too combative, liberal, and unpredictable for either. His strong identification with Reuther and the labor movement would lead to criticism that the new administration was under the influence of the big unions, and Kennedy decided on Arthur Goldberg, a labor lawyer whose past conflicts with construction union officials deflected any claims that his appointment was in deference to labor leaders. The selection of Williams as head of HEW seemed equally dangerous. The fiscal crisis in Michigan had gained Williams a reputation for "prodigality" and would weaken his effectiveness with conservative congressional leaders. "There were just too many difficulties" with Williams, Kennedy concluded. "I just don't think he is the man to go before this Congress and request big spending bills for education and medical care." Kennedy chose Governor Abraham Ribicoff of Connecticut, a far safer pick.[109]

Personal issues as well as political calculations may have influenced Kennedy's reluctance to offer a major appointment to Williams. Animosity between the two Democratic leaders had been constant since Williams's dismissal of Kennedy's abortive run for the vice presidency in 1956. Williams's frequent and outspoken criticism of Kennedy's commitment to civil rights and his rather patronizing tone during their meeting on the issue in Georgetown in August had angered the Massachusetts senator, and the public dissent from the selection of Johnson further distanced the two. Kennedy recognized Williams's campaign skills and popularity with major elements of the Democratic Party, but the governor's strident criticism of

Stevenson, Johnson, and the president elect severely damaged his chances for a significant appointment in the new administration.

There was another consideration that worked against Williams joining the cabinet: Robert McNamara. Staebler knew the Ford Motor Company executive well and had suggested to Kennedy's brother-in-law, Sargent Shriver, that, although he was generally a Republican, McNamara was a liberal on civil rights and other social issues and might be a fine choice to head the Businessmen for Kennedy Committee. Although he was not selected for the position, Kennedy and his aides were impressed with McNamara and were considering him for secretary of defense. McNamara had often voted for Democrats in Michigan, and Kennedy's advisers asked Staebler to find out whether he had voted for their candidate in 1960. They were ecstatic to find that he had supported Kennedy. McNamara, however, had a long and deep loathing of Mennen Williams. He was convinced that Reuther controlled Williams and the UAW had been destructive to the automobile industry. He also believed that the governor's fiscal irresponsibility had driven Michigan to bankruptcy. Although he had voted for Democrats Phil Hart for the Senate and Jim O'Hara for Congress, he had made it publicly known that he would never vote for Soapy Williams. With McNamara as defense secretary, it would have been extremely awkward to have his Michigan rival serving in the same cabinet.[110]

Having ruled out a cabinet-level appointment, Kennedy searched for a position that would appease Williams and capitalize on his strong identification with civil rights. He determined that the best place was as assistant secretary of state for Africa, despite that fact that Williams had no experience in foreign affairs.

Kennedy had made a major issue of Republican inattention to Africa in his presidential campaign, and with over a dozen nations on the continent scheduled for independence in 1961 the area was one of increasing significance. The position as head of a traditionally minor agency in the State Department was, however, a far cry from being a member of the cabinet. When

Kennedy called to tell him of his appointment as head of the African Bureau, Williams was bitterly disappointed and refused to agree to an announcement. Kennedy contacted former Connecticut governor Chester Bowles, a longtime friend of Williams who had worked with him on the civil rights issue in 1960, and urged him to lobby the Michigan governor to accept. He also had his historian in residence, Arthur M. Schlesinger Jr., an associate of Williams in Americans for Democratic Action, call to urge him to take the position in the State Department. Bowles and Schlesinger both argued that African policy was an extremely important issue for the new administration and Williams could provide a crucial liberal voice in American foreign policy.[111]

Despite pressure from the two liberals, Williams remained ambivalent. He felt he deserved a cabinet position and had little interest in confronting the bureaucratic maze of the State Department. He had long distrusted Kennedy's liberalism and the refusal to offer him a cabinet position seemed to confirm his suspicion that the President-elect favored pragmatism over principle whether selecting a vice president or appointing a cabinet. Williams, however, had few options. He had rejected another run for governor of Michigan and staked his political future on a Democratic victory in 1960 and an appointment in Washington. There were no attractive alternatives and Williams finally called Kennedy and accepted.

Williams flew to Washington on November 30, and the next day Kennedy announced his appointment at a press conference at his Georgetown home. Kennedy made a valiant attempt to argue for the significance of Williams's new position by contending that it was the very first appointment of his new administration and showed the vital importance of Africa. He claimed that "the fate of Africa, which is now the object of a giant Communist offensive, will affect the security of every citizen in the United States" and Williams brought "long experience, energy, compassion, imagination, and devotion to the future of his county" to the crucial post. When Williams spoke he stressed his previous travel to Africa and echoed Kennedy's cold war rhetoric by calling Africa a battleground between "the expansion of freedom" and "the further encroachment of Communism upon the free world." Schlesinger later asked Kennedy if Williams had been disappointed with his new position, and Kennedy responded: "He was at first, but I think he is feeling better now. After all, you could hardly ask for a more challenging job." Later that same day Kennedy introduced Ribicoff as the head of HEW.[112]

Heading the African Bureau may have been "challenging," but it was far from the position of power or influence Williams had anticipated. A year earlier he had every reason to expect he might be president elect; now he was headed to Washington as the leader of traditionally the least important area of the State Department. The challenge to Williams was not just running the African Bureau but reasserting his influence in his party and securing the support of the new president. He was determined not only to make Africa a center of American foreign policy but to establish himself as a major force in Kennedy's New Frontier.

VI

AFRICA FOR THE AFRICANS

Williams and the New Frontier, 1961–63

What we want for the African is what the
Africans want for themselves.

—*G. Mennen Williams in Nairobi,*
Kenya, February 1961

In late 1958, Soapy Williams was a major contender for his
party's presidential nomination. Even after his campaign for the
White House collapsed following Michigan's financial crisis, he
had every reason be believe that he would be selected for a
major cabinet position in the new administration. In 1960, he
was forty-nine years old, and as secretary of labor or the head of
Health, Education, and Welfare he would remain a national
figure and could still pursue the presidency in 1968. His selection as assistant secretary of state for African affairs, however,
looked like a quick path to political obscurity. The African
Bureau had only been created in 1958, and it was the least
prominent of all the geographical divisions of the State Department. As an assistant secretary he would likely have little direct
access to the president and would receive scant attention from
the press. Williams was used to power and attention, and both
would be difficult to obtain in the New Frontier.[1]

Although Kennedy's cabinet rebuff was a major disappointment, Williams's innate optimism reemerged, as he decided
that he would go to Washington as a minor figure but use his
position to capture the attention of Kennedy and the public.
Williams quickly determined that the African Bureau offered a
chance to reclaim his role as a leading figure in the Democratic

Party. The champion of civil rights at home would become the spokesman for racial equality and majority rule abroad.

Liberals were generally delighted by Williams's appointment and saw it as symbolic of the new importance of Africa for America. Disappointed that Kennedy had not selected Stevenson or Bowles to head the State Department, they hailed Williams as a strong and necessary voice for liberalism in the new administration. (Stevenson was appointed ambassador to the United Nations and Bowles undersecretary of state). Africans were also impressed that Kennedy had chosen a man of Williams's stature for the position and assumed the nominee would have access to the president to implement a new approach to the continent. Bureaucrats in the African Bureau were also pleased, as they saw Williams's selection as an indication Kennedy would give Africa a high priority in his administration. (The bureau's existing director, Joseph Satterthwaite, noted that he was "most fascinated to learn that I'd been filling a position 'second to none' in the administration.")[2]

Not all reaction to the appointment was as positive. *Newsday* ran a long piece highly critical of Williams's selection. The paper noted that Africa "could be the most important area of the world" in the next four years and Williams was completely unprepared for the job. Not only did he lack any diplomatic experience, but he had "plunged his state into economic morass." His was "purely a political appointment," as his only qualification was that he had "delivered Michigan to the Democratic column." It concluded: "Soapy Williams as the top man on Africa—oh no!" Barry Goldwater sarcastically commented: "I'm glad they sent Soapy Williams to Africa. If we'd been elected, that's exactly where we'd have sent him!"[3]

Williams became convinced his new position had the potential to be of major importance. In 1960, seventeen African nations had gained independence and most of the rest of the continent was moving rapidly toward the end of colonialism. Kennedy had made Africa a major campaign issue in his battle with Nixon, chastising Republicans for their inattention to the continent and their reluctance to support a rapid end to European rule. When the State Department refused funds to transport African students to the United States, Kennedy arranged for a grant of one hundred thousand dollars from the Joseph Kennedy Foundation to pay their expenses, and after the leader of Guinea expressed an interest in meeting the Democratic nominee Kennedy sent a helicopter to fly him to Disneyland for a brief discussion. Williams also was aware that Kennedy had chaired the Senate Subcommittee on Africa and had provoked the wrath of many in the foreign policy establishment with a highly publicized speech critical of France's refusal to consider independence for Algeria.[4]

Given Kennedy's past interest in Africa, Williams assumed his new post would ensure direct access to the president and the chance to play a major role in designing a new U.S. approach to the continent. He wrote Schlesinger: "Jack has really convinced me that as of the moment this African adventure is the greatest challenge I could hope to meet. I am completely happy with the idea and am looking forward with great anticipation to it."[5]

Kennedy's interest in Africa and support of decolonization were in contrast to the conservative approach that had characterized the Eisenhower administration, under which Washington had been reluctant to commit to the end of European rule and warned that "premature independence" would lead to unstable nations unable to resist the "new imperialism" of the Soviet Union. Secretary of State John Foster Dulles was convinced that Moscow was directing the anticolonial effort and had denounced African neutralism in the cold war as "a transitional stage to communism." Eisenhower claimed that African nationalism "resembled a torrent over-running everything in its path, including, frequently, the best interests of those concerned." America in the 1950s remained closely identified with its European allies and hesitant to endorse the end of colonialism. Aid to African nations continued to be controlled by the European Bureau in the State Department rather than the African Bureau, and African diplomats claimed that wives of U.S. officials often slipped on gloves before shaking hands with a black African. The outgoing administration indicated its lack of concern with Africa when after Kennedy's election it tried to appoint a number of older career State Department bureaucrats to ambassadorships on the continent. Only the protests of Robert Kennedy, Bowles, and Williams prevented the move.[6]

From his appointment on December 1, 1960, to the Kennedy inauguration on January 20, 1961, Williams planned a strategy to revitalize the African Bureau and realign U.S. foreign policy in favor of an "African first" position. Williams had traveled to Africa, but had little direct knowledge of the continent. He was fortunate to find an assistant with a strong background in African affairs. Wayne Fredericks had worked for the Kellogg Company in Battle Creek, Michigan, overseeing marketing in Africa and had also served in the Defense Department and the Ford Foundation. He was a close friend of Neil Staebler and had considered running for Congress from Michigan's Third District. Following Williams's appointment, Staebler arranged for him to meet with Fredericks at Staebler's home in Ann Arbor, where they found they shared a commitment to racial equality and a stronger American identification with independent Africa. Williams persuaded Kennedy to appoint Fredericks deputy assistant secretary for African affairs in the State Department, where he would run the daily operations of the bureau. Williams also retained Henry Tosca, a veteran of the State Department with strong ties to business, as third in command. Williams judged Tosca "a tremendous realist" who understood Washington's complex politics and could handle much of the paperwork, leaving Williams and Fredericks to deal with "the more general field of leadership."[7]

While Williams and Fredericks prepared to revitalize the African Bureau and make Africa a focus of U.S. foreign policy, there were strong indications that the incoming administration shared their commitment to a new emphasis on the continent. During the 1960 campaign Kennedy had sent Harriman on a fact-finding mission to Africa, and the former New York governor concluded that the United States was "doing an awful job." Harriman, who had been a close associate of Williams in the Democratic Advisory Council in the 1950s, encouraged Kennedy to make Africa a campaign issue and commit to major changes in Washington's policies toward the region.[8]

Kennedy's preinaugural Task Force on Africa echoed Harriman's call for a more vigorous American approach. It urged more U.S. aid; younger, more energetic diplomats; and the acceptance of African neutralism. The group contended that "African radicalism envisages an African order, not a communist one" and America "should not presume that the time has come in Africa to 'choose up sides.'" It concluded that "nonalignment of African states in the Cold War is in no sense detrimental to our interests," as true neutralism was a denial of communist advances.[9]

In the interim between Williams's appointment and confirmation, he and Fredericks developed a number of initiatives to illustrate Washington's new commitment to the continent. Williams was convinced that first he and Kennedy had to show a personal interest in Africa and its diplomats. Under Eisenhower, African officials had rarely been invited to the White House, and the president had little contact with African leaders. To Williams, it was crucial that Kennedy personally meet and court African leaders, and he made this his first goal when he took office. He also felt that he had to demonstrate his own interest through travel to Africa. Many African leaders had never met a U.S. official, and Williams was determined to change their perception that Africa was of little importance to the United States by becoming "the American ambassador to Africa." During his five years in Washington, Williams would travel to Africa eleven times and visit every nation on the continent with the exception of South Africa.

Aside from vigorous personal diplomacy by Kennedy and Williams, the former governor also was convinced that he needed to be the "spokesman" for Africa at home by showing the American public and Congress the importance of the region and the need for more direct U.S. involvement. In his first year in office he would deliver thirty-three speeches across the nation to try to convince Americans of the significance of the continent.

Williams also argued that Washington had to abandon its distrust of African neutralism in the cold war battle between America and the Soviet Union. The condemnation of African nonalignment that characterized the Eisenhower years had alienated Africans and, ironically, worked to make them more likely to seek aid from the Soviet Union. To Williams, it was not necessary for any African nation "to align itself with us and seek the exact world we seek." America had only to persuade African countries to reject "the subservience communism demands." By denying communist control, neutralism was actually a victory for America, as it denied the Marxist theory of inevitable revolution. Washington could "win" the cold war in Africa simply by not losing it to communism. The United States also needed to recognize that the anti-Western rhetoric of some African leaders was a heritage of colonialism, not a sign of Moscow's influence.[10]

Williams was also convinced of the need for a major increase in foreign aid to the continent. As African states were naturally reluctant to continue their economic dependence on their former colonial masters, the United States had to become a major source of financial assistance to prevent them from turning to communist nations for help. He argued that America had been "too cautious" in its aid programs and there was "too much paper work" for African officials, who, unlike Europeans, did not have "a lot of economists" familiar with U.S. procedures. He made it clear that he would reverse the existing policy of funneling requests for foreign aid to the European Bureau and would work for increased assistance throughout the continent, even to nations such as Ghana and Guinea, which were perceived as "anti-American."[11]

He also planned to change U.S. policy in three specific areas: the Congo, South Africa, and the Portuguese colonies of Angola and Mozambique. The Congo had degenerated into factionalism and chaos immediately after it gained its independence from Belgium in the summer of 1960. Although Eisenhower had supported a unified Congo and intervention by the United Nations, Williams judged his actions as too closely aligned with European support of a divided Congo and too distrustful of the UN. America also needed a clearer policy in support of the immediate decolonization of the Portuguese colonies and had to move beyond mere verbal condemnation of South Africa's racist policy of apartheid.

In the ten weeks between his appointment and confirmation Williams had developed an ambitious agenda: He would persuade Kennedy to become personally involved with African diplomats and would demonstrate the importance of Africa through his own foreign travel and an extensive domestic speaking tour. He would convince Washington of the benefits of African neutralism, increase dramatically U.S. aid to the continent, and force a more aggressive American policy toward the Congo, Portugal, and South Africa. He would concentrate on symbolism before substance, as he would first demonstrate to Africans their significance for America and then move to implement specific policies. This approach was consistent with Williams's flamboyance and love of the dramatic and his impatience with the details of policy. One State Department official recalled: "Soapy Williams was a wonderful guy" who "was interested in establishing a general relationship with the Africans that was favorable and friendly . . . he was just not as interested in the day-to-day business."[12]

Williams knew there were major obstacles to his vision of an African first foreign policy, as many in the State and Defense Departments were highly skeptical of the importance of Africa and reluctant to challenge European allies on African issues. "Europeanists" in Washington were unconvinced of the need to place Africa above Europe and remained distrustful of neutralism in the cold war. Strategic and military considerations such as the preservation of the North Atlantic Treaty Organization (NATO) and the continued presence of missile-tracking stations in South Africa seemed more important than cultivating nations that, according to Undersecretary of State George Ball, had "names that seemed like typographical errors." Congress also was reluctant to allocate substantial aid to a continent lacking the geographical proximity of Latin America, the assumed strategic importance of Asia, or the cultural ties of Europe.[13]

There was another major restraint on Williams's plans for a dramatic new approach to Africa: America's racial situation. Segregation was a powerful handicap to maintaining friendly relations with Africa, and each example of violent resistance to the civil rights movement was monitored carefully in Africa and fueled Soviet propaganda. In addition, African diplomats suffered near daily humiliation in their travels within the United States, particularly in segregated restaurants on the road between New York and Washington, D.C. Williams warned that American segregation was a major burden in establishing a good relationship with Africans: "A pin does not drop here that the sound is picked up all over Africa." He later recalled that "our reputation with Africans would go up and down" depending on the racial situation in America.[14]

Williams was eager to begin the reversal of U.S. inattention to Africa. In early January he left Nancy in Michigan and flew to Washington and the family's new home at 1401 Thirty-first Street in Georgetown (next door to Jackie Kennedy's mother.) When Nancy arrived a few days later she found a sign on the front door in Williams's trademark green ink on African Bureau stationery: "Welcome to Washington sweetheart! It'll be good to see you! All my love, Soapy."[15]

Although he had not been formally confirmed, Williams immediately arranged an appointment with Joseph Satterthwaite, the outgoing head of the African Bureau, and had his first encounter with the bureaucratic maze of Washington. Kennedy had designated Clark Clifford, Truman's secretary of defense, to coordinate all foreign policy appointments, and he told Satterthwaite that he could not talk to Williams until after the appointee had consulted with him. Williams ignored protocol and met with Satterthwaite at the State Department to discuss the organization of the bureau and its existing policies. He was appalled by the shabby furnishings and cramped offices on the seventh floor (Satterthwaite called the African Bureau "skid row") and found most employees demoralized by the inattention of the Eisenhower administration. Williams suggested that he travel to Africa even before the inauguration to demonstrate the importance of the continent, but Republican secretary of state Christian Herder rejected the plan.[16]

On the day of Kennedy's inaugural, Williams held a meeting with the staff of the African Bureau and Bowles to discuss a new and aggressive approach to Africa. That night he and Nancy attended cocktail parties at the homes of Bowles and Robert Kennedy and a reception for David Dubansky of the United Garment Workers before going to the inaugural ball. The next morning he was at the State Department at 8:00 a.m. to plan his first trip to Africa.[17]

Before he could depart for Africa, Williams had to be confirmed, and on January 24 he appeared before the Senate Foreign Relations Committee. He explained that the Mennen Company had no interests in Africa and stressed his travels to the continent. Although Senator Earl Long of Louisiana launched into a long monologue against foreign aid and civil rights, Williams showed uncharacteristic restraint and refused to be drawn into a debate. When Senator Frank Church of Idaho focused on Williams's statements defending African neutralism in the cold war, the nominee explained that they must "expect a certain amount of this neutralism" but reaffirmed his view that such policies would be beneficial to the United States. After twenty minutes the committee was finished, and Williams was confirmed unanimously[18]

Once in office, Williams's first priority was to convince Kennedy of the importance of paying personal attention to African diplomats. Many in the New Frontier assumed that the ultraliberal Williams would have little direct influence with the president, as Kennedy and his aides stressed toughness, focus, and a cool and unemotional style, all absent in the new head of the African Bureau. Williams, however, had significant influence, as Kennedy respected his political success and knew of his popularity among labor leaders, blacks, and liberals. Roger Hilsman, the State Department's director of intelligence and research, observed that Williams "had a big enough reputation to command a public audience at will" and enjoyed "a special relationship" with Kennedy. Carl Kaysen of the National Security Council noted that Kennedy always treated Williams with great respect: "He treated anybody who was a successful elective official with a special respect, because he thought this was a very tough competition and anybody who could win it deserved, you know, that kind of treatment."[19]

Williams immediately used his access to Kennedy to arrange

personal visits to the White House for nearly every African leader who visited Washington. Eleven Africans would meet with Kennedy in 1961, ten in 1962, and seven in 1963. The president even took time during the Cuban missile crisis to spend a few minutes with Milton Obote of Uganda. Williams was crucial in establishing and ensuring the success of these Oval Office encounters. He sent Kennedy handwritten briefs before each meeting with information about the individual and his country and the major issues involved. He also met with each official in his office in the State Department and accompanied him to the White House. After their few minutes with Kennedy, Williams generally hosted a luncheon or reception for the guest.[20]

Kennedy was extremely effective in his personal diplomacy with African leaders. He digested Williams's notes and made certain to mention at least one specific issue or event related to the country of each guest. Tom Mboya of Kenya, for example, was amazed to find that the president could discuss the various labor factions in his nation. Sekou Toure, the mercurial leader of Guinea, left the White House convinced Kennedy was not only informed about Africa but also dedicated to significant changes in U.S. policy. He was especially impressed that the president took him upstairs to meet his wife and children. At times Kennedy was a bit overenthusiastic and promised several officials that he would make a trip to Africa when there were no plans for such a visit.[21]

Williams's ability to involve Kennedy with Africans directly was one of his major triumphs in Washington. The president's meetings with leaders of the continent generated headlines throughout Africa, and even those critical of his policies were impressed with his personal commitment to visiting officials. Williams followed by making his own efforts to establish a rapport with Africans in the capital. He and Nancy hosted a "French only" dinner at his home for Africans from former French colonies. The menu was classic French, and only French could be spoken. Williams, who arranged for private French lessons in his office at the State Department every Thursday at 3:30 (he even conjugated French verbs on scraps of paper during meetings), offered a long toast in French to a new era of U.S.-African relations. Although technically correct, Williams never mastered fluent pronunciation. (Kennedy once quipped: "I'm not very good at conversing in French, but I can under-stand every word Soapy says in French—it sounds so much like English!"). Africans, however, were appreciative of his efforts.[22]

Williams followed with a more informal and controversial event: a square dance for African diplomats at the State Depart-ment. For years Williams had enjoyed square dancing in the ethnic clubs and churches of Michigan, and he decided that Africans should be a part of this American tradition. Williams had the tables and chairs removed from the cafeteria and hired a Western band to play. Dressed in a plaid flannel shirt and handmade black wing tip shoes, he first gave instructions and then served as the "caller" while Africans tried to negotiate the "Virginia Reel." Many staid State Department officials were appalled by the event and thought it undignified and designed as a publicity stunt to gain Williams press coverage, but the Africans were overjoyed by the affair. Williams argued that they appreciated the informality of his approach in contrast to the rigid social rules of their former colonial masters.[23]

Gestures such as the square dance, the French dinner, and Kennedy's receptions for Africans were immensely successful. Although they did not represent any change in policy, they met the intended goal of showing Africans that America was inter-ested in their ideas and they now had the attention of U.S. officials. The most dramatic symbol of Washington's new con-cern for Africa was the extensive trips Williams took to the continent.

Even as a young boy Williams had been a ceaseless traveler. He had accompanied his parents on several of their overseas vacations and in college had made a long trip to Europe. He and Nancy had visited the Middle East, Latin America, and Europe several times, and in 1958 they made a trip to Africa. Given his love of travel, it was natural that Williams would become the first major U.S. official to visit Africa.

His trips were not only the result of his own enjoyment of foreign travel. To Williams they served a crucial diplomatic function, as he was convinced that Africans had felt neglected under Eisenhower and he could demonstrate the importance of the region through personal visits. He also believed strongly in personal diplomacy and assumed that the contacts he made with African leaders would strengthen their ties to the United States. Finally, he saw his travels as a way to bond with the African people. In many ways his African trips were similar to his exhaustive campaigns for governor in Michigan. All included the standard receptions, press conferences, and dinners, but they also involved personal interaction between Williams and the African people. He transferred his handshaking style from the auto plants of Michigan to the streets of Nairobi, Lagos, and Tunis as he plunged into the crowds offering greetings in English and French and shaking every hand available. Critics charged that his trips were extravagant, self-indulgent, and did little to influence policy, but to Williams they were essential to setting a new tone in American relations with Africa.

Williams's African travels were lengthy and exhausting. On February 15, 1961, less than a month after taking office, he left for a whirlwind trip to twelve countries that lasted over a month. Nancy accompanied him, as she would on several of his trips, and Williams insisted on paying her expenses out of his own pocket. When the couple arrived in an African country, Soapy generally went to the embassy to consult with the ambassador and staff while Nancy toured hospitals and schools. She wrote her own reports on health, education, and the condition of women and used the trips to arrange shipments of books, medicine, and clothing from American churches, charities, and corporations. When his wife could not accompany him, Williams wrote her daily letters describing the landscape and people. In Ghana he delayed his plane to go back to the hotel to buy her an anniversary gift.[24]

Both Soapy and Nancy were stunned by the poverty they found in Africa. They were shocked to find children in Uganda who had "never eaten meat, eggs, fish, had never drunk milk" and their first look at the economic conditions reinforced Williams's determination to fight for a major increase in U.S. aid to the continent.[25]

After touring the embassy, Williams usually met with the nation's leaders at a reception or formal dinner, where he gave out autographed copies of Kennedy's book, *A Strategy for Peace*. On these occasions he generally avoided discussion of specific policies and instead tried to establish a personal relationship with the African leader. When he met Kenyan prime minister Jomo Kenyatta the African wore the traditional red rosebud representing his political party in his lapel, and Williams quickly removed his green bow tie so the two leaders could exchange their symbols. At an outdoor black tie dinner hosted by Ivory Coast leader Felix Houphouet-Boigny, the Williamses were warned that snakes were common after dark. During the dinner Nancy felt something cold on her foot. Terrified, but not wanting to disrupt the program, she discreetly called a waiter, who removed Boigny's Pekinese puppy.[26]

The formal dinners were customary for visiting officials, but the State Department was not prepared for Williams's forays into campaignlike personal diplomacy. An American consul in Algeria reported that Williams was not concerned with meeting political leaders but was interested "primarily in seeing as many people and projects as time permitted." He addressed both formal and informal gatherings in "highly accented French" and repeatedly stopped his motorcade to talk with construction workers and shopkeepers. When he found a food center displaying bags of string beans labeled "A Gift from Michigan," he offered a long description of farming techniques in his home state. In Nyasaland, President Hastings Banda gave Williams a fly whisk, symbolic of wisdom and authority, and made him an honorary Malawi chief, the only white man ever so honored.[27]

Williams's visit to Ethiopia on February 23–24, 1961, was typical of his intense pace and personal diplomacy. After an exhausting four-hour flight, he and the sixteen people who had accompanied him were escorted in a motorcade to a dinner for one hundred guests at Emperor Haile Selassie's palace. When it was his turn to speak, Williams abandoned his prepared text (although copies had already been circulated to the press) and gave an impromptu address on American relations with Africa in his college French, unaware that the emperor did not speak the language. The next day he had a forty-five-minute meeting with Selassie and a luncheon with Ethiopian business leaders and journalists, followed by a visit to a local hospital and an unscheduled walk through the central market, where he talked with vendors. At five he held a press conference and that night hosted a reception at the embassy.[28]

The visits by Williams and his party strained the often meager resources of American embassies, as officials had to arrange transportation, lodging, security, and food for nearly two dozen staff members and reporters. Many African airports did not have lights, so officials had to avoid night landings. Although Soapy and Nancy usually stayed at the embassy, there was the need to find housing for others in the party; to hire cars, drivers, and security guards; and to meet the costs of formal receptions and dinners. Typical expenses for a two-day visit by Williams included $400 for local transportation, $300 for added staff, $400 for increased telegraph costs, $300 for insurance, and over $1,000 for a formal reception. When Williams arrived in Gabon, Ambassador Charles Darlington and his wife had to borrow plates, silverware, napkins, and chairs and hire six waiters for a luncheon with ninety guests and an evening reception for four hundred.[29]

Despite the expense and inconvenience, U.S. diplomats in Africa were eager to host Williams, as his visits generated favorable publicity and indicated the importance of Africa for the new administration. They also used Williams to lobby local officials. Ambassador William Mahoney had a stormy relationship with Ghanian leader Kwame Nkrumah and asked Williams to help ease the tensions. He told the assistant secretary that Nkrumah would no longer meet with him, but he "knows quite a bit about you: your consistent liberal record as Governor of Michigan, your long fight for social justice, your defense of the interests of organized labor, I think he admires you for this." Mahoney suggested that only Williams had the prestige to convince Nkrumah to moderate his anti-American rhetoric[30]

Williams made three extensive trips to Africa during his first year in office (February 15 to March 19; July 19 to September

1; and September 29 to October 24), and both Africans and "Africanists" judged them extremely effective. African leaders were flattered to receive a high-ranking American official and were buoyed by Williams's energy and repeated assurances of the importance of the continent to the United States. The trips also raised morale among American diplomats in Africa, who felt that they were part of a new approach to the region and now had a firm advocate in Washington for a stronger "African first" stance. Members of the African Bureau also were energized by their leader's travel, as the trips captured the attention of the media and made African issues more prominent. Williams was ecstatic with the reception he received in Africa and was even further convinced of the importance of such "hands-on," personal diplomacy. He wrote Kennedy that his trips showed the value of "the person-to-person approach," as "many Africans had never shaken hands with an American or exchanged words with a foreign official." One historian concluded: "The most symbolic success of the Kennedy African policy was Governor Williams himself. No other wandering official foreigner had ever been so liked and trusted in Africa."[31]

Not everyone in Washington shared this positive appraisal of his frequent travels. Some in the State Department and White House felt that the trips were designed more to generate publicity for Soapy than to influence policy and noted that his constant absences from Washington for travel and speeches left a void in the African Bureau. Many in the bureaucracy also found that the lengthy summaries of his trips, which he sent to Secretary of State Dean Rusk and President Kennedy, were more like travel accounts than specific policy recommendations. Williams always wrote long, detailed descriptions of farming, clothing, geography, religion, customs, and education that had little to do with foreign policy. These personal observations often ran to twenty-five or thirty single-spaced pages, hardly examples of the precision and focus most valued in the Kennedy administration. After his second trip to Africa, Williams sent a twenty-eight-page memo with his comments on dress, dances, and geography to Kennedy. National Security Adviser McGeorge Bundy quickly condensed it into a one-page summary with a note to the president that "this is all you need to read!"[32]

Although Bundy did not appreciate Williams's verbosity, his hands-on approach to international relations found a curious ally when Vice President Lyndon Johnson toured Africa in April 1961. Bored and despondent over his lack of influence in Washington, Johnson eagerly accepted Kennedy's suggestion that he represent the United States at the anniversary of the independence of Senegal. Like Williams, Johnson approached the trip like a campaign stop and ignored his formal itinerary to plunge into crowds to shake hands and pass out American flag pins. To the shock of embassy officials, he abandoned his prepared text and declared that Washington was going to "send a lot of aid to Africa." He then went on an impromptu visit to a fishing village, where he promised to send an outboard motor to help improve the villagers' catch. An embassy observer noted:

> This is perhaps the first time the Senegalese public has been exposed to the out-going and informal approach of the veteran American political campaigner . . . smiling, shaking hands and greeting pleased and astonished by-standers who most certainly have not been accustomed to such informality on the part of their former French mentors.

State Department officials were appalled by Johnson's treatment of a diplomatic mission as a political rally, but Williams was delighted. He thought LBJ had "campaigned Senegal as he might have campaigned Texas" and that his informal style and energy were exactly the approach needed to gain the goodwill of the Africans.[33]

Williams's personal diplomacy stressed informality and spontaneity over traditional diplomatic procedure and careful statements. This approach led to the most controversial incident of his career in Washington when he caused a diplomatic storm with his comments in Nairobi, Kenya, during his first trip to Africa.

Prior to his departure, Williams met with Kennedy to discuss the need to make African issues a top priority in the administration and claimed that the president agreed that America wanted only "what the Africans wanted for themselves." When he arrived in Kenya, Williams met the press and was asked what American goals on the continent were. He responded: "What we want for the African is what the Africans want for themselves." The press reported that Williams had declared that "Africa is for the Africans," and the reaction was immediate, intense, and sustained.[34]

Whites in South Africa, Rhodesia, Angola, and other European colonies charged that Williams had called for the end of their presence on the continent. At his next stop a reporter asked: "Why do you want to drive all the whites out of Africa?" The South African foreign minister demanded that Williams be fired, as it was clear he meant Africa was only for blacks, and asked if his "ultraliberal" views were shared by the rest of the U.S. government. Portuguese officials called his remarks "irresponsible lunacy," and British diplomats claimed that he had "roughly pushed aside" white Kenyans, saying he only wanted to meet with blacks.[35]

Shocked by the intensity of the response, Williams tried to clarify his remarks. He cabled Rusk that he had never said "Africa is for the Africans" but only "what we want for Africa is what the Africans want for themselves" and explained that he included whites and Asians in his definition of *Africans*. He told the secretary of state: "I honestly believe my actual remarks were within the context of the Administration's statements, although I of course accept all responsibility for any error."[36]

The more Williams tried to explain his comments the more the controversy intensified. The press soon reported a second inflammatory statement. Warning Kenyans about the dangers of communist aggression, he cautioned them to be careful not to let colonialism "be replaced by another tyranny." Reporters then asked if he considered British rule in Africa to have been tyranny. He denied any criticism of Britain, but the remark quickly joined the "Africa is for the Africans" comment as a focus of reaction.[37]

While Williams floundered in attempts to clarify his remarks, the State Department tried to control the damage. Rusk sent a telegram to all the American embassies in Africa stating that "concerning his remarks QUOTE Africa for the Africans END QUOTE Mr. Williams has stated that press reports omitted his statement that these remarks apply to all people regardless of their race or color." Rusk also cabled Williams that

> in view of the propensity of the press to exploit selected frag-
> ments of your recent statements in controversial terms, I
> believe it would help if you would turn aside further ques-
> tions seeking replies to comments others have made on your
> remarks [to avoid further complicating] this tangled
> situation.[38]

While Williams maintained silence, at a press conference on March 1 a reporter asked Kennedy:

> Your roving Ambassador to Africa has been widely criticized
> for some of the statements he has made, that is Mr. Williams,
> including the one of 'Africa for the Africans' and the like. Do
> you find any validity in this criticism, and would you con-
> sider his tour of Africa has been a plus for United States' pol-
> icy?

The president was prepared for the question and replied:

> I think Governor Williams has done very well and I am
> wholly satisfied with his mission. . . . The statement 'Africa
> for the Africans' does not seem to me to be a very unreason-
> able statement. He made it clear that he was talking about all
> those who felt they were Africans, whatever their color
> might be, whatever their race might be. I do not know who
> else Africa should be for.

Williams was grateful for Kennedy's comments and immediately cabled the president: "[I] deeply appreciate your expression of support for me in your press conference."[39]

A few weeks later Kennedy joked about the issue at the Washington press corps' annual Gridiron Dinner when he claimed he had received a telegram from Williams asking whether he could extend his visit to Africa. The president noted that he had replied: "No, Soapy, Africa is for the Africans!" Williams tried to make light of the incident by sending Kennedy a set of cuff links engraved with the initials AFTA (Africa for the Africans) and naming his new French poodle AFTA. Privately Kennedy was less sanguine, as he felt Williams's comments had been rash and his attempted clarifications contradictory. He ordered Bowles to meet with Williams and ask the assistant secretary to clear all future public statements with the State Department.[40]

The controversy over Williams's "Africa for the Africans" comment showed both the strengths and weakness of his personal diplomacy and eagerness to assert a new American commitment to Africa. Despite his later hedging, Williams *did* believe Africa belonged to the Africans, and he meant *black* Africans. The entire basis of his African first strategy was that colonialism was dead and the white enclaves of South Africa, Angola, and Rhodesia were doomed. Washington needed to stop its temporizing and deference to Europeans and white South Africans and align itself with the aspirations of black Africa. He later noted:

> Had I deliberately set out to capture African sympathies with a slogan, I could hardly have done better than my statement. It made America's position toward Africa perfectly clear, and it reached and pleased Africans more immediately than could a thousand diplomatic communiqués.[41]

Williams was accurate, but the frenzied reaction to his remarks demonstrated that there was still strong opposition in Africa, Europe, and Washington to such a radical alteration of U.S. priorities and that the complete black rule of Africa was still a highly volatile issue. The depth of emotion over an African first policy was illustrated immediately following his controversial comments in Kenya when Williams went to Northern Rhodesia. While he was trying to explain his remarks in Nairobi, a white Rhodesian charged the podium and punched Williams in the face. The attacker was arrested and later charged with assault. The next day Williams met with the black leader of Nyasaland, who proclaimed him a "hero" for his call for an end to white rule on the continent.[42]

In his first few months in office Williams had achieved two

of his most important goals: He had persuaded Kennedy to show an active interest in Africa by opening the White House to visiting leaders, and his travels had demonstrated a new concern for the continent. He quickly moved toward a third goal of teaching the American public and Congress of the importance of Africa and educating them about the continent. During his trips he had been the "American ambassador to Africa"; now he would be "Africa's ambassador to America."

Most Americans had little knowledge of either the history or the current situation in Africa. Missionary slides in church basements, Ernest Hemingway short stories, and images of savagery and cannibalism had shaped the general American image of the continent. The violence in the Congo had sharpened the prevailing negative public view of Africa, and the often shrill rhetoric of the continent's leaders led to the impression that the area was generally hostile to the United States. In addition, many in Africa embraced the idea of "African socialism" and one-party rule, and much of the American public saw the region not only as primitive and violent but as communistic and undemocratic. Most committees in Congress were chaired by segregationist southerners decidedly hostile to black Africa and resentful of its leaders' frequent attacks on America's racial problems. Williams faced a sizable challenge in "selling" the public and politicians on the significance of Africa for America.

In 1961, Williams gave thirty-three major speeches across the nation on Africa. As he was overseas for thirteen weeks, he averaged nearly one address a week when home. Some of his talks dealt with specific issues such as policy in the Congo and Washington's decision to support UN resolutions critical of Portugal and South Africa, but most were a more general attempt to educate the public about Africa and to convince the nation of the need for a more active policy toward the continent.

He repeatedly called for America to abandon its lingering ties to Europe and identify more directly with the new independent nations of Africa. In an address at Northwestern University Williams urged a "national commitment" to Africa, as the continent was a "test case." Would the United States support its values of self-determination by pushing for a complete end to colonialism and assisting newly independent states? In Boston he criticized U.S. African policy as "slow in action and cautious in moving." Washington needed to move more quickly to align itself with independent nations and "measure up to the dynamism of the times." He called for an American pledge to ensure the complete independence of "all of Africa" by 1970, hinting that this included the Portuguese colonies and South Africa.[43]

Williams also tried to explain that African socialism was not Marxism but part of a traditional African heritage of communal farming and that one-party rule was necessary to avoid tribal conflict and only "a short-term, transitional arrangement." He also sought to alter the public perception of African violence against whites by pointing out that the Mau Mau rebels in Kenya in the 1950s had killed only ninety whites while more than eleven thousand blacks had died. Finally, Williams repeated his view that African neutralism was a natural result of the inhabitants' colonial heritage and lingering distrust of Europe. Nonalignment was "a manifestation of African independence" not hostility toward the United States. Nonalignment did not mean "nonpreference," as most Africans had a highly favorable image of America. The danger in Africa was not "what the Communists are doing" but "what we are not doing." If America were to firmly support the independence of all of Africa, offer substantial economic aid, and abandon its demands for alignment with the West, Africa would be in no danger of coming under the control of Moscow.[44]

While he tried to change the public perception of Africa, Williams found a more formidable barrier to cordial relations in America's continued racial conflicts. Even before moving to the State Department, Williams had charged that segregation damaged U.S. foreign policy by giving communists a source of propaganda and by making the nation appear hypocritical in its rhetoric about freedom. When he got to Washington, he found segregation the largest burden in establishing a rapport with African leaders. In a speech at the University of Oklahoma after his first trip to Africa, he called racial discrimination "a blight on America" and poisonous to developing good relations with Africa. He was particularly embarrassed and angry by the humiliation segregation forced on African diplomats in the United States.[45]

African representatives had complained for years about the difficulties of obtaining housing, service in restaurants and barbershops, and quality schools for their children in the Washington, D.C. area and about discrimination in motels and restaurants along Route 40, which connected the capital with New York. With the surge of independence in Africa in 1960 and 1961, the problem escalated, as there were now several hundred African diplomats in America. Williams saw the issue of discrimination against Africans as more than an embarrassment; it was a direct burden on establishing favorable relations between the new administration and Africa countries.[46]

As soon as he took office Williams set up a system to monitor incidents of discrimination against Africans in the Washington area and along Route 40 and met with Chief of Protocol Angier Biddle Duke to try to lobby restaurants and motels to open their facilities to all races. In a speech delivered to representatives of the governors of the states along the highway, he stressed that communists focused on each example of discrimination in their propaganda efforts in Africa and lashed out at the continued mistreatment of Africans: "It is a disgrace to the United States when diplomats and other visitors from Africa suffer from incidents of racial discrimination."[47]

Williams found an ally in Bowles, who issued a press release after a number of Africans were denied service at restaurants in Delaware and Maryland, denouncing the incidents as "not only morally wrong" but also "to the detriment of our foreign policy." He was less successful in trying to get Kennedy involved in the issue. When newspapers reported that another group of African diplomats had been denied service at restaurants along Route 40, Kennedy phoned Duke, who immediately responded that they were "working very actively" to solve the problem. Kennedy interrupted him.

> That's not what I'm calling you about! I'm calling to tell
> these African Ambassadors to fly. You tell them I wouldn't

think of driving from New York to Washington. Why the
hell would anyone want to drive down Route 40 when you
can fly today? Tell them to wake up to the world and fly!

Duke phoned Harris Wofford, Kennedy's adviser on civil
rights, and asked: "Are you sure the President is fully behind
our efforts?" Williams was also unable to persuade the secretary
of state to speak out on the issue. Although he was opposed to
segregation, Rusk cautioned patience and argued that the issue
would not be solved through "violent public controversy."
Another U.S. official even suggested that Africans wear a
"unique type of pin or button" to indicate that they were not
American blacks. Williams continued to speak out on the issue
and arranged meetings with restaurant and motel owners on
Route 40, and some eventually agreed to end their whites only
policies.[48]

His concern with the treatment of African diplomats was part
of Williams's efforts to show a new attitude in Washington and
to demonstrate that Africa was a high priority for the new
administration. To show a commitment to the continent, he
lobbied the U.S. Information Agency director Edward R.
Murrow to increase his efforts on the continent, pointing out
that the Soviet Union and China broadcast over 260 hours a
week in Africa while the Voice of America offered only 90.
Williams also eagerly embraced the Peace Corps and pushed for
a major volunteer effort in Africa. To Williams the program
represented American idealism, allowed for personal interaction
between Americans and Africans, and would counter the negative images of segregation in the African media. Under his
prodding, the Peace Corps would send more than four thousand volunteers to twenty-one African nations in its first three
years.[49]

He also made a concerted effort to recruit black Foreign Service officers. He found that most African Americans assumed
the State Department was "for whites only" and gave a number
of speeches actively soliciting black applicants for the diplomatic corps. In large part due to Williams's efforts, the number
of African Americans in the Foreign Service tripled in the first
two years of the Kennedy administration.[50]

Following up on his success in persuading Kennedy to meet regularly with African diplomats, Williams encouraged other symbolic acts to show a commitment to Africa. When Chief Albert Luthuli, the leader of the African National Congress, a banned anti-apartheid organization, was awarded the Nobel Prize for Peace in 1961, Williams suggested that Kennedy send a letter of congratulations. State and Defense Department officials strongly opposed the move as an unnecessary affront to the South African government, but Kennedy sent the note.[51]

Williams's initial efforts to promote an African first attitude in the administration were extremely successful. Kennedy's courting of African diplomats and Williams's repeated tours of Africa were largely symbolic but effective gestures, as African leaders felt they had finally gained the attention of Washington and had a strong advocate for their interests in the State Department. They also were impressed by Williams's frequent speeches designed to show the importance of the region, his efforts on behalf of African diplomats, and his lobbying for a stronger U.S. position in support of the end of colonialism and white rule on the continent.

Although Africans appreciated Williams's advocacy of a new approach to the area, many in the administration were less enthusiastic. Europeanists were convinced that Williams was too willing to sacrifice traditional allies for the support of insignificant new nations in Africa. They were appalled by his Africa for the Africans remarks and his outspoken criticism of South Africa, Portugal, and the heritage of colonialism. The disastrous Bay of Pigs invasion in April 1961, the stormy meeting between Kennedy and Soviet leader Nikita Khrushchev in Vienna, and the construction of the Berlin Wall in August, all led to a new emphasis on Western solidarity and a new commitment in the White House to "toughness" and "winning" the battle with communism.

Williams's push for a reorientation of American policy toward Africa was more of a general attitude than a set of specific policies, and he articulated his ideas in broad generalities rather than specifics. Such an approach was out of touch with most in the Kennedy administration. As Schlesinger noted: "The New Frontier put a premium on quick, tough, laconic, decided people; it was easily exasperated by more meditative types." After six months in office, Kennedy determined that the State Department was too cautious, bureaucratic, and indecisive, and he decided that the main problem was Undersecretary of State Chester Bowles.[52]

Bowles had worked closely with Williams in the 1960 battle for a strong civil rights platform and in the State Department had joined in the call for a major change in America's approach to Africa. Like Williams, he had urged a break with the traditional deference to Europe, had supported stronger action against apartheid, and shared Williams's view that Washington needed to demand independence for the Portuguese colonies. When he heard rumors that Bowles might be replaced, Williams led the campaign to save his liberal ally. He immediately contacted Stevenson, Wofford, and other members of the "Chet set" to urge them to lobby to retain Bowles. He and Stevenson wrote to Kennedy, and Williams phoned the president to plead for Bowles's retention. Bowles told Stevenson that he was being forced out of office by "the Achesons" (former secretary of state Dean Acheson, a vocal advocate of the Europeanist view, and his colleagues), who opposed his demands for a clear commitment to Africa. Bowles predicted that Stevenson and Williams would be the next to go. He claimed that Kennedy was not a true liberal in either foreign or domestic affairs and did not want liberals around him. Williams's efforts only delayed the process, and in November 1961 Kennedy removed Bowles from office, replacing him with George Ball, a strong advocate of a "Europe first" orientation. Bowles was appointed to the vague position of special adviser for African, Asian, and Latin American affairs.[53]

The sacrifice of Bowles led many to expect that Williams might also be removed. Wofford reported that one State Department official had observed: "The trouble with Bowles and Williams was that when they saw a band of black baboons beating tom-toms they saw George Washington." Another chanted: "One down and Williams to go!" Such expectations were wishful thinking on the part of Williams's enemies, as

Kennedy was impressed with his energy, his close relations with African leaders, and his effectiveness in reenergizing the African Bureau. Hilsman observed that "the only part of the [State] department that has come in for any praise was the Bureau of African Affairs and G. Mennen Williams." Williams had "taken charge" and "inspired a once demoralized staff."[54]

All of Williams's successful initiatives to show Africans their importance to the new administration led to expectations that Washington would follow with bold new policies demonstrating a clear commitment to an African first position. He found, however, that shaping America's image was easier than altering its actions. Williams's strengths were his energy and public relations skills, and he used both effectively, but he was less talented at negotiating the murky bureaucratic process of policy-making.

Williams quickly judged the State Department to be "an amorphous mass" and found that making decisions was a cumbersome process, as he had to deal with dozens of agencies and departments before an action was implemented. Any specific policy regarding Africa required consultation and negotiation with the State Department, the National Security Council, Congress, the Department of Defense, the White House staff, the Central Intelligence Agency, and, in some cases, the Departments of Agriculture and Commerce. He knew he had access to Kennedy "because of my political background and associations with the President," but he was frustrated by the endless conferences, paperwork, and political infighting in Washington. He lamented the need for policy decisions to work their way slowly through the bureaucracy and the lack of "any vertical clearance" for quick action. He also acknowledged that he was sometimes "brash and impatient."[55]

He was particularly frustrated in his dealings with Rusk and National Security Adviser McGeorge Bundy. Rusk was cautious on all issues, particularly those involving Africa, and often refused to take a position on crucial decisions. Carl Kaysen of the National Security Council noted sardonically that "the Secretary of State never stood for anything." Bundy, the epitome of the New Frontier's emphasis on precision and specifics, abhorred Williams's unabashed idealism and verbosity and often tried to limit his access to Kennedy. Williams also found the president hesitant to embrace all of the bold initiatives he advocated. Although he supported the idea of a new approach to the continent, Kennedy was preoccupied with more immediate and strategic issues such as the situations in Berlin, Cuba, and Laos. Deputy Secretary of State for Political Affairs U. Alexis Johnson noted that the president was "reluctant to deal with anything except the immediate specific issue," and Bowles observed that Kennedy had a "crisis philosophy" approach to diplomacy.[56]

A final problem for Williams was his own lack of experience in foreign policy and his frequent absences from Washington. As a governor, he had never dealt with international affairs and did not appreciate the subtle nuances of diplomacy. He was often frustrated by hours of debate over the wording of a UN resolution or a note to a foreign government. Harlan Cleveland of the State Department recalled chairing a meeting on Africa that included Williams, Bowles, Stevenson, and Harriman and being struck that all were former governors with no past direct involvement in foreign affairs. Williams was often absent from the capital during the debates and negotiations over policy decisions. His frequent trips to Africa and his speaking commitments led him to delegate responsibilities for bureaucratic battles to lower-level officials, a major handicap in Washington, where political power is often linked to your title.[57]

Williams's first venture in the tangled area of policy formation involved the chaotic and controversial issue of the Congo, the most significant African issue in the Kennedy administration and one of the few that directly involved the president and all of his major advisers. Kennedy inherited the convoluted crisis from Eisenhower. Belgium had done virtually nothing to prepare its giant colony for independence, and when the Congo gained its freedom on June 30, 1960, it quickly degenerated into violence and anarchy after Congolese troops mutinied against their white officers. Attacks on whites and reports of atrocities led Belgium to send troops to protect its citizens, and the mineral-rich province of Katanga declared itself to be a separate nation under the pro-Belgian Moise

Tshombe. Prime Minister Patrice Lumumba dismissed President Joseph Kasavubu, and Kasavubu fired Lumumba. Within a few months the Congo had four separate governments.[58]

To regain unity and force Katanga back into the nation, Lumumba appealed to the Soviet Union for military aid. The director of the Central Intelligence Agency, Allan Dulles, concluded that Lumumba had been "bought by the communists" and the agency made several attempts to assassinate him. On November 30, 1960, with the aid of CIA agents, Lumumba was arrested and imprisoned in Leopoldville. When Kennedy took office, the Congo was wracked by succession, foreign intervention, and anarchy. Hilsman observed that "history could hardly have devised a more battling and frustrating test for the new administration than the Congo."[59]

Kennedy wanted a unified Congo and an end to foreign military intervention but feared that if the volatile Lumumba regained power the nation could become "another Cuba" spreading radicalism throughout Africa. The importance of the Congo became clear to Williams on his first day in office, when he was summoned to a lengthy briefing by the CIA followed by meetings with State Department officials.[60]

On February 1, Kennedy devised a new initiative in the Congo, calling for disarmament of all troops, release of all political prisoners, removal of all foreign military personnel, and control of the nation by the UN. He retained doubts about Lumumba, however, and sent Williams to a secret briefing of Congress, where he made it clear that the United States did not want Lumumba back in power. He called Lumumba "the best rabble-rouser" in the Congo and complained that "you lock him up like a Houdini and somehow he winds up running the show." Williams stressed that when a new government was formed "we do not want Lumumba there."[61]

Ironically, while Williams was testifying that America "did not want Lumumba there," the Congolese leader was already dead, murdered by Katangan soldiers on January 17, 1961, after being flown to Elizabethville. Lumumba's death did not become public until February 13, the day before Williams departed for his first trip to Africa. African leaders were outraged by Lumumba's murder, and many blamed the United States. Williams spent much of his trip denying charges that Washington had engineered the murder and reassuring Africans that the United States supported a united Congo.[62]

Williams had little involvement in the development of the "Kennedy Plan" of February 1, as he deferred to those with more experience in foreign policy, but the death of Lumumba led him to become more assertive in Congo policy. He had found that many Africans were convinced America was not really dedicated to true independence and unity in the Congo and felt that Washington saw the situation more as a battle in the fight against communism than an issue of African independence from Europe. Williams argued that the real threat in the Congo was not communism but the continued presence of Belgian troops and the lingering succession of Katanga under the "Belgian stooge" Tshombe. To Williams, America needed to make it clear that it wanted all Belgian troops withdrawn, the Katangan succession ended, and a new government formed. He felt he had the ideal candidate to head the Congo in labor leader Cyrille Adoula, a liberal anticommunist and Congolese nationalist, who, unlike Tshombe, was respected by Africans. His chief rivals were military leader Joseph Mobutu and Lumumba's protégé, Antoine Gizenga. Rusk agreed that Adoula was "the strongest and most attractive of the moderate Congolese leaders."[63]

Washington quickly arranged a conference under UN supervision at Louvanium University near Leopoldville to form a new government in the Congo. Williams and other American officials were confident that Adoula would triumph and were shocked when early votes showed strong support for the radical Gizinga. Kennedy was furious, as both the CIA and the State Department had assured him of an Adoula victory. After a tense meeting with the president, Rusk ordered American agents to "use all means" to help Adoula. Distributing cash and automobiles to delegates, CIA operatives "simply outbid" the competition, and the delegates picked Adoula to head a new government.[64]

Although he was a bit uneasy with the tactics used, Williams was pleased with the selection of Adoula. Having helped to find a leader for the Congo, he now pushed for action on a second issue: the immediate end of Katanga's succession, but he found strong opposition both within and outside of the government. Like African leaders, Williams saw the independence of Katanga under the pro-Belgian Tshombe as a continuation of colonialism and devastating to the economic viability of the Congo. He was convinced that economic sanctions and even military force would be necessary to restore Congolese unity, but many in Washington disagreed. Most in the Europeanist faction of the administration shared the goal of a unified Congo but were reluctant to support a military move against Katanga. They argued that Belgium, England, and other European allies supported Katangan independence and the United States risked placing a strain on the NATO alliance. Many in Washington also saw Katanga as a pro-Western bastion of stability in the chaotic Congo and were highly distrustful of the ability of the UN to maintain order in the nation. In addition, Katanga used Belgian money to launch a massive public relations campaign in the American press designed to show that it was the only capitalist, anticommunist part of the Congo and linking its right to independence to America's break with England in 1776. In Congress, Senators Barry Goldwater of Arizona and Thomas Dodd of Connecticut (known in the State Department "the Senator from Katanga") became the leading spokesmen for Tshombe and accused Kennedy of planning to turn the Congo over to the "communist-leaning UN." The American Committee to Aid Katangan Freedom Fighters took out full-page ads in the *New York Times* and nineteen other newspapers, proclaiming, "Katanga is the Hungary of 1961." Senator John Tower of Texas spoke for many in Congress when he argued that "Tshombe is friendly to the West. He seeks preservation of a capitalistic economy. His area is the richest and most stable in the Belgian Congo. Its seems a strange paradox that he should feel our wrath."[65]

Given the strong opposition within his administration and in Congress and the new stress on NATO unity after the Berlin crisis, Kennedy equivocated. Williams, Bowles, and Stevenson all lobbied Kennedy to commit America to supporting a UN military intervention against Katanga, but he refused. Given the situation in Europe, Kennedy felt that "it was the better part of valor to go slow with any bold 'New Africa' policy." In the words of Hilsman, America's Congo policy was "squirming on dead center."[66]

To Williams, Kennedy's inaction was precisely the hesitant, European-first approach that the New Frontier was pledged to overturn and was doing major damage to the favorable relations with the continent he had so carefully cultivated. The longer Katanga survived, the worse it would be for America, as Africans saw Washington as supporting a puppet regime that continued white rule. Finally Williams's impatience with the infighting and delay in Washington led him to "go public," despite warnings from Washington officials to remain silent. On October 25, he charged that Belgian support of Katanga was "pushing the Congo toward communism." In a speech in Detroit he assailed Dodd, the Katangan lobby, and the reluctance of America to move against Tshombe. Given Williams's frustration and fear that all his efforts to cultivate Africa were in jeopardy, his actions were understandable, but they also were damaging to his power in Washington. Undersecretary of State George McGhee called a press conference and told reporters that the government had not approved Williams's comments. Journalist William White claimed that Williams had a "sheer evangelical zeal" and was "seized with a holy mission" to align America with Africa at the expense of its traditional and more important European allies.[67]

Despite the public rebuke, Williams refused to remain silent, and throughout 1962 a bureaucratic battle between Africanists and Europeanists raged in Washington. Kaysen recalled: "Soapy Williams and the people in AF [the African Bureau] were hawks. . . . They really wanted a more positive American intention on behalf of the central government and against Tshombe." Bowles's replacement, George Ball, demanded that Williams stop his public demands for military action against Katanga, but Williams refused. Ball responded by insisting that all speeches, press releases, and position papers from the African

Bureau receive his personal clearance. Williams then enlisted Stevenson, American ambassador to the Congo Edmund Gillion, and others outside the bureau to lobby Kennedy to support the use of force to topple Tshombe. Ball called the African Bureau's views on the Congo "a bunch of mush," and Williams privately judged the Kennedy administration "as bad as Eisenhower."[68]

In early 1962, Williams and Stevenson hosted a dinner for Adoula at the Waldorf-Astoria Hotel in New York. The assistant secretary became livid when conservatives demanded that Tshombe also be allowed to visit America. He wrote a blistering note to Kennedy, pointing out that such a trip would damage U.S. relations with Africa, and the president invoked a legal technicality to deny Tshombe a visa.[69]

Williams's triumph was short-lived, as Kennedy, responding to a suggestion from Dodd, decided to send Undersecretary McGhee to meet with Tshombe to try to arrange a reunification of the Congo. Williams was outraged that Kennedy would give Tshombe a sense of legitimacy by talking with him and was humiliated that McGhee, the person who had publicly rebuked him for speaking out on the Congo, would be his representative. He saw the move as "an attempt to appease the Dodd kinds" and a personal affront. Kaysen recalled that "Soapy was just terribly discouraged" and felt "McGhee was wrong; that Rusk was backing McGhee" and State Department Europeanists were destroying his African policies. He told Kaysen: "We were going to be in for trouble with the rest of Africa and he couldn't get Kennedy to see this." He mentioned that he had written a letter of resignation. Kaysen persuaded him that resigning would put an additional burden on Kennedy in a time of crisis, and Williams never sent the letter.[70]

When McGhee arrived in Katanga, he was greeted with signs that read "Welcome Mr. McGhee, Down with Guillon, the Enemy of Katanga," a reference to the U.S. ambassador, a strong ally of Williams. At a banquet for the visiting American, Tshombe offered a toast, saying, "I spit in the face of the racist Guillon." As he had done numerous times, Tshombe promised to disarm and provide financial support to the central government, but as soon as McGhee's plane left he disavowed all of his agreements.[71]

Tshombe's duplicity finally led even Ball and Rusk to support Williams's recommendation that the United States support a UN military action against Katanga, but Kennedy still hesitated. Finally, without any American commitment, the UN launched an attack on Katanga on Christmas Eve of 1962 and, to the surprise of many, quickly routed Tshombe's forces. The Congo was finally, albeit temporarily, united.

Williams had secured a unified Congo under moderate leadership but only after a bruising bureaucratic battle and personal humiliation. His first encounters with the intricacies of policymaking showed the power of the Europeanist faction, the need to work within the bureaucracy, and the dangers of public criticism of the administration. He would apply these lessons in his dealings with the other major diplomatic issues involving Africa.

First, as he had done in Michigan during his conflicts with the legislature, Williams turned to those outside of the government to mobilize support for his policies. He explained that "I as Governor had always employed citizens' commissions most extensively and had found them useful" in both gaining information and supporting policies, and he sought to duplicate the strategy in Washington. He formed the Advisory Council on African Affairs to meet and engage in "freewheeling discussions" of new policy initiatives. Williams wanted to make sure the group "wasn't a usual State Department operation" and selected journalists, ministers, civil rights activists, and academics specializing in African politics and economics. Professor Vernon McKay of Johns Hopkins University chaired the fifty-member group, and, not unexpectedly, it criticized America's reluctance to use force in the Congo, hesitancy in confronting Portugal over Angola, and the lack of U.S. financial assistance to the continent. Williams was pleased with such public support of his recommendations, but the group had little impact outside of the African Bureau. One State Department official forwarded the council's report with the notation, "the best way to get rid of this dreary paper is to read the Press Release and forget the rest!"[72]

Williams also urged black leaders to speak out in favor of a stronger approach to Africa. In response, the American Negro Leadership Conference on Africa adopted resolutions demanding economic sanctions and military force to end Katangan independence and more U.S. pressure on South Africa to end apartheid.[73]

Initially Williams seemed to be successful in influencing Kennedy when the administration faced the issue of independence for the Portuguese colonies of Angola and Mozambique. Unlike other European nations, Portugal refused to consider any discussion of independence for its African colonies. Its dictator, Antonio de Oliveria Salazar, claimed that his nation had no "colonies," only "overseas possessions," and that its African holdings were a "part of Portugal." Portugal was militantly anticommunist, a member of NATO, and leased a key military base in the Azores Islands to America. Europeanists felt that any pressure on Portugal to abandon its African colonies would jeopardize European unity and risk the loss of a military installation that defense officials considered "vital." To Williams and others dedicated to an African first approach, firm opposition to Portugal's obstinacy was a clear test of Washington's commitment to African independence and far more important than maintaining good relations with a European dictator.[74]

Two weeks after Kennedy took office Angolans stormed a prison in the capital of Luanda to free anticolonial activists and police killed thirty-three people in the crowd. African and Asian states followed with a UN Security Council resolution calling for an investigation of the incident and, more importantly, demanding an end to Portuguese colonization in Africa. Williams, Bowles, and Stevenson saw an opportunity to show African nations a new stance by the United States and lobbied hard for support of the resolution. After lengthy debate, the Africanists triumphed, and on March 15 America voted in favor of the resolution, although France, Britain, and four other nations abstained and the motion failed. The same day Africans in Angola attacked white farms, police stations, and army bases. Portugal now faced a full-scale revolt in Africa.

Williams was delighted with the symbolic UN vote, but the

action led to a storm of criticism. Conservatives in Congress and the executive branch joined European leaders in condemning the abandonment of a faithful ally and jeopardizing the crucial Azores base. Dean Acheson, a great admirer of Salazar, led the assault on Washington's "misguided idealism" and "the crumbling of America to the pressures of the new nations," which risked the loss of "the most important U.S. base in Europe." When UN ambassador Stevenson voted for a second resolution calling for Portugal to set "a timetable for independence" for Angola, attacks on the administration intensified. Conservative columnist James Burnham claimed that Williams was behind the shift in policy, as the assistant secretary held "the illusion that the primitive jungles of Africa are more important than the advanced men, ideas, and machines of Europe."[75]

Not unexpectedly, Portugal claimed that the new U.S. policy was a threat to NATO unity and the continuation of the Azores lease, which would expire at the end of 1962. Lisbon was convinced that Williams had engineered Washington's "betrayal" and that claimed statements by "high United States officials" had encouraged the "communist-inspired" revolt in Angola. In a rare interview, Salazar remarked that he had been "confused" by Williams's Africa for the Africans comment and was "perplexed" by his anti–Portuguese statements.[76]

Convinced that Williams and Bowles had taken control of U.S. foreign policy, Portugal, like Katanga, began an intense public relations campaign to rally support. Lisbon hired a New York advertising agency, Selvage and Lee, to persuade the American people that the revolt in Angola was controlled by Moscow and that Portugal was an important U.S. ally. The campaign had a budget of one hundred thousand dollars for 1961, and its leader, Martin Camacho, promised that he could shift U.S. opinion away from the ideas "of such men as Chester Bowles, Williams, and Adlai Stevenson."[77]

Despite the hostile response to the new Angolan policy, Williams was certain he had an ally on the issue in the White House. When Kennedy met with French leader Charles de Gaulle in May, Angola was an important item on the agenda. De Gaulle cautioned that too firm a stance might topple Salazar and lead to the establishment of a communist regime in Portugal, but Kennedy defended the new policy, noting that African independence was inevitable and Washington would offer its support. A gleeful Williams cabled: "Appreciate your vigorous stand on Angola!"[78]

His euphoria was short-lived, as Kennedy quickly became convinced of the possible hazards of continuing a strong policy on Angola. At his stormy meeting with Khrushchev in Vienna, he asked whether the revolt in Angola was an example of what the Soviet leader had called "wars of national liberation." Khrushchev denied any direct involvement in Angola but warned that all wars against colonialism were "sacred." The construction of the Berlin Wall that followed reaffirmed the need for the Azores base, as it was deemed critical for any military operation in Europe.[79]

To Williams, however, the administration needed to continue its pressure on Lisbon to abandon Africa, even if it meant the loss of the Azores. In June he formed the Task Force on the Portuguese Territories in Africa, which proposed a series of strong actions against Salazar to force him to accept a "timetable for independence" for his African colonies. The group recommended economic sanctions, an end to arms sales, and a massive propaganda campaign to show that Portugal's intransigence was driving Angola toward communism. Williams acknowledged that Washington was "faced with a true dilemma in which our policy posture toward newly emerging nations will bring a conflict with our policy posture toward our NATO allies," but the United States needed to make it clear that it stood with Africa. The report concluded that the Defense Department should develop contingency plans for the possible loss of the Azores base. Williams persuaded Stevenson and Bowles to send letters to Kennedy endorsing this "bold move."[80]

Officials in the Defense and State Departments and many in the White House found Williams's recommendations appalling and were stunned that anyone would seriously consider abandoning the Azores. One official suggested that Bundy "get down to brass tacks with Governor Williams" and make it clear that the entire report was unacceptable. Williams responded by

arguing that freedom in Angola was just as important as freedom in Berlin, and he scheduled meetings with officials in the
Defense Department and the National Security Council to
convince them of the need to "get tough" with Portugal.[81]

Undeterred, Williams continued his verbal assault on
Salazar's refusal to consider independence for Angola, prompt-
ing Portugal to deliver a rare official protest to the State Department. When the European Bureau passed the complaint along
to Williams, he responded: "Pray tell, what particularly roused
his Excellency's ire?"[82]

On July 14, Kennedy met with the National Security Council to discuss Williams's proposals for a tough stance against
Portugal, and the group rejected them. Given the crisis in
Europe, it was not a good time to disrupt NATO or risk losing
the base in the Azores. The NSC suggested that Washington
offer Salazar a large financial aid package if he agreed to abandon Angola.[83]

When he heard of Kennedy's cautious approach, Williams
told Rusk that "time was running out" for America to show its
commitment to Africa by standing up to Portugal. He suggested that Kennedy's forthcoming speech to the UN was too
concerned with Berlin and "white man's freedom" rather than
freedom for blacks in Angola.[84]

Although Williams continued to pressure Kennedy, it was
clear the president was abandoning his earlier tough stance on
Angola. He told America's ambassador to Portugal that "it
might be wise for the U.S. to abstain on some of the votes
affecting Portugal in the UN." Even some of Williams's allies
began to doubt to wisdom of continuing U.S. demands on Lisbon. The policy had alienated Europeans and seemed to have
generated little goodwill among Africans, who charged that
America continued to supply Portugal with the NATO
weapons being used to kill Angolans. Kwame Nkrumah of
Ghana suggested that if America really was supportive of
Angolan independence it should expel Lisbon from NATO and
"Portugal's colonial rule would collapse the day after." Even
Stevenson complained that Africans did not appreciate Amer-
ica's efforts to pressure Lisbon, and he looked forward to the

time "when the last black-faced comedian has quit preaching about colonialism so the UN could move on to the more crucial issues like disarmament."[85]

While Williams pushed for a "get tough" policy toward Portugal, he found Kennedy preoccupied with military issues. He wrote Fredericks that "the Azores side seems to be the one receiving disproportional, if not exclusive consideration" in the White House. With Williams's encouragement, the U.S. ambassador to Guinea, William Atwood, met with Kennedy to try to convince him to stand firm on Angola, but the president mentioned "the problem he had with the European Bureau" and the military's emphasis on the Azores. He asked Atwood: "What would they say if there was a tidal wave, and the Azores just disappeared under the sea? Are they all that vital?"[86]

Kennedy eventually concluded that they were vital. The CIA predicted that Salazar would continue to permit America to use the Azores without any formal agreement as long as Washington did not renew its demands for Angolan independence. Kennedy then instructed Stevenson to "sit back and let others take the lead" on issues involving Portugal at the UN. When Stevenson helped write a resolution mildly critical of Lisbon, Kennedy angrily ordered him to abstain on the motion he had drafted. Encouraged by the diplomatic retreat in Washington, Salazar rejected U.S. offers of massive economic aid in exchange for Angolan independence, declaring that "Portugal overseas is not for sale" and vowing to continue his nation's "civilizing efforts" in Africa.[87]

Kennedy's hesitation and eventual retreat on Angolan policy was a bitter defeat for Williams. Combined with the administration's reluctance to use force in the Congo, it showed that the New Frontier was still closely wedded to Europe and that military and strategic interests dominated African issues. Williams had been successful in altering the tone and image of America, but he found it more difficult to make major changes in policy, as the Azores issue trumped any need to align the United States with African nationalism. The Portuguese ambassador concluded: "It is obvious that only the fear of not having the Azores agreement renewed moderated the New Frontier's sympathy with anti-colonialist policy." Bowles agreed and later claimed that "we missed the boat" on Portugal, as cold war military issues led Kennedy to "begin to play to the right side of the fence." Williams was a bit more pensive. He noted Kennedy's personal attention to Africans and that his own trips and speeches had raised expectations. Africans "had much higher hopes . . . from us than we had any ability to deliver."[88]

Frustrated by Kennedy's hesitations on the Congo and Angola, Williams began a new effort to convince the president to take a strong position against South Africa and its policy of apartheid. Under Eisenhower, the United States had verbally condemned South Africa's official policy, which mandated strict racial separatism and reserved all political and economic power for the white minority, but had rejected exerting any economic or political pressure on Pretoria. Like Portugal, South Africa had important strategic implications for the United States, as it contained essential missile-tracking stations and provided America with diamonds, gold, platinum, and other crucial minerals. The white minority government seemed to many conservatives to be a bastion of capitalism, Christianity, and stability on an increasingly radical and chaotic continent.

Ever since he took office, Williams had been outspoken in demanding an end to the "middle road" position of denouncing apartheid but taking no action against South Africa. He viewed apartheid, like American segregation, as morally wrong and was particularly appalled that many white South Africans used religion to justify their racial policies. To Williams Christianity demanded equality, and he was outraged that South Africans would try to use it to support institutional racism. He also saw American inaction on apartheid as shortsighted and a major barrier to good relations with black Africa, as it was clear that the end of white rule was inevitable. Throughout 1961, he conducted a verbal assault on South Africa, denouncing apartheid as "a wrong headed policy, fraught with dangers not only to the people of South Africa, but to international peace," and pledged that the new administration would "stand up and be counted" in its opposition to Pretoria. Within the government he pushed for an end to International Monetary Fund loans to South Africa, as "they subsidize apartheid"; a cutback in arms sales to the nation; and active "discouragement" of new American investments. He condemned U.S. business leaders for being "cowed by the apartheid government" into adopting a "when in Rome, do as the Romans" approach, saying: "I think we've got to be better citizens than we are."[89]

Williams's ceaseless criticism of apartheid won him the admiration of liberals and African Americans at home and African leaders abroad and the deep hatred of South African officials. Pretoria's foreign minister, Eric Louw, even summoned the U.S. ambassador to complain about Williams and to ask whether he spoke for Kennedy. When Williams requested a visa to visit South Africa, Louw replied that he was the "last person" he would ever allow into his nation.[90]

Williams also found that many of America's European allies were reluctant to confront Pretoria. When he met with British officials in 1961 to discuss South Africa it was a stormy session. Foreign Office representatives expected the usual diplomatic cordiality and consideration of technical issues, but Williams immediately pushed them to join America in taking a strong stance against apartheid. When a British diplomat reminded him that South Africa contained key radar stations and provided America and England with crucial minerals, Williams interrupted and declared that Washington "was unwilling to compromise its principles to maintain those interests." The head of the British delegation, Sir Roger Stevens, cautioned Williams to "be careful you don't do more harm that good," but the American insisted that it was "necessary to do something about apartheid." Stevens warned Williams that he would "bear a grave responsibility" if he encouraged "an overthrow of the South African Government." Williams then announced that he was going to insist that all social events and receptions at the U.S. embassy in South Africa be multiracial in direct defiance of apartheid. Stevens stressed the diplomatic impact of such a policy and added: "I presume the U.S. does not want to provoke a break in diplomatic relations with South Africa." Williams replied that he did not, but he was willing to risk it if South Africa tried to prevent interracial gatherings.[91]

Williams also faced strong opposition within the government for any new initiatives against South Africa. Not only did Defense and Commerce Department officials favor continuing the current policy, but Rusk and the American ambassador to South Africa, Joseph Satterthwaite, also resisted a tougher policy. Although he was a strong advocate of civil rights at home, Rusk did not feel America had the obligation or power to impose its policies on the rest of the world. Responding to the battle between Williams and his critics within the government, Rusk developed an official "Guidelines for Policy and Operations" regarding South Africa, which called for Washington "to distinguish between non-cooperation in matters directly or indirectly related to apartheid policy, and cooperation in all other fields." Satterthwaite, Williams's predecessor as head of the African Bureau, felt his job was to "be a stabilizing influence" on Williams's desire to "take an extreme line against the South African Government." He thought his replacement did not understand "the facts of life" about South Africa and was unrealistic to expect any quick end to apartheid. He often judged Williams's instructions to be "unwise" and sent his cables directly to Rusk, bypassing the African Bureau.[92]

Williams was outraged by Rusk's seeming continuance of past "middle road" policies and scornful of Satterthwaite's close relationship with officials in Pretoria. He argued that lack of pressure on South Africa, along with temporizing on Angola, was undoing the progress America had made in its relations with Africa. What Williams wanted was strict economic sanctions against South Africa, but he knew Rusk, Kennedy, and most in the State Department opposed sanctions as impracticable, selective, and impossible to sell to Congress. Convinced that he could never get support for sanctions, in 1963 he determined to push for an embargo on the sale of military equipment to South Africa.[93]

Important in gaining support for an arms embargo was growing African anger at the violent response to peaceful efforts to end segregation in the American South. Africans monitored closely the growing activism of the civil rights movement and were outraged at the violent resistance to the integration of southern schools and public facilities. Many linked the U.S.

refusal to accept racial equality at home with its continued tolerance of white supremacy in South Africa.

In 1963, Africans formed the Organization of African Unity
(OAU) to coordinate efforts to free Angola and end white rule
in South Africa. The first meeting of the group in Ethiopia
coincided with violent attacks on civil rights demonstrators in
Birmingham, Alabama, and images of the use of fire hoses and
police dogs against black children filled African newspapers.
Milton Obote of Uganda told reporters that "nothing is more
paradoxical" than America posing as "the champion of freedom" while those asking for liberty in Alabama were "blasted
with fire hoses."[94]

Williams immediately called for a dramatic gesture to counteract the negative image of Birmingham. He warned Kennedy
that communists were using the white resistance to civil rights
in their propaganda throughout Africa and convinced Rusk to
let him form a "working group" on civil rights and foreign policy. On June 14, he called for "a more vigorous stance against
apartheid" to counteract the anger shown at the OAU and suggested an immediate ban on the sale of arms to South Africa.

> We can no longer rest our case on a condemnation of
> apartheid. We must be ready to back our condemnation with
> some form of meaningful action. . . . A total arms embargo
> . . . is the only way we can convince both the world and
> domestic opinion that we mean business in our disapproval
> of Apartheid.[95]

Rusk was reluctant, pointing out that "it would be hard to
find a single state" that did not have differences with the United
States and suggesting that America "is not the self-elected gen-
darme" of the world, but Kennedy was intrigued with
Williams's idea. It was the sort of grand gesture he liked, and it
did not involve sanctions in other areas. He ordered an assistant,
Ralph Dungan, to survey opinion on a weapons ban. Dungan
found strong opposition in the Defense and Commerce
Departments but support everywhere else. Even George Ball,
the leading voice of the Europeanist faction, endorsed the
move, provided it was not a first step toward general economic
sanctions.[96]

Aware of Kennedy's interest, Williams sent a more detailed rationale for the move, contending that "A complete arms embargo is the least the U.S. can do to maintain our position of influence with the Africans and our ability to prevent more radical and violent action on their part." By mid-July, Kennedy was committed to an embargo but wanted it to be unilateral and its announcement to be a surprise. On July 16, Tanganyikan leader Julius Nyerere visited the White House, and the president could not restrain himself. He leaked the news that America was going to declare a ban on all military sales to South Africa but asked Nyerere to keep the move secret. Rusk then informed Pretoria of the plan, and on August 2 Stevenson announced to the UN that America would end sales of military equipment to South Africa by the end of the year.[97]

The South African arms embargo was a significant personal triumph for Williams. Unlike the Congo and Angola, he was able to overcome strong opposition within the administration and to counter the usually persuasive strategic considerations such as the missile-tracking stations and dependence on South African minerals. Foreshadowing U.S. policy two decades later, Williams argued that the end of arms sales was only a first step, as strict economic sanctions and the end of all American investments in the country would be necessary to force majority rule, but he was unable to implement such dramatic actions.

Along with convincing Kennedy to end arms sales to South Africa, Williams was also able to persuade the president to tolerate African neutralism in the cold war. Many in Washington continued to see nonalignment as anti-American or a cynical attempt to play the United States against Russia and attract more economic aid. Williams repeatedly argued that the refusal of new nations to join with the West was a natural reaction to colonialism and represented a reluctance to align with their former masters. "The erratic behavior of some African countries in foreign affairs" was the result of "their particular experiences (and lack of experiences) and is likely to continue for some time." Washington should not react to African rhetoric, as it was often a show of independence intended for domestic political effect.[98]

Williams tried to show the need to align with African

nationalism and accept neutralism early in his term when he established contacts with leaders of the independence movement in Algeria, provoking vocal opposition from France and the European Bureau of the State Department. When Algeria gained independence in 1962, he campaigned for a major U.S. foreign aid package, despite the radical rhetoric of its leader, Ahmed Ben Bella. When the Algerian welcomed Cuban revolutionary Che Guevara to Algiers, Williams explained that it was not a move toward communism but merely a way to demonstrate his independence by refusing to join either side in the cold war. He also was influential in convincing Kennedy to continue U.S. funding of the massive Volta River Dam project in Ghana. Eisenhower had first offered aid for the project, but many of Kennedy's advisers argued that America should abandon Volta, as Ghana's Nkrumah had become a leading critic of U.S. policy in the Congo (even calling Kennedy a murderer after the death of Lumumba), had supported the diplomatic recognition of China, and had sent troops to Russia for training. Williams argued that withdrawing promised funding would destroy Kennedy's credibility and indicate a rejection of Africa's right to neutralism. With considerable reluctance, Kennedy finally approved the project.[99]

Williams was less successful in his push for massive American economic aid to Africa. Throughout his years as governor, he had called for expanded humanitarian efforts for the poor and in 1958 had urged America to end starvation and poverty throughout the world by sharing its immense wealth. His trips to Africa intensified his Christian commitment to feed the hungry and clothe the naked. Africa's poverty provoked an emotional response from both Mennen and Nancy Williams, but he also saw an American commitment to helping Africa as sound policy. Africans were understandably reluctant to ask for funds from their former colonial masters, and if the United States ignored their needs they had only Russia and China as options. Washington should offer major assistance to all African nations, not just those that supported America in the cold war, as "today's ugly African may be tomorrow's friend (and vice versa)."[100]

Many in Washington did not share the goal of a massive aid program for Africa. They contended that France and England should carry the major burden for their former colonies and the United States should concentrate its funds in a few selected "showpiece" countries. Williams wrote Bowles that he was "concerned by what appears to be a disposition to agree to the expenditures of funds in a few countries to the neglect of a great many" and in late 1961 warned Rusk: "Time is running out on us."[101]

Throughout his first two years in Washington Williams found that there "always was a constant tension between our bureau and AID [the Agency for International Development]," but he remained confident that Kennedy would see the wisdom of providing increased assistance to all African nations. With strong opposition to foreign aid in Congress and a growing balance of payments crisis, Kennedy was hesitant to make a major commitment to Africa and instead commissioned General Lucius Clay to undertake a total review of U.S. aid policy. The Clay Committee would prove to be disastrous to Williams's goal of increased funding for Africa.[102]

The Clay Committee first met in September 1962 and issued its report in March of 1963, concluding that Washington was trying "to do too much in too many places" and recommending major cuts in foreign aid. Its suggestions regarding Africa were devastating to Williams, who noted: "The Committee regards Africa as an area where the Western European countries should logically bear most of the necessary aid burden. . . . In light of its other responsibilities, the United States cannot undertake to support all of the African countries." It judged most aid to Africa as ineffective and producing little significant change. Washington should limit its financial commitment in Africa to two or three nations and leave the rest of the continent to Europe.[103]

Williams was outraged by the committee's conclusions, and many in the State Department shared his anger. Labor leader George Meany, a member of the group and a close associate of Williams, offered a vigorous dissent, but Kennedy, fearing that if he rejected the recommendations Clay would testify in Congress in favor of even larger cuts, approved the document. Clay then told the press that aid could be reduced even further. Congressional critics of foreign aid were ecstatic and slashed Kennedy's request from $4.9 to $3.2 billion, the lowest total since 1958. Direct aid to Africa plunged from $315 million in 1962 to $239 million in 1963 and $198 million in 1964.[104]

The severe cut in economic assistance to Africa was a bitter blow to Williams. Combined with Kennedy's temporizing on Angola and the Congo, it led him to consider resigning. He wrote his family that "the chance to be doing something in the New Frontier is great" but "I miss some of the things in Michigan, especially the chance to get right out with the people from time to time." In 1963, his daughter Nancy was in her second year at Smith College (where she found "all the girls are tall and thin") and son Gery was completing his degree at Princeton after marrying Lee Ann Monroe on June 30, 1962, in St. Paul's in Detroit. (She and Nancy spent hours paring the initial invitation list down from over six thousand on the groom's side alone.) It seemed a good time to consider leaving the African Bureau, but there were few other options. There were no electoral vacancies in Michigan, and it was unlikely that Kennedy would appoint him to another position in Washington. Despite his disappointments Williams decided to stay in Washington until Kennedy completed his first term.[105]

In November Williams received word that Elma Williams had died at the age of eighty-three and flew to Detroit for the funeral. Although she had remained a staunch Republican, his mother had been supportive of her son's run for the presidency and had given a substantial amount of her fortune to her children before her death. Williams stayed in Michigan for a few days and on November 22 was lunching at the Detroit Athletic Club when he received word of Kennedy's assassination. He rushed to the club's barbershop and listened to the details of the shooting on the radio. He immediately caught a flight to Washington, where he attended the president's funeral wearing a formal gray cutaway coat and his trademark green and white polka-dot bow tie.[106]

Although Kennedy had not implemented all of the bold

policies in Africa that Williams had expected, the president had established a new rapport with leaders on the continent and had generated an amazing amount of goodwill among the African people. Despite strong internal opposition to the importance of Africa for America, Williams had convinced Kennedy to demonstrate a personal interest through meetings with African leaders, had persuaded him to embargo arms to South Africa, and had encouraged his acceptance of neutralism on the continent. Williams was also grateful that Kennedy had kept him in office despite the often open hostility of critics in Washington. Although Kennedy often disagreed with Williams on policy issues, he retained his respect and admiration for the head of the African Bureau.[107]

It was uncertain whether Williams would have the same support from the new president. Lyndon Johnson's views on Africa, as on many other issues, were unknown. What was clear was the history of conflict between Johnson and Williams, which had culminated in the infamous public opposition to the vice president's nomination in 1960. After Kennedy's funeral, Williams waited to see if he would remain in office and if he would have the personal respect in the White House he had enjoyed during the previous three years.

VII

FROM WASHINGTON
TO MICHIGAN TO MANILA

The Johnson Years, Electoral Defeat, &
Ambassador to the Philippines, 1964–69

> Some of you fellows fired me but the
> President just rehired me!
>
> —*G. Mennen Williams at a White House*
> *press conference, April 4, 1965*

Soapy Williams had arrived in Washington in January 1961 with an aggressive agenda. Disappointed by his failure to secure a cabinet appointment, he was determined to use his position as head of the African Bureau to both reorient American foreign policy and regain his position as a leader of the Democratic Party. Despite his outspokenness, lack of diplomatic subtlety, and failure to conform to the New Frontier's preference for cool detachment, he managed to achieve many of his goals in his three years under Kennedy. He had persuaded the president to devote considerable time to meeting with Africans; he had pushed the administration to condemn Portugal's continued obstinacy in decolonization and to vote against Lisbon at the UN (although he was unable to overcome the strategic value of the Azores base to implement more substantial actions); he had led the fight to end arms sales to the white regime in South Africa; and, despite bruising bureaucratic battles, he had helped unify the Congo under a more moderate leadership. His frequent trips had convinced African leaders that they had a strong advocate in Washington and, combined with his speaking efforts to "educate" the American public about the continent, had gained him considerable media attention. No previous assistant secretary of state had generated the press coverage that Soapy Williams did.

His success was largely the result of access to and influence with the president. Although he was unable to convince Kennedy to abandon completely a Europe first orientation, he did persuade the president to symbolically recognize the importance of Africa and, in the case of South Africa, to adopt a significant new policy orientation.

Kennedy's assassination seemed a major blow to Williams's influence and his hope for an African first policy. Williams's long criticism of Lyndon Johnson, culminating in his solitary and vocal dissent from the Texan's nomination for the vice presidency in 1960, jeopardized his continued access to the White House and perhaps even put his job at risk. Johnson rarely forgot political or personal criticism, and it was only three years since he had responded to the Michigan leader's opposition to his selection by declaring "piss on Mennen Williams!"

Aside from past personal animosity, Johnson's views on foreign policy generally and Africa in particular were largely unknown, and it was unclear whether he would continue any of the initiatives Williams had sought to implement under Kennedy. It was also uncertain whether the new executive would maintain personal diplomacy with Africans or endorse Williams's view of the importance of the continent for America.

Williams also worried about how Africans would react to the new president. As Johnson was a southerner with seemingly only a marginal interest in civil rights, many Africans were skeptical of his commitment to the continent and racial equality. Williams noted that Kennedy's death had led him to fear that "the association that the United States had built up with Africans, and a feeling for them, a sympathetic feeling, was all over." Sekou Toure of Guinea spoke for many Africans when he informed Williams that he was deeply distrustful of Johnson and doubtful whether Washington would pressure the remaining white governments on the continent to accept majority rule. He told Williams that "the only people I have ever trusted were you and Kennedy."[1]

Williams had other concerns aside from Lyndon Johnson. By the time of Kennedy's death many liberals had become disillusioned with Africa and dubious of its importance for America. Three years of violence, corruption, coups, and dictatorships had convinced many academics, journalists, and politicians that the continent was increasingly chaotic and undemocratic. The heady idealism that followed the rush of African nations to independence in 1960 had given way to apathy and cynicism by late 1963. African Americans, always the leading advocates for a stronger commitment to Africa, had also grown less interested in the region. As the American civil rights movement accelerated, symbolized by the massive march on Washington in August 1963, many black leaders focused on domestic racial issues more than distant Africa.[2]

A final issue that jeopardized Williams's position and policies was the "Robert Kennedy factor." The attorney general had grown increasingly interested in U.S. relations with Africa and three days before his brother's death wrote a memo to Bundy suggesting the formation of a new group to review American policy toward the continent and consider more aggressive diplomacy. It was clear that the younger Kennedy expected to lead the effort. He concluded: "I gather we don't really have much of a policy or are just beginning to develop one." Although Johnson had maintained cordial relations with John Kennedy, he had a deep and visceral hatred of his younger brother and, if Robert Kennedy emerged as an advocate for a stronger U.S. position toward Africa it would hardly garner much support in the White House.[3]

Like all Kennedy appointees, Williams was apprehensive about his position and influence with the new president, but despite his concerns a number of forces made Johnson receptive to the head of the African Bureau. First, although he had been Kennedy's first appointee, Williams was not as identified as a "Kennedy man" as were many others in the administration. He had not been close to Kennedy before 1960 and had never been a part of his often ruthless political machine. While Johnson vowed not to remove any of his predecessor's advisers, many Kennedy appointees, such as Schlesinger, Sorensen, Salinger, and Kenneth O'Donnell, felt a deep loyalty to their murdered leader and sensed Johnson's coolness.[4]

Johnson and Williams also shared a deep affection for Franklin Roosevelt, and their early experiences in the New Deal gave them a common history. They had first met in 1936 when Williams was at the Social Security Agency and Johnson worked for the National Youth Administration. For the next twenty-five years whenever they met Johnson reminded Williams that they had been "two young fellows saving the world." Williams was only six years older than Kennedy (and three years younger than Johnson), but in many ways he seemed to be of a different generation than the late president. Nancy Williams recalled that Johnson was "more of our age" and more approachable than the often detached Kennedy.[5]

Williams also benefited from a close rapport between his wife and Lady Bird Johnson They both had daughters and had met to discuss marriage plans, and Nancy would later invite Mrs. Johnson and her daughter to the Williams's home on Mackinac Island and to her daughter's wedding. Partly due to the closeness of their spouses, the Williamses would be frequent guests at dinners and receptions at the Johnson White House (they attended ten formal affairs in 1964 and 1965), and Lady Bird Johnson would also invite Nancy to eleven luncheons, teas, and receptions.[6]

Soapy Williams's style was closer to Johnson's than Kennedy's. Both loved personal campaigning, where they could meet people and "press the flesh" by shaking hands, and disliked the cool aloofness of Kennedy. Like his predecessor, Johnson also admired Williams's electoral success, as, unlike many other Kennedy appointees, he had held elective office for twelve years before coming to Washington, a trait much valued by the new president.

Despite his apprehensions, it soon seemed that Johnson would not only retain Williams but also offer continued access to the White House. Ten days after Kennedy's death, Johnson phoned Williams and assured him "you are going to be as welcome and as effective in the White House as you had been with Kennedy." He dismissed Williams's hostility to his nomination in 1960, claiming it would not jeopardize their relationship: "We've pulled down the curtain on Los Angeles that night. We're a team." Johnson encouraged Williams to offer new initiatives on civil rights, noting that "you have operated in Michigan so long that you are bound to know some things you've done that will be good in Mississippi" and urging him to "get ideas on our Negro community." The president said he wanted "new fresh things and I want to rely on you to do that," as "you've had more experience than any of us" on racial issues.[7]

Williams was greatly encouraged by the president's support, his dismissal of the conflict in Los Angeles, and his solicitation of ideas on civil rights. With characteristic energy, he immediately tried to persuade Johnson to continue Kennedy's personal diplomacy with African leaders, and the new president responded by writing personal letters to nearly all of the heads of state in Africa, assuring them of his interest in the region and his support of Williams. Although he rarely scheduled one-on-one meetings with Africans in the Oval Office, as Kennedy had done, Johnson hosted regular luncheons for African diplomats in the White House. Johnson did not eat with the guests but would enter during dessert to make a few comments, always acknowledging the vital importance of Mennen Williams. Williams noted that "Johnson always did his homework" and was very effective with Africans.[8]

Although he was dutiful in his attendance, Johnson occasionally mocked the frequent social events that Williams arranged. After a state dinner for the president of Upper Volta, he joked with Robert McNamara that the defense secretary should be grateful for not having to attend the affair, as all Johnson remembered was "dancing with a 280 pound woman about one o'clock!"[9]

Despite his grousing, Johnson continued Kennedy's personal diplomacy with Africans until he became preoccupied with the war in Vietnam in 1965. Eventually, to Williams's delight, he would host African ambassadors on an elaborate dinner cruise on the presidential yacht *Sequoia*. Williams concluded that "while obviously with Kennedy I had the closer prior relationship, I didn't feel that I had really lost much effectiveness when Johnson came in."[10]

Encouraged by Johnson's willingness to meet with Africans, Williams besieged him with candidates for visits to the White House, and eventually the president had had enough. When Williams phoned him to arrange a meeting with two Kenyan officials in early 1964, Johnson responded: "God, Mennen, no! I just can't be seeing individuals like that." He suggested that Williams talk with them and "write a paragraph" for his night reading.[11]

In the first few months of the new administration, Johnson made it clear that not only would Williams remain in office but he would have the attention and support of the president. Williams found, however, that it was more difficult to convince the new administration to adopt the policies the African Bureau favored. Johnson saw himself as a domestic president and initially was deferential in foreign affairs. He was, however, obsessed with fears of "losing" the cold war struggle with communism and was determined not to appear "weak" in the global battle with the Soviet Union. As one student of his foreign policy summarized it: "Johnson fully and uncritically shared the assumptions, axioms, and dictates that composed the American Cold War mindset."[12]

The same could be said of his predecessor, but Kennedy often moderated his cold war militancy when dealing with Africa. As noted, he and Williams generally accepted African neutralism and acknowledged that much of the harsh, anti-American rhetoric of its leaders was intended for domestic consumption. Johnson was far more traditional in his view of Africa as a battleground in the conflict between communism and freedom, where any "loss" was a Soviet "gain."

Johnson's bipolar view of international affairs became even more pronounced as America was drawn into an ever-expanding military involvement in Vietnam. By early 1965, the conflict in Asia was absorbing the president's attention and dominating all other areas of foreign affairs. Like the rest of the world, U.S. diplomacy in Africa came to be shaped largely by its relationship to the war in Vietnam.

Within a few months of Johnson's taking office the tone of Washington's relations with Africa changed, as there was a sudden and strong stress on blocking communist advances in the region. Many in the new administration were convinced that radicalism was on the march throughout the continent and that China would be the leader in turning Africa toward Marxism. Policy analysts argued that the Chinese had a close identification with Africans, as both were non-European and had largely rural societies. The CIA warned that "the Chinese Communists view Africa as a land of opportunity, an area where long-term gains might be won. . . . Unable to afford massive economic and technical assistance programs, the Chinese rely mainly on propaganda, diplomatic maneuver, and personal contact." In late 1963, Chinese foreign minister Chou En-Lai made a lengthy visit to Africa that seemed to confirm Washington's fear that Beijing was the new threat in the region. The agency later warned of the possibility of "a marked growth of Communist influence in tropical Africa," with "African style satellites" controlled by China.[13]

Williams tried to counter the sudden fear of a "CHICOM" (Chinese Communist) offensive by repeating his argument that Africans jealously guarded their independence and would be unwilling to surrender their freedom to either China or Russia. Despite his rhetoric, U.S. concern over possible communist satellites in Africa intensified when John Okello, an obscure Ugandan, seized control of the island nation of Zanzibar a month after its independence, proclaimed himself "Field Marshall of the People's Republic of Zanzibar," and appointed a number of officials with close ties to China. The takeover of an insignificant nation by a comic dictator hardly seemed to pose a major threat to U.S. security, but both the government and the press responded with alarm. The *New York Times* raised the specter of "another Cuba off the coast of Africa," and the American ambassador to Zanzibar warned that the coup have given "CHICOMS and Cubans a strategic base off the East African coast." Johnson phoned Williams and expressed his fear that Zanzibar could "turn into another Cuba."[14]

Williams immediately moved to defuse the assumed crisis by

convincing other African nations to respond and eventually helped persuade Tanganyika's president, Julius Neyere, to annex Zanzibar and create the new nation of Tanzania. Williams felt triumphant and publicly hailed the move as a clear example of the way Africa "could solve its own problems" without foreign intervention. Johnson called him and after listening to a summary of the situation concluded: "Thank you Mennen. You are mighty good!"[15]

Despite his success in Zanzibar, the failure of the United States to predict or block the coup led many in Washington to criticize the African Bureau. Although he had praised Williams for his actions, in April Johnson appointed Averell Harriman as ambassador at large with responsibility for overseeing policy in Africa. Although Williams and Harriman had a long relationship, beginning with their formation of the Democratic Advisory Committee in the 1950s, the former New York governor's elevation was a major blow to Williams. While he publicly commended the move and noted their long friendship, Williams recognized that Harriman's insatiable lust for power and reputation as a master of bureaucratic politics would threaten his influence. He was accurate.[16]

The appointment of the blunt and cagey Harriman (nicknamed "The Crocodile" for his silence and craftiness) to direct African policy was in part due to the administration's general distrust of the glacial process of decision making in the State Department and an effort to diminish the continuing "Kennedy influence" on foreign policy. Ball had already fired Hilsman for perceived arrogance, concluding: "He was so full of his own omniscience." The White House felt Harriman's appointment would signal a new toughness and hardheadedness in policy that had been lacking under JFK.[17]

At the press conference following his appointment, Harriman made it clear that he was in charge of Africa and Williams would report directly to him rather than Rusk. He told reporters that the president wanted "a seventh floor man" in charge, not "a sixth floor person." (The African Bureau was now on level 6.) The newspapers quickly concluded that Williams had been demoted and attributed his reduced role to lingering friction over his opposition to Johnson's selection as vice president.[18]

Johnson was outraged by both Harriman's comments and the press reaction. In a phone conversation with Press Secretary George Reedy he called Harriman "totally irresponsible" and criticized him for humiliating Williams. He told Reedy that Williams "works hard and has my complete confidence. He and his wife have been as diligent and responsive as any two people in the government. I'm very fond of both of them." He ordered the press secretary to tell reporters that the move was not a reflection on Williams and had nothing to do with the 1960 convention. Reedy promised to "blow the hell out of the story."[19]

After talking with Reedy, the president was still seething. He called Rusk and asked: "Dean, have you seen all this stuff Averell's been spewing out about Mennen Williams?" Rusk responded that he was working to counter the press coverage and that Harriman had "just got tangled up." Johnson was not appeased and launched into a tirade against Harriman and the State Department. He ordered Rusk to tell Harriman to call reporters and explain that there had been no demotion of Williams and to apologize to him: "Be God damn sure to make him walk the carpet or apologize or resign. I just think this is awful." He told Rusk that

> if Harriman can't get it straightened out, I can because I'll
> have one [a press conference] and I'll damn sure make it
> clear. Tell him those fellows that sit round in their armchairs
> and mouth over in the State Department on background
> how God-damned important they are ought to get out. I'm
> not pleased with Harriman's griping around here all through
> this thing. Ever since I took over he's been mouthing about
> something, and now he's promoting himself. . . . I am no
> intimate of Williams as you know, but I think it's cruel and
> unfair and I don't play that way. And I think you ought to
> tell Harriman that. If you don't want to tell him, I will.

He then read Rusk a United Press International story on Harriman's comments that suggested some in the State Department were happy to see Williams's authority diminished. "All these damned officials over there talking instead of doing something," he concluded, and hung up on his secretary of state.[20]

Johnson's rage was real, but the damage had been done. Harriman immediately demonstrated his power when over Williams's objections he ordered the removal of William Mahoney as U.S. ambassador to Ghana. The press and many in the government continued to see the Harriman appointment as a direct affront to Williams, and the assistant secretary even called Reedy requesting an appointment with Johnson "as an offset to the Harriman thing." Staffers in the National Security Council suggested that the president personally announce the assistant secretary's next trip to Africa to "please Soapy" and stop "the gossip" about his reduced role. The White House quickly issued a press release praising Williams, noting Johnson's confidence in his ability, and hailing the forthcoming trip to Africa.[21]

Despite such symbolic gestures, many in Washington assumed that Williams might resign following the Harriman appointment. Rusk even phoned Johnson suggesting that Williams be appointed to head the Peace Corps, but Soapy did not resign. He had endured bureaucratic battles before and was determined to pursue his African first policy despite the sudden ascendancy of Harriman. He soon found, however, that the Johnson administration was less interested in Africa for the Africans than in the struggle against communism. The shift in Washington was most dramatic in the convoluted issue of the Congo.

Kennedy's response to the chaotic situation in the Congo had been to support the nation's unity by opposing Katanga's succession under the pro-Belgian Moise Tshombe, to oppose intervention by Belgium or other nations, and to assist a "moderate" Congolese government. At the time of Kennedy's assassination, Williams and other Africanists were generally satisfied that they had met their objectives. United Nations' troops were maintaining order, Tshombe had fled to Spain, and the Congo was unified under the leadership of Williams's personal choice, Cyril Adoula. In June 1964, the U.S. ambassador wrote Williams that "all of us share your optimism that the economic and political progress made in the Congo in the past four years will . . continue and that the pace will accelerate." In less than six months the Congo would again collapse into chaos; Tshombe, despised by most Africans and the African Bureau, would be in power; and the United States would alienate the entire continent by supporting the use of white mercenaries to preserve order in the nation.[22]

Despite the apparent success of American efforts for a united Congo, the nation was still deeply divided by ethnic and political factions, and only the continued presence of UN soldiers maintained order. Constant haggling in the UN over funding led the organization to announce that it was withdrawing its peacekeeping force in June 1964. As UN troops prepared to depart, a revolt swept the nation. The Simba rebels were a strange mixture of political radicalism and mysticism. Some were former followers of Patrice Lumumba who were convinced Adoula was an American puppet, while others claimed to have magical powers that made them immune to bullets. The Congolese army refused to attack the insurgents and launched its own rampage of looting and violence. The revolt spread, and by July the Congo was again in anarchy. Adoula resigned, and, sensing a chance to regain power, Tshombe returned to Africa.[23]

Many in Washington were convinced that the revolt in the Congo was guided by the Chinese to give them a foothold in Central Africa. Although he had repeatedly argued against viewing Africa as a cold war battleground, Williams recognized the new dominance of anticommunism in Washington and echoed the prevailing view of a Marxist threat. He claimed that "Mao Tse-tung's tract on guerilla warfare circulated throughout the eastern Congo, and the rebels were supplied with large amounts of Chinese and Russian military equipment." On August 5, the rebels captured Stanleyville, and the next day, to the shock of Williams and the African Bureau, President Joseph Kassavubu appointed Tshombe prime minister. African leaders were appalled that the "Belgian stooge" who had led Katanga's succession was now the leader of the Congo and charged that America had engineered his appointment. Williams denied that he "or any other State Department official" had any warning of Tshombe's selection. He hung a handwritten sign "GONE TO THE CONGO!" on his office door and immediately flew to meet with the new leader in Leopoldville.[24]

Williams arrived in the Congo on August 15 in a C-130 plane guarded by fifty U.S. paratroopers to talk with Tshombe. It was, in his words, a "prickly" discussion. Three years earlier he had denounced Tshombe as a Belgian puppet who had destroyed Congolese unity and encouraged civil war and charged him with indirectly fostering communism by dividing his country. Tshombe, in turn, had attacked Williams for leading the campaign to remove him from power. The battles had been vitriolic and personal, but now the two enemies sat down to try to devise a strategy to subdue the rebellion in the Congo. It was humiliating for Williams to shake hands with the man he had publicly condemned and who was despised by most African leaders. Williams claimed that sometimes it was necessary to "walk across the bridge with the devil himself to get to the other side" and suppression of the revolt was more important than personal animosity.[25]

Williams was aware that both Johnson and Harriman admired Tshombe and had been lukewarm to U.S. attempts to end Katangan independence. He also was convinced that unless the revolt was crushed there was the potential for a communist presence in the Congo. A few days earlier Johnson had presided at a National Security Council meeting on the Congo, where it was agreed that European or African troops would be needed to end the rebellion. Harriman had unsuccessfully lobbied Belgian officials to send soldiers, and Williams had urged African nations to intervene, but they had no desire to aid the hated Tshombe. Johnson concluded that "time is running out and the Congo must be saved."[26]

At their meeting Williams pressed Tshombe to appeal to the Organization of African Unity for troops to fight the rebels, but he found that the prime minister "was not convinced of our sincerity" and distrusted other African leaders, as they had denounced him when he led Katanga out of the Congo and had mocked his selection as prime minister. He argued that the

only way to destroy the rebels would be to hire white mercenaries to fight them.[27]

Williams knew that the use of white mercenaries would
infuriate nearly all of Africa, as they symbolized colonialism and
violated the principle of African solutions to the continent's
problems. Two years earlier he had denounced Tshombe's use
of hired white soldiers in Katanga, but now he agreed that they
were the only solution. In a memo to Rusk he acknowledged
that, given Belgian's refusal to intervene and African opposition
to helping Tshombe, foreign mercenaries would be the only
way to end the revolt. Williams and Tshombe agreed that the
United States would help fund the recruitment of white mercenaries from South Africa, Rhodesia, Belgium, and other
countries. By October 1964, more than a thousand hired troops
(all of them white) were being paid by the CIA to fight for
Tshombe.[28]

Predictably, the image of hired whites killing black Africans
in support of Tshombe ("the murderer of Lumumba") outraged African leaders. Nearly every African nation denounced
the mercenaries and the United States and several began to provide military support to the rebels. In April 1965 Cuba also sent
troops and guerilla leader Che Guevara to the Congo.[29]

African anger peaked when Washington dispatched twelve
C-130 planes to airlift Belgian paratroopers to free white
hostages held by the rebels in Stanleyville. Under constant
attack by Tshombe's mercenaries, the Simbas arrested about
three hundred whites, including a popular U.S. medical missionary, Dr. Paul Carlson. Fearful that the rebels would execute
their white prisoners, America agreed to airlift five hundred
Belgian troops to Stanleyville, where they succeeded in freeing
most of the hostages, though twenty prisoners, including Carlson, were executed. Williams defended the raid as a humanitarian move intended to save innocent lives, but Africans were
nearly unanimous in denouncing intervention by the hated
Belgians. After listening to nearly every African delegate attack
the United States, UN Ambassador Stevenson claimed that he
had "never heard such irrational, irresponsible, insulting, and
repugnant language in these chambers!"[30]

Tshombe's reign in the Congo was short-lived, as military leader Joseph Mobutu soon seized power and Tshombe fled to Katanga, where he again announced its secession. America may have prevented a communist gain, but its policies helped pave the way for Mobutu's takeover and the beginning of over two decades of an oppressive and corrupt dictatorship.

Three years earlier it would have been inconceivable for Mennen Williams, the advocate of Africa for the Africans and removal of Africa from the cold war competitive game, to endorse the use of white mercenaries, Belgian intervention, and the return of the despised Tshombe to power. His actions in 1964 seem a complete reversal of his earlier positions and can only be understood within the context of the changed mood in Washington after Kennedy's death. Although Williams defended African neutralism and called for Africa to solve its problems without foreign intervention, he also recognized the dominance of anticommunism in the Johnson administration. The elevation of Harriman was a clear indication that preventing the spread of communism on the continent was the first priority and that the press, public, and Congress all viewed Africa within the bipolar cold war framework. He noted that whenever he spoke he could be sure of only one question: how are you doing in Africa compared to the Communists? Despite his liberal proclamations, Williams himself believed that communism was a global menace that had targeted Africa and was convinced that the Congo "was going to go downhill and the Communists were going to take over" unless Washington acted. He knew that he would be judged by the president and the public on the basis of preventing any Soviet or Chinese gains and concluded that his endorsement of Tshombe and white mercenaries was necessary to prevent the possibility of a communist state in Africa. He never questioned the basic cold war assumptions of the communist commitment to expansion, and in the case of the Congo was willing to compromise earlier positions to avoid the charge that he had been unwilling or unable to block a Sino-Soviet victory.[31]

Williams's support of Johnson's policies in the Congo may have been a political necessity for survival in the new administration, but the cost was high. Many Africans felt he had betrayed his earlier principles and abandoned his African first policy. He hoped that Johnson's leadership in the battle for civil rights would temper African hostility by showing America's commitment to racial equality.

Nothing was more important to Williams than civil rights. For twelve years in Michigan he had worked to end racial discrimination, and he had been the most vocal white critic of legalized segregation in America. Since arriving in Washington, he had repeatedly argued that racial equality was not only a matter of principle but a necessity if the nation was to win the cold war battle with communism in Africa. To Williams, it was the height of hypocrisy for Washington to call for freedom and liberty while denying equality at home, and he insisted that Africans would not be convinced of American sincerity until segregation was abolished. As he wrote to Rusk, "more and more African self-determination and Negro equality in the U.S. are linked together."[32]

Given his long record opposing racism, Williams was delighted when Johnson pushed the Civil Rights Act through Congress in July 1964, ending discrimination in public facilities. Williams immediately wrote to all the African leaders, pointing out that America was now a nation of true equality for all races.[33]

Typically, however, Williams was not content with passage of a single bill and pushed for continued efforts to guarantee equal rights. When African Americans formed the Mississippi Freedom Democratic Party (MFDP) to challenge white segregationist delegates to the 1964 Democratic National Convention in Atlantic City, Williams urged that they be seated in place of regular delegates. Johnson, however, feared a fractious floor flight and dispatched Hubert Humphrey to arrange a compromise in which two blacks would be seated as "delegates at large" and the regular Mississippi delegation would be recognized. Civil rights activists were outraged, and so was Williams. Throughout his political career he had denounced any "compromise" of principle. As blacks in Mississippi were not allowed to vote, the regular delegation was fraudulent, and offering only two at-large delegates was a betrayal of democracy. Williams decided to defy Johnson, Humphrey, and their unprincipled compromise.

Williams was a member of the Michigan delegation, which had passed a resolution in support of seating the Mississippi Freedom Democratic Party. Although he declined to attend a meeting of those opposed to Johnson's compromise solution, he, his old ADA colleague Joseph Rauh, and Oregon senator Wayne Morse secretly provided credentials to MFDP delegates so they could get on the floor of the convention. Johnson, who was monitoring the convention from the Oval Office, was outraged to see blacks confronting white Mississippi delegates and ordered aide Walter Jenkins to find out who was giving them credentials. The president never knew that it was his assistant secretary of state who was offering Mississippi blacks access to the convention.[34]

Despite his maneuverings in Atlantic City, Williams was delighted that Johnson had passed significant civil rights legislation and buoyed by the president's overwhelming victory over Peg Johnson's husband, Barry Goldwater, in 1964. He was particularly excited by Johnson's pledge for major economic and social reform at home and his call for "a massive world-wide approach to uplifting the less developed nations." Since 1948, Williams had urged an expansion of national educational, welfare, and housing programs, and during his tenure in the African Bureau he had repeatedly lobbied for a dramatic increase in U.S. aid to the continent. It now seemed that his former foe from Texas would implement both objectives. Even before the election, he wrote vice presidential nominee Humphrey of his delight with the president's plans for expanded aid to Africa and urged him to "set the tone" for a new approach to the continent by duplicating LBJ's famous trip to Africa in 1961.[35]

Johnson's call for "a New Deal" for the third world was only campaign rhetoric, but Williams seized on the pledge as an opportunity to regain prestige and show Africans that they still were important to America. By 1965, Williams badly needed a major policy victory. He had come to Washington to revitalize and reorient America's African policy and maintain his influence within the Democratic Party. Four years later both were in jeopardy. Washington's heavy-handed Congo policy had undone most of his efforts to show Africa that the United States opposed foreign intervention and did not view Africa as merely a cold war battleground. Johnson had been reluctant to renew the demands on Portugal to abandon its African colonies and had shown no willingness to confront the white regime in South Africa. As the "African advocate" in Washington, Williams needed to demonstrate the continued importance of the continent.

Williams also had lost much of the power and publicity that had marked his years under Kennedy. The press continued to focus on the expanded influence of Harriman and the assumed diminished role of Williams. Bundy wrote Johnson that morale was low in the African Bureau due to "confusion as to who is responsible for African decisions—Harriman or Williams." The *Washington Post* and *New York Times* both ran stories that Williams was planning to resign in protest over his loss of power. *U.S. News and World Report* followed with a piece reporting that Williams had been an "unwelcome guest" at Kennedy's hotel suite in Los Angeles at the 1960 convention and had "crashed" a meeting of southern governors lobbying for Johnson. The story concluded that Williams was being forced out due to his past opposition to Johnson's vice presidential nomination. Williams sent a letter denying the story and forwarded a copy to Johnson. The president immediately called the head of the African Bureau to the White House and alerted the press to wait outside. Johnson then assured Williams that there were no plans to remove him. When Williams emerged, reporters asked him if he had any announcements. He was silent for a few minutes but soon broke into a wide grin and said: "Some of you fellows fired me but the President just rehired me!"[36]

Despite Johnson's reassurances, Williams began to think seriously about life after the State Department. He never abandoned hopes of electoral office, and there were rumors that Pat McNamara was ill and might not seek reelection to the Senate from Michigan. Williams was a natural replacement.

To show his continued influence and perhaps prepare for a

return to elected office, Williams needed to make a dramatic gesture, and a massive economic aid program for Africa seemed to be the perfect move. He immediately drafted a cable to be sent by Rusk to all the U.S. ambassadors in Africa, instructing them to prepare for a "new and critical look at overall American policy" that would "shape future U.S. policy toward Africa with the same energy and imagination that generated programs of the Great Society at home." He then called a meeting in Addis Ababa to develop "the Johnson Plan" for a vast increase in economic assistance to Africa.[37]

Williams wanted a major increase in aid to all African nations. His notes for the Addis Ababa meeting suggested "doubling" current aid levels. He justified the new economic commitment as necessary to block Marxism, as communist nations were contributing $714 million to Africa annually, 65 percent of their total aid throughout the world, while the United States was spending only $549 million, less than 8 percent of its global funding. "If the total of Western aid falls too far short of meeting African expectations, the compulsion upon African political leaders to accept communist aid will become irresistible," he concluded. The Johnson Plan was not only symbolic of American idealism and the country's desire to help the poor of Africa; it was a practical necessity to prevent "the establishment of a single Communist center for subversion in Africa."[38]

Williams was in high spirits as he worked on details of the Johnson Plan. He quickly reviewed the situation in each nation, indicated the proposed increase in aid, and listed the programs that could result. He was convinced that the aid program would be Johnson's major initiative in Africa and would appeal to the president's desire to leave a lasting mark on foreign affairs. It would be the "centerpiece" of Johnson's legacy. The Johnson Plan was also the "Williams Plan," as it would restore his prestige with Africans, propel his name back into the headlines, and serve as a launching pad for his campaign for the Senate. He would be bitterly disappointed.[39]

Even before he formally presented his recommendations there was strong opposition in Washington. Ulrich Haynes, the black NSC African specialist, attended the conference in Addis

Ababa and reported that Williams's proposal was too large and unfocused and could not be financed given the pressures of spending on the Great Society and the expanded military involvement in Vietnam.[40]

On May 10, 1965, Williams presented his Johnson Plan for Africa to the National Security Council. It was a long, unwieldy, hundred-page list of dozens of programs, including "high level visits by the President, Vice-President, Secretary of State, Governors etc.," a "White House conference on Africa" to be chaired by Johnson, and a near doubling of aid to every nation on the continent. The reception was chilly. The NSC judged the document "a laundry list" that was "way up there in the clouds," with "something in it to satisfy everyone." It was a "long, verbose, platitudinous effort" that was too expensive and would never be approved by Congress. Robert Komer of the NSC wrote a scathing memo to Johnson, arguing that Williams thought all of Africa's problems could be solved with infusions of U.S. money and suggesting that Africa was so primitive that increased American aid would do little good.[41]

Incensed by the harsh criticism, Williams tried to enlist White House aide Bill Moyers and U.S. Information Agency director Carl Rowan, an African American, to lobby for approval. NSC staffers phoned Moyers and explained their opposition to the proposal, and over drinks Haynes told Rowan that the plan was "still under review."[42] Williams continued to push for a dramatic increase in aid to Africa, but the project was doomed. By the summer of 1965, Johnson had implemented most of his Great Society's social and economic programs and was beginning a massive military involvement in Vietnam. The cost of domestic reform and the war in Asia were already straining the budget, and few were convinced that it was time to double aid to Africa. Many in the White House argued the opposite: given the costs of the Great Society and the conflict in Vietnam, it was a time to slash aid to Africa and other areas not considered vital. Johnson agreed and appointed former U.S. ambassador to Ethiopia Edward Korry to prepare a "comprehensive study of Africa" with suggestions on how to focus U.S. assistance where it would have the most impact.[43]

Korry ignored Williams, the man who had arranged his appointment to Ethiopia, and argued that Africa was "for the most part outside the main areas of U.S. attention" and lacked the "historic ties of Latin America" or "the strategic interests of Asia." He concluded that aid was scattered in too many countries and funded too many programs. U.S. assistance policy had been "a reflection of the unrealistic expectations found in both the United States and in Africa." He urged Johnson to drastically cut most aid programs, to focus on a "few strategic countries," and to stress education, rural development, and "the promotion of private enterprise."[44]

Korry's recommendations were perfectly timed, as the cost of the Great Society and the war in Vietnam had made many in Washington favorable to reducing spending in all other areas. It was also a direct repudiation of Mennen Williams. His Johnson Plan had envisioned a major escalation in American aid spread throughout the continent, a New Deal for Africa that would be both the president's and Williams's signature gesture of a deep commitment to the continent. Korry's call for a cut in aid and a focus on a few nations was the exact opposite, and Williams felt betrayed. He argued that Korry's recommendations were

> contrary to what we had discussed over a period of time— and I say all, I mean all of the African Ambassadors and all of our staff—had come up with a general program of development. Korry advocated the concentration of aid programs in a few countries. I thought that was wrong.

He phoned Johnson, Rusk, and others and bombarded the White House with memos trying to justify a broad program of increased aid throughout Africa, but he found that the president and his staff "had leant their ears to Ed Korry."[45]

By late 1965, it was clear that the battle had been lost. There would be no Johnson Plan for Africa and no stunning triumph for Soapy Williams. He felt Johnson had deceived him and Korry had betrayed him. He later recalled that the major failure of his career in the State Department was when "somebody fell off the boat and filed that Korry plan." The always optimistic and buoyant Williams was depressed and angry, and many in the administration thought he would publicly denounce Korry's recommendations and perhaps even resign. Bundy dispatched Komer to talk with Williams and get him to follow "the administration line." He noted that Williams "doesn't take guidance easily" but Komer should "give it to him hard!"[46]

Williams did not "go public" or immediately resign, but the "Korry Report" sapped his energy. He would remain at the State Department until March 1966, but increasingly he focused on a possible return to elected office. In August Walter Reuther phoned Johnson and urged him to appoint Williams to the U.S.-Canadian Border Commission so he could return to Michigan and "cut [George] Romney down more nearly to size." Romney had defeated Neil Staebler in the race for governor in Michigan and had emerged as a leading contender for the Republican presidential nomination in 1968. Reuther argued that "Soapy can do a better job cutting Romney down to size than anybody else." Johnson agreed that Williams could "murder them damn Republicans," but it was up to Williams whether he wanted to leave Washington.[47]

Despite Reuther's desire for Williams to return to Michigan immediately, Soapy was not yet ready to leave Washington. He had already decided that if McNamara did not run he would campaign for the Senate in 1966, but the election was over a year away. He would stay in the State Department until the spring of 1966, but he showed little of the flair and flamboyance that had characterized his first four years in Washington. He continued to lobby for a stronger stance in favor of the end of white rule in Africa and would become deeply engaged in America's response to the unilateral declaration of independence of the white minority government in Rhodesia, but by late 1965 his mind was more focused on a triumphant return to Michigan and election to the Senate than on policy battles in Washington.

During his last year at the African Bureau the ever-expanding war in Vietnam dominated U.S. foreign policy. In October 1965, Williams left for his thirteenth trip to Africa and found that the war in Asia was the major issue for African leaders. Like Johnson and others who came of age during World War II and

the cold war, Williams accepted the battle in Vietnam as necessary to block the expansion of communism. He defended the
war in his talks with African leaders but repeatedly assured them
that it would be brief and would end in a negotiated settlement.
He wrote Rusk that "almost all" Africans supported "our Vietnam policy."[48]

When he returned from Africa, Williams went to Michigan
for Christmas and was sitting in his dentist's chair in Detroit
having a filling replaced when he received a phone call asking
him to return to the capital immediately for an urgent meeting
with Rusk. The secretary of state informed him that Johnson
had ordered a halt to American bombing in Vietnam and issued
a call for a cease-fire and multinational negotiations to end the
war. Williams was to depart immediately to explain the proposal to African leaders and pressure them to publicly support
the "Johnson peace offensive."[49]

After he developed his plan for a bombing halt Johnson
arranged visits by U.S. officials to nearly all foreign governments to solicit support. Rusk and Bundy had urged him to
send Williams's aide Wayne Fredericks to Africa, but Johnson
argued that Williams "was so much better with the liberals."
The president feared that liberals were turning against the war
and hoped the endorsement of the peace initiative by Williams
would help keep them in line. "Williams is a symbol," he told
Rusk, and ordered the secretary of state to "give him
[Williams] enough education so he doesn't get you in trouble."[50]

Williams immediately left Washington for a frantic ten-day
trip to Morocco, Tunisia, Liberia, Senegal, the Ivory Coast,
Algeria, Kenya, Tanzania, Uganda, Guinea, Mali, and Ethiopia
to persuade Africans that Johnson was seeking "an honorable
and peaceful settlement in Vietnam." Most African leaders
endorsed the effort, but Tanzanian leader Neyere was skeptical
and suggested that America should withdraw its troops and let
the Vietnamese decide their future.[51]

Johnson was pleased with Williams's efforts, but the bombing halt did not result in negotiations and the war resumed.
When Williams met Johnson at a luncheon meeting to argue

for a renewal of pressure on Portugal to abandon Angola, the president only wanted to discuss Vietnam.[52]

Johnson was also uninterested in any new efforts to oppose apartheid. He continued Kennedy's arms embargo but rejected Williams's suggestion that he consider more general economic sanctions against South Africa. When Williams routinely submitted a draft of a speech he was to deliver at the Harvard Law School criticizing apartheid, he was stunned to find it had been rejected by officials as "too provocative," as it implied that sanctions might be necessary to end apartheid. Ambassador Satterthwaite applauded the effort to restrain the outspoken Williams and contended that the head of the African Bureau was more concerned with preserving his reputation among American liberals than using "quiet diplomacy" to moderate apartheid. South African officials were quick to recognize the softening of the rhetorical attacks on apartheid, and its ambassador remarked to Williams: "You haven't been too horrible to us recently!"[53]

Given the lack of initiatives in Africa, Williams was left with only symbolic gestures to show Africans that they still mattered in Washington. Johnson sent autographed copies of his speech proposing a voting rights act to all African leaders with the inscription: "Recognizing your personal interest in the great problems of achieving human dignity." This posed a problem for the leader of South Africa, and the note on his copy was changed to "recognizing your Government's awareness of the importance of racial problems." On July 15, the president hosted African diplomats on a cruise of the Potomac on the presidential yacht. Williams and Rusk joined him as he told stories of his childhood in Texas and reaffirmed his dedication to racial equality. The next day Williams sent a note informing Johnson that the Africans "went away bubbling with enthusiasm!"[54]

While he appreciated Johnson's symbolic efforts, Williams was increasingly frustrated with the seeming lack of attention to Africa. Although he supported the war in Vietnam, he was dismayed that it seemed to override other diplomatic interests. Williams was finally able to push Johnson into an active role in

Africa in response to the crisis in Rhodesia, his last major issue as head of the African Bureau.

Rhodesia had been a problem for America for nearly five years before it became a crisis in November 1965. As most of Africa moved toward independence in the late 1950s and early 1960s, the white minority in Rhodesia (less than 10 percent of the population) refused to grant any political rights to the black majority and argued that their nation, like the rest of Britain's colonies, should be granted independence. As early as 1962, Williams had warned that Rhodesia was "the new African time bomb." The bomb exploded when whites elected Ian Smith as prime minister of Rhodesia and he announced that he would defy Britain and declare independence unilaterally. Washington made it clear that it would support London's efforts to prevent Rhodesian independence without guarantees of equal political rights for its black citizens. Despite threats of economic sanctions from Britain, the United States, and the UN, on November 11, 1965, Smith declared Rhodesia independent.[55]

To Williams and other Africanists, Rhodesia's defiance of Britain and the international community demanded a strong response from the United States. Many in the White House and the State Department argued that Rhodesia was "England's problem" and Washington had little to gain from opposing the white minority in a tiny African nation, but to Williams Rhodesia was another test of America's commitment to racial equality and majority rule. The nation had finally abolished formal racial discrimination at home and needed to show that its dedication to equality did not end at its borders. Africans were united in their opposition to Rhodesian independence, and America would be judged by its response. A forceful policy toward Smith and the white minority would help undo the damage caused by Washington's intervention in the Congo. Williams led the fight to persuade Johnson to impose strict economic sanctions on Rhodesia, and, despite opposition within the Defense and State Departments, he triumphed. The United States joined England in declaring an end to all economic contact with Rhodesia.[56]

Williams was convinced that sanctions would produce a

"quick kill" and force Smith to compromise, but the whites in Rhodesia proved to be determined and resourceful. They were able to covertly purchase oil and other products in defiance of sanctions and immediately launched an effective propaganda campaign to convince Americans that they were only duplicating the U.S. break with England in 1776. The Rhodesian lobby gained support from many American conservatives, who saw the white minority as a bastion of stability and anticommunism in Africa. They also pointed out that, while Rhodesia supported U.S. efforts to stop communism in Vietnam, Britain and its prime minister, Harold Wilson, were critical of the war and continued to trade with North Vietnam. By early 1966, the Rhodesian Information Agency had established a weekly newsletter and a monthly magazine explaining the country's position and created two powerful lobbying groups, the Friends of Rhodesian Independence and the American–Southern African Council. They enlisted support from the Liberty Lobby, the John Birch Society, and conservative radio commentators Carl McIntyre, Dan Smoot, and Fulton Lewis II. Many conservatives in Congress also defended Rhodesia, and the State Department had to hire extra secretaries to handle the thousands of letters it received demanding repeal of sanctions against "Brave Rhodesia."

While the administration waited for sanctions to drive Rhodesia back to Britain, Williams led the campaign against Smith and his U.S. allies. He gave over a dozen speeches in the four months following Rhodesia's declaration of independence defending America's actions as both morally and politically correct. In an address to a hostile audience at the national convention of the American Legion, he charged that it was a violation of American ideals to allow "220,000 whites to maintain a 'George Wallace type' of racial supremacy over millions of black Africans." He also claimed that unless Washington acted "the Communists would be happy to rush into the situation." Rhodesia was a test of the U.S. commitment to racial equality and a challenge to its determination to resist communism. He contended that economic sanctions would work and Smith would give in by early summer.[57]

Despite his predictions, the sanctions were largely ineffective, and there was no "quick kill." Black Rhodesians began an armed revolt, and in 1971 Congress adopted the Byrd Amendment (named after Virginia Senator Harry Byrd) lifting the ban on imports of Rhodesian chrome and other "strategic materials." It would take over a decade of war to finally establish majority rule in Rhodesia.

While leading the attack on Rhodesia, Williams was already preparing for his return to Michigan. As expected, in February McNamara announced that he was too sick to seek reelection. When he died of cancer on April 30, Governor Romney appointed Congressman Robert Griffin to complete his term. Williams contacted a number of Michigan Democrats indicating that he would be willing to run for the Senate in 1966. Reporters in Michigan and Washington quickly picked up the story and predicted Williams's departure. By late February it was clear that he was leaving, and NSC staffers noted that "Williams' domestic political ambitions" would soon outweigh his interest in African issues and they should look for a replacement. After listening to Williams's attempts to justify the lack of economic sanctions against South Africa under withering questioning from New York representative Benjamin Rosenthal, *The Nation* suggested it was time for him to "go back to Michigan," where he could "create his own foolish positions . . . and not have to defend those created for him by the Administration."[58]

Williams delayed his resignation, however, as he had one final goal in Washington. He wanted Johnson to deliver a major address to African diplomats on the third anniversary of the formation of the Organization of African Unity reaffirming American dedication to racial equality and majority rule in Africa. Johnson agreed and eventually gave the talk on May 26. In a speech largely drafted by Williams, the president declared that America was committed to the abolition of racial discrimination throughout the world and to control of Africa "by Africans." It was all that Williams had hoped for. Joseph Palmer, his replacement as head of the African Bureau, recalled that Johnson's speech was "wonderful" and he "out Soapied Soapy Williams!"[59]

Williams and John F. Kennedy on Mackinac Island in June 1960. When his own campaign for the presidency collapsed, Williams endorsed Kennedy, despite concerns about the senator's commitment to civil rights. (G. Mennen Williams Papers, 1883–1988, Box 6-P, courtesy of the Bentley Historical Library, University of Michigan.)

Williams with President Lyndon Johnson in 1965. Although Williams's lone and vocal dissent from Johnson's nomination for vice president in 1960 strained relations, he retained his position as head of the African Bureau after the death of Kennedy. (G. Mennen Williams Papers, 1883–1988, Box 6-P, courtesy of the Bentley Historical Library, University of Michigan.)

Williams being invested as an honorary chief of Kpelle tribe in Liberia in 1962.
(Photograph by USIS staff. G. Mennen Williams Papers, 1883–1988, Box 10-P, courtesy of the Bentley
Historical Library, University of Michigan.)

Soapy and Nancy with Martin Luther King. Throughout his political career, Williams was an outspoken advocate of racial equality and a vocal critic of segregation, a stance that often alienated influential Democrats. (G. Mennen Williams Papers, 1883–1988, Box 6-P, courtesy of the Bentley Historical Library, University of Michigan.)

Senator Ted Kennedy and Williams
campaigning during the latter's failed
Senate run in 1966. Despite winning six
consecutive terms as governor, Williams
suffered his only electoral defeat when
he lost the U.S. Senate race to Robert
Griffin. (G. Mennen Williams Papers, 1883–1988,
Box 6-P, courtesy of the Bentley Historical Library,
University of Michigan.)

Williams riding a water buffalo while
serving as U.S. ambassador to the
Philippines in 1968. His appointment as
the United States' chief representative in
Manila was his last position in the State
Department. (G. Mennen Williams Papers,
1883–1988, Box 11-P, courtesy of the Bentley
Historical Library, University of Michigan.)

Soapy and Nancy dancing at the Sweetheart Ball a month before his death. Williams spent most of his brief retirement defending his liberal ideology and trying to establish his significance in American political history. (G. Mennen Williams Papers, 1883–1988, Box 1-P, courtesy of the Bentley Historical Library, University of Michigan.)

Michigan Supreme Court justice G. Mennen Williams. Williams served on the
court for sixteen years (the last three as chief justice) and was best known for his
efforts to modernize and computerize the state's courts. (G. Mennen Williams Papers,
1883–1988, Box 11-P, courtesy of the Bentley Historical Library, University of Michigan.)

Williams's casket before his burial on Mackinac Island in 1987. After a temporary
burial in Detroit, Williams's body was moved to his beloved Mackinac Island.
He was buried within sight of the bridge connecting the two halves of
Michigan. (Photograph © *The Detroit Free Press*. G. Mennen Williams Papers, 1883–1988, Box 1-P,
courtesy of the Bentley Historical Library, University of Michigan.)

Assured of Johnson's intentions to make the speech, Williams wrote the president on March 1 that he would be resigning to run for the Senate. On March 11, they held a joint press conference, where Williams praised Johnson for his attention to Africa and urged him to continue his peace initiative in Vietnam. Johnson responded by hailing Williams's service "during the most critical period" of American involvement in Africa. A White House press release added that he had "set the tone for American actions in the still-troubled areas of southern Africa" and "it is noteworthy that there have been no Communist satellites established on the African continent" during Williams's tour.[60]

Williams hoped that the administration would continue his efforts to make Africa a major priority and strongly endorsed his top aide, Wayne Fredericks, as his successor at the African Bureau. But Fredericks had repeatedly clashed with Rusk over African policy and was not considered. Blacks, led by Michigan congressman Charles Diggs and noted historian John Hope Franklin, lobbied for an African American to replace Williams. Eventually Johnson made the safe selection of career diplomat Joseph Palmer.[61]

No assistant secretary of state provoked as much controversy or publicity as G. Mennen Williams. Most State Department bureaucrats never get their name in the paper or attract public praise or criticism. Williams's flamboyance, outspokenness, and travel kept him in the public eye throughout his five years in Washington. His infamous "Africa is for the Africans" speech in 1961 symbolized both his goals and his style, earning the praise of Africans and unrelenting criticism from his opponents. He defied most of the rules of diplomacy, and that was the source of both his successes and his failures. To liberals and Africans, he was a solitary voice for an African first orientation in U.S. policy that demanded the nation live up to its ideals of equality, democracy, and freedom. To critics, Williams was a publicity-seeking politician who did not understand the process and protocol of policy-making and had the unrealistic expectation that Washington should champion Africa regardless of the cost of alienating traditional allies and jeopardizing strategic interests.

No one can deny Williams's ability to generate publicity, and, given the fierce opposition to his goals, he was able to achieve remarkable success. He managed to convince both Kennedy and Johnson to demonstrate the importance of Africa through personal diplomacy, and his frequent trips succeeded in showing Africans their significance for America. He pushed Kennedy to take some steps to prod Portugal toward granting independence to its African colonies, and the arms embargo on South Africa was a major personal victory. His efforts to ensure a united, anticommunist Congo were consistent but modified by the realities of power politics. Williams's leadership in mobilizing opposition to the illegal independence of Rhodesia marked a final policy victory.

When he arrived in Washington in early 1961, Williams was dedicated to showing Africans their importance to the United States, to reorientating American policy to be less deferential to Europe, to becoming the "voice of Africa" in the United States, to moving Washington toward acceptance of African neutrality, and to lead the effort to end minority rule on the continent. It was an ambitious agenda, and, given the dominance of cold war strategic interests and global anticommunism, he was amazing successful. Underneath the colorful quotes, the flamboyant behavior, and the insatiable travel, there were solid diplomatic triumphs. Africa was never at the center of American foreign policy, but never before or again would it be as significant to U.S. diplomacy as it was in the Williams years.

His second goal in accepting the appointment to head the African Bureau was more personal: to keep himself politically alive by maintaining a public presence. He was certain his efforts in Washington had been successful in generating publicity that would lead to a second political career beginning with election to the Senate. The White House was still a possibility, as Williams was fifty-five in 1966, still young by political standards and not too old for a run at the presidency in 1972. If he could revive his Democratic machine in Michigan and win the Senate race against Griffin (thereby humiliating George Romney, the likely 1968 presidential nominee, in the process), Johnson and other party leaders might support him for the nomination in 1972. Nancy Williams wrote to Lady Bird Johnson that "Soapy's reentry into Michigan Politics seems to have given Michigan Democrats a new lease on life which may be especially important in view of George Romney's ambitions."[62]

In 1948, a nearly unknown Soapy Williams was a seemingly hopeless underdog in the battle for the governorship. Eighteen years later he returned to his home state to run for the Senate. Far from the obscure member of the Michigan Liquor Control Commission, he was now the best-known politician in his state, so famous that he did not even need to put his name on billboards, only a picture of a bow tie. He had remade the Democratic Party into one of the most efficient political machines in the country and had the ample financial support of Michigan's unions. Many observers believed he would easily sweep past his Republican opponent and regain his title as "Michigan's greatest vote getter."

Williams had changed from underdog to favorite, but much else had also changed in Michigan and the nation. The Vietnam War and urban riots had badly divided the nation, the Michigan Democratic Party, and Williams's major source of support, unions. George Romney had emerged as the new dominant force in Michigan politics, and it was clear he would have little difficulty gaining reelection in 1966. Increasingly, television, never one of Williams's strengths, was the most important element in elections. He learned that younger members of his party had their own political ambitions and were not deferential to the former "boy wonder." Williams also found that his political organization had declined dramatically during his five years in Washington. Staebler, Weber, Murray, and many other advisers were no longer active, and he would need to find replacements. Finally, Williams was no longer the aggressive newcomer but approaching "elder statesman" status. Younger voters were not familiar with his style and not responsive to his 1950s brand of political liberalism.

Williams would soon discover these barriers to his triumphant return to electoral politics, but in the spring of 1966 he was supremely confident. Although his resignation from the African Bureau did not officially take effect until March 23, he left Washington immediately after his press conference with Johnson and blitzed the state, shaking hands and renewing old political acquaintances. On the first day back he traveled to Detroit, Grand Rapids, Muskegon, and Flint and told reporters: "It is going very well indeed!" The next day he officially announced his candidacy for the Senate before a raucous crowd of party officials and union leaders at the Detroit Sheraton-Cadillac Hotel. He promised to work for racial harmony, for continuation of Johnson's Great Society, and to be "a supporter of the Administration's policy" on Vietnam, which he characterized as working for "a negotiated settlement."[63]

Williams was buoyant and confident, but his campaign showed early signs of major problems. Buffy Berthelot had managed his last two campaigns for governor, but she had also been in charge of Staebler's disastrous run against Romney in 1964, and Williams selected Ed McGloin, a former teacher, to run his organization. To replace Weber as his press secretary he picked former reporter Jim Robinson, who had never been in a top position in a campaign. Noting the lack of veteran politicians, Robinson concluded that "this is essentially an amateur staff."[64]

To show his commitment to Detroit's decrepit inner city, Williams located his campaign headquarters downtown in the abandoned Fuller Hotel. The neighborhood was overrun with prostitutes and drug dealers, and Williams was propositioned several times. Many of his staff members were afraid to work at night and ventured out to their parked cars in groups of three or four.[65]

More important than staff or buildings was the decision of Detroit mayor Jerome "Jerry" Cavanaugh to challenge him for the nomination. Michigan Democrats had urged Cavanaugh to run against Romney for governor, but the Republican seemed invulnerable and he chose to battle Williams for the nomination for the Senate seat. Cavanaugh was young (at thirty-eight he was only a year older than Williams when he was elected governor in 1948), aggressive, articulate, and popular with black voters. He had won two terms as mayor and served as the head of both the National League of Cities and the U.S. Conference of Mayors. He argued that Williams was "a tired old war horse" who had been crucial in reviving the Democratic Party in the 1950s but was out of touch with the issues and voters of the 1960s. He was also a fervent opponent of the war in Vietnam.

Few in Michigan or the nation gave the young mayor a chance. The *Wall Street Journal* noted that Williams's name "was still magic" and Michigan was "solid for Soapy." The *New York Times,* however, predicted "a hard fight." Lyndon Johnson was angered by Cavanaugh's criticism of Vietnam and urged Williams to challenge him on the issue.[66]

Few expected Cavanaugh to defeat Williams, but his decision to contest the nomination meant a costly primary in early August, which taxed the finances and energy of the campaign. Cavanaugh ran an aggressive campaign focused on the need for "younger leadership" and an immediate cease-fire in Vietnam. Williams largely ignored his Democratic opponent, concentrating his attacks on Griffin and Romney. He refused to debate Cavanaugh on the war, and when the Detroit mayor hired a team of media consultants Williams charged that he was controlled by "Madison Avenue–Miami mercenaries." Cavanaugh, who had swept the black vote in his mayoral campaign in 1964, made a major blunder when he endorsed a "stop and frisk" law to permit police to search individuals without a warrant. Williams seized on the comment and denounced the proposal as racist and a violation of civil liberties.[67]

Williams ran his usual frantic hands-on campaign. A *Time* reporter noted that "it was a old-fashioned, personal handshaking, back slapping campaign in the age of TV—which Soapy largely ignored" and marveled that "he never stopped campaigning." In a typical day he shook hands with "everyone," including "bums on Detroit's Skid Row"; played pool with "unemployed Negroes"; and greeted wedding guests in Polish and mourners at a wake in German. Williams easily defeated Cavanaugh by a margin of 435,848 to 289,643, winning by 60 percent in Detroit and carrying the African American vote by a twelve-to-one margin. To the national media, Williams was back and his political organization and personal appeal were as strong as ever. Five years in Washington had done nothing to diminish his political power. *Time, The Reporter, U.S. News and World Report,* and the *New York Times* all predicted an easy win in November.[68]

Despite his impressive victory, the battle with Cavanaugh showed some weaknesses that would emerge more fully in the run against Griffin. Clearly Williams was still able to work a crowd and establish a rapport with the people, but his energy level was not as high as when he was younger. His distrust of TV was a handicap given its increasing importance. The primary showed that Williams could still mobilize his base in the Democratic Party, but in November he would have to broaden his appeal, as it was clear Romney would win the governorship easily and he would have to again convince voters to split their tickets. The primary also showed that younger voters were not as easily influenced by his folksy style. One observer noted that his past victories had "attained the status of party myth," but they did not resonate with those who did not remember them. Finally, the run against Cavanaugh had cost more than three hundred thousand dollars. Griffin was running unopposed and had a sizable financial advantage.[69]

Williams was largely oblivious to these weaknesses and immediately flew to Washington to confer with Johnson. He hoped the president would campaign for him in Michigan and stress "favorably and affirmatively his work with the State Department," and Johnson agreed to appear at a Labor Day rally in Detroit. When he returned to Detroit he restructured his campaign organization, appointing Berthelot to mange the effort against Griffin.[70]

As they prepared for the general election, the campaign suffered a major setback when Williams developed severe kidney stones. He was hospitalized for a week and spent nearly a month recovering. Lyndon Johnson, in Michigan to campaign, visited him in the hospital, and entertainer Sammy Davis Jr. had to cancel a fund-raising concert, as Williams was too ill to attend. His son Gery filled in at political rallies, but the loss of the candidate for five weeks was a disaster. His illness led to rumors that Williams was dying of cancer, and against the advice of his doctors he rushed back to the campaign, looking gaunt, pale, and fatigued.[71]

The frail Williams soon discovered another major problem: his running mate. When Cavanaugh declined to challenge Romney, Democrats selected their glib and sarcastic state party chairman, Zolton Ferency. Although he knew he had little chance against Romney, Ferency loved the role of political gadfly and spent nearly as much time during his campaign attacking Mennen Williams as his Republican opponent. A strident critic of Johnson and the war in Vietnam, he criticized Williams for his support of the war. Like Cavanaugh, he showed little respect for the man who had remade the party in Michigan and quipped that "the only new thing to come out of Soapy Williams in years was a kidney stone." Ferency refused to make joint appearances with Williams and rejected meetings to coordinate campaign strategy. Williams's advisers were frustrated and suggested they cut all ties with the Democratic nominee for governor, but Williams argued that party loyalty compelled him to continue to endorse Ferency.[72]

By late September the campaign was lurching from one disaster to another. Griffin relied heavily on television and attacked his opponent for refusing to debate him. Romney barely campaigned against Ferency, spending his time attacking Williams. He charged that Williams was "known for his ties, not for any accomplishments" and that the only thing Kennedy and Johnson consulted with Williams on was "how to get Kennedy elected." When Williams finally went back to the campaign trail he headed to the Democratic stronghold of the Upper Peninsula, but three days of torrential rain forced him to cancel most of his schedule. Crowds at his endless personal appearances were small, and one observer, noting a half-filled church in Lansing, remarked that "this church would have been filled when he was running for Governor." Even appearances by Robert and Ted Kennedy did little to revive the flagging campaign.[73]

Williams also found it difficult to find appealing issues with which to define his campaign. In at attempt to appeal to young voters, he endorsed lowering the voting age to eighteen, a highly unpopular stance, as a referendum on the issue would be defeated by a two-to-one margin. He also showed a lack of understanding of the growing militancy among African Americans. Williams had been an advocate of civil rights for nearly twenty years, but when asked about the new cry of "black power" he replied that the only issue was "voting power." When a *Detroit News* poll showed Griffin with a narrow lead, Williams reverted to the attack strategy that had been effective in his earlier campaigns and charged that Griffin was a right winger who was known as "Senator No" for his refusal to support housing, education, and health programs. Griffin was "anti-progress, anti-people, anti city and anti-labor" and had voted "against widows, orphans, school kids, college students . . . against food for the hungry, against decent housing, and against a living wage for the working-man." He also focused on his opponent's role in drafting the Landum-Griffin Bill of 1959 calling for stricter regulation of labor unions to end corruption and called the legislation an attempt to destroy unions. Griffin countered by pointing out that senators John Kennedy, Hubert Humphrey, and Lyndon Johnson had all voted for the bill. Forced to criticize his party's leaders, Williams backed down and claimed that he was "neutral" on repeal of the bill. Griffin immediately accused his opponent of not taking a position, arguing that in the Senate you have to vote yes or no, as the "clerk doesn't register a response of 'I am neutral.'"[74]

As the campaign stumbled along, Williams developed a severe case of laryngitis and during the two weeks before the election could barely speak. He also seemed to be resigned to defeat. In the final week a tired and hoarse Williams canceled most of his appearances. Rather than the whirlwind finale that had characterized his earlier campaigns, he made only two or three appearances a day. Two days before the election he failed to show up for a 5:30 a.m. appearance at a Chrysler plant, and on the last day of the campaign, while Griffin saturated the state with TV ads, Soapy Williams spoke to fifty senior citizens at the Polish Club in Detroit and then went home for an afternoon nap.[75]

G. Mennen Williams had never lost an election, but in 1966 he not only lost but was crushed, as Griffin won by more than three hundred thousand votes. Romney defeated the maverick Ferency by a 61 to 39 percent landslide. Williams's political career was over, and analysts who had predicted a triumphant return for the "boy wonder" were left to explain the disaster. Most argued that Williams was just out of touch with the times and the voters. Writing in the *Detroit News,* columnist Allan Blanchard concluded: "Soapy has not changed. But the times had." His health problems, distrust of TV, old-fashioned populist campaign style, the inability to link himself with Kennedy and Johnson, and his flip-flop in the Landum-Griffin issue had all contributed to his defeat. He also had underestimated Romney's popularity and Griffin's skills as a campaigner. Equally important, he was no longer the energetic Soapy Williams but an old, tired man who had not adjusted his style or ideas to a new decade. In an editorial on his defeat entitled "Old Democrats Lose," the *New York Times* linked his loss with those of Senator Paul Douglass of Illinois and Governor Pat Brown of California and concluded they all were out of touch with the times. "Familiarity breeds boredom" and "overexposure," and lack of "vigor" had doomed all three. Others suggested that Williams's loss showed the diminished power of organized labor and demonstrated that "the UAW is still significant but it hasn't the clout it used to." Nancy Williams argued it was "that Cavanaugh fellow" who cost them the election.[76]

Regardless of the reasons, the 1966 defeat was both a political and a personal disaster for Williams. His faint dream of the White House was finally dead, and he had little chance of ever being elected to office again. For nearly three decades he had been running Michigan or the African Bureau. He now had nothing to run. He was a professional politician without a position or any prospects. He wrote Berthelot that

> the loss in the Senatorial election was a shattering experience and there were some really dark days and nights following it. I guess there are other places I can go too [*sic*] . . . but I haven't got things worked out yet the way I would like and haven't been able to approach full steam yet.[77]

There were not many "other places" for him to go. He was too young to retire, had never been interested in business or law, and had no prospects of a major political appointment. Whatever his future, he did not have to worry about money. He had established $1 million trust funds for each of his three children and owned over $1 million in tax-exempt bonds, which he used to pay his living costs He also had $3 million in stocks, $100,000 in other investments, $85,000 in high-risk oil-drilling stock, and an unspecified number of shares in the Mennen Company worth many millions more. In the early 1960s, he had purchased a number of Holiday Inn hotels (insisting that they be open to all races). Despite his affluence, he and his wife still lived frugally, and when his son experienced some financial problems Williams wrote him a lengthy letter, noting that he and Nancy had "managed to save money when making only $2000 a year" and urging Gery to "keep a monthly budget" and send it to him for review. He advised his son to contribute to "the church, the Democratic Party, and the NAACP," but cut all other expenditures.[78]

Throughout 1967, Williams pondered his future. He and Nancy kept busy planning the wedding of their daughter Nancy to Theodore Ketter in April at Saint Paul's Cathedral Church in Detroit, and he served on a commission that investigated the causes of the 1967 Detroit race riot. He also watched his political party self-destruct over Vietnam and found his own views on the war changing. When Ferency resigned as the state Democratic chairman in protest of the war, Williams issued a statement that he "understood" the decision but argued that Ferency "did not represent the viewpoint of the vast majority of the Democratic Party." After Eugene McCarthy and Robert Kennedy challenged Johnson for the 1968 Democratic nomination, Williams refused to endorse his former boss, saying only that he would support the convention's choice.[79]

While Williams brooded, others worked to find a way for him to return to public service. There were rumors that he would become the head the Peace Corps. Michigan Democrats wrote Johnson, urging that he be appointed head of the Department of Health, Education, and Welfare or be nominated for the U.S. Supreme Court. In early 1968, Williams received a call from John Macy, Johnson's aide in charge of appointments, asking whether he would consider serving as U.S. ambassador to the Philippines. He declined, saying later, "my wife and I had pretty much decided that we weren't going to do anything outside of the state of Michigan." Johnson, however, was determined and had Rusk phone to explain that the ambassadorship was "an urgent job" and the nation needed him. A few hours later Williams accepted.[80]

Johnson and Rusk had considered a number of candidates to fill the vacant position in Manila, and from a final list of eighteen that included former California governor Pat Brown and Eisenhower's secretary of state Christian Herder decided on Williams. Ambassadorships were a standard reward for party service, and Johnson appreciated Williams's defense of his Vietnam policy and work in the African Bureau. Despite the fact that Johnson had announced he would not seek reelection, he wanted international support for the war in Vietnam and felt Williams might convince the Filipinos to contribute more to the effort. Also Williams's early political mentor, Frank Murphy, had served as governor general and later high commissioner of the Philippines and the University of Michigan was known as a center for the study of the islands.[81]

On April 16, Johnson announced Williams's selection, and on April 25 he sent the nomination to the Senate Foreign Relations Committee. The committee was chaired by one of the leading critics of the United States' involvement in Vietnam, J. William Fulbright of Arkansas, and there were concerns that he would use the hearings to debate the war. Michigan senator Phil Hart convinced Fulbright that as the position had been vacant for six months prolonged hearings would be seen as an insult in Manila. The confirmation hearings were, in Williams's words, "an easy trot," and he was approved unanimously.[82]

On May 1, Williams met with Johnson prior to his departure for the Philippines, and the president made it clear that the major issue was to increase Filipino support for the war. "Philippines' contribution to South Vietnam is relatively small and the government is encountering difficulties in maintaining the current level," he concluded. Williams was to show Filipinos that it would be "in their own interests and in the interest of the free world position in South Vietnam" to provide more troops for the war. At a second meeting, Johnson repeated that the "top priority" was to generate more support for the war. A Johnson aide, Walt Rostow, observed that the Philippines had a "rather vicious" political system, but "as a veteran of the political wars, Governor Williams should be particularly well-fitted to understand and operate effectively in this atmosphere."[83]

Not much was expected from an ambassador serving a lame duck president, but Mennen Williams was not prepared for a leisurely and sedate sinecure. He planned his arrival in the Philippines "like a political campaign" and sketched out a month of whirlwind travel to "meet the people." For four weeks he and Nancy stormed the Philippines as if they were running for governor of Michigan again. Williams commandeered a military plane, and instead of meeting with his staff in Manila toured sixty of the eighty provinces of the island nation. He met with mayors and other officials, school groups, and business leaders and visited rice farms, factories, and colleges while Nancy went to clinics, schools, and women's organizations. In one village the new ambassador put on his swimsuit and rode a water buffalo into a rice paddy. The resulting photo made the front page of many U.S. newspapers, and one reporter concluded that Williams "was acting like a Filipino candidate for office in mixing with the people." On June 22, he joined President Ferdinand Marcos to dedicate a memorial to U.S. and Filipino soldiers who had died in World War II. Soapy Williams was back in the headlines.[84]

Not content to rely only on the press, he sent Johnson a constant stream of memos, photos, and clippings from local newspapers documenting his triumphant tour of the islands, explaining "my first effort has been to establish rapport with the Filipinos." Rostow was overwhelmed with the material flowing daily from the new ambassador, but he urged the president to write a note complementing Williams on his efforts to establish contacts with the Filipino people.[85]

Eventually Soapy and Nancy reluctantly abandoned their public relations campaign and returned to the U.S. embassy in Manila. The previous ambassador, William McCormack Blair (the Stevenson aide who had criticized Williams for his attacks on Stevenson's moderation speech) had suffered through a stormy term, and his wife had hated the assignment. When Nancy met with her she found that "Mrs. Blair was so unhappy that she had nothing nice to say about it and I finally gave up talking to her as she was only depressing." More seriously, the shooting by a U.S. soldier of a Filipino citizen accused of stealing a bike had provoked a crisis, as Washington insisted on a trial by a U.S. military court while Filipinos wanted a criminal trial in their courts. Williams's agreed with the Filipinos, but members of Congress lobbied for U.S. jurisdiction and he reluctantly went along. He soon faced a second issue when a State Department official stated that a section of North Borneo claimed by the Philippines was a part of Malaysia. Williams claimed the comment "raised unshirted hell" for him and led to anti–American riots, but he worked out a compromise, calling for negotiations on the issue.[86]

These incidents were minor compared to his major goal: getting a stronger commitment to the war in Vietnam. Marcos had already sent a small engineering force to Vietnam, and the United States had paid them a "combat bonus." The opposition press claimed that Washington was using "Filipino mercenaries" to fight the war. Williams found the Filipino press "just unbelievable . . . they really are scandalous," but it had an impact, and he was unable to persuade Marcos to send more troops to Vietnam.[87]

Despite the continued problem of Vietnam, Soapy and Nancy Williams enjoyed their stay in Manila. He inherited a "first-rate deputy head of mission, Jim Wilson," who was "a real crackerjack" and ran the day-to-day business of the embassy, leaving Nancy and Soapy time for leisurely walks with their dogs on the beach and shopping for food in local markets. Nancy began buying carved Chinese porcelain figures left on graves, and she accumulated a major collection, which she later donated to the Detroit Institute of Fine Arts, Eastern Michigan

University, and the University of Michigan. They found their residence "old and touched with a pleasant feeling of gracious living" but far too small for entertaining, so they ordered construction of a reception annex. Nancy wrote Lady Bird Johnson that she and Soapy "were very happy" with the post.[88]

Williams's service in Manila was a welcome respite from his devastating defeat by Griffin and the disappointments of his last year in the African Bureau. It also offered an escape from the traumas America was experiencing during one of the most painful years in its history. In 1968, the nation endured massive protests against the war in Vietnam, the assassinations of Martin Luther King and Robert Kennedy, the violence at the Democratic National Convention in Chicago, and the peak of the urban riots. America was a far different nation than forty years earlier when Williams won his shocking victory over Kim Sigler. The eloquent vision of King's nonviolent campaign against segregation had been replaced with violence, black separatism, and a white backlash against the civil rights movement. Williams's beloved Democratic Party was fractured by the war in Vietnam, and his dream of an expanded national commitment to economic equality and social welfare programs, symbolized by Johnson's Great Society, was already unraveling. The unexpected power of George Wallace's presidential campaign and the election of Richard Nixon illustrated the rapid demise of support for Williams's 1950s liberalism.

Not only had the political landscape changed, but social and cultural forces had transformed American society. The counterculture, the radical student protests, the emerging feminist and gay rights movements, the prevalence of violence, and shrill political debate had made the nation nearly unrecognizable from the society Williams had envisioned. He had come of age in an era when acceptance of authority was the standard, elections were won by shaking hands, and the traditional male-dominated family was assumed to be the norm. The folksy, Bible-quoting, bow-tied Soapy Williams seemed to be from another age in a time of free love, drugs, and rock music.

Williams retained his optimism for both himself and his country, but he was increasingly dismayed by the new forces unleashed in the 1960s. He was moved to tears by the death of King (whom he had met in Detroit only three weeks earlier) and hailed the civil rights leader as "a minister of God" who had "died a martyr in the causes of human brotherhood and peace." He flew to Atlanta for the funeral, where he was seated with former football star Jim Brown, basketball player Wilt Chamberlain, and novelist James Baldwin. He wrote his children that he hoped "the American people would respond to his martyr's death" by "giving equal rights to our Negro brothers and sisters." He was shocked by the reemergence of Nixon, one of the few politicians he despised, and dismayed that Vietnam continued to divide America.[89]

By 1969, Williams had lost not only his first election but much of his constituency and the issues that had defined his career. The political climate in America was not conducive to an unrepentant liberal who still argued for the moral sanctity of equal rights and the need for continued economic reform. He was only fifty-eight when he returned from the Philippines, but he seemed to be of an ancient political generation. He still harbored dreams of running for office, but the prospects of an electoral victory were bleak. Williams would soon find a new forum in which to express his ideology in the less raucous chambers of the Michigan Supreme Court.

VIII
TO DO JUSTLY

The Supreme Court Years, 1970–86

My judicial philosophy is simple: "What doth the
Lord require of thee, but to do justly, and to love
mercy, and to walk humbly with thy God."

—G. *Mennen Williams in a speech to*
the Economic Club of Detroit, 1970

His diplomatic service in the Philippines offered Williams a
badly needed return to prominence after his humiliating loss in
the 1966 Senate election. When he returned to Michigan in
1969, many Democrats assumed he would retire to the role of
elder statesman, but Williams was not yet ready to abandon
politics. At fifty-eight he felt he was still young enough for
another campaign for elected office. Phil Hart would run for
reelection to the Senate, and it was too late to gain the Democratic nomination to challenge incumbent Republican governor William Milliken, but in two years Robert Griffin's term
would be up and Williams would have the opportunity to
avenge the bitter 1966 defeat. To challenge Griffin in 1972, he
would need a prominent public position that would keep the
voters' attention and convince Democrats that he was still popular enough to win an election. Typical of Williams's energy
and confidence, he simultaneously sought two possible step-
ping-stones to later electoral office.

As soon as he returned from Manila, he decided to pursue
the presidency of Michigan State University. Michigan State
had always suffered in comparison with its more prestigious
rival in Ann Arbor, and the selection of a "big name" president

who was well known in the state might be a tempting move for the school. The post would offer Williams a chance to keep his name in the news as an interim stop before a future run for elected office. While he actively lobbied for the job at Michigan State he also organized a campaign for election to the Michigan Supreme Court in 1970. Although theoretically this was a nonpartisan position, candidates for the court were endorsed by the two major parties, and a successful campaign could help Williams regain his influence with the Democratic Party.

In February 1969, he wrote a lengthy memo entitled "Supreme Court Strategy" and sent it to a number of former advisers. It outlined a yearlong effort to first secure endorsements from prominent lawyers, then to lobby influential Democrats, and finally to organize a whirlwind campaign similar to those of his successful runs for governor.[1]

It would be fifteen months before Williams would officially announce his candidacy for the court, and during that time he conducted a vigorous effort to obtain the presidency of Michigan State. Williams called on his old political adviser, John Murray, to help him "run for the MSU job" and asked his former aide: "What does a college president do?" Murray responded that the head of a university needed to raise money from both the legislature and private donors, promote athletics, and host dinners for "Dr. Whoozits" and others who visited the school. Williams was certain he would excel in these roles. He immediately began to lobby members of the Board of Trustees and organized a petition drive among the school's faculty in support of his nomination.[2]

Murray was stunned by Williams's aggressive campaign and told him that, unlike governmental positions, "it is considered gauche to apply for the job, or to give the appearance in any manner" of wanting the appointment. He cautioned Williams to call off the personal lobbying and instead work behind the scenes to marshal support from students, faculty, foundation leaders, and other university presidents. "There is a legitimate question whether the traditional courting dance done for this position should be thrown out and a direct move made—simply kicking over the supposed sensitivity in this area," Murray cautioned, and he urged Williams to tone down his efforts and leave the actual campaigning to Staebler, labor leaders, and Democratic officials. Williams should continue to contact supporters, but "it is very important that this be done orally rather than in writing. Let's keep as much NOT WRITTEN as possible. . . . Great care should be taken to avert any look that you applied."[3]

As Murray warned, Williams's early and aggressive lobbying alienated many at the school. More than one hundred faculty members signed "An Open Letter to G. Mennen Williams," which noted their personal admiration but criticized his attempt to interject politics into the search for the head of the university. They concluded that "it would be disastrous for both you and the University if you were to become its President under such partisan circumstances." More important, his active campaign for the office had angered members of the Board of Trustees. The group was evenly divided, with four Republicans and four Democrats, and GOP members were united in their determination that Soapy Williams would never be selected. The Republicans resented his "steamrolling" tactics and did not want to put the former governor in any position that might help him make a political comeback in the state. To contain the "Williams for MSU" movement, they delayed the formal discussion of candidates for nearly a year and did not interview applicants until the early fall of 1970. By then Williams was actively running for the Michigan Supreme Court, though he continued to let it be known that he was interested in becoming MSU president.[4]

It unclear whether Williams would have abandoned his run for the court to accept the presidency of Michigan State, but he never withdrew his name, even while he was campaigning hard for the judiciary. The MSU job was extremely attractive, as it was far more public than the court and seemed more likely to eventually lead to an elected office, but it also was more difficult to obtain. For over two decades Williams had campaigned long and hard in six races for governor and in his Senate campaign. A slow and subtle effort was not a part of his makeup, and it was nearly impossible for him to "pretend" that he was uninterested in a position. Less than a month before the election for the court, the Michigan State Board of Trustees saved him from having to choose between the Supreme Court and academia.

Partly due to the lengthy delay in the process, by the summer of 1970 the initial list of over a dozen contenders for the MSU job seemed to be down to only three: Williams, Oakland University chancellor D. B. Varner, and the acting president, economics professor Walter Adams. The four Republican trustees were adamantly opposed to Williams and were unimpressed by Varner. When Adams announced that he would not accept a permanent appointment they quickly sought an alternative to Williams. They finally fixed on Dr. Clifton R. Wharton, an African American and vice president of the Agricultural Development Council in New York, and flew east to interview him without consulting the Democratic trustees. Republican support of a black candidate was shrewd, as it made it difficult for Democrats to attack Wharton, but Williams's supporters denounced the move as a secret end run designed to prevent the former governor's appointment and blocked any attempt to offer the position to Wharton.

On October 16, after six weeks of argument, the MSU trustees met for a decision, and the discussion quickly became a bitter battle fought along party lines. When Republicans moved the appointment of Wharton, Democrat Frank Hartman of Flint, an outspoken Williams advocate, called for a delay in the vote and when his motion failed threatened a filibuster. After several hours of wrangling, recesses, and shouting, Democrat Don Stevens of Okemos finally broke ranks and joined the Republicans and the board voted five to three to offer the position to Wharton. Ironically, Republican opposition to Williams, the longtime advocate of civil rights, led to the appointment of Michigan's first black college president.[5]

It had been nearly a year since Williams returned from the Philippines and launched his effort to gain the MSU job. Impatient with the political maneuvering and delays, he had thrown himself into a campaign for election to the Michigan Supreme

Court. If he was disappointed with his rejection for the job in East Lansing, he did not show it and concentrated instead on winning a "real" election as a justice of the state's highest court.

In March 1970, while awaiting word on his effort to gain the presidency of Michigan State, Williams contacted Staebler and other prominent Democrats, told them he would run for one of two open positions on the court, and asked for names of influential lawyers who would endorse his candidacy. A month later he wrote a "personal and confidential" letter in his trademark green ink to fifty lawyers across the state, telling them he was "thinking of running" for the court as a way to "offer a genuine and significant service to the people of Michigan." On May 19, with his granddaughter Lee Ann Monroe Williams holding his hand, he made an official announcement of his candidacy and outlined his major theme: "I firmly believe that a judge must at all times be mindful of the biblical injunction 'to do justly, and to love mercy, and to walk humbly with thy God.'" Williams's invocation of the Old Testament prophet Micah illustrated his continued belief that the Bible offered the best guide to politics and also showed his desire to appear as a principled statesman rather than a partisan politician in running for the court. "To Do Justly" immediately became his campaign slogan.[6]

All four Detroit TV stations, six radio stations, and both of the city's major newspapers covered the announcement that he was running for the court and the press conference that followed. The same day Williams issued a lengthy list of union leaders, academics, lawyers, and others who had endorsed his campaign, including John D. Voelker, a former Michigan Supreme Court justice and author of the best-selling novel *Anatomy of a Murder,* and Otis M. Smith, the first African American to serve on the court. Smith noted: "I did not become a confirmed Democrat until I heard Governor G. Mennen Williams speak. . . . He was the first politician I had ever met who did not insult the voter's intelligence." Williams would feature Smith in campaign material aimed at black voters.[7]

Williams immediately plunged into a campaign for the court that mirrored his energetic runs for governor. He appointed

Paul Donahue campaign manager, with Paul Seldenright and Barbara Patterson as assistants. They hired a full-time staff of twelve and opened a "Williams for Supreme Court" campaign headquarters at 1248 Washington Boulevard in Detroit. There was a budget of $250,000, most of it provided by the candidate.[8]

Williams quickly found that a campaign for the court was different from running for governor. Although he had a law degree, it had been nearly twenty-five years since he had been in a courtroom and he had no experience as a judge. Second, the court was supposedly nonpartisan and there were concerns that he was too liberal and too closely identified with the Democratic Party to attract the independent votes necessary for success. Finally, he faced a field of nine candidates for the two open positions on the court. Justice Harry F. Kelly (Williams's opponent in the 1950 race for governor) had reached the mandatory retirement age of seventy, but incumbent John Dethmers (who had over thirty years of experience) was seeking reelection. Williams's former protégé John Swainson and Robert Evans, an African American, were also in the field. Unlike his campaigns for governor, he would not be able to run by attacking a single opponent.

His staff was well aware that Williams had a major advantage in name recognition but also knew that he had some significant weaknesses. They commissioned Marketing Strategies, Inc., to interview five hundred registered voters. The pollsters found that Williams was known by nearly all of those polled and still had strong support among union members and African Americans but many others saw him as more of a politician than a judge. They also noted that many voters were concerned about his unabashed political liberalism and warned: "Governor Williams is still maintaining a strong liberal ideology in the face of voter movement toward a more moderate political position."[9]

Despite warnings that he should not appear to be "too much of a partisan Democrat," Williams was eager to duplicate the frantic campaign style that had been successful in six elections as governor. He filled two spiral notebooks with issues, slogans, and strategies and mapped out a schedule nearly identical to his efforts in the 1950s. He compiled lists of ethnic groups and festivals for campaign stops, rosters of union officials for endorsements, and the dates of all of Michigan's county fairs. Aides had to remind him that he should "not run too hard" and should try to appear "judicial."[10]

He also found that the issues for election to the court were far different from those that had been the focus of his campaigns for governor. In 1970, the Vietnam War deeply divided the nation and voters were increasingly concerned about student protests on campuses and occasional violent opposition to the conflict. Two years earlier Richard Nixon had successfully appealed to the "silent majority" of Americans who did not join protest marches or attack the government, and Williams and his aides realized that he, too, had to reach out to this group.

Like the rest of the nation, the people of Michigan were alarmed by the continued militancy of African Americans identified with the urban riots of the 1960s and the black power movement. It had only been three years since Detroit was nearly burned to the ground in one of the most violent racial conflicts of the decade. Much of the destroyed area had not been rebuilt, and there had been a mass white exodus from the city. Rather than discussing welfare, roads, taxes, and teachers' salaries, Williams would have to take a position on draft card burning, campus protests, and black unrest. "Law and order" was the major theme for most voters, and Williams was not identified as a proponent of the "toughness" many wanted in their courts.

As the campaign progressed, Williams toned down his frantic campaign style in an attempt to appear judicial and tried to show that he would be "tough on crime." Polls by the Williams's campaign found he had a slight lead but was still seen as too liberal and "soft" on crime. The consultants concluded: "We recommend that the Governor speak on issues that have moderate voter appeal." Aware of the public's overriding interest in law and order, Williams changed his campaign style and rhetoric.[11]

While he still made his usual appearances at ethnic clubs and local fairs, he began to devote more time to meetings of professional organizations of business leaders, lawyers, and law enforcement officials. Along with shaking hands at factory gates he also campaigned at suburban shopping malls, where he distributed pamphlets in his trademark green and white, showing him sitting at a desk wearing glasses and reading a law book. The caption was "Integrity. Ability. Experience."[12]

He addressed the issue of campus unrest and student protest by taking a middle road, defending the legality of peaceful protest but arguing that it should never be allowed to interfere with "the right to teach and learn." He also suggested that universities had been too slow to respond to legitimate demands and had overreacted to attempts to make colleges more responsive to their students. Commenting on the violent demonstrations at Columbia University, he noted that "there were many reforms long overdue and when the students moved they had much justice in their demands." He make few references to the war in Vietnam, claiming it was not an issue for the Supreme Court, but promised to be stern with violent actions on campus or elsewhere that showed "overt acts of disrespect for our government, its laws, and its institutions."[13]

He was generally vague on issues such as drugs, the environment, and gun control. He called for tough sentences for drug dealers and rehabilitation for drug users and promised to support laws controlling pollution but pledged to oppose unnecessary regulations that would harm business. Reacting to the shootings of Martin Luther King and Robert Kennedy, he suggested a need for "some restrictions" on handguns but avoided calling for their ban. One of his major themes (and a later focus of his judicial years) was the need to modernize the court system in Michigan. He reminded voters that the Supreme Court had two major duties—to hear cases and oversee the lower courts in the state—and vowed to increase the efficiency of justice in Michigan. At every campaign stop he repeated his major slogan: "A judge must at all times be mindful of the Biblical injunction 'to do justly, and to love mercy, and to walk humbly with thy God.'"[14]

Williams's attempt to appear less partisan and more centralist did not convince Michigan Republicans that he had moderated his liberalism. They attacked his "judicial activism" ideology, which would allow the court to legislate and make policy, and contended that his record as governor showed he was soft on crime and criminals. They also raised the traditional charge that he would be under the control of organized labor.[15]

Although the campaign was supposedly nonpartisan, it quickly became a contest between Democrats Williams and Swainson and Republicans Dethmers and Wayne County circuit court judge Edward Piggins. Also on the November 3 ballot were contests for the Senate and the governorship. It looked like Hart would be an easy winner over Lenore Romney, wife of the former governor, and the Democrats had nominated Sander Levin to challenge William Milliken for the governorship.

Both Detroit newspapers endorsed Piggins and Dethmers, but polls showed Swainson and Williams with a slight lead three days before the election. Heavy rains flooded the state on election day, lowering turnout in traditionally Democratic Wayne County. Also Michigan had recently adopted a punch card ballot, which led to numerous technical problems. In a replay of his recount victories in 1950 and 1952, it took fifty-seven hours to determine the results. When the votes were finally counted on November 6, Swainson led the field with 1.2 million votes and Williams was second with just over 1 million. Piggins received 855,000 and Dethmers 785,000. Hart crushed Romney, and Milliken had defeated Levin.[16]

Williams's victory was largely due to his incredible name recognition in the state. Polls showed that over 90 percent of voters knew him, far more than any other candidate. Although somewhat disappointed that he ran second to Swainson, Williams was pleased that he could still win a statewide election. Although he worked hard to prepare for his new position, it was clear that he saw the court as only a temporary stop before a return to the governorship or the Senate. In the study of his Grosse Pointe Farms home he set up two desks with separate secretaries, one for his duties on the court and the second for political issues.[17]

The election of Williams and Swainson led to a major realignment of the court. Previously there had been three Republicans, three Democrats, and one independent, but now the court had five Democrats, one Republican, and an independent. Although he was new to the court, Williams was familiar with its members. There were two Thomas Kavanaughs. Chief Justice Thomas M. Kavanaugh (nicknamed "Thomas the Mighty") had served as Williams's attorney general from 1954 to 1958. Thomas G. Kavanaugh (known as "Thomas the Good") had been an active Democrat in the late 1950s and had campaigned for Williams in 1956 and 1958. Eugene Black, a former Republican, had switched to the Democratic Party after Williams's election in 1948 and had been appointed by Williams to the Thirty-first Circuit Court. Justice Paul Adams had been a classmate at the University of Michigan Law School. The other new judge, John Swainson, had been Williams's attorney general and his successor as governor. Thomas E. Brennan, the lone Republican on the court, was the only judge without a direct personal link to Soapy Williams.

He quickly found that his duties on the court were not as time consuming as those of the governor and that he needed to spend only two or three days a week in Lansing, where he stayed at the Capitol Park Motel. This left him ample time for social events, political gatherings, and travel. In the first three weeks after his inauguration on January 1, 1971, he attended two brief organizational meetings of the court, three concerts of the Detroit Symphony Orchestra, two Detroit Pistons basketball games, and four plays. He also gave six speeches to local civic groups. He then left with Nancy for a week in New York, where he dined at 21 and Sardis and attended three Broadway musicals.[18]

Like most justices, Williams depended heavily on his clerks to outline cases, conduct research, and draft opinions. Most of his clerks had degrees from Michigan law schools, and in appointing them he was less concerned with their grades than their enthusiasm and commitment to hard work, traits he had exhibited throughout his own career. He also preferred those who were married over single applicants.[19]

Although most expected Williams to be a liberal justice dedicated to preserving individual rights, highly critical of business, and an advocate of an activist judiciary, his record on the court was much more complex. His judicial philosophy was simple: "Real justice . . . must be the product not only of fine legal honing but of broad human experience and deep insight and religious perception." One of his clerks summarized Williams's legal ideology as "the common sense, people-oriented approach" that meant "read the statute and do what it plainly says."[20]

Williams may well have believed in a "common sense, people-oriented approach" to the law, but his votes and decisions reflect the complexity of the issues that came before the court. In his sixteen years on the Michigan Supreme Court Williams wrote 402 opinions beginning with *Higgins v. Henry Ford Hospital* in May 1971 and concluding with *The State of Michigan v. Krezen* in December 1986. His votes, writings, and interactions with his peers all showed a new moderation and a tempering of his earlier, often combative political style. In his first term he generally sided with a "liberal" interpretation of the law, but he also showed a more centralist approach in cases involving the rights of accused and claims against business. He also was forced to confront new issues, such as abortion, the environment, drugs, and equal rights for women, that had emerged in the decade since he served as governor.[21]

Based on his long battles with business interests in Michigan, it was assumed that Williams would side with those making claims against corporations, and in most cases in his first term he generally supported plaintiffs seeking damages from corporations. He consistently voted in favor of those suing for workman's compensation settlements, including an auto worker who had lost a leg on the job even though he had failed to inform his employer that he was blind in one eye. He also repeatedly voted against insurance companies that tried to deny payment of claims due to legal technicalities, arguing that "it would be unconscionable to permit insurance companies to collect premiums with one hand and try to take coverage away with the other." He was the lone dissenter in a case in which

General Motors lowered workman's compensation benefits for
employees over the age of sixty-five.[22]

Given Williams's long advocacy of direct democracy and
union rights, it was not surprising that he strongly dissented
when the court denied the right of citizens to seek a referendum for changes in zoning requirements, arguing that "the
right of referendum" was essential in "our democratic society."
He also defended the right of teachers to strike and supported
civil service workers' claims that they had been fired for political reasons.[23]

Votes against insurance companies and in favor of workman's compensation payments, the right to strike, and allowing
the people to vote on issues affecting their lives were consistent
with Williams's lifelong liberalism, but on issues relating to
crime he was less clearly ideological. The U.S. Supreme Court
decisions of the 1960s such as *Gideon v. Wainwright* and *Miranda
v. Arizona* established complex new procedures for interroga-
tion of suspects, guaranteed the right to counsel, and established
strict procedures for police searches. As a result, state courts
were besieged with new cases alleging violations of individual
rights by the police and prosecutors. Like all state judges,
Williams faced the dilemma of balancing the need to follow the
new requirements with the desire to avoid being seen as soft on
crime. Williams was particularly vulnerable, as he was perceived as an extreme "liberal" too committed to "coddling
criminals." In his decisions on criminal cases he took a moderate position, voting almost equally in favor of guaranteeing the
rights of suspects and supporting the police.

In three important cases Williams decided that prosecutors
had abused suspect rights by searching a car without a proper
warrant, by repeatedly charging an individual with contempt
for refusing to answer questions, and for making references to a
defendant's unemployment in closing arguments. "Whether a
defendant was rich or poor, employed or unemployed has
nothing to do with guilt," he wrote.[24]

He balanced these decisions with others in which he upheld
police actions. In *People v. Enoch Chism* he voted against overturning the conviction of a man who had mailed an exploding

package that killed the recipient despite charges that the police had made an illegal search and the judge had offered prejudicial instructions to the jury. In another case police asked a rape victim to identify her attacker by offering three photos of suspects. The accused was an Indian, and two of the three pictures were of Caucasians. When she selected the one photo of a Native American, the defendant appealed. Williams, however, defended the process and voted to uphold the conviction.[25]

The flood of "victims' rights" appeals was accompanied by a surge in drug-related cases. The puritanical Williams was appalled by the rise in drug use, but he argued against the existing harsh penalties for marijuana use. He attacked a decision to sentence a young woman to nine years in prison for possession of two marijuana cigarettes and wrote the court's decision overturning her conviction. Later, in a speech defending his actions, he argued that the court needed to distinguish between "hard" and "soft" drugs.

> Heroin and marijuana have neither the same pharmacological characteristics nor physical effects and consequences and consequently a law lumping them together and providing the same penalties denied equal protection of the laws.[26]

He faced another new issue with the sudden concerns for women's rights and reproductive freedom. Although he was of a generation in which male dominance was assumed and women were seen as subservient, Williams also had been influenced by a powerful and independent mother and wife. Throughout his career he had been an advocate of equality for women, had appointed a number of females to his advisory committees, and had made Helen Berthelot his campaign manager in two campaigns for governor. On the court he was a leader in reforming divorce, inheritance, and property laws that discriminated against women.[27]

Williams found it far more difficult to decide on the more controversial issue of abortion. He personally opposed abortion, based largely on religious convictions, but eventually became convinced that women had the right to control their bodies. His court decisions reflected the struggle between his personal beliefs and his acceptance of women's reproductive freedom. In 1972, he provoked the wrath of antiabortion advocates when he voted to deny a referendum calling for a complete ban on abortions in the state, but he explained he had not ruled on the issue of abortion itself but only that the proposition had come to the court too near the election date. He later angered the pro-choice lobby when he upheld the right of suits seeking damages from the death of a fetus claiming "science now recognizes a separate life in the unborn." After the U.S. Supreme Court legalized abortion, Williams argued *Roe v. Wade* did not permit non-physicians to terminate pregnancies or allow for the sale of medications that induced abortion. He also voted in favor of making an attack on a pregnant woman that caused the death of a "quick child" (a fetus in the second trimester) subject to prosecution as manslaughter.[28]

No such ambiguity marked his rulings on the growing number of cases dealing with the environment. As early as his 1948 campaign for governor, he had called for strict laws regulating air and water pollution, and once on the court he became its leading advocate of protecting Michigan's environment. In 1974, he wrote the court's decision allowing public access to the records of companies accused of air and water pollution. The next year he and the court gained national attention in *Ray v. Mason County Drain Commission,* when they upheld Michigan's Environmental Protection Act and ruled that the public had the right to bring suit against any building project that might be harmful to the environment. Dozens of conservation organizations applauded the decision, and it was cited in a number of law reviews. The *New York Times* ran an editorial hailing the ruling as a landmark of environmental protection.[29]

Although he was the best-known member of the court, Williams generally deferred to his senior colleagues during his first term. He admitted he was "no great legal scholar" and felt his "greatest talent was as an administrator." It was in this administrative role that he made his most lasting contribution to the court by vigorously leading a campaign to modernize Michigan's system of justice.[30]

During his 1970 campaign Williams had repeatedly argued

that the court had two equally important functions: to rule on cases and to oversee the other courts in the state. He charged that Michigan's courts were slow and inefficient and too often "justice delayed was justice denied." After his election, Chief Justice Kavanaugh appointed Williams to head the Supreme Court Computer Committee, which was charged with bringing "increased speed, efficiency and quality in the administration of justice in the Michigan Court System." For the next five years he devoted much of his time and energy to meeting this goal.[31]

Overseeing a program to modernize the courts was an ideal project for the new justice. Williams had contacts among politicians, prosecutors, and court officials throughout the state, and the assignment was a perfect outlet for his boundless energy and enthusiasm. His wife recalled that, while he enjoyed legal discussions and decisions, he became truly energized when he was working on reforming the justice system.[32]

Creating a more efficient court system does not sound like a compelling issue, but Williams saw a chance to again be a leader and reformer and immediately plunged into the project, often devoting more time to this goal than to pending cases. After two organizational meetings of the group, he concluded that the courts lagged far behind other organizations in the use of computers, as many judges and law enforcement officials were either unaware of the new technology or opposed to its use. Williams mocked Michigan's courts for still being dependent on "work in longhand by men with green eye shades." He called for establishment of "at least a preliminary computer system in operation next year at this time" but acknowledged the need to "change attitudes of courts, clerks, lawyers etc." He designated Einar Bohlin, the hardworking director of systems for the Supreme Court, and one of his clerks, Rick Witte, to survey all state courts and recommend steps to implement a uniform computer system. Williams promised that he would personally undertake the task of educating court personnel.[33]

Totally committed to using the new technology, Williams soon discovered a problem: He knew virtually nothing about computers! Like most in his generation, Williams had grown up in an era of manual typewriters, carbon paper, ditto fluid, and hand-cranked adding machines. He was vaguely aware of the potential of computers but had never used one. He immediately began a crash course in the new invention and contacted information experts at Ford and Chrysler, asking them to explain computer technology. He also attended two seminars on computers hosted by the International Business Machines Corporation (IBM) and drew handwritten charts on how they worked. His notes included many questions: "What is magnetic tape?" "How do you 'create' a program?" "What is COBOL?" At the State Department he had regularly made lists of irregular French verbs; now he compiled "vocabulary lists" of computer terms such as *input, processing, hard copy,* and *function key.* In early 1973, he spent ten days in California "studying computers" and later wrote to the National Center for Automated Information Retrieval in New York asking for copies of technical papers on computer applications. By the end of his first year on the court, the sixty-two-year-old justice, who two years earlier had never used a computer, was familiar with data-processing technology, usage, terminology, and even the latest programs on the market.[34]

Williams ordered Bohlin to write weekly reports on the progress of computer usage in the courts and to start a newsletter for all court officials discussing possible applications of the new technology. After reading Bohlin's memos, Williams sent personal letters to court and law enforcement officials congratulating them on any attempts to incorporate computers and electronic data processing into their work. He also lobbied reluctant administrators, urging them to shift to computerized records and data retrieval. At one meeting he pointed out that lists of Michigan prison inmates were still handwritten and kept in separate files grouped by case numbers, names, aliases, social security numbers, local police departments, driver's licenses, state police numbers, and FBI numbers, with none of them cross-listed. He then explained how all of these could be combined and cross-referenced using computers. When a Wayne County clerk wrote asking about computer costs, he sent a detailed reply with prices for various terminals and programs.[35]

Williams also took his case for modernizing the court to the public. In a speech to the Economic Club of Detroit, he asserted "it is common knowledge that there is a breakdown in the administration of justice" in Michigan, as it took over two years to hear most civil cases and over six months for criminal cases. He promised to "bring Michigan courts out of the quill pen era into the electronic age." In a talk to the Detroit chapter of the Federal Bar Association he pledged to have every court in the state linked with computers and all court records stored electronically.[36]

Despite Williams's energy and prodding, computerizing the courts was a slow process. Many officials distrusted the new technology, and court employees feared they would be replaced because they lacked computer expertise. Lawyers argued that electronic storage of data raised issues of privacy and confidentiality, as records could be accessed by outsiders and various courts had purchased different machines and found they could not communicate with each other. When Williams finally got the records of Detroit's Traffic Court computerized, the air conditioning failed and the entire system crashed, destroying most of the data.[37]

While he was well aware of the technical and personal problems involved, Williams argued that "the general public should be the one to receive the maximum benefits of our efforts. . . . We are all in this together. We are changing old ways into new ways." He also was blunt in criticizing those reluctant to accept new technology. When the mayor of Detroit reported that it was difficult to hire personnel with computer expertise and bickering among brokers made it hard to purchase computer equipment, Williams wrote him that he knew there were problems but the mayor must "resolve them as soon as possible!"[38]

Williams also insisted that all "existing and new clerks in the state" be required to take a course in data processing. He pushed judges to subscribe to Lexis, a new, computer-assisted legal research service, and to Westlaw's summaries of state court cases.[39]

In 1971, Michigan had 300 different courts with 500 judges and 6,500 other employees handling over 90,000 transactions a day. To get the entire system to adopt new technology, train workers to use it, and store all records electronically was an immense task. Under the constant prodding of Justice Williams, it was virtually completed in six years. By 1977, all of the largest courts had shifted to computerized record keeping and all but the smallest were linked electronically. It as an immense achievement, a testimony to Williams's energy and effort, and his most significant contribution to the state's justice system.

During his term on the court Williams had settled into a comfortable life. He continued to spend most of his time in his Grosse Pointe Farms home attending musical performances and plays and speaking to civic and legal groups. His efforts to modernize the state's court system had been amazingly successful, and it was assumed that he would easily be elected to a second term and likely be selected as chief justice.

Despite his pleasant lifestyle and rewarding career on the court, Williams still longed for another political office. He had decided not to run for the Senate in 1972 but badly wanted to challenge incumbent governor William Milliken in 1978. Williams was far from the "boy wonder" who had upset Kim Sigler in 1948. He was sixty-seven years old and had little direct influence in the Michigan Democratic Party. Most of his advisers were dead or retired, and his last partisan campaign had ended in a disastrous loss to Robert Griffin. Soapy, however, wanted one last political battle and the chance to return to the state house in Lansing. He encouraged formation of Williams for Governor Committees and responded to pleas from Democrats that he challenge Milliken with notes observing that "it is an exciting prospect" and "something I must give real consideration." He wrote to old colleagues seeking their advice and to his surprise found strong opposition. Berthelot spoke for most when she wrote that he was too old for a "brutal campaign," concluding: "You can't go back, you have to keep moving forward. We all look back with such nostalgia to the golden years when you were Governor—but we tend to only remember the happy times and like childbirth forget the pain. Maybe it's time to count your blessings and see what you can do on the court." After receiving similar responses from other former advisers, he wrote Berthelot that "most of them have the same reaction as you." With some reluctance, he decided to seek a second term on the court.[40]

Even before his unsuccessful trial balloon efforts for the governorship, Williams began preparations for reelection to the Supreme Court. In late 1976, he hired Frank Jefferis a 1974 graduate of Kalamazoo College with a master's degree from the Lyndon B. Johnson School of Public Affairs in Texas, to work with Paul Donahue on the campaign for the court. Jefferis noted that "the number one issue" in Michigan was crime and Williams needed to show that he was tough on criminals. The public's concern with crime was brought home to Williams dramatically when he was brutally mugged in Detroit.[41]

At 10:30 p.m. on June 2, 1976, Williams parked his car in the lot next to the apartment of his administrative assistant, Barbara Patterson, at 1000 Trevor Place in downtown Detroit. Patterson was visiting her mother in Missouri, and Williams had promised to take in her mail and newspapers and check on the apartment, as it was in a high crime area, directly across from the Martin Luther King housing complex. As soon as Williams left his car, three young black men attacked him from behind, beating him and throwing him to the ground. They took his wallet and the key to Patterson's apartment and dragged him inside, where they tied his arms behind his back with the telephone cord and put a pair of pantyhose over his head. After rummaging through the apartment for about ten minutes, they left with some cash, the television, and a stereo. Fifteen minutes later Williams freed himself and called the police.[42]

At 11:10, the police arrived and found the judge bleeding from the mouth. They did not take him to the local hospital, Detroit General, but drove to St. John's Hospital on the far East Side of the city, where he was treated in the emergency room for a cut lip and driven home to Grosse Pointe. Williams lost some credit cards, seventy dollars in cash, fifty dollars in traveler's checks, and his car keys. The next day he met with reporters in his office in Lansing and told them: "I just got mugged!" He told them he was "stunned" and that "it happened so fast" that he could not identify his attackers. That night he and Nancy attended a testimonial dinner for Elner White, the retiring head of the Michigan Press Association in Lansing. His swollen lip made it hard to talk, but he told the press that he had promised to check Patterson's apartment and was "surprised this could happen on a main street."[43]

Ever eager for some hint of scandal in the life of the notoriously clean-living Williams, Detroit newspapers ran large photos of Patterson and noted that she was thirty-six years old, single, and "a stunning redhead" who had worked for Williams for ten years. Neighbors, however, told reporters that Patterson had alerted them that Williams would regularly check her apartment while she was out of town and they had never seen him stay in her apartment for more than a few minutes.[44]

Although Williams claimed to be "surprised" by the attack, many in Detroit were almost gleeful that the liberal justice had been a victim of the rampant crime in the city. One letter to the *Detroit News* simply stated: "Welcome to the club!" Another argued that it would be "poetic justice" if those who mugged Williams had been "set free by stupid decisions of the Michigan Supreme Court." One writer concluded: "While I sympathize with Williams, he always has been known as an ultra-liberal. It is precisely the ultra-liberal, permissive policies of politicians like Williams that have led to our current nightmare of crime and degeneracy."[45]

Partly in response to his attack and partly due to the public preoccupation with crime, Williams's 1978 reelection campaign tried to make the case that he would be tough on criminals. Few in the state knew of his efforts to reform and modernize the courts, but nearly every voter was aware of crime.

Although he was not running for governor, he campaigned as it he were, trying to duplicate his successful efforts of the 1950s. His advisers developed a budget of $160,000 for the election (Williams personally donated $100,000) and urged him to "be as apolitical as possible" and run "as a nonpartisan judge." They reminded him again that his biggest weakness was the perception that he was soft on crime. On July 5, 1978, he formally announced his candidacy for reelection and listed "the environment, individual privacy, and public safety" as the major issues.[46]

Although his advisers had urged him to run a nonpartisan campaign, they did not recommend a passive effort. Williams knew this would be his last campaign and was determined to show the energy and enthusiasm that had marked his runs for governor in the 1950s. It was almost 1948 all over again, as the sixty-seven-year-old Williams began to work eighteen-hour days across the state. On a typical day in Allegan, he was up at six shaking hands at the Rockwell plant, followed by a breakfast with local officials, and a luncheon with the Bar Association. At two he led the parade at the county fair, gave two radio interviews, and left for a four-hour drive to Bay City for a repeat of the grueling schedule the next day. As in his races for governor, he also tried to appeal to the state's ethnic groups with a series of cocktail parties for Italians, Irish, Germans, Mexicans, Hungarians, and Poles in Detroit. Guests got drinks, a photo with Williams, and an appeal for a campaign donation.[47]

Williams opened nearly every campaign speech by telling a story of running into an old friend, who asked: "Soapy, what are you doing these days?" The justice had had to remind his friend that he was on the Michigan Supreme Court. Sensitive to the importance of the crime issue, he had his clerks compile a list of cases in which he had shown that he was tough on crime, and he scheduled numerous appearances before law enforcement groups. He also called for mandatory sentences for violent criminals and stressed how his reform of the court system had led to swifter justice for offenders.[48]

As in 1978, there were two openings on the court. Williams and Saginaw judge Gary McDonald received the endorsement of the Democrats, while incumbent James Ryan and Oakland County Circuit judge Alice Gilbert were nominated by the Republicans. Ryan had replaced Williams's protégé John Swainson in 1975 when the former governor had been accused of taking a bribe. Democrat William Fitzgerald ran against Milliken for the governorship, while Carl Levin, a former Detroit city council president, challenged Griffin for the Senate seat. Williams and Ryan retained their seats by a large majority, and Milliken easily won a third term as governor. Surprisingly Levin did what Williams had been unable to do: he defeated Griffin for the Senate. (Ironically, Griffin would later be appointed to the court, where he served under Chief Justice G. Mennen Williams.)

When Williams was sworn in for his second term, he knew it would be his last, as Michigan law stipulated that no one over the age of seventy could be elected to the court. Having completed his efforts to computerize the justice system, he now sought selection as chief justice as a capstone of his career and to symbolize three decades of service to his state.

In his first term on the court Williams had enjoyed cordial relations with his fellow justices. In 1971, five of his six colleagues had been in his cabinet, appointed by Williams to the court, or a classmate. They did not defer to their more famous associate, but they did offer him more authority and respect than was common for the most junior member of the court. When he took office in 1979, the makeup of the court had changed dramatically. Of the seven justices serving in 1971, only Williams and Thomas G. Kavanaugh remained on the bench, and, with the exception of Blair Moody Jr., the son of Williams's liberal colleague of the 1950s, none had direct ties to the former governor. Although Williams made it known that he would like to be chief justice, the court selected Mary Coleman, elected two years after Williams, for the position.[49]

Although disappointed by Coleman's election, Williams understood that being selected to lead the court was not like running for public office. Rather than appealing to thousands of voters it was necessary to court six people who were convinced of their own power and independence. He observed that "to be Chief Justice, it's not important so much to be learned in the law, but to recognize that each judge in the system thinks he or she is a king or a queen." He knew Coleman was close to retirement and waited for his opportunity.[50]

Freed from ever having to run another campaign, Williams began to speak on issues far removed from the law. When he was named American of the Year by the Religious Town Meeting group in Dallas, he used the opportunity to call for tolerance and diversity. For thirty years he had championed equal rights for African Americans, but now he expanded his plea for acceptance of all races and religions: "The symbol of

America is not the gray of the melting pot. The symbol of America is the vibrancy of the rainbow." He also repeated the twin themes of his political career: religion and making government an instrument to help others. In a speech to the National Prayer Breakfast he affirmed his long-held belief that service to God is the crucial element in government. He acknowledged the importance of the separation of church and state but argued that all politics must be based on recognition of "a divine providence and God as our creator." His eulogy at the death of Justice Blair Moody Jr., the son of his old liberal colleague, argued that the "greatest sin" was "politics without principle" and concluded that it was ironic that Moody's heart gave out, as it had "never failed anybody else."[51]

Finally, in April 1983, Coleman retired and his peers elected Williams as chief justice. He was delighted both by the honor and for the opportunity to return to the role of administrator. In his first term he had led the campaign to computerize the courts. He now began a move to increase their efficiency and secure more financial support. For the last time Mennen Williams was back on center stage.

In his final term on the court, and especially after being selected chief justice, Williams showed a significant moderation in both his style and his interpretation of the law. The outspoken, often combative "conscience of the Democratic Party" had evolved into an elder statesman. As head of the court he assumed the role of moderator of disputes and facilitator of consensus. He was scrupulously fair in assigning opinions, rarely reserving the honor of speaking for the court for himself and actually wrote fewer decisions as chief justice than he had as an associate. Williams also generally remained silent in court deliberations until all the other judges had spoken. One colleague noted:

> He knew the art of consensus making. In the difficult, heated, and sometimes contentious process of collegial Supreme Court decision making, he was constantly a calm voice of reasoned moderation. . . . During an age in which style and grace are too all infrequently seen in major public figures, Mennen Williams was an enviable example of both. He was incapable of being uncharitable.

His associates were often surprised by his restraint and lack of ideological fervor and his willingness to look for a centralist decision that would gain majority support.[52]

"Reasoned moderation" seems a strange phrase to describe Mennen Williams, but both the times and the man had changed since his years as governor and head of the African Bureau. The ideological battles over civil rights, expanded social welfare programs, and an American commitment to the third world had been replaced with the political conservatism of the 1980s. Ronald Reagan was in the White House, in part due to his attack on social programs and government itself, and the idealistic campaign to end legal segregation had given way to a white backlash over affirmative action, busing, and other issues. America was largely unconcerned with Africa and more focused on the arms race with the Soviet Union. Most Democrats shunned the term *liberal* and reflected the times by moving toward the center.

Williams's behavior on the court also reflected changes in the man. He was seventy-two when he became chief justice, and it was clear it would be his last public position. He was no longer the boy wonder attacking conservatives in the legislature, uncaring businessmen, segregationist southerners, or Europeanists in the State Department. There would be no more campaigns, no more offices, and no more battles. His legacy on the court would not be based on ideology but compassion, tolerance, and affability.

He also reflected this new moderation in his decisions. Williams continued to support individuals in workman's compensation suits and those alleging racial or gender discrimination, and he remained a strong advocate for protecting the environment. Unlike his first term, however, he was far more sympathetic to business and insurance interests in liability cases. When a motorcycle rider sued the company that sold him a defective vehicle, Williams voted to deny the claim, agreeing that by neglecting to obtain a motorcycle driver's permit the plaintiff had failed to show "reasonable care" in operation of the machine. In a complex insurance case in which a woman was injured while driving a pickup truck insured by her husband's business, the chief justice agonized over the opposing claims. The woman's lawyers argued that the insurance policy was complex, vague, and incomprehensible and that the driver naturally assumed she was covered by the policy. The insurance company responded that the policy clearly stated that it covered only "the owner" of the vehicle, not his spouse. In his opinion, Williams wrote:

> On the one hand, this Court is made up of human beings, who are aware that very few insured will try to read the detailed, cross-referenced, standardized, mass-produced insurance forms, nor necessarily understand it if he or she does. Thus courts have gradually moved away from the traditional viewpoint of *caveat emptor* realizing that the modern insurance contract is not made between parties of equal bargaining strengths. On the other hand, this Court, as a court of law, cannot ignore the fact that an insurance contract is still a contract and must be enforced.

He finally sided with the sanctity of contracts and voted against the woman's claim.[53]

He also continued his middle of the road rulings on crime and the rights of the accused. Despite his mixed opinions during his first term, he was accused of being soft on crime during his reelection campaign but continued to alternate between endorsing strict limits on police and prosecutors and endorsing their right to gather evidence. In one case, when the police arrested a woman for a vehicle infraction, she left her purse on the front seat. The officers instructed her to unlock her car and get her purse before taking her to jail and found cocaine in her handbag. The court overturned the drug conviction as an illegal search, but Williams dissented and argued that police had the right to use the drugs as evidence.[54]

At the same time Williams delivered a harsh tongue-lashing in his verbal examination of a prosecutor defending the validity of a confession given by an accused rapist while undergoing a polygraph test without his attorney present. Even though his attorney had been told that the results of the lie detector exam could not be used in court, the district attorney contended that the defendant had waived his right to having a lawyer present.

Williams repeatedly asked the state attorney: "Would *you* ever allow a client to take a polygraph without counsel?" and wrote the court's decision overturning the conviction.[55]

Despite his rather centralist approach on insurance claims and criminal issues, Williams remained consistent in his defense of democracy and the people's right to be heard in government. When a local government levied a "fee" on apartment complexes to avoid a vote on a tax increase, the chief justice offered a civics lesson: "A tax is a revenue raising exercise of the government's taxing power, while a fee is an exercise of the police power. The government may not raise revenue through an enactment of police power." Taxes require the consent of the governed, and officials could not use arbitrary power to avoid the will of the people. Democracy, Williams concluded, was based on the power of the people, not the whims of politicians.[56]

Williams's conciliatory style and more moderate interpretation of the law were also partly a result of his new role as advocate for Michigan courts and lobbyist for their funding. Much of his last five years on the court were spent speaking to the state legislature, testifying before legislative committees, and trying to generate public support for better facilities and increased salaries for judges. In his first term he had devoted much of his time and energy to modernizing the justice system. In his second he focused on improving the quality of the courts.

When elected chief justice, Williams immediately turned to a technique that had served him well as governor, appointing "blue ribbon" citizens committees to determine the public's view of the courts and to suggest changes in the administration of justice. He then used their ideas to try to convince the legislature to build better facilities and increase salaries to speed up the legal system and make it more responsive to the people. In his first "State of the Judiciary" speech to the legislature in 1983, he noted that it had been more than twenty years since he last addressed the group. At that time legislators lacked staff and worked out of cramped offices. Now, he argued, it was the courts that were overcrowded and lacked necessary personnel. He pointed out that some courthouses were formerly "gas stations and funeral homes" and one had been "a meat locker." Michigan needed a massive program to renovate buildings and hire more staff for its courts.[57]

He also lobbied for more jails and parole and probation officers, claiming that some judges were reluctant to send criminals to overcrowded prisons or to decide on probation with so few qualified staff. As a result, too many criminals were allowed to go free. He noted that he had long advocated mandatory sentences for violent offenders, but there were not enough jails to hold them.[58]

Aside from attempting to convince the state to increase spending on the justice system, he began his own efforts to speed up the backlog of cases. After surveying judges around the state he found that the major complaints were delays, public dismay with the system, and a lack of adequate funding. He then drafted a "Program to Improve the Michigan Court System during 1986–1987," calling for more judges, an educational program to explain the courts to the public, and new facilities. He also suggested hiring retired judges on a part-time basis to help relieve court congestion and increasing salaries and retirement benefits for judges to prevent them from leaving for more lucrative positions in private practice.[59]

Despite Williams's aggressive lobbying, the legislature was reluctant to increase funds for the court in the budget-cutting 1980s. Three decades earlier he had battled representatives to increase spending for social programs; now he fought for more funds for the courts. When Governor Milliken proposed cutting fifteen full-time judges to help balance the budget, Williams personally intervened and managed to have six positions restored. He also was able to negotiate moderate raises for judges, an improved pension program, and modernization of a number of court buildings.[60]

As he neared the end of his final term on the court, he faced the prospect of retirement with considerable reluctance. He knew Michigan law did not permit a judge to seek election once he or she had turned seventy, but he was not ready to abandon public service or the public's attention. When he spoke to the legislature for the last time it was a nostalgic and

emotional event. For twelve years as governor and five as chief
justice he had addressed legislators, at times berating them for
their lack of support for his reform programs and more recently
attempting to convince them to allocate more funds for the
legal system. On April 10, 1986, he walked to the podium in
the state House of Representatives for the last time. After a
lengthy standing ovation by members of both parties, he paused
to gather his composure and noted that this was the twenty-
fourth time he had addressed them, "and in all probability this
is the last time I shall have this honor." He recalled that he had
served with a number of their fathers and in one case a member's grandfather. "I only wish I could go on to serve further
with you and then with your children and grandchildren," he
concluded. Although he was now seventy-five, his desire and
ambition were undiminished. He left dabbing tears from his
eyes to another standing ovation.[61]

While Williams may still have wanted to hold some public
office, there were no opportunities for any significant elected
position. As he prepared to leave the court he wrote a friend:

> While I haven't really had time to figure out what I'm going
> to do after the first of the year, I think I may do a little
> teaching and I want to do some writing. The chief thing I
> want to write about is to set the record straight on the '48
> election.[62]

He did teach, but he also became more and more concerned
with his lasting reputation and the need to correct what he saw
as historical errors. A number of schools wanted the prestige of
having Williams on their faculty. In January 1987, a week after
his formal retirement, he taught a two-credit course at the University of Detroit School of Law entitled "Judicial Power in
Practice." That fall he offered a class called "Leadership" at
Oakland University, which included readings from Plato,
Machiavelli, Lao Tzu, and the liberal historian Arthur M.
Schlesinger Jr. Professor Williams supplemented the texts with
anecdotes drawn from his career as governor, his service in the
State Department, and his years on the court. He was popular
with students and repeated the course in the spring.[63]

He enjoyed teaching but began to spend more and more time gathering material on his career as governor. Governor Milliken appointed him to chair the celebration of the twenty-fifth anniversary of the completion of the Mackinac Bridge, and he was overjoyed with the chance to celebrate his most lasting and tangible achievement. He even wrote a brief history of the project to be added to his papers, which he had donated to the University of Michigan a decade earlier (receiving a large tax deduction in return). He also retrieved an early manuscript he had begun on "1948 Gubernatorial Campaign History," but he completed only three pages before he decided he needed to solicit material from others involved in the election. He developed a questionnaire for campaign workers to fill out and wrote to many former colleagues asking them to write or record on cassette their memories of the election. He acknowledged the efforts of the Michigan History Project to conduct oral history interviews but noted that many who had been involved in the campaign had died and he needed to get the recollections of others before the "all-valuable but slow moving oral history program."[64]

Williams's near preoccupation with his 1948 election victory was partly the result of his anger over accounts that attributed his success almost solely to the efforts of organized labor. He wrote that most analysts "seem to feel that the UAW won the election for me." To Williams the 1948 victory was not just due to the efforts of the unions but was "a grass root movement of those untouched by politics." It "was a people's movement" of volunteers who became involved due to his own energy and passion. He admitted that he would not have won without the crucial support of the unions but maintained that "we wouldn't have won with just the unions."[65]

Williams felt that those who had studied the 1948 election and his subsequent victories had missed the main point. His success was the result of the triumph of direct democracy, as people throughout the state were invigorated and empowered by his campaign and the issues it raised. The lesson of his six gubernatorial victories was not that unions had influence but that when properly motivated ordinary citizens will act. The

key to his success was the direct participation of the people of
Michigan in the political process, and the reason for their
involvement was Mennen Williams. In a fragment written in
his trademark green ink on a yellow legal pad, he jotted down:
"Who Won the 1948 Michigan Governorship?" and contended that his victory was a lesson to the nation of the potential power of an inspired public unleashed by the inspiration of
an idealistic leader: "What I propose to you political leaders of
America is that you yourself can be the catalyst that can bring
together a movement to achieve the objectives you hold dear
and to move America nearer the heart's desire."[66]

In one of his last public speeches he addressed the Wayne
State University Local History Conference and again returned
to his 1948 upset. He now connected the victory to the other
dominant issue of his public life, civil rights, and told the group
that his win in 1948 was crucial in forcing America to embrace
the idea of racial equality. The Michigan election led to a
national focus on civil rights and later he personally "provided
an educational experience for Senator Kennedy, particularly as
what his position should be on the then important issue of civil
rights sit–in strategy." He even argued that his opposition to the
nomination of Lyndon Johnson in 1960 was instrumental in
moving the Texan toward endorsing racial equality: "Michigan's no vote on Vice President Lyndon Johnson must have
been a force in causing him to embrace civil rights so fervently
and effectively."[67]

His linking of his personal electoral victory with the nation's
eventual endorsement of racial equality was an attempt to
confirm his own historical importance for the nation. Not only
did he revive and remake the Democratic Party in Michigan,
but he also was influential in achieving the American dream of
equality. In defending his lecturing tone toward Kennedy in
their June 1960 meeting, and even contending that his solitary
opposition to Johnson's selection for the vice presidency led to
the Civil Rights Act of 1964, Williams showed a deep concern
for establishing his place in American history and for stressing
the centrality of his 1948 victory for the nation. Without his
upset victory over Sigler, the country and its leaders would not

have moved as rapidly toward equal rights. Without his leadership and commitment, segregation would have endured far longer.

Williams's argument was problematic and self-serving, but it is an indication of why he was so determined to provide a "real" account of 1948. Sporadically Williams had tried to organize material on the 1948 election and wrote to several students working on Michigan political history, encouraging their efforts and suggesting that they look beyond labor as the key. He roughed out a chapter on the campaign that was to be part of a complete autobiography but put the project on hold until after his retirement.

After he left the court Williams basked in the accolades of retirement dinners and testimonies. Michigan Democrats organized a gala affair to commemorate his career, which featured a massive cake with his trademark green frosting. Berthelot reminded the audience: "It's hard for many younger members of the party to realize that 'before Soapy,' Democrats in Michigan were as rare as whooping cranes." He had personally saved the party from extinction and made it into the most powerful state organization in the nation.[68]

While he worked on documenting his political career, Williams also felt the need to defend his liberal ideology. He told his Princeton classmates that it was "no left wing tract or teacher" that led him to liberalism but reading about the hardships of medieval serfs and "the suffering of the women and the cries of the children in the mills and mines during England's Industrial Revolution." As a result, "something very strong and compelling happened inside me almost 50 years ago. . . . Then and there I determined to fight for the underdog."[69]

Forty years after he gained the attention of the nation with his election as governor, both Williams and his unabashed liberalism were out of date. During his sixteen years on the court he had accomplished much, but it was not like being governor or even serving in the State Department. In his retirement years he would show the importance of his career, correct the mistaken view of the 1948 election, and defend his liberal philosophy. He was only seventy-six and in excellent health. He had never smoked, rarely drank, and had been a physical fitness devotee since his early teens. There would be plenty of time to set the record straight on the reasons for his 1948 victory and its impact on the nation.

On February 2, 1988, barely a week before his seventy-seventh birthday and a year after he had retired from the court, Williams began his day as he had every morning since he was a young boy, with vigorous exercise. He got up at his usual time of 5:30 a.m., did fifty sit-ups, and rode his stationary bicycle for half an hour. After his morning workout, he devoted several hours to corresponding with friends and political figures, took a forty-five-minute nap after lunch, and spent much of the afternoon on the phone. At 10:00 p.m. he changed into green linen pajamas to prepare for bed. He told Nancy that he had "a terrible headache," turned away, and collapsed to the floor of their bedroom. An ambulance rushed him to St. John's Hospital in Detroit, where emergency room physicians diagnosed a massive cerebral hemorrhage. He never regained consciousness and was pronounced dead at 2:22 a.m. on February 3.[70]

The next day all of the major Michigan newspapers prepared special supplements summarizing his career, running photos, and offering eulogies. Even old opponents such as George Romney and William Milliken joined the tributes. "He ennobled the political process," Milliken noted. Detroit mayor Coleman Young concluded: "He was a giant." The *Detroit News,* always a bitter enemy, ran a cartoon showing a giant bow tie linking lower and upper Michigan with the caption "Evergreen."[71]

Williams's son Gery flew to Michigan to organize the funeral, and Nancy opened their home in Grosse Pointe Farms for two days of visitation. From 2:00 to 10:00 p.m. each day thousands waited for up to two hours to enter the home, pause at the open casket, and view the body dressed in a black suit and the trademark green and white polka-dot bow tie. Next to the casket was an American flag decorated with his World War II medals. Police estimated that more than twelve thousand persons paid their respects. Buffy Berthelot caught an all-night train from Florida, and when she paused in front of the body she told his son: "There is only one thing wrong. His tie is on straight."[72]

Cards, telegrams, and letters arrived from leaders around the world and eventually filled three large cardboard boxes. Lady Bird Johnson, John Kenneth Galbraith, Sergeant Shriver, Ted Kennedy, Dean Rusk, Eppie Lederer (the advice columnist Ann Landers), the chief justice of Australia, fourteen European leaders, and the heads of state of every African nation except South Africa sent tributes. There were telegrams from more than six hundred Michigan and national politicians and hundreds of other notes from friends and colleagues at the Salisbury School, Princeton University, and the University of Michigan and from World War II navy veterans and State Department officials. More than five hundred charities send condolences in memory of one of their major contributors, as did one hundred grade and high schools in the state and fifty ethnic clubs. The national NAACP, the Congress of Racial Equality, and supreme court justices from a dozen states sent notes. The U.S. Congress, the Michigan legislature, the Michigan Bar Association, more than one hundred labor organizations, and Democratic committees in each of Michigan's counties passed formal resolutions memorializing Williams.[73]

While the cables, cards, and resolutions from leaders and organizations displayed at his home were a testament to his impact, Williams may well have been more moved by the nearly three thousand letters that eventually were stored in a box labeled "Common Citizens of Michigan." Many were written in pencil on cheap notebook paper or plain postcards, and nearly all mentioned a personal encounter with Williams at a county fair, local picnic, square dance, or church supper. One read:

> When I was five years old my dad was a union greeter. My brother and I were the only little ones there. I remember him giving my brother a sticker—apparently the last one as he gave me a dime—I was so thrilled. He will be missed by all who knew him but by many people he never even knew.

A woman from the Upper Peninsula wrote Nancy:

I met your husband only once when he came into our small town. Never met a more sincere and honest person. I considered him a friend.

A woman from Grand Rapids recalled:

Soapy tickled my baby's chin at a food store in 1952. It's in her baby book! I was given a paper bow tie too. The bow tie was kept on the visor of our cars and I gave it to my daughter years ago.

A young attorney from Gaylord recalled:

It was not until Mennen's death that I realized how much his life and ideals affected my development. I was raised by parents who were middle class, Irish and fervent Democrats. Soapy influenced my parents very much. They in turn instilled into me a deep sense that we are here to serve a higher purpose than our own day to day concerns of financial gains.

And a black woman from Detroit remembered:

I walked by your church many a day on my way to the library. I sure wanted to go in. But, being young and black, I didn't have the courage to venture in. Soapy gave others and me the courage we needed! Every black person says, God bless him![74]

The military funeral and high mass were scheduled for 11:00 a.m. on Friday, February 5, at his beloved Cathedral Church of St. Paul. The first people arrived at seven and by ten all of the twelve hundred public seats were filled. The church staff quickly arranged a TV monitor in an adjoining room for two hundred more visitors. Nearly a thousand others, unable to get into the church, stood outside in the twelve-degree weather as a sharp northern wind gusted along Woodward Avenue.

A rabbi, a Roman Catholic priest, and a black Baptist minister offered prayers, and the Very Reverend Bertram N. Herling, dean of the cathedral, presided. In his homily he described Williams's accomplishments in Michigan and Washington and noted the governor's pride in building the Mackinac Bridge: "He has now crossed the last bridge." During the funeral service all the tollbooths on the bridge were closed for one minute in tribute.

Williams's son Gery, Governor James Blanchard, Supreme Court Justice Dennis Archer, and U.S. District Judge Horace Gilmore delivered the eulogies. Blanchard concluded, "Soapy Williams made Michigan a model for the nation. Everybody in Michigan shook his hand—twice!" When the family rose to take communion, a group of civil rights leaders and union officials seated in the rear spontaneously began to sing "We Shall Overcome," and the rest of the audience joined in the civil rights anthem. As the casket was wheeled out, the organist played the "Battle Hymn of the Republic."[75]

The family placed Williams's body in a temporary crypt in Evergreen Cemetery in Detroit. In June a hearse drove him north to Mackinac Island. The body was transferred from the Mackinac Island ferry to a horse-drawn carriage, which carried it to the tiny Trinity Episcopal Church for a private family service. The body was then put back on the carriage for a slow trip through the town, passing the governor's summer residence, the original fort, and the Grand Hotel (where the thirteen flags were lowered to half-mast and the staff assembled with heads bowed on the front steps), and finally to a secluded cemetery for burial. If you stand behind the grave and the wind blows hard enough to sway the trees, you can see the top of the Mackinac Bridge uniting the state of Michigan.

CONCLUSION

Coming Clean with Soapy

A "no" uttered from the deepest conviction
is better than a "yes" merely uttered to please,
or worse, to avoid trouble.

—*Mahatma Gandhi*

The first question asked at history conventions is "Do you know of any jobs?" The second is "What are you working on?" For the past three years my answers have been "There are no jobs, and I am working on a biography of G. Mennen Williams." The typical reaction is awkward silence. After my standard two-minute biography, some recall his dissent from the nomination of Lyndon Johnson, a few know a bit about his years in the African Bureau, and a handful remember that he wore bow ties.

The response of nonhistorians is even more bleak. Most of my students were toddlers when Williams died and know little about any American politician before Bill Clinton. I once told a few about Williams's commitment to civil rights and showed them his picture. Their response was that his bow tie made him look "dorky." My colleagues were vaguely aware that I was writing about somebody from Michigan but were never sure exactly who. One recently asked: "Are you still working on *Soupy*?"

Occasionally a mention of Williams does stir a response. Once I was eating breakfast at a diner in Ann Arbor seated at the counter next to an old guy wearing a Detroit Tigers hat.

After a while we began to discuss the usual topics acceptable for strangers. We agreed that the weather was terrible, the Lions were worse, and coffee should be included in the breakfast specials. After a brief silence he asked if I was from Ann Arbor, and I explained that I was in town to do some research. That usually is a sure way to end all conversation, but he asked what I was studying. "Well, I'm working on a biography of a guy who was from Michigan named G. Mennen Williams," I answered. He stuck his spoon in his oatmeal, turned toward me, and replied: "You mean old Soapy? Boy, he was quite a character. They don't make politicians like that anymore!" He was right. Old Soapy *was* quite a character, and we *don't* have politicians like him anymore.

There are any number of physical monuments to Williams's long career. There is a highway in the Upper Peninsula named after him. In 1987, Governor John Engler dedicated the G. Mennen Williams Building in Lansing, which houses the State Law Library, the Supreme Court, and the offices of the attorney general. There is a G. Mennen Williams Auditorium at Ferris State University in Big Rapids, an endowed lecture series in his name at Wayne State, and a room named in his honor at the Bentley Historical Library in Ann Arbor. His collection of African masks at the Detroit Institute of Fine Arts bears his name, as does his wife's donation of Chinese porcelains. It is unlikely, however, that most who drive on his road, enter his buildings, or view his art know much about the man after whom they are named.

Williams's current obscurity is understandable. If history is not always "written *by* winners" but it is usually *about* winners. The subjects of most political biographies are the powerful, the important, the influential, the winners. Kings, generals, popes, and presidents are always good bets, as well as long-term leaders in Congress and demonstrably significant presidential advisers. A bit of sexual or financial scandal is also good. The historiography of the nation's political "lovable losers" is pretty thin.

Both Mennen Williams's style and his ideology make him seem of a distant age. In the five and a half decades since he scored his upset victory in 1948 American politics has changed immeasurably. His unabashed liberalism, belief in an ever-expanding welfare state, and moral pronouncements on racial equality seem like dusty relics in our era of distrust of government, racial polarity, and endorsement of political moderation. Williams was the epitome of the "big-spending liberal," now scorned by even his own political party. Ronald Reagan's famous pronouncement that "government is not the *solution* to our problems; government *is* the problem" would be unfathomable to Williams, as he was convinced that government was the designated instrument of economic and racial equality.

His ideas on foreign affairs seem similarly obsolete. The belated independence of Angola and Rhodesia and the collapse of apartheid in South Africa finally led to his vision of "Africa for the Africans," but the results are not what he or others in the idealistic 1960s expected. In the twenty-first century Africa is far removed from the attention of most Americans and makes the news only with the latest exposé of corruption, brutal dictatorships, and foreign military intervention or accounts of the ravages of the AIDS epidemic. It is doubtful Williams's vision of African liberation included Idi Amin, Robert Mugabe, or U.S. troops in Somalia and Liberia.

Even his most cherished goal, the dream of racial equality, seems to be of another era. The idealistic image of racial cooperation, peaceful integration, and Christian brotherhood is a reflection of a time when a mixed audience singing "We Shall Overcome" was seen as a certain sign that America was moving toward the elimination of racism. While legal segregation ended, the urban riots of the 1960s, the black power movement, and the battles over busing and affirmative action, have all eroded the noble but simplistic idealism of Williams's efforts in the 1950s.

If Williams's unflinching liberalism and commitment to expanded government seem out of date, his campaign style and personality are even more archaic. In an era of focus groups, sophisticated polling, and carefully cultivated media images, Soapy's fervent populist campaign style seems ever more distant and obsolete. A tall, gangly, bow-tied, gravelly voiced millionaire named Soapy shaking hands at factory gates, calling square

dances at ethnic clubs, and selling raffle tickets at county fairs is
not the way to "sell" a politician in our time of candidates in
matching blue suits mouthing carefully rehearsed poll-tested
responses on TV. It is doubtful that any current U.S. official
would organize a square dance for diplomats in the State
Department cafeteria, take off his shoes during a TV debate, or
ride a water buffalo into a rice paddy in the Philippines.
Williams's folksy approach and flair for the dramatic gesture
would likely provoke more ridicule than admiration from an
ever more cynical public and press.

Williams's fusion of Christianity and politics, the core of his
ideology, is also largely absent in contemporary America.
Politicians still invoke the name of God, but only the conservative Christian Right still links religion and policy. Few to the
left of center dare to claim Jesus as their political model or
advocate that the government's goal should be the creation of
God's kingdom on earth.

Mennen Williams was a loser measured by the usual standards of American politics. He never was nominated for the
presidency. He never gained a cabinet position. He built a
potent political machine in Michigan, but it collapsed under the
stress of racial issues and the war in Vietnam. He was a strong
and often successful advocate for reorienting American foreign
policy away from a "Europe first" stance toward greater attention to the third world, but he was unable to overcome completely the prevailing bipolar cold war ideology and the bureaucratic infighting in Washington. He lost his comeback
campaign for the Senate and spent his final sixteen years in pursuit of the important but hardly captivating goal of modernizing Michigan's courts.

What elevated Williams above the other political figures of his
age was his uncompromising moral vision of the promise of
America and his stubborn refusal to accept a diluted version of
that ideal. Certain that government was obligated to feed the
hungry, clothe the naked, and help the poor, he defied his
Republican opponents, drove his state into bankruptcy, and
destroyed his presidential ambitions. The dominant moral issue
of his career was civil rights, and he was convinced that the goal

of racial equality could not be adjusted by means of political cal-
culation. He would not equivocate on the subject and would not
remain silent when others in his party temporized on the topic.

To Williams, politics was a battle between right and wrong,
good and evil, and one could not betray what was right and
good for popularity and power. His absolute conviction that he
was correct infuriated his critics in both political parties but was
the essence of his energy and appeal. His confidence in the
moral superiority of his positions led him to a seeming self-
righteousness and a belief that he had the duty to point out the
moral failures of others. His was a hectoring humanitarianism
characterized by a strident tone, and it carried a high price.

Historian Alonzo Hamby has argued that Franklin Roosevelt
"established as the dominant theme of American politics a tradition of New Deal liberalism" that was gradually eroded by the
emphasis on cultural issues and the cold war. To Hamby, the best
way to examine the changing fortunes of liberalism is through "a
biographical approach to the history of American politics," as
both personality and issues affect policies and elections.[1]

G. Mennen Williams's career demonstrated both the power
of and the challenges to twentieth-century American liberalism
and the interaction between personality and policy. His six
electoral victories in Michigan were largely the result of his
flamboyance and fervent campaign style, but he found that
winning elections did not ensure reform in his state, as personal
popularity was no guarantee of legislative success. Unlike most
of his Democratic contemporaries, Williams rejected the necessity of compromise and pragmatism. His refusal to adjust to the
political realities of Michigan left his ideology undiluted but his
concrete achievements limited.

While many other Democrats shared his commitment to liberalism, what made Williams unique was the fusion of progressive politics and religious belief. Christianity has often served as
the basis for political activism in the United States, but in the
post–World War II era the American Left grew increasingly
secular and appeals to a religious basis for politics became
largely the province of conservatives. The major exception to
this trend was the civil rights movement. The legal attack on

segregation was accompanied by direct action organized by the black church and justified in religious language. Martin Luther King condemned racism as a violation of Christ's teachings, and his rhetoric stressed the biblical injunctions to love your enemy, forgive your oppressor, and accept all people as equal before God. While direct religious references waned among white liberals, they became central to the black struggle for equality.

It is ironic that the white, millionaire, Princeton-educated Williams had more in common with African American activists than with most in his political party. Just as he refused to compromise with the Michigan legislature, he was also unwilling to abandon the religious basis for politics and government that had shaped his life. Most liberals shunned overt religious language, but Williams remained consistent in resting his ideology on a biblical base.

In *The Vital Center,* his primer for postwar liberals, Arthur M. Schlesinger Jr. contended that "compromise is the strategy of democracy" and cautioned against relying on the Christian belief in the perfectibility of man. To Schlesinger, only tough, pragmatic realists could protect liberalism from assault by both the Left and the Right. It is not surprising that John Kennedy rather than Mennen Williams would become his model. Kennedy viewed civil rights as a political rather than a moral issue and accepted the need to retain southern support in Congress by moving cautiously on race. Less concerned with expanding social programs at home than with aggressively pursuing the cold war conflict with communism abroad, his legacy is his victory in the Cuban missile crisis, not leadership in the assault on segregation. While Soapy Williams may have been the conscience of the Democratic Party, the pragmatic John Kennedy and the deal-making Lyndon Johnson were its captains. Williams may have been an excellent chaplain, but the captain sails the ship.[2]

Williams claimed Franklin D. Roosevelt as his inspiration and political model, but his ideology and style more nearly resembled those of earlier American leaders. Like the militant abolitionist William Lloyd Garrison, he decried compromise on the great moral issue of his era. The contentious Garrison had announced "I do not want to think or speak or write with moderation" and challenged critics of his abrasive style to "tell a man whose house is on fire, to give a 'moderate' alarm." Like Walter Rauschenbusch and others who advocated the social gospel to alleviate the hardships of industrial America, Williams saw politics and policies as having a biblical blueprint. He echoed Rauschenbusch's view that "The sense of equality is the only basis of Christian morality" and shared the theologian's belief that "nations do not die by wealth, but by injustice." He combined Garrison's moral certainty and abrasiveness with Rauschenbusch's vision of a more equal and just society. Unfortunately, unlike Garrison and Rauschenbusch, he was an elected politician and had to deal with the political consequences of his outspokenness. Garrison never had to worry about alienating powerful members of his political party, and Rauschenbusch never had to work with John Kennedy or Lyndon Johnson.[3]

Had he compromised with the Michigan legislature, abandoned some of his social programs, and accepted a modified tax program, he could have avoided the fiscal crisis of 1959 and perhaps have had a chance for the presidential or vice presidential nomination. Had he ignored Adlai Stevenson's call for moderation, he would not have alienated his party's presidential nominee. Had he moderated his liberalism and restrained his patronizing lectures to Kennedy about civil rights, he almost certainly would have received a cabinet position. Had he toned down his ceaseless demands for immediate racial equality, he could well have become a far more powerful figure within the Democratic Party. Had he remained silent when Lyndon Johnson was nominated for the vice presidency, he would likely have had far more influence with the future president. But had he done any of these he would not have been Soapy Williams, the conscience of the Democratic Party.

It is his very refusal to compromise, modify, or moderate his positions that makes him admirable. The very traits that doomed his political career are those that are most deserving of praise. My oatmeal-eating breakfast partner had it right: "Old Soapy was quite a character. They don't make politicians like that anymore!"

NOTES

CHAPTER I

1. There are two main sources for the history of Williams's family and early life. In 1980, he developed a strong interest in his ancestors and commissioned an exhaustive genealogical review of his family. He also wrote an account of his early life entitled "Family Story." This material is in "Genealogical Files," box 103, G. Mennen Williams Nongubernatorial Papers, Bentley Historical Library, Ann Arbor, Michigan (hereafter GMWN, meaning nongubernatorial). Papers in the vast G. Mennen Williams collection in the Bentley are organized into two broad categories: materials on his years as governor of Michigan and those covering his years before 1949 and after 1960. References to his career as governor are cited as GMW. References to all other materials in the collection are cited as GMWN. When he considered a run for the presidency, Williams chose Frank McNaughton to write a campaign biography entitled *Mennen Williams of Michigan: Fighter for Progress* (New York: Oceana Publishing, 1960). Like most campaign biographies, it offers little criticism of its subject but provides a good summary of his early life. McNaughton's notes and outlines are in the "Frank McNaughton Files," box 419, GMWN.

2. "Family Story," box 103, GMWN.

3. Ibid.

4. Ibid.

5. Williams's account of his early religious ideas are in "Cathedral Church of St. Paul," box 91, GMWN.

6. "Family Story."

7. Ibid.; Nancy Williams Gram, interview with author, April 23, 2001.

8. "Family Story."

9. Nancy Williams Gram, interview with author.

10. William Weddon, *Michigan Governors: Their Life Stories* (Lansing: Michigan State Historical Society, 1994), 149.

11. "Family Story."

12. "Salisbury Files," box 1, GMWN.

13. McNaughton, *Mennen Williams of Michigan*, 50.

14. "Family Story." See also his letters to his parents in "Salisbury Files."

15. Diary of G. Mennen Williams, September 17, 1930, box 1, GMWN.

16. "Family Story"; Williams Diary, September 30, 1930.

17. "Family Story."

18. Application Letter to Princeton University, box 1, GMWN.

19. Williams Diary, November 23, 1930. Williams's grades and papers are in "Princeton Files," box 1, GMWN.

20. Williams Diary, January 7, 1931, and March 1, 1931; "Prodigy's Progress," *Time,* September 15, 1952, 26–29. See also Beverly Smith Jr., "Soapy, the Boy Wonder," *Saturday Evening Post,* November 9, 1957, 27–29.

21. Williams Diary, September 17, 1930; September 30, 1930.

22. "Margaret Johnson Obituary," *The Star* (Muncie, Indiana), December 12, 1985.

23. Williams Diary, September 17, 1930.

24. Ibid., November 6, 1930.

25. Ibid.

26. Ibid., January 4, 1931; January 5, 1931.

27. Ibid., January 5, 1931.

28. Ibid., January 10, 1931; February 3, 1931.

29. Ibid., February 3, 1931.

30. Ibid., February 10, 1931.

31. Ibid., April 11, 1931; May 11, 1931; May 13, 1931.

32. Ibid., May 13, 1931.

33. Ibid., May 24, 1931; June 1, 1931.

34. Ibid., June 2, 1931.

35. Peg Johnson to Mennen Williams, September 18, 1931, box 2, GMWN; Williams Diary, September 18, 1932; June 7, 1932.

36. *The Star* (Muncie, Indiana), October 6, 1964. See also Barry Goldwater, *No Apologies* (New York: William Morrow, 1979), 29–41.

37. *New York Times,* December 14, 1960. Although they usually disagreed, Williams met regularly with Goldwater during his years in the State Department to inform him about African issues. See, for example, "Talking Points for Governor Williams's Meeting with Senator Gold-

water," undated, Department of State Records, G. Mennen Williams Papers, box 17, National Archives, College Park, Maryland.

38. Williams Diary, February 3, 1931.

39. Stock Transfer Deed, February 27, 1932; Henry Williams to Mennen Williams, March 11, 1933; Edward Warner to Mennen Williams, March 16, 1933, box 2, GMWN.

40. Williams Diary, September 30, 1930.

41. Williams's account of his trip is in "Travel Correspondence," box 2, GMWN. See also Williams Diary, September 23, 1932; and G. Mennen Williams, *A Governor's Notes* (Ann Arbor: Michigan Institute of Public Affairs, 1961), 1.

42. William Barry Furlong, "A Boy Wonder Begins to Wonder," *New York Times Magazine,* November 22, 1958.

43. G. Mennen Williams, "The Social Significance of Henry Ford," senior honors thesis, May, 1933, box 2, GMWN.

44. *Nassau Herald,* 1933, Seeley-Mudd Library, Princeton University.

45. Travel Correspondence, box 2, GMWN.

46. Williams Diary, February 3, 1931.

47. McNaughton, *Mennen Williams of Michigan,* 60. Williams's law school papers and honors are in "University of Michigan School of Law," box 2, GMWN.

48. G. Mennen Williams, oral history, October 1981, box 103, GMWN. Williams granted three lengthy oral history interviews. The one in the Bentley Library is cited as Williams oral history, GMWN. The one in the John F. Kennedy Presidential Library in Boston is cited as Williams oral history, JFKL. The one in the Lyndon B. Johnson Presidential Library in Austin is cited as Williams oral history, LBJL.

49. Neil Staebler, *Out of the Smoked-Filled Room: A Memoir of Michigan Politics* (Ann Arbor: George Wahr, 1991), 29–31. Williams kept a copy of the Liberal Club Constitution for the rest of his life. It is in box 3, GMWN.

50. McNaughton, *Mennen Williams of Michigan,* 59–60; G. Mennen Williams to Henry Williams, January 25, 1935, box 3, GMWN.

51. Michael Parrish, *Felix Frankfurter and His Times* (New York: Free Press, 1982), 199–200.

52. "Family Story."

53. Nancy Williams Gram, interview with author. See also McNaughton, *Mennen Williams of Michigan,* 62–63.

54. McNaughton, *Mennen Williams of Michigan,* 62–63.

55. Nancy Lace Quirk, "Poverty," paper prepared for the class "Poverty and Dependence," May 21, 1936, box 105, GMWN.

56. Nancy Williams, "The Christian in Politics," remarks delivered at a governor's reception, January 1, 1955, box 105, GMWN.

57. Helen Washburn Berthelot, *Win Some, Lose Some: G. Mennen Williams and the New Democrats* (Detroit: Wayne State University Press, 1995), 49.

CHAPTER 2

1. McNaughton, *Mennen Williams of Michigan,* 69–70.

2. "Family Story."

3. For Murphy's background and career, see Sidney Fine, *Frank Murphy: The Detroit Years* (Ann Arbor: University of Michigan Press, 1975); and *Frank Murphy: The New Deal Years* (Chicago: University of Chicago Press, 1979).

4. J. Woodford Howard, *Mr. Justice Murphy: A Political Biography* (Princeton: Princeton University Press, 1968).

5. Williams oral history, GMWN.

6. McNaughton, *Mennen Williams of Michigan,* 70–72.

7. Fine, *Murphy: New Deal Years,* 280–81.

8. Ibid. See also McNaughton, *Mennen Williams of Michigan,* 71.

9. For the details of Williams's involvement with the milk-pricing bill, see "Milk Bill," box 4, GMWN.

10. Ibid.

11. Fine, *Murphy: New Deal Years,* 457–60.

12. McNaughton, *Mennen Williams of Michigan,* 74–75.

13. Howard, *Mr. Justice Murphy,* 189.

14. Nancy Williams Gram, interview with author.

15. Williams oral history, GMWN.

16. McNaughton, *Mennen Williams of Michigan,* 80–82.

17. Ibid., 84–86.

18. Details of Williams commission, training, and wartime experiences are in "Navy Files," box 4, GMWN.

19. "Biographical Sketch of Mrs. Williams," box 105, GMWN.

20. "Navy Files," box 4, GMWN.

21. Ibid. For Williams's involvement in veterans affairs, see "Veterans," box 414, GMW.

22. Williams Diary, January 7, 1946.

23. Williams oral history, GMWN. See also George Weeks, *Stewards of the State: The Governors of Michigan* (Ann Arbor: Detroit News and Historical Society, 1987), 112–14.

24. "1948 Campaign Memoirs." In 1981, Williams wrote this lengthy account of his nomination and election "to set the record straight." It is in box 103, GMWN.

25. Ibid.

26. McNaughton, *Mennen Williams of Michigan,* 97–98.

27. *Life,* November 28, 1955, 19.

28. Staebler, *Out of the Smoke-Filled Room,* 30–32.

29. Ibid., 50–51. In 1962, Staebler was elected to Congress and in 1964 lost a campaign to George Romney for governor of Michigan. For details of his organizational genius, see Robert Lee Sawyer, *The Democratic State Central Committee in Michigan, 1949–1959* (Ann Arbor: Ann Arbor Institute for Public Administration, 1960); and Christine Weidman, *Neil Staebler: His Career and Legacy* (Ann Arbor: Bentley Historical Library, 1987). Staebler's papers are in the Bentley Historical Library in Ann Arbor.

30. Williams oral history, GMWN; "1948 Campaign Memoirs."

31. Minutes of Meeting of members of the Michigan Liquor Commission, Detroit, May 9, 1947; Public Meeting of the Michigan Liquor Control Commission, Port Huron, November 24, 1947. Both are in Michigan Liquor Control Files, box 4, GMWN.

32. "1948 Campaign Memoirs."

33. Mennen Williams, Travel Voucher, May 1947, Michigan Liquor Control Files, box 4, GMWN.

34. "1948 Campaign Memoirs."

35. Sawyer, *The Democratic State Central Committee in Michigan*, 3–7.

36. Carolyn Stiebler, *The Politics of Change in Michigan* (Lansing: Michigan State University Press, 1970), 8.

37. Sawyer, *The Democratic State Central Committee in Michigan*, 8. See also Dudley Buffa, *Union Power and American Democracy: The UAW and the Democratic Party, 1935–1972* (Ann Arbor: University of Michigan Press, 1984), 15–16; and "Labor in Politics," *Newsweek*, October 25, 1948, 37–38.

38. An excellent account of Hoffa's political maneuverings is in Thaddeus Russell, *Out of the Jungle: Jimmy Hoffa and the American Working Class* (New York: Knopf, 2001), 153–70. See also Buffa, *Union Power and American Democracy*, 30–32.

39. Staebler, *Out of the Smoke-Filled Room*, 30–31; Russell, *Out of the Jungle*, 157. For details of the lengthy battle between Williams and Hoffa, see "Hoffa Folder," box 29, Staebler papers.

40. Resolution Adopted by the Michigan CIO-PAC, March 13, 1948, box 13, Staebler papers.

41. There are numerous accounts of the meeting at the Griffiths home. See Staebler, *Out of the Smoke-Filled Room*, 30–32; McNaughton, *Mennen Williams of Michigan*, 99–100; and Buffa, *Union Power and American Democracy*, 13–14. Williams's recollections are in "1948 Campaign Memoirs."

42. Berthelot, *Win Some, Lose Some*, 25–28.

43. "1948 Campaign Memoirs."

44. Staebler, *Out of the Smoke-Filled Room*, 32. See also Williams oral history, GMWN

45. "1948 Campaign Memoirs"; Staebler, *Out of the Smoke-Filled Room*, 33.

46. "1948 Campaign Memoirs." See also Paul Weber oral history, Michigan Oral History Project, box 2, Bentley Historical Library.

47. Ruth Ellen Wasem, "The Michigan Democratic Party in 1948," manuscript, box 103, GMWN; Staebler, *Out of the Smoke-Filled Room,* 55.

48. Wasem, "Michigan Democrtic Party in 1948"; Martha Griffiths to Floyd Stevens, August 16, 1948, box 5, GMWN.

49. For Williams's account of his meeting with Scholle, see G. Mennen Williams to Aaron Horowitz, April 1, 1984, box 103, GMWN. See also Buffa, *Union Power and American Democracy,* 15; and Williams oral history, GMWN.

50. Press release, Michigan CIO-PAC, March 13, 1948, box 13, Staebler papers; Buffa, *Union Power and American Democracy,* 16. Southwell is quoted in McNaughton, *Mennen Williams of Michigan,* 110.

51. Russell, *Out of the Jungle,* 157–58; "Labor in Politics," *Newsweek,* October 25, 1948.

52. Williams for Governor press releases, May 15 and July 19, 1948, box 5, GMWN.

53. "From the Desk of G. Mennen Williams," memo, May 15, 1948, box 5, GMWN.

54. "1948 Campaign Memoirs."

55. G. Mennen Williams, "Remarks at Princeton University, September 17, 1984," box 103, GMWN; Chuck Harmon, "Pleasant Politickins," *Michigan Magazine of History,* November-December 1999, 8–9; Williams, *A Governor's Notes,* 14.

56. Nancy Williams oral history, Michigan Oral History Project, box 2, Bentley Historical Library.

57. "Itinerary of Our State Trip, August 7–15, 1948," box 5, GMWN.

58. "1948 Campaign Memoirs"; Berthelot, *Win Some, Lose Some,* 47.

59. Nancy Williams oral history; Williams for Governor press release, August 4, 1948, box 5, GMWN.

60. Buffa, *Union Power and American Democracy,* 17–18.

61. "1948 State Convention," Hoffa folder, box 29, Staebler papers; Nancy Williams oral history.

62. *New York Times,* September 15, 1948.

63. "Volunteers," undated handwritten memo, box 5, GMWN.

64. "1948 Campaign Memoirs"; *Detroit News,* October 11 and October 12, 1948.

65. "'Wandering Willie' [G. Mennen Williams] to Campaign Staff, October 13, 1948," box 6, GMWN; Staebler, *Out of the Smoke-Filled Room,* 33.

66. *Detroit News,* October 13 and October 15, 1948; Williams to Neil Holland, undated; Nancy Williams, "Speech at Sault Ste. Marie, September 27, 1948," box 5, GMWN; *Stars and Stripes,* October 3, 1948.

67. Press releases of campaign speeches, October 14, Bay City; October 19, Battle Creek, box 5, GMWN.

68. Radio address, October 20, 1948; "Public Utilities," G. Mennen Williams speech, October 26, 1948, box 5, GMWN.

69. Weber oral history; radio address, Ypsilanti, October 11, 1948; Press release, "Negroes," October 14, 1948, box 5, GMWN.

70. For background on the Mackinac Bridge and Williams's use of the issue in 1948, see Lawrence A. Rubin, *Building Michigan: The Story of the Mighty Mac* (Detroit: Wayne State University Press, 1985), 4–11.

71. "The Unfulfilled Promises of 'Promisin' Kim Sigler," undated speech, box 5, GMWN.

72. *Detroit News,* September 19 and October 28, 1948.

73. Ibid., September 19, 1948.

74. Campaign speech, Flint, October 25, 1948, box 5, GMWN; *Detroit News,* September 28, 1948.

75. Campaign speeches, Ypsilanti, October 28, 1948, and Adrian, October 29, 1948, box 5, GMWN; "Vote for G. Mennen Williams for Clean Government and Good Schools!" Williams for Governor campaign flyer, box 5, GMWN. See also Berthelot, *Win Some, Lose Some,* 43.

76. Weber oral history; *Detroit News,* October 38 and November 1, 1948.

77. *Detroit News,* October 29, 1948; Williams to Associated Press, October 30, 1948, box 5, GMWN.

78. Correspondence of Office Manager, box 5, GMWN; "1948 Campaign Memoirs."

79. James Lincoln to Mennen Williams, October 28, 1948, box 5, GMWN.

80. *New York Times,* November 5, 1948; *Detroit News,* November 4, 1948.

81. Williams to Mr. and Mrs. Clarence V. Smazel, October 20, 1986, box 103, GMWN; Williams is quoted in Weeks, *Stewards of the State,* 112.

82. G. Mennen Williams, "Who Won the 1948 Michigan Governorship?" box 5, GMWN.

83. Weber oral history.

CHAPTER 3

1. Buffa, *Union Power and American Democracy,* 33–37.

2. Staebler, *Out of the Smoke-Filled Room,* 35; Nancy Williams Gram, interview with author.

3. Nancy Williams, oral history, box 2, Michigan Oral History Project, Bentley Historical Library. In 1955, the house was assessed at $11,700. See City of Lansing Assessment for 1955, box 104, GMWN.

4. Nancy Williams Gram, interview with author; Williams, *A Governor's Notes,* 4.

5. Williams, *A Governor's Notes,* 4.

6. Murphy to Williams, November 3, 1948, box 5, GMWN; *New York Times,* June 4, 1949; Buffa, *Union Power and American Democracy,* 21.

7. Press release, November 27, 1948, box 6, GMWN; radio broadcast, December 20, 1948, box 5, GMWN.

8. For an analysis of the long-term feud between Williams and the legislature, see David W. Winder, "Divided Government in Michigan: Legislative Relations of Governors G. Mennen Williams and William G. Milliken," *Michigan History* 72 (November-December 1988), 36–43.

9. Inaugural address, January 1, 1949, box 423, GMW.

10. *Detroit News,* January 2, 1949; "Message to Sixty-fifth Michigan Legislature," January 6, 1949, box 430, GMW. See also McNaughton, *Mennen Williams of Michigan,* 139–40.

11. "Remarks to the Michigan State Legislature," January 13, 1949, box 430, GMW.

12. "Speech to Michigan State Legislature," February 2, 1949, box 430, GMW..

13. Smith, "Soapy, the Boy Wonder," 27–29.

14. Nancy Williams Gram, interview with author.

15. Williams oral history, GMWN; McNaughton, *Mennen Williams of Michigan,* 168.

16. See William Berman, *The Politics of Civil Rights in the Truman Administration* (Columbus: Ohio State University Press, 1970).

17. Sidney Fine, *Expanding the Frontiers of Civil Rights: Michigan, 1948–1968* (Detroit: Wayne State University Press, 2000) is a comprehensive and meticulously researched account of the battle for equal rights in Michigan in the period 1948–68. Fine examines discrimination and legislation dealing with blacks, women, Native Americans, the handicapped, migrant workers, and the aged during and after Williams's governorship.

18. Fine, *Expanding the Frontiers,* 105–8; B'nai B'rith of Detroit to G. Mennen Williams, "Social Discrimination by Michigan Resorts," August 1, 1949, box 6, GMW.

19. Fine, *Expanding the Frontiers,* 116–18.

20. George Schermer [director, Mayor's Interracial Committee of Detroit] to Francis Haas, December 1, 1948; Advisory Committee on Civil Rights, "Preliminary Report to Governor," December 17, 1948, box 6, GMWN.

21. "Message to Michigan State Legislature," January 6, 1949, box 430, GMW; *Detroit News,* January 7 and January 8, 1949. See also Duane Lockart, *Toward Equal Opportunity: A Study of State and Local Antidiscrimination Laws* (New York: Macmillan, 1968), 40–49.

22. "Address to the Urban League of Flint," February 17, 1949; "Address to AFL-CIO dinner," Detroit, March 22, 1949, box 423, GMW; Fine, *Expanding the Frontiers,* 40.

23. *Detroit News,* April 28 and April 29, 1949.

24. *Battle Creek Inquirer News,* October 18, 1949, clipping in box 451, GMW; Fine, *Expanding the Frontiers,* 42–43.

25. Governor's address, May 26 1950, box 423, GMW; McNaughton, *Mennen Williams of Michigan,* 145.

26. Nancy Williams Gram, interview with author.

27. Weidman, *Neil Staebler,* 2–4.

28. Ibid., 2–6; Staebler, *Out of the Smoke-Filled Room,* 55–66. See Sawyer, *The Democratic State Central Committee in Michigan,* for the details of Staebler's organizational efforts.

29. Staebler, *Out of the Smoke-Filled Room,* 55. See also Staebler to Williams, January 12, 1956, box 494, GMW.

30. Weber oral history.

31. Smith, "Soapy, the Boy Wonder"; Governor's schedules, 1949–50, boxes 438–40, GMW.

32. Radio addresses, 1949–50, boxes 431–32, GMW.

33. Carl Solberg, *Hubert Humphrey: A Biography* (New York: Norton, 1984), 117.

34. David E. Murley, "Un-American Activities at Michigan State College: John Hannah and the Red Scare," M.A. thesis, University of Michigan, 1993, 13–14. See also M. J. Heale, "The Triumph of Liberalism? Red Scare Politics in Michigan, 1948–1954," *Proceedings of the American Philosophical Society* 139 (1995): 44–66.

35. Murley, "Un-American Activities at Michigan State College, 14–15; "Message to Members of the Senate and the House," August 15, August 29, 1950, box 430, GMW. See also "Beans and Communists," April 24, 1950, box 431, GMW.

36. *New York Times,* July 9, 1950; *Detroit News,* July 9 and July 10, 1950.

37. *New York Times,* July 9, 1950; *Detroit News,* July 10, 1950.

38. *Detroit Free Press,* July 10 and July 13, 1950.

39. Haywood Patterson and Earl Conrad, *Scottsboro Boy* (Garden City, N.Y.: Doubleday, 1950), 230–46; *New York Times,* July 11, 1950; *Publisher's Weekly,* July 22, 1950, 98. See also Dan Carter, *Scottsboro: A Tragedy of the American South* (Baton Rouge: Louisiana State University Press, 1969), 413.

40. *New York Times,* December 19, 1950, and September 25, 1951.

41. *New York Times,* June 18, 1949; Address at Probus Club of Detroit, January 5, 1950, box 423, GMW.

42. "Message to Michigan Legislature," March 15, 1950, box 430, GMW; radio address, March 28, 1950, box 430, GMW.

43. "Message to Michigan State Legislature," March 20, 1950, box 430, GMW.

44. Nelson Lichtenstein, *Walter Reuther: The Most Dangerous Man in*

Detroit (Urbana: University of Illinois Press, 1996), 230; John Barnard, *Walter Reuther and the Rise of the Auto Workers* (Boston: Little, Brown, 1983), 289–90; *New York Times,* May 8, 1949. See also Victor Reuther, *The Brothers Reuther: A Memoir* (Boston: Houghton Mifflin, 1976).

45. Williams, *A Governor's Notes,* 2; McNaughton, *Mennen Williams of Michigan,* 152–53.

46. *Detroit Free Press,* September 21, 1950. See also Buffa, *Union Power and American Democracy,* 30–32; and Russell, *Out of the Jungle,* 166–70.

47. *Detroit News,* September 22, 1950.

48. Lichtenstein, *Walter Reuther,* 305–7.

49. Staebler, *Out of the Smoke-Filled Room,* 74–76.

50. *Detroit News,* October 11, October 12, and October 15, 1950.

51. For the background and ideology of the ADA, see Clifton Brock, *Americans for Democratic Action: Its Role in National Politics* (Washington, D.C.: Public Affairs Press, 1962).

52. *Detroit News,* October 15 and October 16, 1950; Weber oral history.

53. Williams, *A Governor's Notes,* 6; Staebler, *Out of the Smoke-Filled Room,* 65–66.

54. *Detroit News,* October 13, 1950.

55. Ibid., October 11 and October 20, 1950.

56. Ibid., October 23, 1950.

57. Ibid., October 26, November 1, and November 3, 1950.

58. Ibid., November 1 and November 4, 1950.

59. Ibid., November 5, 1950.

60. For accounts of the 1950 recount battle, see Berthelot, *Win Some, Lose Some,* 70–72; Staebler, *Out of the Smoke-Filled Room,* 42–45; and McNaughton, *Mennen Williams of Michigan,* 129–32.

61. *Detroit News,* November 10, 1950.

62. Ibid., November 14, 1950; McNaughton, *Mennen Williams of Michigan,* 130.

63. Ibid., November 12, November 14, and November 15; Berthelot, *Win Some, Lose Some,* 71.

64. Staebler, *Out of the Smoke-Filled Room,* 66.

65. *Detroit News,* November 20, 1950; McNaughton, *Mennen Williams of Michigan,* 132.

66. *Detroit News,* November 24, 1950.

67. "1951 Inaugural Address," January 1, 1951, box 423, GMW.

68. Ibid.

69. *Detroit News,* January 2, 1951.

70. "Message of G. Mennen Williams to the Sixty-sixth Michigan Legislature," January 4, 1951, box 423, GMW.

71. Fine, *Expanding the Frontiers,* 43.

72. *Detroit News,* February 9, 1951; Williams to Olive Beasley, March 23, 1951, box 48, GMW.

73. Fine, *Expanding the Frontiers,* 45.

74. *Detroit Free Press,* March 14, 1952.

75. "Fair Elections Committee," press release, October 21, 1952, box 451, GMW.

76. Buffa, *Union Power and American Democracy,* 78.

77. G. Mennen Williams, "Message to Senate and House, June 28, 1951," box 430, GMW; Weber to Williams, "Suggested Program of Action RE: Gas Tax," box 430, GMW.

78. Rubin, *Building Michigan,* 40–41.

79. G. Mennen Williams, "Speech to Upper Peninsula Development Board, Iron River, October 19, 1951," box 423, GMW.

80. *Detroit News,* April 21, 1951.

81. Ibid., April 22 and April 24, 1951.

82. *New York Times,* December 22, 1950.

83. "Prodigy's Progress," *Time,* September 15, 1952, 26–29; Buffa, *Union Power and American Democracy,* 39.

84. Williams oral history, GMWN; *Detroit Free Press,* December 5, 1951.

85. Williams to Stevenson, September 2, 1949, and Stevenson to Williams, September 28, 1949, both in box 89, Adlai Stevenson papers, Seeley-Mudd Manuscript Library, Princeton, New Jersey.

86. Williams to Stevenson, January 22, 1952, box 89, Adlai Stevenson papers, Seeley-Mudd Manuscript Library, Princeton, New Jersey.

87. Williams to Paul Douglass, August 13, 1952, box 490, GMW. See also Charles L. Fontenacy, *Estes Kefauver: A Biography* (Knoxville: University of Tennessee Press, 1980).

88. Ibid.

89. *New York Times,* July 21 and July 22, 1952.

90. Ibid., July 25, 1952; Fontenacy, *Estes Kefauver,* 208–25.

91. "Prodigy's Progress," *Time,* September 15, 1952, 26–29.

CHAPTER 4

1. *New York Times,* February 3 and April 1, 1952.

2. Berthelot, *Win Some, Lose Some,* 99–103.

3. Paul Weber oral history.

4. "Speech, 1952 Kick-Off Dinner," September 2, 1952, box 424, GMW.

5. "Building the People's Plant," undated, box 424, GMW.

6. *Detroit News,* October 7 and October 28, 1952.

7. "Transcript of the debate between Mennen Williams and Frederick Alger at the Economic Club of Detroit," September 15, 1952, box 424, GMW.

8. Ibid.; *Detroit News,* October 18, 1952.

9. *Detroit News,* October 7 and October 8, 1952.

10. Ibid., October 16, 1952.

11. Ibid., October 9, October 31, and November 1, 1952.

12. Ibid., November 2, 1952.

13. Ibid., September 30 and October 17, 1952.

14. "Transcript of television debate between Mennen Williams and Frederick Alger," October 13, 1952, box 424, GMW.

15. *Detroit News,* October 26, 1952.

16. Ibid., November 7, November 16, and November 24, 1952.

17. Berthelot, *Win Some, Lose Some,* 117–19; Detroit *News,* November 16, 1952.

18. *Detroit News,* November 9, 1952; McNaughton, *Mennen Williams of Michigan,* 133; Hubert Humphrey to Williams, November 8, 1950, 150.C.19.8, box 4, Hubert Humphrey papers, Minnesota State Historical Society, Minneapolis.

19. Humphrey to Williams, November 8, 1952, 105C.19.8, box 4, Hubert Humphrey papers.

20. "1953 Inaugural Address," January 1, 1953, box 424, GMW.

21. *Detroit Free Press,* January 2 and January 3, 1953.

22. "Message to the Sixty-seventh Michigan Legislature," January 15, 1953, box 424, GMW.

23. *Detroit News,* January 16 and January 17, 1953.

24. "A Program for Progress, 1954–1955," message to the Sixty-seventh Michigan legislature, box 430, GMW.

25. *Detroit News,* April 21, 1954.

26. Fine, *Expanding the Frontiers,* 51–53; *Detroit Free Press,* March 4, 1953.

27. "Governor Mennen Williams to members of the Senate and House," December 29, 1953, box 451, GMW; Governor G. Mennen Williams to President Dwight D. Eisenhower, January 5, 1954, box 118, GMW; *New York Times,* September 1, 1953.

28. Heale, "The Triumph of Liberalism?" 58–59; *Detroit Free Press,* March 17, 1952.

29. Heale, "The Triumph of Liberalism?" 58–59; Mark E. Engberg, "McCarthyism and the Academic Profession: Power, Politics, and Faculty Purges at the University of Michigan," *American Educational History Journal* 29 (2002): 53–62.

30. *New York Times,* May 1, 1953.

31. Berthelot, *Win Some, Lose Some,* 151.

32. Rubin, *Building Michigan,* 100–2. See also David Steinman and John T. Nevill, *Miracle Bridge at Mackinac* (Grand Rapids.: William Eerdmans, 1957).

33. Williams oral history, GMWN.

34. Governor's schedules, December 1953, box 438, GMW.

35. Williams, *A Governor's Notes,* 7.

36. *New York Times,* September 16 1953; "Speech to Young Demo-

crats of Wisconsin," November 18, 1953, box 424, GMW.

37. *New York Times,* September 2, September 4, and September 10, 1954.

38. McNaughton, *Mennen Williams of Michigan,* 183–84.

39. *New York Times,* February 9, 1954.

40. Will Muller, "Williams Faces Lonely Time as State's Mr. Democrat," *Detroit News,* November 9, 1953; Cabell Phillips, "Who'll Head the Tickets in '56?" *New York Times Magazine,* July 25, 1954.

41. *New York Times,* January 31, 1954.

42. Nancy Williams Gram, interview with author; Williams, *A Governor's Notes,* 1.

43. "It's Adlai versus Stevenson for Democratic Nomination," *Life,* November 28, 1955, 119; McNaughton, *Mennen Williams of Michigan,* 197.

44. Berthelot, *Win Some, Lose Some,* 126–33.

45. For accounts of the Guanca case see Barnard, *Walter Reuther and the Rise of the Auto Workers,* 164–65; Robert W. Ozanne, *The Labor Movement in Wisconsin: A History* (Madison: Wisconsin State Historical Society, 1984), 100–101; and McNaughton, *Mennen Williams of Michigan,* 155–60. Williams offered a detailed summary of the issue and his actions in a 1958 radio address, "The John Guanca Case," in Audio Tapes, box 3, GMW.

46. Barnard, *Walter Reuther and the Rise of the Auto Workers,* 164–65; McNaughton, *Mennen Williams,* 158–60.

47. Ibid. See also *Detroit News,* June 18 and June 19, 1959.

48. Williams radio address, "The John Guanca Case," in Audio Tapes, box 3, GMW; Weber oral history.

49. *Detroit News,* September 27, 1954; Buffa, *Union Power and American Democracy,* 8–10.

50. Russell, *Out of the Jungle,* 169. See also "Jimmy Hoffa Folder," box 29, Staebler papers.

51. Staebler to Humphrey, July 12, 1954, and Humphrey to McNamara, July 16, 1954, both in 150C. 19.8, box 4, Humphrey papers; Berthelot, 148–49.

52. *Detroit News,* October 27 and October 30, 1954.

53. Ibid., October 23 and October 24, 1954: Paul Weber oral history.

54. *Detroit News,* October 30, 1954.

55. Berthelot, *Win Some, Lose Some,* 139–40.

56. The tapes of *Nancy's Scrapbook* are in Audio Tapes, box 1, GMW.

57. *Detroit News,* September 21 and September 22, 1954; Berthelot, *Win Some, Lose Some,* 149.

58. *Detroit News,* October 20, October 28, and October 29, 1954.

59. Williams to Stevenson, October 18, 1954, Stevenson papers, box 89; *Detroit News,* October 21, 1954.

60. *New York Times,* December 12, 1954 and April 10, 1955.

61. "1955 Inaugural Address," January 1, 1955; "Special Message to

the Sixty-eighth Legislature on the Needs of Education in Michigan," January 20, 1955, box 430, GMW.

62. "1955 Inaugural Address," January 1, 1955; "Special Message to the Sixty-eighth Legislature on the Needs of Education in Michigan," January 20, 1955, box 430, GMW. See also *New York Times,* January 13 and January 20, 1955.

63. "G. Mennen Williams to members of the Michigan House and Senate," January 19, 1955, box 451, GMW; *Detroit News,* June 30, 1955; Fine, *Expanding the Frontiers,* 57–59.

64. Press release, Study Commission on Migratory Labor, February 6, 1955, and press release, Michigan Resorts, April 17, 1956, both in box 451, GMW.

65. *New York Times,* February 20 and February 27, 1955.

66. Ibid., June 8, 1955; Russell Baker, "Governors Score Domestic Policy," *New York Times,* May 5, 1955.

67. Michigan Democratic Party, *The Michigan Democratic Story, 1948–1954* (Detroit: Democratic State Central Committee of Michigan, 1955).

68. The Michigan Democratic Party, *The Michigan Declaration, Adopted by the Democratic State Convention, June 2, 1956* (Lansing: Democratic State Committee of Michigan, 1956).

69. Williams, *A Governor's Notes,* 3.

70. Press release, September 29, 1955, box 451, GMW; *New York Times,* September 30, 1955.

71. *New York Times,* September 25 and October 21, 1955.

72. Ibid., September 3 and November 1, 1955.

73. Box 104, GMWN.

74. "Speech to Nationalists Groups Program, Los Angeles," January 3, 1956, box 494, GMW (capitalization in original). See also "Civil Rights," box 494, GMW.

75. *New York Times,* April 30, 1956.

76. Ibid., June 3 and August 19, 1956; audio tape *"Today Show,* May 24, 1956," Audio Tapes, box 1, GMW.

77. The article, with Williams's notations, is in box 494, GMW.

78. Stevenson to Williams, December 10, 1955, and Williams to Stevenson, December 18, 1955, both in box 89, Stevenson papers. Correspondence from Harriman, Symington, Kefauver, and Stevenson to Williams is in box 495, GMW.

79. *New York Times,* December 3, 1955.

80. A copy of the article is in box 89, Stevenson papers.

81. Blair to Staebler, April 10, 1956, and Staebler to Blair, April 23, 1956, both in box 89, Stevenson papers.

82. Paul Butler, Chairman, Democratic National Committee, to Williams, July 24, 1956, box 494, GMW. Letters urging Williams to run for the presidency in 1956 are in box 495, GMW.

83. Staebler to Butler, August 2, 1956, and telegram, Kefauver to Williams, July 31, 1956, both in box 495, GMW.

84. Williams, *A Governor's Notes,* 53.

85. *New York Times,* August 10, 1956. See also Timothy N. Thurber, *The Politics of Equality: Hubert H. Humphrey and the African-American Freedom Struggle* (New York: Columbia University Press, 1999), 98–99; and Joseph Rauh oral history, LBJL.

86. For the details of Johnson's strategy and his relationship with Williams, see Robert Caro, *The Years of Lyndon Johnson: Master of the Senate* (New York: Knopf, 2002), 801–47.

87. *Washington Post,* August 14, 1956.

88. Caro, *The Years of Lyndon Johnson,* 816.

89. Williams oral history, GMWN.

90. Williams to Stevenson, September 15, 1956, box 89, Stevenson papers.

CHAPTER 5

1. Berthelot, *Win Some, Lose Some,* 164–65; Mennen Williams, "1956 Campaign," undated handwritten memo to Paul Weber, box 497, GMW.

2. Press release, May 9, 1958, box 494, GMW.

3. "Cobo File," box 495, GMW; *Detroit Times,* August 24, 1956.

4. Berthelot, *Win Some, Lose Some,* 165, 172.

5. Staebler to Michigan Democratic county chairmen, October 17, 1956, box 494, GMW; *Detroit News,* July 6, 1957.

6. Adelaide Hart to Women division leaders of the Michigan Democratic Party, September 11 and October 9, 1956, and Michigan Federation of Democratic Women of Grand Rapids to Adelaide Hart, August 12, 1956, all in box 494, GMW.

7. Williams to Michigan Democratic Party members of Michigan, September 5, 1956, box 494, GMW.

8. "The Republican Party and the Negro," box 494, GMW.

9. Woolner to Democratic county chairmen, October 9, 1956, box 494, GMW.

10. Committee on Good Government campaign flyer, box 497, GMW; "1956 Campaign Clippings," box 494, GMW.

11. Williams oral history, GMWN; Weber oral history. Williams had his shoes made by the Johnson and Murphy Company in Tennessee. In 1965, his secretary wrote that Williams's feet seemed to have grown and all new shoes were to be made "the same size as his golf shoes" (Cecilia Lucas to Johnson and Murphy Company, July 1, 1965, box 85, GMWN).

12. James Lincoln to Paul Weber, undated, box 495, GMW; "Republicans Back Hoffa," box 494, GMW.

13. *Detroit News,* April 12, 1956; *Tucson Daily Citizen,* May 2, 1956; Staebler to Dick Jenkins, May 21, 1956, box 495, GMW.

14. John Murray, "Cobo-Arizona," undated, box 495, GMW.

15. "1956 Campaign Clippings," box 494, GMW; Berthelot, *Win Some, Lose Some,* 173–75; Smith, "Soapy, the Boy Wonder."

16. "State of Michigan Message of G. Mennen Williams to the Sixty-ninth Legislature," January 10, 1957, and "Governor's Budget Message to Members of the State Legislature," January 25, 1957, both in box 431, GMW.

17. *New York Times,* April 29, May 3, and May 24, 1957.

18. Ibid., February 1, 1957. For background on the DAC, see Averell Harriman oral interview, LBJL.

19. *New York Times,* February 18, September 16, and October 20, 1957, and March 16, 1958.

20. Ibid., December 13, 1957.

21. G. Mennen Williams, "Remarks to the Democratic National Committee Meeting," May 4, 1957, copy in box 89, Adlai Stevenson papers.

22. G. Mennen Williams, "Speech to Young Democrats of Cook County," September 21, 1957, box 428, GMW; G. Mennen Williams, "Little Rock: Challenge to the Democratic Party," *The Nation,* October 7, 1957, 235–37; *New York Times,* September 25, 1957.

23. *New York Times,* October 20, 1957; James Patterson, *Grand Expectations: The United States, 1945–1974* (New York: Oxford University Press, 1976), 418.

24. *New York Times,* November 15, 1957.

25. Williams to Stevenson, January 14, 1958, box 89, Stevenson papers.

26. *New York Times,* April 23, 1958.

27. Ibid., June 16 and October 13, 1958.

28. Smith, "Soapy, the Boy Wonder"; "Suddenly It's 1960," *Time,* April 15, 1957, 34; "Michigan Again and Then Washington?" *U.S. News and World Report,* February 28, 1958, 64–66; D. D. Lloyd, "Figuring the Odds on the Democratic Candidates," *The Reporter,* January 23, 1958, 28.

29. *Detroit News,* November 2 and November 3, 1957; Berthelot, *Win Some, Lose Some,* 178–79.

30. Staebler to Williams, November 16, 1958, box 494, GMW; Williams oral history, GMWN.

31. Williams oral history, GWMN; Nancy Williams Gram, interview with author; Berthelot, *Win Some, Lose Some,* 181–82; "1958 Election," press release, May 1, 1958, box 497, GMW.

32. *Detroit News,* December 19, 1976; G. Mennen Williams to Gery Williams, September 22, 1958, box 85, GMW.

33. *New York Times,* February 14 and March 16, 1958; "Remarks by G. Mennen Williams, WKZO TV, Kalamazoo, October 15, 1958," box 498, GMW.

34. John Murray to Paul Weber, September 5, 1958, John Abernethy to G. Mennen Williams, August 13, 1958, "Know Your Opponent: Republican Voting Record," all in box 498, GMW.

35. Murray to Weber, July, 29 1958, and Staebler to Williams, September 11, 1958, both in box 498, GMW.

36. "Basic Campaign Theme, 1958," confidential staff memo, box 499, GMW; *New York Times,* October 25, 1958.

37. "The Democratic Parade!" and Platform of the Democratic Party of Michigan, August 22–23, 1958, both in box 498, GWM.

38. "Governor's Remarks," September 23, 1958, box 499, GWM.

39. *New York Times,* October 25, 1958; "Bagwell for Governor," press release, October 10, 1958, box 499, GMW.

40. G. Mennen Williams, "Address to the Lions Club of Saginaw," September 25, 1958, box 499, GMW.

41. "Williams for Governor," press release, September 17, 1958, box 499, GMW; G. Mennen Williams, "Remarks at Michigan State Building and Construction Council, Lansing, October 9, 1958," box 499, GMW; "Remarks by G. Mennen Williams, WKZO-TV, Kalamazoo," October 15, 1958, box 498, GMW.

42. The television scripts by W. B. Doner and Company are in box 499, GMW.

43. Williams oral history, GWM.

44. Richard Nelson to William McCormick Blair, December 5, 1958, box 89, Adlai Stevenson papers; *New York Times,* November 13 and November 23, 1958.

45. *New York Times,* December 7, 1958.

46. Williams oral history, GWM.

47. There are a number of accounts of Michigan's 1959 financial crisis and the long and bitter battle between Williams and the legislature. See Staebler, *Out of the Smoke-Filled Room,* 72–77; McNaughton, *Mennen Williams of Michigan,* 8–25; and Judith Larkin, "What Made the Mess in Michigan?" *The Reporter,* March 3, 1960, 33–35.

48. G. Mennen Williams, "Inaugural Address, January 1, 1959," and "Message to the Seventieth Michigan State Legislature, January 15, 1959," both in box 431, GMW.

49. "Message to the Seventieth Michigan State Legislature, February 4, 1959," box 431, GMW.

50. "Transcript of Television Debate, G. Mennen Williams and Frederick Alger, October 13, 1952," box 424, GMW; McNaughton, *Mennen Williams of Michigan,* 17.

51. *Detroit News,* April 22 and April 24, 1959.

52. Ibid., April 30, 1959.

53. D. Duane Angel, *Romney: A Political Biography* (New York: Exposition Press, 1967), 39; McNaughton, *Mennen Williams of Michigan,* 18–19.

54. Staebler, *Out of the Smoke-Filled Room,* 76–78; Angel, *Romney,* 43; G. Mennen Williams to Nancy Williams, March 22, 1959, box 104, GMWN.

55. *Detroit News,* April 29 and April 30, 1959.

56. *Detroit News,* May 1, 1959; *New York Times,* May 1 and May 2, 1959; "A Welfare State Runs into Trouble," *U.S. News and World Report,* February 13, 1959, 49.

57. *Detroit News,* May 3, 1959.

58. *Detroit News,* May 7 and May 9, 1959; *New York Times,* April 19, 1959.

59. "Special Message to the Seventieth Michigan Legislature, May 5, 1959," box 431, GMW; "Remarks to the Michigan State Legislature, May 8, 1959," box 431, GMW; McNaughton, *Mennen Williams of Michigan,* 18–19.

60. Damon Stetson, "Michigan's Plight Curbs Williams," *New York Times,* April 12, 1959; *New York Times,* May 18, 1959; *Detroit News,* May 15, 1959.

61. Staebler, *Out of the Smoke-Filled Room,* 77; Angel, *Romney,* 43: Helen Berthelot to G. Mennen Williams, May 12, 1959, and Mennen Williams to Helen Berthelot, May 14, 1959, reproduced in Berthelot, *Win Some, Lose Some,* 200–201; G. Mennen Williams to Nancy Williams, May 4, 1959, box 104, GMWN.

62. "Address of G. Mennen Williams, Michigan Jefferson-Jackson Day Dinner, Detroit," May 23, 1959, box 949, Pre-presidential Papers, JFKL.

63. *Detroit News,* August 30 and December 19, 1959. See also Staebler, *Out of the Smoke-Filled Room,* 12; and McNaughton, *Mennen Williams of Michigan,* 23–25.

64. Williams oral history, GWM.

65. Ibid.; *New York Times,* July 8 and July 9, 1959.

66. *New York Times,* October 12, November 5, and December 8, 1959, January 24, 1960.

67. For background on the book, see "Frank McNaughton Files," box 419, GMWN. Review in *New York Times,* January 24, 1960.

68. *New York Times,* February 14, 1960.

69. Ibid., February 16, 1960.

70. G. Mennen Williams to Gery Williams, February 26, 1960, and Williams to Dean B. W. Bates, March 28, 1960, both in box 85, GMWN.

71. Berthelot, *Win Some, Lose Some,* 206–7.

72. Williams oral history, GMWN; G. Mennen Williams oral history, LBJL.

73. Berthelot, *Win Some, Lose Some,* 204.

74. Williams oral interview, GWM; *New York Times,* March 3 and March 4, 1960.

75. *Houston Press,* November 19, 1959, clipping in Senate Political Files, box 106, LBJL.

76. "Locke Report: Michigan," March 1960, box 106, LBJL.

77. Transcript of telephone conversation, Bob Oliver and Walter Jenkins, May 17, 1960, and Eugene Locke, "Michigan Appraisal," June 15, 1960, both in box 106, LBJL.

78. Williams oral history, JFKL. See also Herbert Parmet, *Jack: The Struggles of John F. Kennedy* (New York: Dial Press, 1980), 409; and Carl Brauer, *John F. Kennedy and the Second Reconstruction* (New York: Columbia University Press, 1977), 18.

79. Theodore White, *The Making of the President, 1960* (New York: Atheneum, 1961), 161–62.

80. Edward Hindert to Sargent Shriver, July 11, 1957, and Theodore Sorensen to Ed Purdy, May 28, 1959, both in box 949, Pre-presidential Papers, JFKL.

81. Berthelot, *Win Some, Lose Some,* 210–12.

82. Ibid.

83. "Summary of Meeting with John F. Kennedy, June 2, 1960," box 502, GMW. See also Williams oral history, GWM; and Staebler, *Out of the Smoke-Filled Room,* 77.

84. Statement by Governor G. Mennen Williams, June 2, 1960, box 949, Pre-presidential Papers, JFKL.

85. *Detroit News,* June 3, 1960.

86. Harris Wooford to John Kennedy, "Civil Rights," June 9, 1960, copy in box 502, GMW.

87. "Summary of the Washington, D.C., Meeting on Civil Rights between Senator John Kennedy and the Michigan Delegation," box 502, GMW. See also Parmet, *Jack,* 51–52.

88. Williams oral history, JFKL.

89. G. Mennen Williams, "Confidential Memorandum, Kennedy Meeting, June 20, 1960," June 21, 1960, box 502, GMW; Williams oral history, JFKL.

90. G. Mennen Williams, "Statement before the Platform Committee of the Democratic National Convention, July 9, 1960," box 502, GMW; Williams oral history, JFKL.

91. *New York Times,* April 28, 1960.

92. Williams oral history, GMWN; Williams oral history, LBJL.

93. Williams oral history, GMWN; Williams oral history, LBJL.

94. Williams oral history, LBJL.

95. Ibid.

96. Michael Becheloss, ed., *Reaching for Greatness: Lyndon Johnson's Secret Tapes, 1964–1965* (New York: Simon and Schuster, 2001), 442; Williams oral history, LBJL.

97. *New York Times,* July 14, 1960.

98. Williams oral history, JFKL.

99. Letters and telegrams applauding his opposition to Johnson are in box 502, GMW.

100. "Message to the Seventieth Michigan Legislature," January 14, 1960, box 431, GMW.

101. Charles Vanik to G. Mennen Williams, undated, box 502, GMW; *New York Times,* July 15, 1960.

102. "Notes of telephone conversations with Senator John Kennedy," undated, box 504, GMW.

103. "Governor's Report on Meeting with Senator John Kennedy," August 15, 1960, box 504, GMW.

104. Mennen Williams to John Kennedy (Confidential), "Preliminary Estimate of Kennedy Situation, New York," September 12, 1960, and Williams to Kennedy, "California Report," September 30, 1960, box 504, GMW.

105. Williams oral history, LBJL; Williams oral history, GMWN.

106. "Address, Foreign Language Newspaper Editors," Chicago, October 28, 1960, "Address at Valparaiso University," October 10, 1960, "Speech to Pulaski Day Banquet," New York City, October 2, 1960, "Address to Canyon Club," Chicago, October 11, 1960, and "Remarks at Boston Sane Nuclear Policy Dinner," October 1, 1960, all in box 430, GMW.

107. "Itinerary for John Kennedy and Party, Labor Day, and "Senator Kennedy's Visit to Michigan, October 14–15, 1960," box 504, GMW; "Remarks of Welcome to President Eisenhower," October 1, 1960, box 430, GMW.

108. Arthur M. Schlesinger Jr., *A Thousand Days: John F. Kennedy in the White House* (Boston: Houghton Mifflin, 1965), 119.

109. Ibid., 130.

110. David Halberstam, *The Best and the Brightest* (New York: Random House, 1972), 272–75.

111. Williams oral history, GMWN; Howard B. Schaffer, *Chester Bowles: New Dealer in the Cold War* (Cambridge: Harvard University Press, 1993), 194.

112. *New York Times,* December 2, 1960; Schlesinger, *A Thousand Days,* 130.

CHAPTER 6

1. This chapter focuses on the personal goals and impact of Mennen Williams and is not a comprehensive overview of American relations with Africa under Kennedy. For the details of African policy in this period see Richard Mahoney, *JFK: Ordeal in Africa* (New York: Oxford University Press, 1983); Thomas Noer, "New Frontiers and Old Priorities," in *Kennedy's Quest for Victory: American Foreign Policy, 1961–1963,* edited by Thomas G. Paterson, 253–84 (New York: Oxford University Press, 1989);

Ibezim Chukwumerije, "The New Frontier and Africa, 1961–1963," Ph.D. diss., State University of New York at Stony Brook, 1976; and G. Mennen Williams, *Africa for the Africans* (Grand Rapids: William Eerdmans, 1969). Williams's account of his years in the African Bureau is often vague on specific policies, but it is a good summary of his general approach to the continent.

2. Helen Kitchen, "Africa in the Kennedy Era," *New Republic,* December 19, 1960, 17–19; John Morrow, *First American Ambassador to Guinea* (New Brunswick, N.J.: Rutgers University Press, 1968), 214–15; Joseph Satterthwaite oral history, JFKL.

3. *Newsday,* December 6, 1960; Thomas Reeves, *A Question of Character: A Life of John F. Kennedy* (New York: Free Press, 1992), 228.

4. For Kennedy's stress on Africa in the 1960 campaign, see Schlesinger, *A Thousand Days,* 554; and Noer, "New Frontiers," 256.

5. Williams oral history, JFKL: Williams to Schlesinger, December 6, 1960, Schlesinger papers, box 29, JFKL.

6. On Eisenhower and Africa, see Thomas Noer, "Truman, Eisenhower, and South Africa: The 'Middle Road' and Apartheid," *Journal of Ethnic Studies* 11 (spring 1983): 76–104; and Dwight D. Eisenhower, *Waging Peace, 1956–1961* (Garden City, N.J.: Doubleday, 1965), 572–73. See also Chester Bowles oral history, JFKL.

7. Williams oral history, JFKL.

8. Averell Harriman oral history, JFKL.

9. Report to the Honorable John F. Kennedy by the Task Force on Africa (confidential), December 31, 1960, Pre-inaugural Papers, box 949, JFKL.

10. Williams, *Africa for the Africans,* 172. See also Noer, "New Frontiers," 256–58.

11. Williams oral history, JFKL.

12. Harlan Cleveland oral history, JFKL.

13. George Ball, *The Past Has Another Pattern: Memoirs* (New York: Norton, 1982), 228–34. For details of the Africanist/Europeanist split in the Kennedy administration, see Thomas Noer, *Cold War and Black Liberation: The United States and White Rule in Africa, 1948–1968* (Columbia: University of Missouri Press, 1985), 64–67.

14. Department of State press release no. 333, May 19, 1961, National Security Files Africa [hereafter NSF], box 2, JFKL; Williams, *Africa for the Africans,* 174–75.

15. The note is in box 104, GMWN.

16. Satterthwaite oral history, JFKL. The African Bureau's offices were soon remodeled, and Williams began work in temporary quarters on the first floor of the State Department Building.

17. G. Mennen Williams Schedule Book, January 20, 1961, box 93, GMWN.

18. U.S. Senate, *Hearings before the Committee on Foreign Relations, 87th*

Congress, lst Session, January 24, 1961 (Washington, D.C.: U.S. Government Printing Office, 1961), 75–98.

19. Roger Hilsman, *To Move a Nation: The Politics of Foreign Policy in the Administration of John F. Kennedy* (Garden City, N.Y.: Doubleday, 1967), 246, 570; Carl Kaysen oral history, JFKL. See also Joseph Kraft, "Come Back of the State Department," *Harpers* 223 (November 1961), 43–50.

20. G. Mennen Williams, "Notes on Meetings with African Diplomats," box 86, GMWN. See also Williams, *Africa for the Africans,* 160–61.

21. Tom Mboya, Sekou Toure, and William Atwood oral histories, JFKL. See also Schlesinger, *A Thousand Days,* 558–60.

22. G. Mennen Williams Schedule Book, March 1961, box 93, GMWN; Williams speech to 1933 Princeton Class Dinner, Princeton Club, New York, April 3, 1975, box 100, GMWN.

23. Nancy Williams Gram, interview with author.

24. Details of his trips are in "G. Mennen Williams' Trips to Africa," box 93, GMWN. He also wrote lengthy accounts of each trip for the State Department; these are housed in the Kennedy and Johnson libraries. Detailed descriptions set down in letters to his family are in box 104, GMWN. For Nancy Williams's accounts, see "Notes on African Trips," box 105, GMWN.

25. Williams, *Africa for the Africans,* 20–21.

26. Ibid., 23, 64.

27. American Consul Oran to Department of State, March 2, 1963, Records of the Department of State, Central Foreign Policy Files, box 3162, National Archives, College Park, Maryland (hereafter NA); Williams oral history, JFKL.

28. American Embassy Addis Ababa to Department of State, February 23, 1961, "Visit of Assistant Secretary of State Williams to Ethiopia," box 173, NA.

29. Department of State Circular, February 7, 1961, "Visit of Assistant Secretary Williams," box 173, JFKL; Charles Darlington and Alice Darlington, *African Betrayal* (New York: David McCay, 1968), 107–9.

30. William Mahoney to Mennen Williams, May 20, 1963, box 173.

31. Mennen Williams to John Kennedy, "Report of Second Trip to Africa," September 9, 1961, NSF, box 2, JFKL; Russell Howe, *Along the Afric Shore: A History of Two Centuries of U.S.-African Relations* (New York: Barnes and Noble, 1975), 121–22.

32. Williams to Kennedy, "Report of Second Trip to Africa," September 9, 1961; McGeorge Bundy to the White House, September 25, 1961, both in NSF, box 2, JFKL.

33. "Summary of the Vice-President's Trip to Africa," April 5, 1961; U.S. Embassy Dakar to the Department of State, April 13, 1961, both in Vice Presidential Security Files, box 1, LBJL; Williams oral history, JFKL.

34. Williams, *Africa for the Africans,* 159–60.

35. U.S. Embassy South Africa to Secretary of State, February 27, 1961, U.S. Embassy Lisbon to Secretary of State, February 27, 1961, U.S. Embassy London to Secretary of State, February 24, 1961, all in box 173, NA.

36. Williams to Rusk, February 25, 1961, NSF, box 2, JFKL.

37. Williams to Rusk, February 26, 1961, NSF, box 2, JFKL.

38. Rusk to American Embassies, Africa, February 27, 1961, and Rusk to Williams (Eyes Only), February 26, 1961, both in NSF, box 2, JFKL.

39. Transcript of the president's March 1, 1961, press conference, enclosed in Department of State to Governor Williams, March 1, 1961, Central Foreign Policy Files, box 1783, NA; Williams to Kennedy, March 2, 1961, NSF, box 2, JFKL.

40. Schlesinger, *A Thousand Days,* 555–56; Williams, *Africa for the Africans,* 159–60; Bowles to Kennedy, March 3, 1961, box 297, Chester Bowles papers, Sterling Library, Yale University.

41. Williams, *Africa for the Africans,* 160.

42. *New York Times,* February 27, 1961; Williams oral history, JFKL.

43. U.S. Department of State press release no. 762, November 2, 1961, NSF, box 2, JFKL; *U.S. Department of State Bulletin,* October 16, 1961, 638–42; *U.S. Department of State Bulletin,* November 20 1961, 864–65; *U.S. Department of State Bulletin,* November 27, 1961, 885–88.

44. Williams, *Africa for the Africans,* 28–38, 53, 70–72.

45. Department of State press release no. 333, May 19, 1961, NSF, box 2, JFKL.

46. For details of the issue of discrimination against African diplomats, see Michael Krenn, "The Unwelcome Mat: African Diplomats in Washington, D.C., during the Kennedy Years," in *Window on Freedom: Race, Civil Rights, and Foreign Affairs, 1945–1988,* edited by Brenda Gayle Plummer, 163–80 (Chapel Hill: University of North Carolina Press, 2003).

47. John Abernathy to G. Mennen Williams, "Incidents for Governor Williams," April 27, 1961; "Meetings with Representatives of State Governors," April 27, 1961, both in box 2, G. Mennen Williams papers, NA; Department of State press release no. 352, May 29, 1961, NSF, box 2, JFKL.

48. Harris Wofford oral history, JFKL; Rusk to Robert Kennedy, White House Central Files, box 365, JFKL; Krenn, "The Unwelcome Mat."

49. Williams, *Africa for the Africans,* 173, 193–99. See also Julius Amin, *The Peace Corps in Cameroon* (Kent, Ohio: Kent State University Press, 1992), 66.

50. Williams oral history, JFKL.

51. Williams to Kennedy, November 3, 1961, and Kennedy to Luthuli, November 15, 1961, both in NSF, box 2, JFKL.

52. Schlesinger, *A Thousand Days,* 438–39.

53. Wofford to Kennedy, July 15, 1961; Bowles to Stevenson, July 23, 1961, both in box 301, Bowles papers; Bowles oral history, JFKL.

54. Wofford oral history, JFKL; Harris Wofford, *Of Kennedy's and Kings: Making Sense of the Sixties* (New York: Farrar, Straus and Giroux, 1980), 371; Hilsman, *To Move a Nation,* 35.

55. Williams oral history, JFKL; Williams, *Africa for the Africans,* 164–66.

56. Kaysen, Johnson, and Bowles oral histories, JFKL.

57. Cleveland oral history, JFKL.

58. For details of American policy in the Congo, see Stephen Weissman, *American Foreign Policy in the Congo, 1960–1964* (Ithaca: Cornell University Press, 1974); Mahoney, *JFK,* 34–156; Madeline Kalb, *The Congo Cables: The Cold War in Africa from Eisenhower to Kennedy* (New York: Macmillan, 1982); and "Analytical Chronology of the Congo Crisis," January 25, 1961, NSF, box 27, JFKL.

59. Hilsman, *To Move a Nation,* 233.

60. Theodore Sorensen, *Kennedy* (New York: Harper and Row, 1965), 636; G. Mennen Williams Schedule, January 24, 1961, box 93, GMWN.

61. Rusk to Kennedy, "Suggested New United States Policy on the Congo," February 1, 1961, NSF, box 27, JFKL; "Briefing on the Congo, Senate Committee on Foreign Relations," February 6, 1961, box 1, Williams papers, NA.

62. G. Mennen Williams to Dean Rusk, "Report on the Visit of the Assistant Secretary to Africa," April 15, 1961, NSF, box 2, JFKL.

63. Williams to Henry Tosca, February 18, 1961, box 1, Williams papers, NA; Williams's handwritten notes, "Cyrille Adoula," undated, box 86, GMWN; Rusk to Kennedy, "The Congo," August 3, 1961, NSF, box 28, JFKL.

64. Mahoney, *JFK,* 86–87.

65. Noer, "New Frontiers," 265–66; *Congressional Record,* Senate, March 4, 1962, 5907.

66. Hilsman, *To Move a Nation,* 249–50.

67. *Christian Science Monitor,* October 26, 1961; *New York Times,* December 27, 1961; Hilsman, *To Move a Nation,* 257; William S. White, "Which Friends Come First?" *Harpers,* March 1962, 100–105.

68. Kaysen and Guillion oral histories, JFKL; Noer, "New Frontiers," 266–67; Mahoney, *JFK,* 144–45.

69. Williams to "My Family," undated, box 85, GMWN; Williams to Kennedy, "Proposed Tshombe Visit to the United States," February 16, 1962, box 2, Williams papers, NA.

70. Williams oral history, GMWN; Kaysen oral history, JFKL.

71. Mahoney, *JFK,* 147–48.

72. Williams oral history, JFKL; "Proceedings of the Advisory Coun-

cil on African Affairs, June 13–14, 1962," in Wayne Fredericks to Bundy, August 2, 1962; Samuel Belk to Bromley Smith, August 10, 1962, both in NSF, box 2a, JFKL.

73. "Resolutions of the American Negro Leadership Conference on Africa, November, 1962," box 2, Williams papers, NA. See also Roy Wilkins to Adlai Stevenson, January 2, 1963, box 89, Stevenson papers.

74. For a detailed discussion of the conflicts between the United States and Portugal over Africa, see Noer, *Cold War and Black Liberation,* 61–125; and Mahoney, *JFK,* 187–222.

75. *New York Times,* March 21 and March 22, 1961; James Burnham, "Image in What Mirror?" *National Review,* July 15, 1961, 15.

76. *New York Times,* May 28 and May 31, 1961.

77. Daniel M. Friedenberg, "The Public Relations of Colonialism: Salazar's Mouthpiece in the U.S.," *Africa Today* 9 (April 1962): 4–16.

78. Williams to Kennedy, June 7, 1961, box 2, Williams papers, NA.

79. U.S. Department of State, "Talking Points on the Vienna Conversations," undated, box 300, Bowles papers.

80. "Report of the Task Force on the Portuguese Territories in Africa," undated; Stevenson to Rostow, "U.S. Foreign Policy as Seen from New York," June 26, 1961, both in NSF, Angola, box 5, JFKL; Bowles to Kennedy, "Some Requirements of American Foreign Policy," July 1, 1961, box 297, Bowles papers.

81. Belk to Bundy, June 29, 1961; Kenneth Hansen to Bundy, June 28, 1961, both in NSF, box 2a, JFKL; Williams to Fredericks, July 6, 1961, box 1, Williams papers, NA.

82. Williams to European Bureau, June 18, 1962, box 2, Williams papers, NA.

83. National Security Council, "Action Memorandum," July 14, 1961, NSF, Angola, box 5, JFKL.

84. Williams to Rusk, "Report on Second Trip to Africa," September 9, 1961, NSF, box 2, JFKL; "Williams to Harlan Cleveland," September 14, 1962, box 1, Williams papers, NA.

85. Memorandum of a conversation between the president and C. Burke Elbrick, November 27, 1961, NSF, box 154, JFKL; John Bartlow Martin, *Adlai Stevenson and the World* (Garden City, N.Y.: Doubleday, 1977), 711.

86. Williams to Fredericks, April 16, 1962, box 2, Williams papers, NA; Atwood oral history, JFKL.

87. Central Intelligence Agency memorandum, "Significance of the Portuguese and Spanish Colonial Problems for the U.S.," July 11, 1963, NSF, box 154a, JFKL; Martin, *Adlai Stevenson,* 767–68; Elbrick to Rusk, August 13, 1963, NSF, box 154a, JFKL.

88. Perira, Bowles, and Williams oral histories, JFKL.

89. G. Mennen Williams, "South Africa in Transition," *U.S. Depart-*

ment of State Bulletin, October 16, 1961, 638–42; G. Mennen Williams, "The Three 'A's' of Africa: Algeria, Angola, and Apartheid," *U.S. Department of State Bulletin,* November 27, 1961, 280–88; Williams to Fredericks, June 23, 1961, box 1, Williams papers, NA; Williams oral history, JFKL.

90. Satterthwaite oral history, JFKL; U.S. Department of State to Joseph Satterthwaite, August 25, 1961, NSF, box 2, JFKL.

91. Memorandum of conversation, "US/UK Talks, South Africa— Summary Minutes, November 20, 1961," in U.S. Department of State, *Foreign Relations of the United States, Africa, 1961–1963* (Washington, D.C.: U.S. Government Printing Office, 1995), 613–16 (hereafter *FRUS*).

92. U.S. Department of State, "Republic of South Africa: Guidelines for Policy and Operations," May 1961, NSF, box 2, JFKL; Satterthwaite oral history, JFKL.

93. Williams to Rusk, November 1, 1961, box 2, Williams papers, NA.

94. Department of State to Mr. Bundy, "Addis Ababa Meeting and Related African Developments," June 1, 1963, box 3, Williams papers, NA.

95. Williams to Kennedy, "Civil Rights," June 15, 1963, box 3, Williams papers, NA; Williams to Rusk, "U.S. Policy towards South Africa," June 12, 1963, NSF, box 3, JFKL.

96. Rusk to Williams, June 14, 1963, NSF, box 3, JFKL; Rusk to Alexis Johnson, June 15, 1963, NSF, box 159, JFKL; Ralph Dungan, "Background of the South African Problem," July 9, 1962, box 1, Schlesinger papers, JFKL.

97. Williams to Rusk, "Arms Policy and South Africa," July 12, 1963, box 3, Williams papers, NA; A summary of Kennedy meeting with Nyerere is in "Proposed Lockheed Sale to South Africa," September 22, 1964, NSF, box 2, LBJL. See also "Memorandum of Conversation between the Secretary and Ambassador Naude of South Africa," NSF, box 159, JFKL.

98. African Bureau, "Guidelines of U.S. Policy and Operations Concerning Africa," September 2, 1961, NSF, box 2, JFKL.

99. Williams to Alexis Johnson, "Authority to Receive PAG [Provisional Government of Algeria]," March 13, 1962, *FRUS,* 1962, 89–90; Williams to Ball, "Aid to Algeria," October 22, 1962, *FRUS,* 1962, 107–8. For Williams's efforts to save the Volta project, see Thomas Noer, "The New Frontier and African Neutralism: Kennedy, Nkrumah, and the Volta River Project," *Diplomatic History* 8 (winter, 1984): 61–79.

100. African Bureau, "Guidelines of U.S. Policy and Operations concerning Africa," September 22, 1961, NSF, box 2, JFKL.

101. Williams to Bowles, "Aid to Africa," September 29, 1961, box 1, Williams papers, NA; "Report on Assistant Secretary Williams' Third Trip to Africa," November 28, 1961, NSF, box 2, JFKL.

102. Williams oral history, JFKL.

103. Draft Report of the Clay Committee," March 15, 1963, NSF, box 297, JFKL.

104. For criticism of the Clay report, see Robert Komer to Kennedy, March 2, 1963, NSF, box 297, JFKL; Edmund Hutchinson oral history, JFKL; and Schlesinger, *A Thousand Days,* 597–99. See also Meany to John Kennedy, March 19, 1963, NSF, box 297, JFKL.

105. Williams to the Family, January 26, 1963, Nancy Williams to Mom, Dad, and Wendy, September 17, 1962, Williams to Lee Ann Monroe, March 28, 1962, box 85, GMWN.

106. Williams to Nancy Williams, June 21, 1963, ibid.; Williams oral history, JFKL.

107. Williams, *Africa for the Africans,* 160–61.

CHAPTER 7

1. Williams oral history, LBJL. There is far less scholarship on Johnson's African policy than on that of Kennedy. For an overview, see Noer, *Cold War and Black Liberation,* 155–237; Terrance Lyons, "Keeping Africa off the Agenda," in *Lyndon Johnson Confronts the World,* edited by Warren Cohen and Nancy Tucker, 245–78 (New York: Cambridge University Press, 1994); and Henry F. Jackson, *From the Congo to Soweto: U.S. Foreign Policy toward Africa* (New York: Morrow, 1982). On U.S. relations with Rhodesia, see Anthony Lake, *The 'Tar Baby' Option: American Policy toward Southern Rhodesia* (New York: Columbia University Press, 1976); and Andrew DeRoche, *Black, White, and Chrome: The U.S. and Zimbabwe, 1953–1998* (Trenton: Africa World Press, 2001).

2. See Martin Staniland, *American Intellectuals and African Nationalists, 1955–1970* (New Haven: Yale University Press, 1991), esp. chap. 4.

3. Robert Kennedy to Bundy, November 20, 1963, NSF Africa, box 76, LBJL. For details of the strained relationship between Johnson and Robert Kennedy, see Jeff Shesol, *Mutual Contempt: Lyndon Johnson, Robert Kennedy, and the Feud That Defined a Decade* (New York: Norton, 1997).

4. See Paul Henggeler, *In His Steps: Lyndon Johnson and the Kennedy Mystique* (Chicago: Ivan Dee, 1991), 92–118.

5. Williams oral history, LBJL; Nancy Williams Gram, interview with author.

6. W.S. Woodfill to Nancy Williams, June 18, 1964, box 104, GMWN; Lady Bird Johnson to Nancy Williams, March 3, 1966, Social Files, box 2115, LBJL; Social Events Cards, LBJL.

7. White House telephone conversation, Lyndon Johnson and Mennen Williams, December 2, 1963, K6312.01, LBJL.

8. Lyndon B. Johnson, *The Vantage Point: Perspectives on the Presidency, 1963–1969* (New York: Holt, Rinehart, and Winston, 1971), 352; Williams oral history, LBJL.

9. Beschloss, *Reaching for Greatness,* 259.

10. Williams oral history, LBJL. For details of the cruise, see White House Backup Social Diary, box 21, LBJL.

11. Telephone conversation, Lyndon Johnson and Mennen Williams, February 3, 1964, WH6402.03, box 21, LBJL.

12. Waldo Hendrichs, "Lyndon B. Johnson: Change and Continuity," in Cohen and Tucker, *Lyndon Johnson Confronts the World,* 29.

13. CIA Special Reports, "Chinese Communist Activities in Africa," June 19, 1964; "Communist Potentialities in Tropical Africa," December 1, 1964, both in NSF Africa, box 76, LBJL. On Chou's trip, see Williams, *Africa for the Africans,* 82–85.

14. G. Mennen Williams, "Africa's Problems and Progress," *State Department Bulletin,* March 30, 1964, 501–10; *New York Times,* January 14, 1964; American Embassy Zanzibar to Department of State, January 24, 1964, NSF Africa, box 103, LBJL; telephone conversation, Lyndon Johnson and Mennen Williams, February 3, 1964, WH6402.03, LBJL.

15. G. Mennen Williams, "Africa South of the Equator," *State Department Bulletin,* July 13, 1964, 51–54; telephone conversation, Lyndon Johnson and Mennen Williams, February 1, 1964, WH 6402.02, LBJL.

16. *New York Times,* April 4, 1964.

17. George Ball oral history, LBJL.

18. Telephone conversation, Lyndon Johnson and George Reedy, April 4, 1964, WH6404.05, LBJL.

19. Ibid.

20. Telephone conversation, Lyndon Johnson and Dean Rusk, April 4, 1964, LBJL.

21. Williams Brubeck to Bundy, May 1, 1964, NSF Africa, box 76, LBJL; telephone conversation, Lyndon Johnson and George Reedy, May 2, 1964, WH 6405.01, LBJL; White House press release, "Governor Williams' Trip to Africa," May 4, 1964, NSF Africa, box 76, LBJL.

22. G. McMurtrie Godley to Mennen Williams, June 16, 1964, box 29, Williams papers, NA.

23. See Weissman, *American Foreign Policy in the Congo,* 226–54; Pieto Gleijeses, "Flee! The White Giants Are Coming! The United States, the Mercenaries, and the Congo, 1964–1965," *Diplomatic History* 18 (spring 1994): 207–38; and Williams, *Africa for the Africans,* 86–87, 96–103.

24. Williams, *Africa for the Africans,* 98–99.

25. Ibid., 86–87.

26. National Security Council, "Meeting on the Congo," August 11, 1964, NSC Meeting File, box 1, LBJL.

27. Williams, *Africa for the Africans,* 87–88.

28. Williams to Rusk, August 7, 1964, Williams papers, box 12, NA; Gleijeses, "Flee!" 225–26.

29. *New York Times,* August 13, 1964; Gleijeses, "Flee!" 220–21.

30. Richard Walton, *The Remnants of Power: The Tragic Last Years of Adlai Stevenson* (New York: Coward-McCann, 1974), 89.

31. Williams, *Africa for the Africans,* 71; Williams oral history, LBJL

32. Williams to Rusk, *FRUS,* Africa, 1961–63, 532–33.

33. Carl Rowan, United States Information Agency, to Lyndon Johnson, "African Reactions to Recent U.S. Civil Rights Developments," July 21, 1964, NSF Africa, box 76, LBJL.

34. Charles Riggs to Williams, August 12, 1964, box 68, GMWN; *Washington Post,* August 26, 1964; Taylor Branch, *Pillar of Fire: America in the King Years, 1963–1965* (New York: Simon and Schuster, 1998), 472; telephone conversation, Johnson and Walter Jenkins, August 26, 1964, WH 7408.30, LBJL.

35. Williams to Hubert Humphrey, September 3, 1964, NSF: Confidential files, box 6, LBJL.

36. Bundy to Johnson, "Improving U.S. Relations with Africa," March 8, 1965, NSF Africa, box 76, LBJL; "If Kennedy Didn't Pick LBJ," *U.S. News and World Report,* August 2, 1965, 8; Williams to Editors, *U.S. News and World Report,* July 27, 1965; WHCF Name File, box 332, LBJL. Williams's letter was published in the August 9 issue. For an account of his press conference, see Ulrich Haynes, "Memorandum for the Record," April 5, 1965, Ulrich Haynes papers, box 1, LBJL.

37. Rusk to all U.S. Ambassadors in Africa, May 6, 1965, NSF Africa, box 76, LBJL: Haynes to Bundy, "Soapy's Johnson Plan for Africa," April 28, 1965, Haynes papers, box 1.

38. Williams handwritten notes, "The Johnson Plan for Africa," April 23, 1965, box 86, GMWN; Williams to All African Ambassadors and Certain Principle Officers, "Bench Marks for New African Program," May 10, 1965, NSF Africa, box 76, LBJL.

39. Williams's handwritten notes, "Addis Abada Conference," May, 1965, box 86, GMWN.

40. Haynes to Bundy, "A New Policy for Africa," June 5, 1965, Haynes papers, box 1. See also Haynes to Robert Komer, "Governor Williams' Plan for Africa," May 3, 1965, NSF Africa, box 76, LBJL.

41. Haynes to Komer, "Soapy's Johnson Plan for Africa," April 28, 1965, NSF Africa, box 76, LBJL; Haynes to Bundy, "New Program in Africa," May 13, 1965, Haynes papers, box 1; Komer to Johnson, "Memorandum for the President," June 16, 1965, NSF Africa, box 76, LBJL. See also Joseph Palmer oral history, LBJL.

42. Haynes to Moyers, "Governor Williams' Johnson Plan for Africa," May 3, 1965, NSF Africa, box 76, LBJL; Haynes to Komer, "Soapy Williams' Meeting with Bill Moyers," June 8, 1965, Haynes papers, box 1.

43. Johnson, *The Vantage Point,* 354–55.

44. The various drafts of the Korry Report are in NSF Africa, box 77,

LBJL. His plan was formally adopted on October 5, 1966. See NSC Action Memorandum 356, "Implementation of the Korry Report," NSF Africa, box 77, LBJL.

45. Williams oral history, LBJL; African Bureau to Bundy, "Why Are We Aiding So Many African Countries?" November 20, 1965, Bundy papers, box 15, LBJL; Williams, *Africa for the Africans,* 179.

46. Edward Hamilton to Bundy, "Avoiding Confusion on the Aid Program in Africa," February 1, 1966, Bundy to Komer, February 2, 1966, both in Edward Hamilton papers, box 1, LBJL.

47. Telephone conversation, Lyndon Johnson and Walter Reuther, August 20, 1965, WH 6508.08, LBJL.

48. Williams to Rusk, "Thirteenth Trip to Africa," October 18, 1965, Central Policy Files, Administration, box 119, NA.

49. Henry Graff, *The Tuesday Cabinet: Deliberation and Discussion on Peace and War under Lyndon Johnson* (Englewood Cliffs, N.J.: Prentice-Hall, 1970), 74–77.

50. Telephone conversation, Lyndon Johnson and Dean Rusk, December 31, 1965, WH 6512.06, LBJL.

51. Williams to Lyndon Johnson, January 10, 1966, Haynes papers, box 1.

52. Resume of Luncheon Meeting with the President," August 19, 1965, Williams papers, box 5, NA.

53. Satterthwaite to Rusk, March 10, 1964, NSF South Africa, box 2, LBJL; Satterthwaite to Williams, June 17, 1964, Williams papers, box 28, NA; Mennen Williams, "Notes on Conversation," April 19, 1964, Williams papers, box 4, NA.

54. Jack Valenti, Special Assistant to the President, to Williams, November 10, 1965, NSF Africa, box 6, LBJL; Williams to Lyndon Johnson, July 16, 1965, Williams papers, box 4, NA.

55. Williams to Rusk, "Major Conclusions of African Trip," February 24, 1963, Williams papers, box 3, NA.

56. Noer, *Cold War and Black Liberation,* 185–213.

57. Assistant Secretary Williams' Speech to the American Legion, *State Department Bulletin,* January 3, 1966, 13–15; *New York Times,* April 17 and April 20, 1966. See also "Situation Report: The Rhodesian Crisis," January 6, 1966, Haynes papers, box 1.

58. "In Dubious Dialogue," *The Nation,* March 21, 1966, 6.

59. *New York Times,* May 27, 1966; Palmer oral history, LBJL.

60. Williams to Johnson, March 1, 1966; Johnson to Williams, March 11, 1966, both in WHCF Name file, box 332, LBJL; *New York Times,* March 12, 1966; White House press release, March 12, 1966, John Macy files, box 1, LBJL.

61. *Washington Evening Star,* March 21, 1966; telegrams, John Hope Franklin to Lyndon Johnson, March 4, 1966; Charles Diggs to Lyndon

Johnson, March 4, 1966, both in Macy files, box 1, LBJL.

62. Nancy Williams to Lady Bird Johnson, February 25, 1966, White House Social Files, box 2115, LBJL.

63. *New York Times,* March 6 and March 7, 1966.

64. Berthelot, *Win Some, Lose Some,* 253–56.

65. Ibid.

66. *Wall Street Journal,* July 27, 1966; *New York Times,* March 20, 1966; Memorandum for Marvin Watson, May 16, 1966, WHCF, Name File, box 332, LBJL.

67. *New York Times,* July 31 and August 2, 1966.

68. "Return of the Boy Wonder," *Time,* August 12, 1966, 12; "Ballad of the Bow Tie," *The Reporter,* September 8, 1966; "In the Political Spotlight Again," *U.S. News and World Report,* August 15, 1966, 10; *New York Times,* August 1, 1966.

69. Stiebler, *The Politics of Change in Michigan,* 107–8.

70. Robert Kitner, "Memorandum for the President," August 15, 1966, WHCF Name File, box 32, LBJL; Memorandum to Marvin Watson, September 1, 1966, WHCF Name File, box 32, LBJL; Berthelot, *Win Some, Lose Some,* 258–60.

71. 1960 Campaign Schedule, box 93, GWMN; Marcus Childs, "Are a Friendly Smile and a Bow Tie Enough in '66?" *Detroit News,* October 3, 1966.

72. Berthelot, *Win Some, Lose Some,* 261.

73. *Detroit News,* October 11, October 21, and October 23, 1966.

74. Ibid. September 18, September 27, and October 11, 1966; Angel, *Romney,* 137–38.

75. 1966 Campaign Schedule, box 93, GMWN; *Detroit News,* November 4, 1966.

76. Allan Blanchard, "Election Postmortem," *Detroit News,* November 9, 1966; "Old Democrats Lose," *New York Times,* November 10, 1966; Stiebler, *The Politics of Change in Michigan,* 107–8; Nancy Williams Gram, interview with author.

77. Williams to Berthelot, January 25, 1967, in Berthelot, *Win Some, Lose Some,* 285.

78. Williams to Raleigh, Chafee, Bluth, and Co., September 10, 1968, box 104, GMWN. On the Holiday Inn purchases, see Williams to James J. Brown, January 11, 1966, and Williams to Gery Williams, August 24, 1963, both in box 86, GMWN.

79. Nancy Williams to Lady Bird Johnson, undated, Social Files, box 2115, LBJL; "Statement on Ferency Resignation," November 28, 1967; "Statement by G. Mennen Williams," March 16, 1968, both in box 103, GMWN.

80. Eighth Democratic Committee Resolution on G. Mennen Williams to Lyndon B. Johnson, March 9, 1967, William Clifford to

Robert Cox, Special Assistant to the President, March 16, 1967, John Macy to Lyndon Johnson, "Ambassador to the Philippines," February 20, 1968, all in John Macy Files, G. Mennen Williams folder, LBJL; Williams oral history, LBJL.

81. Macy to Johnson, "Ambassador to the Philippines." See also Willis Dunbar, *Michigan: A History of the Wolverine State* (Grand Rapids: Eerdmans, 1995), 456.

82. Williams oral history, LBJL.

83. Rostow to Johnson, "Meeting with Governor G. Mennen Williams," May 1, 1968, Rostow to Johnson, "Your Meeting with Mennen Williams Today," June 6, 1968, both in NSF, box 279, LBJL.

84. Richard Moore, "Analysis of Press and Editorial Reaction to the Arrival of Ambassador Williams," enclosure in Rostow to Lyndon Johnson, July 10, 1968, Confidential files, box 11, LBJL.

85. Williams to Lyndon Johnson, June 25, 1968; Williams to Rostow, July 10, 1968, both in Confidential files, box 11, LBJL.

86. Nancy Williams to Lady Bird Johnson, July 2, 1968, Social files, box 2114, LBJL; Williams oral history, LBJL.

87. CIA intelligence cable, September 23, 1968, NSF, box 79, LBJL; Williams oral history, LBJL.

88. Williams oral history, LBJL; Nancy Williams to Lady Bird Johnson, July 2, 1968, Social files, box 2115, LBJL; Nancy Williams Gram, interview with author.

89. Statement by G. Mennen Williams RE: Martin Luther King, April 5, 1968, Williams to Mr. and Mrs. Gery Williams and Mr. and Mrs. Ted Ketterer, April 8, 1968, both in box 76, GMWN.

CHAPTER 8

1. G. Mennen Williams, "Draft Supreme Court Strategy," February 23, 1969, box 77, GMWN.

2. Williams to John Murray, Neil Staebler, and Paul Weber, "Thoughts about MSU," March 13, 1969, box 103, GMWN; Jim Murray to G. Mennen Williams, "MSU Job," undated, box 77, GMWN.

3. Murray to Williams, "MSU Job," undated, box 77, GMWN.

4. "An Open Letter from Michigan State Faculty to G. Mennen Williams," September 17, 1969, box 103, GMWN.

5. *Detroit News,* October 18, 1970.

6. G. Mennen Williams, "Draft Analysis for Campaign Strategy," April 24, 1970; "Press Release, May 19, 1970," box 77, GMWN.

7. G. Mennen Williams, "Press Release, May 19, 1970"; John Casey to Mennen Williams, "News Coverage of Announcement of Candidacy," May 20, 1970, both in box 77, GMWN; Otis Milton Smith, *Beyond Race: The Life of Otis Milton Smith* (Detroit: Wayne State University Press, 2000), 122. Voelker wrote the introduction to Williams's 1960 campaign biography.

8 G. Mennen Williams, "Campaign Budget," June 15, 1970, box 77, GMWN.

9. "Analysis of Michigan Voters: Michigan Supreme Court, May 22–June 5, 1970," box 77, GMWN.

10. "Supreme Court Candidacy Strategic Program," August 27, 1970, box 77, GMWN.

11. "Analysis of Michigan Voters: Michigan Supreme Court," September 1970, box 77, GMWN.

12. "Trip Reports, 1970 Campaign," box 77, GMWN.

13. Williams to L. Hart Wright, President, University of Michigan Law School, August 27, 1970, Williams to James Miller, President, Western Michigan University, August 27, 1970, both in box 77, GMWN.

14. Williams to Williams for Supreme Court Lawyers, undated, "Supreme Court Campaign Strategic Program," August 27, 1970, both in box 77, GMWN.

15. See "Dethmers for Supreme Court" ads, *Detroit News,* October 31 and November 1, 1970.

16. *Detroit News,* November 4, November 5, and November 6, 1970.

17. Nancy Willliams Gram, interview with author.

18. G. Mennen Williams Schedule, January–February 1971, box 95, GMWN.

19. See Law Clerk Interviews, box 95, GMWN.

20. G. Mennen Williams, "Justice; As I See the Supreme Court's Role," speech to the State Bar Association of Michigan, January 12, 1973, box 100, GMWN; Rich Nederlander to G. Mennen Williams, May 10, 1976, box 78, GMWN.

21. Williams's case files fill thirty-eight large boxes at the Bentley Library but are closed to researchers. Inadvertently, I was allowed to examine over half of them before the staff remembered they were closed. Aside from this material, his clerks prepared summaries of his most significant opinions for his 1978 reelection campaign. Williams also commented on many cases in his speeches and correspondence.

22. For his opinions on workman's compensation, see *Hilton v. Oldsmobile Division of General Motors* (1974), *Thomas v. Certified Refrigeration* (1974), *Lewis v. Crestwood* (1975), and *General Motors v. Cruz* (1978), in "Summary of G. Mennen Williams' Court Decisions," box 78, GMWN. On insurance issues, see *Blakeslee v. Farm Bureau Insurance* (1972) and *Williams v. Polgar* (1974), in boxes 33 and 36, GMWN.

23. *West v. City of Portage* (1974), box 45, GMWN; *Rockwell v. Crestwood School District* (1975), box 43, GMWN; *Viculin v. Department of Civil Service* (1971), in "Summary of G. Mennen Williams' Court Decisions," box 78, GMWN.

24. *Maskalik v. Dunn* (1974), *People v. Walker* (1975), *People v. Johnson* (1975), in "Summary of G. Mennen Williams' Court Decisions," box 78, GMWN.

25. *People v. Enoch Chism* (1973), box 39, GMWN; *People v. Anderson* (1973), box, 43, GMWN.

26. *People v. Sinclair* (1972), in "Summary of G. Mennen Williams' Court Decisions," box 78, GMWN; G. Mennen Williams, "Psychiatry and the Family," speech to Michigan Psychiatric Society, August 12, 1972, box 100, GMWN.

27. G. Mennen Williams, "Status of Married Women's Property Rights," speech to the Women and the Law Seminar, Detroit, October 27, 1978, box 100, GMWN.

28. Williams to Chief Justice Thomas M. Kavanaugh, "Explanation of No Vote on Abortion Referendum," August 31, 1972, box 65, GMWN; G. Mennen Williams, "Justice: As I See the Supreme Court's Role," speech to the State Bar Association of Michigan, January 12, 1973, box 100, GMWN; *People v. Bricker* (1973); *Larkin v. Wayne Prosecutor* (1973), both in Lexis Nexis, May 3, 2003.

29. *Daniels v. Allen Industries* (1974), box 34, GMWN; *Mason v. County Drain Commission* (1975), box 44, GMWN. *New York Times,* February 9, 1975. See also G. Mennen Williams, "Environmental Law: The Long View," speech to the Law Section of the State Bar Association of Michigan, May 20, 1983, box 100, GMWN.

30. Nancy Williams Gram, interview with author.

31. "Minutes of Electronic Computer Committee Meeting," June 7, 1971, box 20, GMWN.

32. Nancy Williams Gram, interview with author.

33. "Description of Court Procedures Technology Committee," August 5, 1971, Williams's handwritten notes, "Technology Committee," undated, both in box 20, GMWN.

34. Mayford L. Roark, Ford Motor Company, to G. Mennen Williams, undated, Williams handwritten notes, "IBM," August 15, 1972, Williams to Edwin Jones, National Center for Automated Informational Retrieval, September 14, 1973, all in box 20, GMWN.

35. Bohlin's weekly reports to Williams and his monthly newsletters are in box 20, GMWN. See also "Minutes of Basic Michigan Court System Steering Committee," March 20, 1975, and Williams to James Killeen, March 18, 1975, both in box 20, GMWN.

36. "To Do Justly," speech to the Economic Club of Detroit, April 7, 1972, "Improving the Delivery of Justice," speech to the Detroit chapter of the Federal Bar Association, November 13, 1975, both in box 100, GMWN.

37. "Systems Technology and the Michigan Courts: Status Report and Plan for Action," October 25, 1972, Richard Wilhelm, Supreme Court Staff, to G. Mennen Williams, "Systems Development," December 12, 1974, both in box 20, GMWN.

38. "Minutes of SMCS Steering Committee," March 20, 1975,

Williams to The Honorable Roman S. Gibbs, June 19, 1972, both in box 20, GMWN.

39. G. Mennen Williams, "Clerks for the New Recorder's Court," September 25, 1972, box 20, GMWN; "Report of Committee on Computerized Research," April 7, 1976, box 21, GMWN.

40. "Draft Williams for Governor" petition, April 30, 1977, Williams to Max Honeyman, May 15, 1977, Helen Berthelot to Nancy and Mennen Williams, May 12, 1977, Williams to Berthelot, May 17, 1977, all in box 78, GMWN.

41. Frank Jefferis to G. M. Williams and Paul Donahue, "Proposed Campaign Appearances Leading up to 1978 Supreme Court Election," November 20, 1976, box 78, GMWN.

42. *Detroit News,* June 3, 1976.

43. Ibid., June 3 and June 4, 1976.

44. Ibid., June 4 and June 5, 1976.

45. Ibid., June 8 and June 9, 1976.

46. Paul Donahue to G. Mennen Williams, "Proposed Campaign Budget," April 4, 1978, "Reelection Announcement," July 5, 1978, both in box 78, GMWN.

47. Campaign Schedule for September 12–13, 1978, "Fundraiser Schedule," July 1978, both in box 78, GMWN.

48. Remarks by G. Mennen Williams, Sault Ste. Marie, June 20, 1978, Speech, "Crime and Punishment," South Grand Rapids Rotary Club, November 1, 1978, "Law Clerks' Response: RE: 1978 Campaign," all in box 78, GMWN.

49. See www.micourthistory.org (accessed April 30, 2003).

50. Kathy Hunt Davis, "Williams Trades Robes for Professional Tweeds," *Michigan Lawyer's Weekly,* January 19, 1987, 8–10.

51. Speech to American Religious Town Meeting, Dallas, Texas, February 19, 1978, box 78, GMWN; Speech to National Prayer Breakfast, February 12, 1981; Eulogy for Blair Moody, November 30, 1982, both in box 101, GMWN.

52. James Ryan, "Remarks about my Colleague, G. Mennen Williams," February 2, 1988, State Bar Association of Michigan, "Resolution of Tribute to the Honorable G. Mennen Williams," March 4, 1988, both in box 104, GMWN.

53. *Klanseck v. Anderson* (1986), box 39, GMWN; *Raska v. Farm Bureau Mutual Insurance* (1986), box 43, GMWN.

54. *People v. Krezen* (1986), box 39, GMWN.

55. *People v. Matthew Leonard* (1985), box 39, GMWN.

56. *Rouge Parkway Associates v. City of Wayne* (1985), box 43, GMWN.

57. "State of the Judiciary Speech to Michigan State Legislature," May 12, 1983, box 29, GMWN.

58. "State of the Judiciary Speech to Michigan State Legislature," April 18, 1985, box 29, GMWN.

59. "Program to Improve the Michigan Court System During 1985–1986," October 22, 1985, box 22, GMWN.

60. Meeting of Joint Judges Association with Chief Justice G. Mennen Williams, March 19, 1986, box 21, GMWN.

61. "State of the Judiciary Address to Michigan State Legislature," April 10, 1986, box 29, GMWN.

62. Williams to Mr. and Mrs. Clarence Smazel, October 20, 1986, box 103, GMWN.

63. "Syllabus for Leadership Course," box 103, GMWN; See also Davis, "Williams Trades Robes for Professional Tweeds."

64. "Mackinac Bridge History," rough draft, undated, Francis X. Blouin, Bentley Historical Library, to G. Mennen Williams, July 20, 1982, "1948 Gubernatorial Campaign History," August 11, 1981, Williams interview with David L. Lewis, October 5, 1981, all in box 103, GMWN.

65. Williams to Mr. and Mrs. Clarence Smazel, October 20, 1986, Williams to Mr. and Mrs. Nick Sroia, December 30, 1985, Williams's handwritten notes, "1948 Campaign Memoirs," all in box 103, GMWN.

66. "Who Won the 1948 Michigan Governorship?" undated, box 103, GMWN.

67. "Remarks at Wayne State University Local History Conference," April 11, 1987, box 101, GMWN.

68. Berthelot, *Win Some, Lose Some,* 10.

69. Speech to 1933 Annual Class Dinner, Princeton Club, New York, April 3, 1976, box 100, GMWN.

70. *Detroit News,* February 4, 1987.

71. *Detroit Times,* February 4, 1987; *Detroit News,* February 4, 1987.

72. *Detroit News,* February 5 and February 6, 1987; Berthelot, *Win Some, Lose Some,* 310.

73. The memorials, letters, tributes and other material on Williams's funeral are in box 105, GMWN.

74. Ibid.

75. *Detroit News,* February 6 and February 7, 1987.

CONCLUSION

1. Alonzo Hamby, *Liberalism and Its Challenges: From FDR to Bush,* 2d ed. (New York: Oxford University Press, 1992), viii. A more recent book argues that the traditional liberal emphasis on economic issues has been defeated by the conservative stress on cultural conflict. See Thomas Frank, *What's the Matter with Kansas? How Conservatives Have Won the Heart of America* (New York: Metropolitan Books, 2004).

2. Arthur M. Schlesinger Jr., *The Vital Center: The Politics of Freedom* (Cambridge: Riverside Press, 1949), 174, 254.

3. William Lloyd Garrison, "To the Public," *The Liberator,* January 1, 1831, reproduced in *William Lloyd Garrison and the Fight against Slavery: Selections from The Liberator,* edited by William Cain (Boston. Bedford Books, 1995), 72; Walter Rauschenbusch, *Christianity and the Social Crisis* (New York: Macmillan, 1908), 284–86.

BIBLIOGRAPHY

UNPUBLISHED DOCUMENTS

Materials in the Bentley Historical Library, Ann Arbor, Michigan
  Neil Staebler Papers
  G. Mennen Williams, Gubernatorial Papers
  G. Mennen Williams, Nongubernatorial Papers
  G. Mennen Williams, Photo Collection
  G. Mennen Williams, Audiovisual Collection
  Nancy Williams Papers
  Oral histories: Paul Weber, G. Mennen Williams, Nancy Williams

Materials in the National Archives, College Park, Maryland
  Department of State Records, G. Mennen Williams Papers
  Department of State Records, Central Foreign Policy Files

Materials in the Seeley-Mudd Library, Princeton University,
    Princeton, New Jersey
  Adlai Stevenson Papers
  Princeton University Annual
  Nassau Herald

Materials in the John F. Kennedy Presidential Library, Boston,
    Massachusetts
  Arthur M. Schlesinger Jr. Files
  Carl Kaysen Files
  National Security Files: Confidential Files, Country Files, Subject Files
  Oral histories: William Atwood, Chester Bowles, Harlan Cleveland,
    Edmund Guillion, Averell Harriman, Edmund Hutchinson, U.
    Alexis Johnson, Carl Kaysen, Pedro Perina, Joseph Satterthwaite,

Sekou Toure, G. Mennen Williams, Harris Wofford
Pre-presidential Papers
White House Central Files

Materials in the Lyndon B. Johnson Presidential Library, Austin, Texas
Edward Hamilton Papers
John Macy Files
Oral histories: George Ball, Averell Harriman, Joseph Palmer,
G. Mennen Williams
National Security Files: Confidential Files, Country Files, Subject Files
Political Files
Senate Files
Social Files
Telephone Tapes
Ulrich Haynes Papers
Vice Presidential Security Files
White House Central Files

Materials in the Minnesota State Historical Society, Minneapolis,
Minnesota
Hubert Humphrey Papers

Materials in the Sterling Library, Yale University, New Haven,
Connecticut
Chester Bowles Papers

PUBLISHED BOOKS AND ARTICLES

Amin, Julius. *The Peace Corps in Cameroon.* Kent, Ohio: Kent State University Press, 1992.

Angel, D. Duane. *Romney: A Political Biography.* New York: Exposition Press, 1967.

Baker, Russell. "Governors Score Domestic Policy." *New York Times,* May 5, 1955.

Ball, George. *The Past Has Another Pattern: Memoirs.* New York: Norton, 1982.

"Ballad of the Bow Tie." *The Reporter,* September 8, 1966.

Barnard, John. *Walter Reuther and the Rise of the Auto Workers.* Boston: Little, Brown, 1983.

Becheloss, Michael, ed. *Reaching for Greatness: Lyndon Johnson's Secret Tapes, 1964–1965.* New York: Simon and Schuster, 2001.

Berman, William. *The Politics of Civil Rights in the Truman Administration.* Columbus: Ohio State University, 1970.

Berthelot, Helen. *Win Some, Lose Some: G. Mennen Williams and the New Democrats.* Detroit: Wayne State University Press, 1995.

Blanchard, Allan, "Election Postmortem." *Detroit News,* November 9, 1966.

Branch, Taylor. *Pillar of Fire: America in the King Years, 1963–1965.* New York: Simon and Schuster, 1998.

Brauer, Carl. *John F. Kennedy and the Second Reconstruction.* New York: Columbia University Press, 1977.

Brock, Clifton. *Americans for Democratic Action: Its Role in National Politics.* Washington, D.C.: Public Affairs Press, 1962.

Buffa, Dudley. *Union Power and American Democracy: The UAW and the Democratic Party, 1935–1972.* Ann Arbor: University of Michigan Press, 1984.

Burnham, James. "Image in What Mirror?" *National Review,* July 15, 1961.

Cain, William, ed. *William Lloyd Garrison and the Fight against Slavery: Selections from The Liberator.* Boston: Bedford Books, 1995.

Caro, Robert. *The Years of Lyndon Johnson: Master of the Senate.* New York: Knopf, 2002.

Carter, Dan. *Scottsboro: A Tragedy of the American South.* Baton Rouge: Louisiana State University Press, 1969.

Childs, Marcus. "Are a Friendly Smile and a Bow Tie Enough in '66?" *Detroit News,* October 3, 1966.

Chukwumerije, Ibezim. "The New Frontier and Africa, 1961–1963," Ph.D. diss., State University of New York at Stony Brook, 1976.

Darlington, Charles, and Alice Darlington. *African Betrayal.* New York: David McCay, 1968.

Davis, Kathy Hunt. "Williams Trades Robes for Professional Tweeds." *Michigan's Lawyer Weekly,* January 19, 1987.

DeRoche, Andrew. *Black, White, and Chrome: The U.S. and Zimbabwe, 1953–1998.* Trenton: Africa World Press, 2001.

Dunbar, Willis. *Michigan: A History of the Wolverine State.* Grand Rapids: Eerdmans, 1995.

Eisenhower, Dwight D. *Waging Peace, 1956–1961.* Garden City, N.Y.: Doubleday, 1965.

Engberg, Mark E. "McCarthyism and the Academic Profession: Power, Politics, and Faculty Purges at the University of Michigan." *American Educational History Journal* 29 (2002): 53–62.

Fine, Sidney. *Expanding the Frontiers of Civil Rights: Michigan, 1948–1968.* Detroit: Wayne State University Press, 2000.

———. *Frank Murphy: The New Deal Years.* Chicago: University of Chicago Press, 1979.

———. *Frank Murphy: The Detroit Years.* Ann Arbor: University of Michigan Press, 1975.

Fontenacy, Charles L. *Estes Kefauver: A Biography.* Knoxville: University of Tennessee Press, 1980.

Frank, Thomas. *What's the Matter with Kansas? How Conservatives Have Won the Heart of America.* New York: Metropolitan Books, 2004.

Friedenberg, Daniel M. "The Public Relations of Colonialism: Salazar's Mouthpiece in the U.S." *Africa Today* 9 (April 1962): 4–16.

Furlong, William Barry. "A Boy Wonder Begins to Wonder." *New York Times Magazine,* November 22, 1958.

Gleijeses, Pieto. "Flee! The White Giants Are Coming! The United States, the Mercenaries, and the Congo, 1964–1965." *Diplomatic History* 18 (spring 1994): 207–38.

Goldwater, Barry. *No Apologies.* New York: Morrow, 1979.

Graff, Henry. *The Tuesday Cabinet: Deliberation and Discussion on Peace and War under Lyndon Johnson.* Englewood Cliffs, N.J.: Prentice-Hall, 1970.

Halberstam, David. *The Best and the Brightest.* New York: Random House, 1972.

Hamby, Alonzo. *Liberalism and Its Challenges: From FDR to Bush.* New York: Oxford University Press, 1992.

Harmon, Chuck. "Pleasant Politickins." *Michigan Magazine of History,* November-December, 1999.

Heale, M. J. "The Triumph of Liberalism? Red Scare Politics in Michigan, 1948–1954." *Proceedings of the American Philosophical Society* 139 (1995): 44–66.

Hendrichs, Waldo. "Lyndon B. Johnson: Change and Continuity." In *Lyndon Johnson Confronts the World,* edited by Warren Cohen and Nancy Tucker. New York: Cambridge University Press, 1994.

Henggeler, Paul. *In His Steps: Lyndon Johnson and the Kennedy Mystique.* Chicago: Ivan Dee, 1991.

Hilsman, Roger. *To Move a Nation: The Politics of Foreign Policy in the Administration of John F. Kennedy.* Garden City, N.Y.: Doubleday, 1967.

Howard, Woodford. *Mr. Justice Murphy: A Political Biography.* Princeton: Princeton University Press, 1968.

Howe, Russell. *Along the Afric Shore: A History of Two Centuries of U.S.-African Relations.* New York: Barnes and Noble, 1975.

"If Kennedy Didn't Pick LBJ." *U.S. News and World Report,* August 2, 1965.

"In Dubious Dialogue." *The Nation,* March 21, 1966.

"In the Political Spotlight Again." *U.S. News and World Report,* August 15, 1966.

"It's Adlai versus Stevenson for Democratic Nomination." *Life,* November 28, 1955.

Jackson, Henry F. *From the Congo to Soweto: U.S. Foreign Policy toward Africa.* New York: Morrow, 1982.

Johnson, Lyndon B. *The Vantage Point: Perspectives on the Presidency, 1963–1969.* New York: Holt, Rinehart, and Winston, 1971.

Kalb, Madeline. *The Congo Cables: The Cold War in Africa from Eisenhower to Kennedy.* New York: Macmillan, 1982.

Kitchen, Helen. "Africa in the Kennedy Era." *New Republic,* December 19, 1960.

Kraft, Joseph. "Come Back of the State Department." *Harpers* 223, November, 1961, 43–50.

Krenn, Michael. "The Unwelcome Mat: African Diplomats in Washington, D.C., during the Kennedy Years." In *Window on Freedom: Race, Civil Rights, and Foreign Affairs, 1945–1988,* edited by Brenda Gayle Plummer. Chapel Hill: University of North Carolina Press, 2003.

"Labor in Politics." *Newsweek,* October 25, 1948.

Lake, Anthony. *The 'Tar Baby' Option: American Foreign Policy toward Southern Rhodesia.* New York: Columbia University Press, 1976.

Larkin, Judith. "Who Made the Mess in Michigan? *The Reporter,* March 3, 1960.

Laski, Harold. *The State in Theory and Practice.* New York: Viking, 1935.

Lichtenstein, Nelson. *Walter Reuther: The Most Dangerous Man in Detroit.* Urbana: University of Illinois Press, 1996.

Lloyd, D. D. "Figuring the Odds on the Democratic Candidates." *The Reporter,* January 23, 1958.

Lockart, Duane. *Toward Equal Opportunity: A Study of State and Local Antidiscrimination Laws.* New York: Macmillan, 1968.

Lyons, Terrance. "Keeping Africa off the Agenda." In *Lyndon Johnson Confronts the World,* edited by Warren Cohen and Nancy Tucker. New York: Cambridge University Press, 1994.

Mahoney, Richard. *JFK: Ordeal in Africa.* New York: Oxford University Press, 1983.

Martin, John Bartlow. *Adlai Stevenson and the World.* Garden City, N.Y.: Doubleday, 1977.

McNaughton, Frank. *Mennen Williams of Michigan: Fighter for Progress.* New York: Oceana Publishing, 1960.

"Michigan Again and Then Washington?" *U.S. News and World Report,* February 28, 1958.

Michigan Democratic Party. *The Michigan Declaration, Adopted by the Democratic State Convention, June 2, 1956.* Lansing: Democratic State Committee of Michigan, 1956.

———. *The Michigan Democratic Story, 1948–1954.* Detroit: Democratic State Central Committee of Michigan, 1955.

Morrow, John. *First American Ambassador to Guinea.* New Brunswick, N.J.: Rutgers University Press, 1968.

Muller, Will. "Williams Faces Lonely Time as State's Mr. Democrat." *Detroit News,* November 9, 1953.

Murley, David E. "Un-American Activities at Michigan State College: John Hanneh and the Red Scare." M.A. thesis, University of Michigan, 1993.

Noer, Thomas J. *Cold War and Black Liberation: The United States and White Rule in Africa, 1948–1968.* Columbia: University of Missouri Press, 1985.

———. "The New Frontier and African Neutralism: Kennedy,

Nkrumah, and the Volta River Project." *Diplomatic History* 8 (Winter, 1984): 61–79.

———. "New Frontiers and Old Priorities in Africa." In *Kennedy's Quest for Victory: American Foreign Policy, 1961–1963,* edited by Thomas G. Patterson. New York: Oxford University Press, 1989.

———. "Truman, Eisenhower, and South Africa: The 'Middle Road' and Apartheid." *Journal of Ethnic Studies* 11 (spring 1983): 76–104.

"Old Democrats Lose." *New York Times,* November 10, 1966.

Ozanne, Robert W. *The Labor Movement in Wisconsin.* Madison: Wisconsin State Historical Society, 1984.

Parmet, Herbert. *Jack: The Struggles of John F. Kennedy.* New York: Dial, 1980.

Parrish, Michael. *Felix Frankfurter and His Times.* New York: Free Press, 1982.

Patterson, Haywood, and Earl Conrad. *Scottsboro Boy.* New York: Doubleday, 1950.

Patterson, James. *Grand Expectations: The United States, 1945–1974.* New York: Oxford University Press, 1976.

Phillips, Cabell. "Who'll Head the Tickets in '56?" *New York Times Magazine,* July 25, 1954.

"Prodigy's Progress." *Time,* September 15, 1952.

Rauschenbusch, Walter. *Christianity and the Social Crisis.* New York: Macmillan, 1908.

Reeves, Thomas. *A Question of Character: A Life of John F. Kennedy.* New York: Free Press, 1992.

"Return of the Boy Wonder." *Time,* August 12, 1966.

Reuther, Victor. *The Brothers Reuther: A Memoir.* Boston: Houghton Mifflin, 1976.

Rubin, Lawrence A. *Building Michigan: The Story of the Mighty Mac.* Detroit: Wayne State University Press, 1985.

Russell, Thaddeus. *Out of the Jungle: Jimmy Hoffa and the American Working Class.* New York: Knopf, 2001.

Sawyer, Robert Lee. *The Democratic State Central Committee of Michigan, 1949–1959.* Ann Arbor: Ann Arbor Institute for Public Affairs, 1960.

Schaffer, Howard B. *Chester Bowles: New Dealer in the Cold War.* Cambridge: Harvard University Press, 1993.

Schlesinger, Arthur M., Jr. *A Thousand Days: John F. Kennedy in the White House.* Boston: Houghton Mifflin, 1965.

———. *The Vital Center: The Politics of Freedom.* Cambridge, Mass.: Riverside Press, 1949.

Shesol, Jeff. *Mutual Contempt: Lyndon Johnson, Robert Kennedy, and the Feud That Defined a Decade.* New York: Norton, 1997.

Smith, Beverly. "Soapy, the Boy Wonder." *Saturday Evening Post,* November 9, 1957.

Smith, Otis Milton. *Beyond Race: The Life of Otis Milton Smith.* Detroit: Wayne State University Press, 2000.

Solberg, Carl. *Hubert Humphrey: A Biography.* New York: Norton, 1984.

Sorensen, Theodore. *Kennedy.* New York: Harper and Row, 1965.

Staebler, Neil. *Out of the Smoke-Filled Room: A Memoir of Michigan Politics.* Ann Arbor: George Wahr, 1991.

Staniland, Martin. *American Intellectuals and African Nationalists, 1955–1970.* New Haven: Yale University Press, 1991.

Steinman, David, and John T. Nevill. *Miracle Bridge at Mackinac.* Grand Rapids: William Eerdmans, 1957.

Stetson, Damon. "Michigan's Plight Curbs Williams." *New York Times,* April 12, 1959.

Stiebler, Carol. *The Politics of Change in Michigan.* Lansing: Michigan State University Press, 1970.

"Suddenly It's 1960." *Time,* April 15, 1957.

Thurber, Timothy N. *The Politics of Equality: Hubert H. Humphrey and the African-American Freedom Struggle.* New York: Columbia University Press, 1999.

U.S. Department of State. *Foreign Relations of the United States, Africa, 1961–1963.* Washington, D.C.: U.S. Government Printing Office, 1995.

U.S. President's Commission on Civil Rights. *To Secure These Rights: Report of the President's Commission on Civil Rights.* Washington D.C.: U.S. Government Printing Office, 1947.

U.S. Senate, *Hearings before the Committee on Foreign Relations, 87th Congress, 1st Session, January 24, 1961.* Washington, D.C.: U.S. Government Printing Office, 1961.

Walton, Richard. *The Remnants of Power: The Tragic Last Years of Adlai Stevenson.* New York: Coward-McCann, 1974.

Weddon, William. *Michigan Governors: Their Life Stories.* Lansing: Michigan Historical Society, 1964.

Weeks, George. *Stewards of the State: The Governors of Michigan.* Ann Arbor: Detroit News and Historical Society, 1987.

Weidman, Christine. *Neil Staebler: His Career and Legacy.* Ann Arbor: Bentley Historical Library, 1978.

Weissman, Stephen. *American Foreign Policy in the Congo, 1960–1964.* Ithaca: Cornell University Press, 1974.

"A Welfare State Runs into Trouble." *U.S. News and World Report,* February 13, 1959.

White, Theodore. *The Making of the President, 1960.* New York: Atheneum, 1961.

White, William S. "Which Friends Come First?" *Harpers,* March 1962.

Williams, G. Mennen. *Africa for the Africans.* Grand Rapids: William Eerdmans, 1969.

————. "Africa South of the Equator." *U.S. State Department Bulletin,* July 13, 1964.

————. "Africa's Problems and Progress." *U.S. State Department Bulletin,* March 30, 1964.

————. "The Three 'A's' of Africa: Algeria, Angola, and Apartheid." *U.S. State Department Bulletin,* November 27, 1961.

————. "South Africa in Transition." *U.S. State Department Bulletin,* October 16, 1961.

————. *A Governor's Notes.* Ann Arbor: Michigan Institute of Public Affairs, 1961.

————. "Little Rock: Challenge to the Democratic Party." *The Nation* 185 (October 7, 1957): 235–37.

Winder, David W. "Divided Government in Michigan: Legislative Relations of Governors G. Mennen Williams and William G. Milliken." *Michigan History* 72 (November–December 1988): 36–43.

Wofford, Harris. *Of Kennedy and Kings: Making Sense of the Sixties.* New York: Farrar, Straus, and Giroux, 1980.

INDEX